TWENTIETH
CENTURY
CANADA
SECOND EDITION

TWENTIETH
CENTURY
CANADA
SECOND EDITION

J. L. Granatstein
York University

Irving M. Abella
Glendon College, York University

David J. Bercuson
University of Calgary

R. Craig Brown
University of Toronto

H. Blair Neatby
Carleton University

McGRAW-HILL RYERSON LIMITED

Toronto   Montreal   New York   Auckland
Bogotá   Cairo   Guatemala   Hamburg
Lisbon   London   Madrid   Mexico   New Delhi
Panama   Paris   San Juan   São Paulo   Singapore
Sydney   Tokyo

TWENTIETH CENTURY CANADA
Second Edition

ISBN 0-07-549074-9

Care has been taken to trace ownership of
copyright material contained in this text.
The publishers will gladly take any information
that will enable them to rectify any reference
or credit in subsequent editions.

4 5 6 7 8 9 0 THB 0 9 8

Printed and bound in Canada

Cover design and photograph by Dave Hader

Canadian Cataloguing in Publication Data

Main entry under title:
Twentieth century Canada

Includes bibliographical references and index.
ISBN 0-07-549074-9

1. Canada — Politics and government — 20th century.
2. Canada — History — 20th century. I. Granatstein, J. L., 1939–

FC600.T94 1986   971.06   C85-090861-2
F1034.2.T94 1986

Contents

Preface

"The twentieth century belongs to Canada." In the popular memory that is the way Sir Wilfrid Laurier's words are usually remembered, even if that is not precisely the way they were uttered. At times, in the years since Laurier spoke, his words have seemed almost a bad joke, particularly when Canadians contemplated the terrible wars of the century and the international and domestic discord they have suffered through. And yet, in a real sense, Laurier was right.

In this century Canada has developed and prospered, giving most of its people, wherever they have come from and however short a time they have resided in Canada, a chance for a good life, an education, and a job. Not without difficulty, the state has put into place and thus far maintained a good system of social welfare, assuring all its residents most of the bare necessities of life. The harsh and repressive attitudes that earlier in our history stifled cultural development and the bitter prejudices that made the lives of women, immigrants, and native peoples often unbearable have eased dramatically, even if they have not disappeared and even if they have sudden, sometimes vicious, recrudescences.

But how did we get to this point? To attempt to answer that question is this book's purpose. The five authors of *Twentieth Century Canada* set out to convey the basic history of Canada and its people from Confederation, giving heaviest emphasis to the years after 1896; but they also wanted to do something more. By focussing in detail on five major themes — the political process and political leadership, the rise of labour, immigration, the bureaucracy, and the new Quebec — they set out to add a new and different dimension to general histories of Canada. This approach has resulted in some repetition in the chronological chapters and the theme chapters, but we do not apologize for this. Some users of the text will only read the chronology; others might only use one or two themes. In the authors' view, it was best to allow the repetition to stand so that every student could get a fair and relatively complete account.

A generation ago there was very little research into the areas covered in the theme chapters. Canadian historians were just beginning to venture hesitantly into social history, to study trade unions or business attitudes, to consider the exploitation of immigrants and the racist attitudes that lay behind government policies, or to move behind the facade of speeches and political posturing to study the party machinery or the bureaucracy that kept the wheels of government spinning. The idea that Quebec might be a worthy area of study, that provincial struggles for power could ever be anything more than dry-as-dust disquisitions on Oliver Mowat and the provincial boundary struggles of the late nineteenth century, say, seemed almost incredible to all but a few specialists. But events change history, and they change historians too. There is a vigorous process of healthy revisionism underway, and this book in each of its chapters reflects it. The bibliographical footnotes, carefully updated to be as current as possible, point to the newest and best work available so that readers can readily pursue specialized topics.

The themes that are studied here and that shape the approach of all twelve chapters of this text represent some of the new research accomplished by the most recent generations of Canadian historians. Professor R. Craig Brown of the University of Toronto is the biographer of Sir Robert Borden and the co-author of *Canada 1896–1921*, the best study of that period, and he is now closely studying the Canadian experience during the Great War. David Bercuson of the University of Calgary is one of the country's pioneer labour historians, the author of the leading studies of the Winnipeg General Strike and Western unionism, and he is currently working on a biography of Brooke Claxton, one of the leading mid-century Liberals. Irving Abella of Glendon College, York University, is also a labour historian, but one who has recently turned his full attention to the study of immigration policy. His book, *None Is Too Many*, examined the ways the government kept Jewish refugees from Hitler out of this promised land, and he is now in the midst of a major study of the Canadian Jewish community. H. Blair Neatby of Carleton University is the official biographer of Mackenzie King, the author of a notable study of Laurier and Quebec, and is currently working on a major study of university education in Canada. And J.L. Granatstein, the coordinating author of this book, has written on politics, the bureaucracy and conscription, and is the author of the final volume in the Centenary series, that covering 1957–1967. The writers, in other words, are all active and prolific publishing scholars and teachers, deeply immersed in the process of trying to discover more about this country, and all assume a collective responsibility for this book and its approach.

Fall 1985

Chapter I

Canada in the
Age of
Sir John A.

"I congratulate you on the legislative sanction which has been given by the Imperial Parliament to the Act of Union, under the provisions of which we are now assembled, and which has laid the foundation of a new nationality." Those were the words of the Governor General, Lord Monck, delivered at the opening of the first session of the first Parliament of Canada in November, 1867, and those key words — "a new nationality" — had been inserted into the Speech from the Throne by His Excellency's advisors. Those advisors, a Cabinet of French- and English-Canadian politicians led by Sir John A. Macdonald, had used that phrase in full awareness of its meaning. They intended that the Dominion of Canada they had created would link together the isolated colonial provinces of New Brunswick, Nova Scotia, Canada East and Canada West, and in some fashion yet unclear meld together the disparate interests of French Canadians and English Canadians, Catholics and Protestants, Maritimers and Ontarians, fisherman, farmer and capitalist. It was an ambitious experiment, a great attempt to create a new nation in the still largely uninhabited regions of British North America.

But for the first thirty years after Confederation, few believed that the promise of 1867 was being realized. The historian Frank Underhill once wrote that a nation is a body of men and women who have done great things together in the past and who hope to do great things together in the future. They become a nation through their shared history and traditions, their experience of living together, their surmounting obstacles together. But in the first years of the new Canada, the obstacles seemed

1

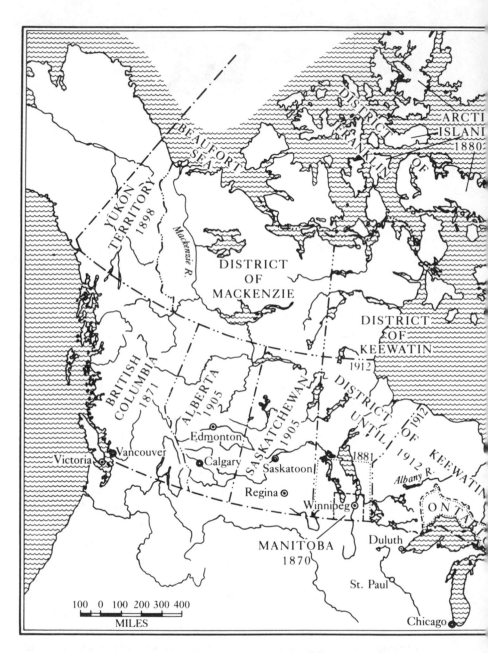

Boundary Changes in Canada Since Confederation

As Canada grew, there were, necessarily, boundary changes. The four provinces of 1867 were joined by Manitoba, British Columbia, and Prince Edward Island, and the Dominion was extended to the north when Britain ceded the Arctic

Boundary 1882   - - - - -
Boundary 1905   - ·· - ·· -

islands. Alberta and Saskatchewan became provinces in 1905, and Newfoundland joined Confederation in 1949, at last making the national motto, A Mari Usque Ad Mare, *a reality. (Adapted from* The Kingdom of Canada *by W.L. Morton, published by Macmillan of Canada, p. 404.)*

almost insurmountable, the traditions disparate, and the experience of living together strained a country divided by language, religion, and geography. There had been great deeds in the past, but too often they represented the struggles of New France against the conquering English, or the efforts of Nova Scotians to break free of the superior power and economic strength of the Canadas. There seemed very little that could be used to unite the four former colonies into a nation.

One uniting force was the first prime minister of Canada. Sir John A. Macdonald — he had been given his knighthood for his services in creating the Confederation bargain — was an Upper Canadian lawyer, a politician of long experience, and a man who suffered from the illnesses of his family and his own drinking problems. That says much, but it says very little of his true genius. Macdonald was a politician's politician, a manipulator of men and a dreamer of dreams, a man with deep feelings but one with the ability to override them when the interests of the state demanded. There seemed to be no man he could not work with — and charm over a good dinner or a drink in the quiet of his office on Parliament Hill. There seemed to be no audience in the country that he could not beguile, and even those who detested his policies could find themselves cheering Sir John when his platform wit and style were in full flight.

Macdonald was a Tory, of course, but he was first and foremost a pragmatist. He looked at Canada as it was, and although he had a vision of what it might become, he had to deal with what was there. This meant that he had to build a balanced Cabinet, carefully giving representation to each region (and to regions within the regions); it meant that he had to have so many Catholics and just so many Protestants, and the correct proportion of Methodists and Presbyterians, too; it meant that he had to have businessmen and farmers among his ministers; and above all it meant that he had to satisfy the aspirations of Quebec for strong representation without alarming his supporters elsewhere with fears of an overweening French influence. To create a Cabinet in such circumstances was a work of art, and John A. set the pattern that all of his successors have followed.

But if the Cabinet had to be so carefully balanced, then it was exceedingly difficult to be dogmatic about policy questions. Ontario might believe vehemently in a particular course, if the big-city newspapers were to be believed. But almost certainly there would be letters and delegations from eastern or southwestern Ontario objecting to such a policy and pronouncing it ruinous to local interests. Some parts of Quebec certainly

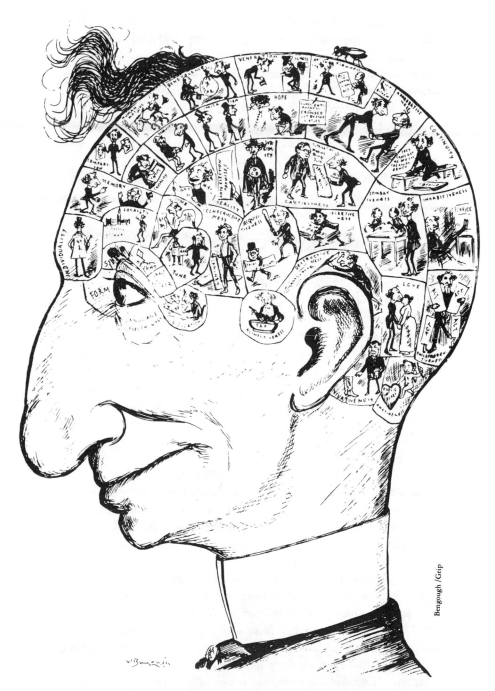

Bengough / Grip

Phrenological Chart of the Head of the Country

would be cool to anything Toronto wanted, and the merchants of Saint John or the apple-growers of the Annapolis Valley had their own interests to protect. Every issue, it seemed, had the potential to create divisions and fissures in the body politic and political troubles for a prime minister. Macdonald quickly learned one of the fundamental truths of Canadian politics: it was often better to do nothing than to act and create bitter animosity. His nickname of "Old Tomorrow" suggested that the Canadian people had become accustomed to the delaying tactics of the old man.

One of the tools Macdonald had at his disposal in his efforts to create a country, and one that he employed with masterly skill, was patronage. To impose a new nationality atop the existing structure of the four colonies was to create the opportunity for new jobs. In a colonial economy jobs were precious gifts, and a good deal of loyalty to the new nation — and, not incidentally, to the Conservative party — could be created with judicious use of the power of appointment. As the departments of the federal government took shape, there were posts to be filled at all levels, positions to be created, money available to smooth out the difficulties. You could be a Nova Scotia Anti-Confederate or a French Canadian dubious of the merits of the 1867 scheme, but the assurance of a job or even the prospect of one in the near future went some distance to easing your concerns. Patronage was the grease that kept the political wheels turning; it was also, to a substantial extent, the glue of nationhood.

Building a Bureaucracy

Patronage was essential glue, but glue does not always allow the wheels of government to function at their best. The country needed a civil service, and the new Dominion government essentially took over the public service that had run the two Canadas, now Ontario and Quebec, before Confederation. Initially only a very few men from Nova Scotia and New Brunswick were brought to the capital, an immediate source of grievance in an era when steady work was scarce and a secure government job was a highly valued commodity. The new Dominion's capital city, Ottawa, was a rough, raw place with few of the amenities of mid-nineteenth century civilization and a reputation as a boozing, brawling lumbering town. "Possibly the place might be fit for habitation in fifty years time," Edmund Meredith, one senior official wrote, "but certainly not before." The Parliament Buildings were grand — and had cost five

Sir John A. in 1888, when he was seventy-three years old. (Ontario Archives, 5.271)

times the original estimate — but little else was, and Meredith complained that the town was "drains, drains, nothing but drains," a blunt and heartfelt comment on the unhealthy nature of life in even the best sections of old Bytown.[1]

But somehow the civil service settled in and made a place for itself. Its numbers were tiny by modern standards, probably no more than four hundred officials and clerks in Ottawa and another two thousand or so scattered across the country. Most of the inside public service, as it was called, was housed in the east Block of the Parliament Buildings, something possible because there were so few departments of government: in 1867 only Customs, Inland Revenue, Agriculture, Public Works, Secretary of State, and the Post Office; the next year Justice and Marine and Fisheries were added; in 1869 Finance and in 1873 the Department of the Interior came into being. Over the next decades, other departments were added in response to perceived need and political necessity — Railways and Canals in 1879, Trade and Commerce in 1892, Labour in 1900, and External Affairs in 1909. Small as it was, understaffed as it must have been — as late as 1885 the staff of the Justice Department was only fifteen men and three or four messengers — the public service performed essential tasks. It moved the paper, it showed the Ministers the ropes (and quite often, critics charged, tried to bind them in red tape so that changes would be impossible at best or slow at worst), and it kept the government functioning in a country that sometimes scarcely even realized it had a federal government, so little money did it have to spend.

Something more was needed to hold the new nation together, and to Macdonald and his men that could only be expansion. The four provinces that formed Canada in 1867 did not come near to filling the present-day map. Nova Scotia and New Brunswick had their present boundaries, but Quebec and Ontario were less than half their size today and remained so until 1912. (In 1927, the Judicial Committee of the Privy Council, the final court of appeal in the empire, greatly expanded Labrador's boundaries at the expense of Quebec, creating a long-lived grievance.) But within a few years of Confederation there was dramatic expansion. The West, the territory wholly owned by the Hudson's Bay Company, was acquired in 1870, not without difficulty as we shall see.

1. A brilliantly written account of life in Ottawa in this period, largely through the eyes of Edmund Meredith, can be found in Sandra Gwyn's *The Private Capital: Ambition and Love in the Age of Macdonald and Laurier* (Toronto, 1984). For a more scholarly study of the early public service from which the Dominion structure sprang, see J.E. Hodgetts, *Pioneer Public Service: An Administrative History of the United Canadas, 1841-1867* (Toronto, 1955).

The next year, seduced by the promise of a railway to the East, British Columbia joined. And in 1873, its economy in ruins through too-rapid railway expansion, Prince Edward Island tied its fate to Canada's. The nation now stretched from sea to sea, and with the British cession of the Arctic Islands in 1880 and the entry into Confederation of Newfoundland in 1949, Canada was complete.

Expansion was a powerful force in a new nation. Even if it had only just completed its own terrible Civil War, the United States remained a testimony to the virtues of growth. The Americans had pushed west inexorably, settling the land, beginning to tap its great riches, and creating the infrastructure of a continental economy. If the Americans could do it, then surely the Canadians could do so as well. But who would control the West economically? Who would settle it?

Riel and the Future of the West

To French Canadians, still a little less than certain about their place in the new Dominion, it seemed absolutely fundamental that they have an equal share in the settling of the West, the patrimony of the whole nation. But to English-speaking Canadians, and particularly to those in Ontario, the West was theirs, theirs to settle, theirs to control, and theirs to shape. In the clash between those attitudes were the seeds of misunderstanding and tragedy between the races and between regions, for just before the Hudson's Bay Company passed control of its vast lands in the west to the new federal government at Ottawa in 1870, there was a brief vacuum of power at the Red River. To the few Ontario settlers at Fort Garry, the one "town" of any size on the Prairies, this was the opportunity to demonstrate that they were ready, indeed eager, to become the new rulers over the land; other whites, less militant, simply wanted to be certain that their interests were not forgotten in the transition.

For the Métis, descendants of French and English fur traders and their native wives, who comprised the great majority in the Red River area, this transfer of authority without their consent or, indeed, even without consultation, was a chance to take power, and by creating their own "new nation," to prevent the destruction of their unique way of life by what they feared would be an uncaring federal power or by the often racist Ontarians at the settlement.

Led by Louis Riel, a charismatic young Métis educated in the seminaries of Quebec, the Métis seized control of the territory out of the faltering hands of the Hudson's Bay Company and imposed the power of the majority on the whole population. They established a Convention and then a Provisional Government to extract concessions from the Canadian government. Some of the Canadians at Red River became obstreperous and Riel, the head of the Provisional Government, had one particularly ill-disciplined settler, Thomas Scott from Ontario, executed for a number of less-than-serious offences, largely to cow the other settlers and to impress Ottawa with the Métis leadership's seriousness. His killing — murder, it was called in the East, but to the Provisional Government it was the maintenance of order — inflamed opinion across English Canada and led to ferocious calls for vengeance against Riel.

The always delicate relations between French- and English-speaking Canadians and between Protestant and Catholic were seriously jeopardized for the first time since Confederation, and there were plenty of hotheads among the Orangemen in Ontario or the militant young Catholics in Quebec willing to damn a whole race or religion for the errors of a few. A military force, hurriedly prepared from the British garrison still stationed in Canada, was sent westward over difficult country while political negotiations with the emissaries from the Red River went on in Ottawa. The inevitable result was that Riel, fearing for his life, fled the advancing troops. More surprisingly, Manitoba was proclaimed a province, though its territory was confined to a small square of land around what became the city of Winnipeg, and French- and English-speaking inhabitants of the new province were given equal language and schooling rights. Less surprisingly, the new province was denied control over its lands and resources so the federal government alone could control the planning of the future of the West.

To French Canadians in Quebec and elsewhere, the Manitoba Act of 1870 was a vindication and a victory, an undertaking from the new federal government that the West was to belong to both of the founding races. But that victory, if that is what it was, was destined to be short-lived, and Riel again was the man who brought matters to the point of crisis. Louis Riel, who had been in exile in the United States for most of the time since his flight in 1870, returned fifteen years later and led the Métis into rebellion once more, this time farther to the west in the lightly populated Northwest Territories around the South Saskatchewan River settlement of Batoche. The Territories, created by Ottawa in 1870, had initially been under the control of the Lieutenant-Governor of Manitoba, wearing an extra hat as Governor of the Northwest Territories, and his appointed council. Five years later, Ottawa named a separate Lieutenant-Governor for the Territories and laid the groundwork for the transition to

Louis Riel, from a photograph taken around 1873. Riel was only twenty-nine at the time, although he appears much older. (C-18084/Public Archives Canada)

A Riel Ugly Position

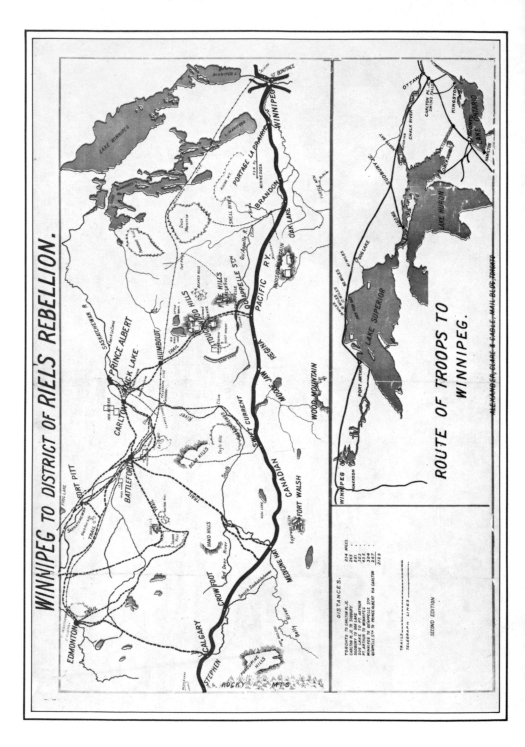

◄ *The Route Taken by Troops to Reach the Rebellion*
This contemporary sketch showed the route of the troops from the east to the rebellion. Note on the map at the bottom the gaps in the rail line around Lake Superior, gaps that caused the raw militia soldiers terrible difficulties in moving over the still-frozen land and water. But note, too, the unbroken line from Winnipeg to Calgary, the government's major advantage in moving quickly against Riel.

Source: W.A. Oppen, *The Riel Rebellions: A Cartographic History* (Toronto, 1979) p. 103. Printed by permission, National Map Collection, Public Archives of Canada.

representative government. But the settlers were still living in a virtual colony, even though they had the vote in local and federal elections. Ottawa controlled the lands and resources. Ottawa dealt with the Indians. Ottawa, so far away, set the policy on virtually every question of importance. The sense of grievance was powerful and not limited only to the Métis or the Indian tribes, but the whites in the Territories would not go so far as to take up arms against Ottawa. The restless native tribes, however, fearing for their future once white settlers flooded west, did join in the uprising, and for a brief period there was terror in the scattered settlements and near-panic in Ottawa. But troops of the Canadian Militia from English and French Canada were quickly despatched to the scene under the command of General Fred Middleton, the obese British General Officer Commanding the militia. The news of the uprising had been instantly carried to the east on the newly strung telegraph wires and the hurriedly mobilized troops travelled west on the not-yet-completed Canadian Pacific Railway. The first troops from the East reached the Territories in nine days, striking proof of the value of the rail line. The revolt was quickly squashed after a few sharp skirmishes, though not without substantial difficulty. Led militarily by Gabriel Dumont, a skillful tactician who had grasped the idea that fighting from rifle pits gave his lightly armed soldiers a better chance against the artillery and Gatling guns of the militia, the Métis had proven a tougher nut to crack than the cocky militia colonels and the editorialists back home had predicted.

Riel himself was caught and tried for "levying war upon Her Majesty." His able defence lawyers' arguments that he was insane were rejected by the Court — and by Riel himself, who spoke with great passion and fatally impressive clarity in his own defence — although, by this century's definition, he was almost certainly unbalanced. He had visions, heard voices, and had messianic dreams. Nonetheless, the Court ordered Riel to be hanged by the neck until dead. After Macdonald's Cabinet, including its five Quebec representatives, decided not to commute the sentence, the Métis leader was executed on a gibbet at Regina in November 1885[2]. The hangman, a Scotsman who had been a friend of Thomas Scott, executed by Riel fifteen years earlier at the Red River, had seized the opportunity as he put the noose around the Métis rebel's neck to whisper to Riel, "You cannot escape from me today."

To Quebec, the execution of Riel was a slap in the face. French Canada had solidly condemned the uprising in the spring of 1885 when it began, but public opinion had shifted by the fall until mercy for the Métis chief had become an almost unanimous demand. In Ontario, and also in the New Brunswick and Nova Scotia, the execution was largely considered justifiable — John Thompson, the Nova Scotian (and Roman Catholic) who had just been appointed Macdonald's Justice Minister called Riel "a paltry hero who struggled so long and so hard for the privilege of hanging" — and certainly there were some in the English provinces who wanted Riel's head to demonstrate Anglo-Protestant power over Catholic and French-speaking rebels. But opinion was probably less racist than popular memory and some modern historians would have it. Much of the English-language press (and especially — and not surprisingly — the Liberal newspapers) condemned Sir John A. Macdonald and his government for the administrative incompetence that had produced the rebellion just as much as they attacked Riel. The Prime Minister himself had no doubts of Riel's guilt, and certainly he wanted him to be executed as an object lesson that Canada would take strong action to preserve the West and to keep the peace. The Americans, still occasionally casting covetous eyes north, got the message. So did any native tribes that might have desired to resist the government's policy of settling the Prairies, as had Indians in the United States. The Indians who had risen in revolt at the same time as Riel were herded back onto the reservations Ottawa had created for them, small remnants of the lands over which they had once roamed freely. The system of treaties and reserves that now confined the tribes had removed aboriginal title — for all time, government thought, until the courts in the 1970s and 1980s differed. The chiefs who had signed the treaties almost certainly did not understand the implications; but all the Indians could see that resistance was futile and would lead only to wars they could not hope to win against the machine guns and artillery that Ottawa could dispose against them.

2. The best biography of Riel is G.F.G. Stanley's *Louis Riel* (Toronto, 1963). See also Thomas Flanagan, ed., *The Diaries of Louis Riel* (Edmonton, 1976) and his *Riel and the Rebellion: 1885 Reconsidered* (Saskatoon, 1983); Desmond Morton, ed. *The Queen v. Louis Riel* (Toronto, 1974); and the immensely valuable book by Stanley, *The Birth of Western Canada* (Toronto, 1960).

Quebec got the message too. Its popular protests, even its five ministers in the Cabinet in Ottawa, were insufficient to give French Canada what it wanted. That lesson was reinforced in the next few years when Manitoba moved to restrict dramatically the rights of the Roman Catholic minority, and almost incidentally limited the rights of French-speaking Manitobans to receive schooling in their own language. The Manitoba School Question, as it was known then and as it is known in our own day, was in train. The Manitoba Act of 1870, to Quebec's great chagrin, had been overtaken by events and overturned by a government and people heedless of the past and heedless of the rights of their Roman Catholic and French-speaking compatriots, suddenly in a minority in the province. Legislation alone, it appeared, could not definitively determine the character of the West; the population had to be in place before that could occur. And the reality was that few French Canadians except those who thought in missionary terms were willing to leave Quebec for the forbidding climate of the Prairies, where a short growing season and the limited strains of wheat then available seemed to curtail the possibilities of earning a living. In 1872 *L'Evenement*, a Quebec newspaper, expressed its concern that the need for settlers in the West might slow the settlement of unopened regions of French Canada's own province, "For our part, we think that public opinion is not eager to go looking for *the key to colonization* so far away. As long as it hasn't undone the lock that closes the gates to the colonization of the St. Maurice, the Saguenay, etc., it will hardly be eager to pay out millions for the key to colonization in the North-West." That attitude continued, and those who chose to leave their ancestral habitations along the St. Lawrence and the Richelieu instead went to the factories of Montreal or the cotton mills of New England to seek the better life that very few found in the crowded city slums, rife with disease and, all too often, immorality and political corruption.

Indeed, few people from anywhere seemed eager to go west — or to any part of Canada — in the years after Confederation. There was still good land available to settlers in the United States either free or at low prices, and European immigrants were convinced that the streets of America, not Canada, were paved with gold. Immigration to the United States boomed, as even British settlers chose the States over Canada in vast numbers. The population of Canada, about 3.5 million at Confederation, rose slowly with a growth rate to 1901 of only 1 per cent a year. During 1851–61, by comparison, the rate had been 2.9 per cent a year, and in the 1901–11 decade, on a much larger base, it would be 3 per cent a year. In fact, in the first ten years of the twentieth century, as many immigrants came to Canada as had arrived during the preceding forty years. Worse yet, in each decade from 1861 to 1901 more Canadians had left Canada than immigrants had arrived, the total net loss amounting to 480 000 men, women, and children. Only a very high birth rate allowed the population to increase at all.

What was it that kept immigrants away and drove the native-born to the United States? In Canada, the opportunities seemed fewer and the climate harsher than in the U.S. This was a small country, battling against vast geography; in the United States, with its much larger population and vast amounts of good soil, an ambitious man could start a business or farm and have a fair chance at prosperity. The United States also seemed more open to upward mobility than Canada, saddled as it was with some vestiges of a mock-British class system. Here people were expected to know their place and to doff their caps to their betters, and while that fostered order and stability, it did tend to diminish opportunity. In the United States, rougher and freer as it was, one's past seemed to matter less than one's abilities. Naturally enough, those Canadians who resisted the lure of the "Boston States" or the cities like New York or Chicago or the prairies of Kansas had to persuade themselves that their virtue was superior to that of the emigrés. There was a price that had to be paid to be Canadian, and one of the results was an assumption of superiority, usually unfounded, to Americans and their ways.

The Tariff

After 1879 there would be another price to pay for being Canadian. The National Policy, the politically clever name that Macdonald gave to his policy or tariff protection for Canadian manufactured goods (and that was later expanded to include the completion of the railway to the Pacific and the peopling of the Prairies), raised the costs of imported products in an effort to encourage the development of manufacturing in Canada and so stimulate a laggard economy. The Government's reasoning was simple and clear. If Canadians were leaving Canada to find work and opportunity, then some way had to be found to create jobs for them in Canada. One way was to encourage manufacturing to take root, and one method of achieving that goal was to raise the costs of imported goods by slapping a substantial tariff on them. In other words, if widgets made in the United States before the National Policy was in place entered Canada at 3 cents each, a price that no Canadian manufacturer could meet, given the smaller size of the Canadian market and the relative backwardness of Canadian techology, then by placing a tariff of, say, 33 per cent on widgets, the cost

WANTED--PROTECTION!!

A Grip *cartoon from 1876 shows Uncle Sam striking down Canadian industry while Alexander Mackenzie watches idly.*

would be raised to 4 cents here. That price might allow a manufacturer to begin widget production in Montreal, to employ twenty workers, and to sell his product at 3.8 cents each. That was a victory for the National Policy — jobs, profits, Canadian sales for a Canadian product. Another result, of course, was that widget users were paying more for the product, and that increase in costs had to be passed on to the consumer in every product that incorporated widgets. The cost of living increased, an unfortunate counterpoint to the benefits of the policy.

There were other difficulties inherent in the National Policy. Macdonald's Government had put it in place in 1879 for sound national reasons, but the tariff also served to bind businessmen to the Government and to the Conservative party. If you wanted a tariff to protect your industry, then it helped to be a Tory and a contributor to the party's election coffers. That was the rule of the 1880s, and that was unhealthy for political democracy.

The tariff also allowed businessmen to be rather more cautious and less innovative than they might otherwise have been. It provided a comfortable cushion that allowed the inefficient manufacturer to survive, free of the rigours of foreign competition. Why modernize plant in such circumstances? Why press forward with new processes and new inventions? Many Canadian businessmen (but not all), sheltering behind the tariff wall erected by the National Policy, became cautious and backward almost from its very birth, and although they preached the gospels of competition and free enterprise with a fervour equal to that of businessmen in the United States, in fact they tended to seek out pleasant arrangements that minimized unhealthy competition and preserved "a living profit" for them all.

Labour organizations also benefited from the National Policy. The tariff created manufacturing jobs and gradually increased the number of skilled craftsmen, and once Macdonald's Government made trade unions legal in 1872 there was a slow but steady growth and development of unions. Initially labour's organizational efforts were concentrated within specific crafts or trades. There would be a carpenters' union and a plumbers' union, in other words, but not a union of general labourers. The issues of the era were not dissimilar to those of the present day. Workers wanted more pay, better working conditions, and a shorter work week. Nonetheless the struggle was much more fierce than it is now. The businessmen of the nineteenth century may have been lacking in innovative ideas, but they believed in the divine right of capital and were absolutely convinced that if they owned the factory their word was and should be law. A union in attempting to win a say for the workers was challenging a credo, and labour organization was viewed as anathema. Very often a union could be crushed by the simple expedient of firing the troublemakers and hiring new men, often recent immigrants who were willing to endure terrible conditions and low wages out of direst necessity. To the workers, this hiring of cheap labour was a sin, and unions struggled to win exclusive rights to certify who could or could not work at their craft. There was also an unhappy tendency for workers to be opposed to immigration, a not unnatural response to their employers' hiring practices.

Most important, perhaps, was the fact that the tariff seemed designed to serve the interests of central Canada alone. It was Ontario and Quebec that had the population, and it was Ontario and Quebec that got the factories. But for someone in New Brunswick or in Manitoba or British Columbia the net effect of the National Policy was higher prices. Everything cost more, they could and did say with increasing vehemence, and only Toronto and Montreal got the benefits. So long as Ontario and Quebec had the votes in Parliament, that situation did not alter very much, although there were repeated assaults on the principle of protection.

The tariff had at least one additional effect, one that the Government had considered. If American firms could not export freely to Canada because of a high tariff, then they might be encouraged to set up branch plants in the Dominion. That would allow them to crawl under the protective wall and regain their Canadian markets. To Ottawa, this was a positive step. An American (or German or French) firm brought capital into the country and created employment; it enhanced the manufacturing capacity of the nation; and it kept Canadians in Canada. If there were long-term implications in this policy, in 1879 the Government might be forgiven for not seeing them.

A New Nationalism

Not that the government was unaware of potential dangers from the United States. To a substantial extent, Confederation itself had been a product of the military threat from the south, the fear that Washington might seek to bind up the wounds caused by the Civil War by staging a glorious invasion to wrest British North America from England's grasp. Separate British colonies would have no chance against the hardened veterans of Gettysburg and Vicksburg; together, and with British help, they just might have a slim possibility of survival. War was averted, however, though not without the Fenian invasions in the 1860s that helped persuade the reluctant in New Brunswick and Nova Scotia and Lower Canada to favour union. But over the next four decades the Americans remained a potentially hostile presence. There was the threat to the West in 1870. There were the negotiations for the Treaty of Washington in 1871 when the shrewd Yankee traders had blustered the British, acting on behalf of Canada with Sir John A. Macdonald sitting almost impotent at the bargaining table, into sacrificing Canadian interests to Washington in compensation for claims that had arisen during the American Civil War. "I stand alone," Sir John had written back to Ottawa, "the Americans are constantly depreciating the value of our property, and making absurdly low offers, which my [British] colleagues, in their anxiety for a settlement, are constantly pressing me to yield to." There were war scares over the Venezuela boundary dispute that troubled Anglo-American relations in the 1890s, a demonstration that a British dispute with the United States in some far-off part of the world could lead the politicians and generals in Washington to believe that seizing Canada was the best way to strike at London. And at the turn of the century there would be the Alaska Boundary Dispute — important enough to merit capitalization — when the British, in the judgment of the Canadian government and people, again sold out Canada for the potential benefits of American friendship.

To some Canadians, the only possible answer to the difficulties of relying on Mother England was to put Canada first. In other words, Canadians had to take control of their own destiny and manage their foreign policy just as they did their domestic affairs. Only in that way could they be sure that their interests would not be bargained away by the British. If that sounded like a cry for independence from the Mother Country, it wasn't, at least not yet. The same nationalists who talked of Canada First in the early 1870s looked south at a bellicose and powerful United States and concluded quickly and sensibly that their only protection lay in a close relationship with Britain. Indeed, some of them even dreamed of a day when Canada, with its great territory, vast and untouched resources, and its potential to support a larger population than the cramped British Isles, might become more powerful than Britain and, naturally, as a son or daughter takes over the running of the family business from an aged parent, assume control of the Empire.[3]

That vision of a Canadian Empire was a pipe dream, of course, but it absorbed many otherwise sensible people, and the conflicts it dramatized in the Canadian psyche were very real. While French Canadians largely wanted to be left alone, English Canadians of the nineteenth century wanted to be independent in some ways, but they also identified strongly and emotionally with Britain, with the Queen-Empress, with the glories of Nelson and Wellington, and of the great Empire on which the sun never set. But the essential problem still remained: how could an independent foreign policy or an independent nation be created as long as Canada relied on the British army, the Royal Navy, and London's great prestige as its first and only line of defence? That conundrum would not be resolved in the nineteenth century or for a good part of the twentieth; it only became clear when Britain's power decreased and America's intentions to Canada altered from military seizure to a more benign economic control. But for the first decades after Confederation, Canadians co-existed uneasily with the United States while never quite trusting the good intentions or continued devotion to Canadian interests of Great Britain.

3. The best book on Canadian nationalism in the late nineteenth century is Carl Berger's *The Sense of Power: Studies in the Ideas of Canadian Imperialism, 1867-1914* (Toronto, 1970). See also Berger's collection of documents, *Imperialism and Nationalism, 1884-1914: A Conflict in Canadian Thought* (Toronto, 1969).

The Great Railway

If foreign policy was not the strongest suit for Macdonald's government, there was a better record in national development. The Dominion government had sunk large sums of money into the building of the Canadian Pacific Railway. Macdonald and his Cabinet and most of the educated opinion in the country had agreed that Canada could never be a nation as long as there was no iron road to connect the Atlantic, Central Canada, the Prairies, and the Pacific together; the railway was absolutely essential. But the costs were huge, and almost certainly they were beyond the capacities of private enterprise in the years after Confederation. Macdonald's first efforts to get the railway built had culminated in the Pacific Scandal, revealed in 1873, when it became apparent that the year before money for electoral campaign purposes had flowed from the railway entrepreneurs to the government's always desperate candidates.

The Liberal Party, captained by the dour Scot, Alexander Mackenzie, was the beneficiary of the Scandal. Facing defeat in the House, Macdonald resigned office in November, 1873, and the Liberals took power. The Grits, wracked with dissension between their French- and English-speaking wings and cursed with an uncommonly large number of prima donnas on their front benches, did not govern happily. Mackenzie won the election of 1874 with a handsome majority but, bedevilled by Macdonald's men in the Opposition, his government found its freedom of manoeuvre limited by the nation's tiny fiscal resources in a period of economic difficulty. The Mackenzie government had no choice but to favour a go-slow policy of building the railway to keep pace with the infinitesimally slow movement of settlement and population to the West. That probably made sense economically, but it did seem too cautious for a new nation that thought the future was its to seize. Certainly it was too slow for John A., and when he came back into office in the election of 1878, and once he had found himself a syndicate of entrepreneurs to build the railway, he again stepped up the pace of railway construction.

The C.P.R.'s contractors brought in thousands of Chinese "coolies" to work in the difficult and mountainous terrain of British Columbia, to be subjected to the unbridled racism of the whites, and the corruption of the labour merchants. Hundreds, perhaps thousands, died in building the line through the mountains, and there were even stories, probably uttered half in jest, that the dead had been boiled and canned for sale in China as rabbit meat. While the work proceeded slowly in British Columbia, at the same time huge work gangs built the line across the Prairies, moving at great speed. There were constant crises to be overcome in the construction as the engineers were forced to improvise and solve problems that Canadian contractors had never before faced, and the Canadian Pacific was always on the verge of going bankrupt, always in need of more government money or more grants of land. But somehow the railway was completed, the government willing to put up the last-minute grants that allowed completion, and the last spike was driven in at Craigellachie, British Columbia on a dull, wet November morning in 1885.[4]

The impact of the railway was tremendous. Whole cities sprang up on the Prairies where the C.P.R. pitched its camps and sited its depots, division points, and repair shops; fortunes were made one day — and lost the next — by land speculators at the mercy of decisions made back east, and farmers quickly became dependent on the railway to get their produce to the markets in the east. Eventually, the immigrants came too, first crossing the Atlantic in steerage, then riding a C.P.R. colonist car — equipped with rough seats and bunk-like slats that pulled down from the ceiling to form a makeshift bed — to a sparse station or to a spot on the still unbroken Prairie where they would be let off with their pathetic bundles of belongings. Then it was a hike into the wild, a search for the surveyor's stakes that marked their acres, a struggle for survival the first winter in a rough sod hut, and for the lucky and skillful farmers among them the chance to thrive and prosper and grow wheat; for the government, that settler and his family, whether from England, the United States, the Ukraine, or less often Ontario and the Maritimes, was an increase in the West's population and a potential increase in the Gross National Product.

For the C.P.R., those immigrants were fares and possible future shippers of wheat. Later, of course, the monopoly in Western Canada that Macdonald had given to the C.P.R. to protect it from the competition of U.S. lines became hated by the same settlers the railway had carried west. How could farmers make a decent living when, they claimed, the railway charged them exorbitant rates to move grain to market? How could they sell their wheat when prices were at their peak if the C.P.R. controlled the supply of the railway cars necessary to carry grain to market? Premier John Norquay's Conservative government of Manitoba backed the angry farmers and battled Macdonald, challenging Ottawa's right singlehandedly to determine transportation policies in the region. Norquay issued a charter to build a line from Winnipeg to the border where it could connect with an American line, and a constitutional war almost became a shooting war when the provincially authorized line tried to cross the C.P.R.'s main line.

4. On the building of the railway, see Pierre Berton's two volumes, *The National Dream* and *The Last Spike* (Toronto, 1970 and 1971); and Hugh Dempsey, ed., *The CPR West: The Iron Road and the Making of a Nation* (Vancouver, 1984), a very fine collection of essays.

The Canadian Pacific rushed trains and crews to the spot and tried to hold off the interlopers. In 1888, finally, Macdonald and the government relented, revoked the C.P.R. monopoly, and offered the angry company financial concessions in return. The farmers of Manitoba and the Territories were not long assuaged, however, and they now charged that the C.P.R. was conspiring to allow only elevator companies it favoured to build along the main line; that, they maintained, obliged them to use those elevators as there were no others around to compete. Only time, competing railways, and an influx of population that would eventually give the Prairies political clout could resolve matters.

Thus Canadians in the first quarter-century after Confederation had domestic and foreign problems aplenty to concern them: immigration, labour, tariffs, French-English difficulties, federal-provincial struggles, a stagnant economy, and worries about the enormous power of the United States; the problems sound familiar still.

The Nineteenth Century Woman

There were other issues, however, of a more philosophical kind. Some women were unhappy with their sex's subservient place in Canadian society (and in Western society generally), and some were actually violating the taboos of the day by trying to seek entry to universities and, more daring still, to medical schools. There were more difficulties once they broke down the admission barriers, of course. Elizabeth Smith, a young Ontario woman of good family who made her way to Queen's University's medical school in the early 1880s, noted in her diary the comment of one professor that "any good looks a girl may have were given her purely and solely to get a husband with," an attitude, then and later, that was very common. As Smith noted with more than a hint of bitterness, that offhand remark clearly implied that "as we were quite lacking in that respect we look to medicine in despair, never dreaming of such a hope in that state of life." The idea that a woman, attractive or not, might want to be a doctor — or a lawyer or a notary — for professional or economic reasons, and not because there was no potential husband in the offing, scarcely crossed the male mind. The idea that a woman might want the right to exercise the vote was similarly hard for men to grasp, and in truth many women seemed content to play their traditional role and forgo a share in the professional world of work or in governing the country. That attitude was beginning to be shaken by the efforts of Elizabeth Smith and her bold sisters.

But for most women in Canada, there was little chance even to dream of a professional career. Women's work was no longer limited to the household, difficult as that was in an era before labour-saving conveniences. On the farms, women worked as they had for centuries in the barns and fields, toiling just as hard as the men. In the towns and cities, there was factory work, usually hard, often dangerous, and almost always repetitive — and inevitably the pay was lower than men received. Other work, except for domestic service, was scarce, and women were often driven into prostitution in the desperate struggle to earn enough to survive.

Other than nuns, the church was still closed to women. Clergymen were not any more troubled by this than the country's surgeons, but they worried over great issues nonetheless. Was there some way to reconcile religion with the harsh effects of the industrial revolution that were all too readily apparent in the factories and slums of the cities? How could they help integrate the polyglot immigrants into the British-Canadian way of life and teach them to forget their barbarous languages and habits? Missions and settlement houses in the inner city neighbourhoods were one answer that seemed to hold out promise. So were the campaigns to prohibit the sale of alcohol. In Quebec, the curés were more concerned with their own compatriots. How could they be kept on the land and discouraged from immigration to the Boston States or elsewhere in Canada? To some, as we have seen, the answer was to encourage the colonization of uninhabited parts of Quebec; to others, the answer lay in encouraging industry to set up factories in small towns in an effort to provide work close at hand and to preserve the people from the moral pollution of the cities.

Canadians were also beginning to take a lively interest in culture. British and American magazines and books circulated widely, and Canadian periodicals, though not large in number, had a substantial circulation. Scholarship was still rather scanty, but Canadian history was beginning to be a field of study and some academics — Adam Shortt of Queen's University was the best example — had come to believe that the consideration of public policy was a worthy task. There were even novelists and poets, painters and portraitists, although much of their work was imitative of European trends.

Above all, until his death in 1891, there was John A. himself. The grand old man had symbolized Canada in a way that is difficult to realize from this distance. He had seemingly always been there, applying the soothing balm of political blarney where it was needed and fighting vigorously for the national interest where that was necessary. Macdonald had fought the political wars through bad times and good, and he had held the public attention like no man before or since. Against him the Liberals could do nothing. Alexander Mackenzie, the Kingston stonemason, had ruled for five years with a Scots rectitude, but the electorate had again succumbed happily to John A.'s wiles at the first opportunity. Edward Blake, Mackenzie's successor, was an intellectual giant, but he lacked Macdonald's human touch, and his successor, Wilfrid Laurier, was an unknown quantity but, being a French Canadian, was suspect to most outside of Quebec — and to many *bleus* — Quebec Conservatives — inside it too.

But after leading the Conservative party to victory one last time in 1891, Macdonald was gone. He had campaigned on the slogan of "The Old Flag, The Old Policy, The Old Leader," and he had denounced the Liberals' efforts to seek a major trade arrangement — unrestricted reciprocity — with the Americans as verging on treason. Characteristically, Macdonald himself had earlier sought just such an arrangement with the United States, and only after he had realized it would be impossible to achieve on reasonable terms did he come out against it and for "The Old Policy." But now the politician who had set the pattern for all successful Canadian prime ministers was gone and with him went his almost uncanny skill in political management.[5]

For the next five years, under a succession of leaders, the Tories drifted, wracked by racial and religious tensions as the Manitoba School Question tore the Cabinet, caucus, and country apart. Those tensions were an accurate reflection of the national mood, for Canada, after almost three decades of existence, was still a country unsure of its course and direction.

5. The classic biography of *John A. Macdonald* is Donald Creighton's two volume study (Toronto, 1952, 1955). On *The Man From Halifax: Sir John Thompson, Prime Minister* (Toronto, 1985), see Peter Waite's able biography. On Alexander Mackenzie and Edward Blake, the Liberals they opposed, see Dale Thomson, *Alexander Mackenzie: Clear Grit* (Toronto, 1960) and Joseph Schull, *Edward Blake* (2 vols., Toronto, 1975, 1976).

Chapter II

1896-1911:
The
Laurier
Years

It was Tuesday evening, June 20, 1893, and Ottawa, whose basic industry was politics, was agog with excitement. The carriages and drivers outside the large old Rideau Rink had brought the Liberal faithful from Parliament Hill, from the provincial capitals, from constituencies across the land to the arena. Inside, the workmen had finished their chores; the chairs had been set out in rows with military precision and draped Union Jacks, freshly cut boughs and early summer blooms were in place. On the platform sat the potentates of the Liberal party in strict order of prominence and seniority. The main event of the first national political party convention ever to be called in Canada was at hand.

The man standing at the podium was known to all of the delegates, alternates, newsmen, and visitors who had crowded into every cranny and corner of the rink. And — it was only one of his remarkable talents — he knew most of them, had probably given many a kindly word of greeting or encouragement at some time, in some place, during the seven years he had been party leader. He was fifty-two: tall, erect, handsome, his flowing hair starting to grey, his warm smile balancing the alert, piercing gaze of his deep-set eyes. His dress, the high, white collar, the silk cravat, the high-buttoned coat, was formal. About his bearing there was a formality, an aristocratic touch, befitting a leader of men. But the delegates also knew him as a friendly man whose approach to politics, and life, was seemingly easy-going, almost lazy, though governed by a deep commitment to moderation, conciliation, and tolerance.

Wilfrid Laurier, the son of a land surveyor of modest means, had been born in L'Assomption County, Lower Canada, in 1841.[1] His early schooling at a classical college was followed by studies in law at McGill University. After admission to the Lower Canada Bar in 1864 he practised his profession in Montreal for two years and then took up the editorship of a small newspaper, *Le défricheur*, in Arthabaska County. The radical politics of the Institut Canadien and *parti rouge*, of which Laurier had been a member in his student days, found expression in the journal, incurring the profound displeasure of the very conservative Bishop Laflèche. It was the first of a lifelong series of ideological conflicts between the liberal-minded Laurier and the superiors of his church over the role of the Church and churchmen in the affairs of state. Within months, *Le défricheur* was banned. By then Laurier was again practising law in Arthabaskaville.

The briefs and busy work of a small law office were not enough to contain his ambition. That ambition found its outlet in politics where, as he told a friend, his goal was "making my ideas triumph." In 1871, Laurier won election to the Legislative Assembly of Quebec. Three years later, he was elected for the first time to the House of Commons in Ottawa. Laurier was quickly recognized as a young man of uncommon talent and in 1877 he joined the Cabinet of Alexander Mackenzie's Liberal Government and became leader of the federal Liberals in Quebec. When Mackenzie retired after Sir John A. Macdonald's victory in the 1878 election, Edward Blake, the new leader of the Liberal party, depended heavily upon Laurier as a friend and advisor. Then, when Blake himself retired in 1887, the Liberal caucus chose Laurier as their national leader.

The early years of Laurier's leadership had been neither easy nor rewarding. His reputation for fairness and moderation in addressing the great and decisive questions of English-French relations in the 1880s, the Riel question and the use of the French language in the Northwest Territories, was firmly established. However, many English-Canadian members of the party worried as much about Laurier's Roman Catholicism and his defence of the rights of French Canadians as French-Canadian

1. The standard biography of Laurier is O.D. Skelton, *Life and Letters of Sir Wilfrid Laurier*, 2 vols. (Toronto, 1921). Other accounts include Joseph Schull, *Laurier: The First Canadian* (Toronto, 1965); Richard Clippingdale, *Laurier, His Life and World* (Toronto, 1979); J.S. Willison, *Sir Wilfrid Laurier and the Liberal Party*, 2 vols. (Toronto, 1903); and J.W. Dafoe, *Laurier, A Study in Canadian Politics* (Toronto, 1922). A masterful analysis of Laurier's political career is H. Blair Neatby, *Laurier and a Liberal Quebec: A Study in Political Management* (Toronto, 1973).

members fretted about his tendency to compromise what they perceived to be the essential rights and privileges of French Canadians in Confederation. Moreover, when he assumed the leadership, Laurier knew that his party was desperately in need of a policy alternative to the Macdonald Government's National Policy of tariff protection to promote industrial and agricultural development. He quickly embraced unrestricted reciprocity, with its demand for complete free trade with the United States and, in the 1891 election, was humiliatingly defeated and charged with disloyalty by Macdonald.

The Ottawa convention had been called two years later to restore party confidence, to encourage party organization and, Laurier hoped, to adopt a new program that would at last put the Liberals on the path to victory. As Laurier waited for the cheers that greeted him to die, he noted the bold banners displayed throughout the hall. Like all the other convention arrangements, they had been carefully prepared to draw the delegates' attention to a single point:

> Protection is a National Folly and a National Crime.
> The Tory Tariff Oppresses the Farmer.
> Millions for Necessity — Not a Cent for Monopoly.
> Protection is Legalized Robbery.
> Liberty to Commerce.

Delegates were being reminded of fifteen years of Tory protectionism, of courting the big interests, of neglect of farmers and workers. Macdonald, the Father of Confederation, the champion of the National Policy, was dead. But the Conservatives still ruled on Parliament Hill and it was easy enough on that warm summer evening for Laurier's followers to believe that baneful Tory policies were the cause of the depressed trade and low farm prices which wracked Canada in the mid-1890s.[2]

That was Laurier's theme. "One of the plagues of Egypt took away the first-born of each family," the Liberal press reported him as saying, "but under Canada's National Policy the whole issue of the people was being taken away. (CHEERS) The ideal fiscal system was the British system of

2. On the National Policy see O.J. McDiarmid, *Commercial Policy in the Canadian Economy* (Cambridge, 1946); J.H. Perry, *Taxes, Tariffs, and Subsidies: A History of Canadian Fiscal Development*, 2 vols. (Toronto, 1955); and J.H. Dales, *The Protective Tariff in Canada's Development* (Toronto, 1966). R.C. Brown examines "The Nationalism of the National Policy" in Peter Russell, ed., *Nationalism in Canada* (Toronto, 1966). See also Michael Bliss, "Canadianizing American Business: The Roots of the Branch Plant" in Ian Lumsden, ed., *Close the 49th Parallel; The Americanization of Canada* (Toronto, 1970). A valuable retrospective is "The National Policy, 1879–1979," *Journal of Canadian Studies*, XIV, Fall, 1979.

Another Adventurous Inventor

Performer Laurier: "Yes, my friends, I'm going over in this machine—my own invention—I feel sure it will take me safely through."

Kahrs /Daily Mail and Empire

free trade. (GREAT APPLAUSE) It was the policy of the Liberal Party to get as near that ideal policy as the requirements of revenue would permit. Free trade was the goal towards which they should struggle. (CHEERS) He was, before all things, a Canadian. TARIFF REDUCTION AND RECIPROCITY ought to form the two main planks in the platform of the party. (GREAT APPLAUSE)."

Ever so skillfully the banners, Laurier's speech, and the resolutions adopted the next day began to move the party away from total reliance on the dangerous doctrine of unrestricted reciprocity and towards a new tariff policy which could accommodate the manufacturing and commercial interests which the National Policy had nurtured. The "requirements of revenue" could cover many concessions to these interests. The "goal" of free trade — *freer* trade with Great Britain and the United States was the way the tariff resolution put it — held out hope to the farmers.

No less carefully, the banners, the speech, and the resolutions of the convention were silent on the other great issue which bedeviled Canadian politics in the 1890s, the Manitoba school question. At that moment the issue was before the courts and that was an excuse for silence. More important, members of the Liberal party, like their opponents, were deeply divided on the issue. There was little that could be said that would not offend one or another faction of the party whereas silence, and deflection of the party's interest to other issues, like the tariff, would promote party unity.

The Liberal Party Convention of 1893 marked the turning point in Wilfrid Laurier's political fortunes. The next general election was still a few years away, but the convention stimulated party loyalty and organization and established the strategy and the programs that the Liberals would carry into the contest. Over the months ahead Laurier would keep his counsel on the schools question and reassert, again and again, the party's safe if ambiguous trade policy. When followers strayed away and urged him to take a stand on the schools issue, they were brought back into line. "Let us bring back public opinion to the tariff," he told a Liberal editor in Ontario in 1895.

The Schools Question

Like Laurier, the leaders of the Conservative Party in the 1890s fondly hoped to "bring back public opinion to the tariff." Unlike Laurier, the governing party in Ottawa had to deal with the schools question. Its history traced back to 1870 when the Province of Manitoba, with its tiny population of about 12 000 inhabitants of European origin, a majority of whom were Roman Catholic and French speaking, entered Confederation. The institutions of the new province reflected its dual culture. French and English were recognized as official languages of government and a publicly financed system of denominational schools was established. By 1891 the population of the province had grown to more than 150 000 and less than 20 per cent of Manitobans were Catholic. As the province grew, so too did the perception, especially in the rapidly expanding western districts, that government financing of the dual school system favoured schools in older settlements along the Red River where the Catholic and French-speaking population was concentrated. Criticism of the dual school system crystalized in 1889 when Joseph Martin, M.L.A. for Portage La Prairie and Attorney General in the Manitoba Government, announced his support for a radical revision of the school system and for the abolition of printing of government documents in French. The following year Premier Thomas Greenway's Liberal Government abolished the status of French as an official language and passed the Manitoba Schools Act (1890), which eliminated public support for denominational schools. Henceforth, provincial funding for education would be channelled only to a new, non-denominational, "national" public school system. Denominational schools would be dependent on private support for their continued existence.

The Catholic minority, with strong encouragement from the Church in Quebec, immediately petitioned Macdonald's Government in Ottawa to disallow the Schools Act. A host of issues fundamental to the very nature of Confederation was raised by the petition. It assumed that Ottawa's constitutional power to disallow provincial legislation would apply to the Schools Act. But the disallowance power itself had been repeatedly challenged by the provinces in the 1880s and, moreover, Section 92 of the British North America Act clearly assigned public education to the jurisdiction of the provinces. More important still, the petition raised the most important issue of Confederation itself: What was the nature and scope of the agreement between French and English Canadians in 1867? That too had been the subject of angry debate in the 1870s and 1880s, and Macdonald's Government had already lost significant support in Quebec as a result of its decision to hang Louis Riel after the rebellion in 1885. Macdonald knew that he would soon have to call a general election and he dreaded raising such fundamental legal and political issues in the political forum. Instead of disallowing the Schools Act, he encouraged the minority to challenge the legislation in the courts.

The court cases dragged out over the next five years. By 1895 it had been determined that Manitoba *did* have the power to enact the Schools Act. But the courts also determined that the minority had the right to appeal to the Ottawa Government for redress if its educational rights were upset. By then Sir Mackenzie Bowell, the third Conservative leader to head the Government since Macdonald's death, was Prime Minister. In March, 1895, after hearing the minority's case, the Government ordered Manitoba to restore public support to the province's Roman Catholic schools. At this point the issue became a contest of political will between the Liberal Government in Winnipeg and the Conservative Government in Ottawa.

Greenway was obstructive. He first proposed a commission of enquiry and then called an election on the issue which resulted in a healthy majority for his Government. Though he threatened remedial legislation, Bowell was indecisive. In January, 1896, several of his ministers, impatient with the Prime Minister's dithering, resigned. To resolve the Cabinet crisis Sir Charles Tupper, the High Commissioner in London, was brought back to lead the Government and shepherd remedial legislation through Parliament. Tupper's situation was truly desperate. By the time the remedial legislation came to the House of Commons for debate the Government's five-year parliamentary term had only a few short weeks to run. The Liberals filibustered the bill and forced a general election in June, 1896.[3]

If voters in the election sensed that neither party was giving them clear choices on the schools question or the tariff issue, they were correct. Where appropriate, and especially in Quebec, both parties suggested that if necessary Greenway would be brought to heel by remedial action from Ottawa. Elsewhere, and especially in Ontario where sympathy for Greenway's stand was strong, both parties alluded to less coercive resolutions to the schools question. Similarly, while the Conservative defence of the National Policy tariff was as strong as ever, the ambiguous approach to the tariff by the Liberals, and the presence of a number of prominent protectionists as Liberal candidates, left open the possibility that a Liberal victory would not threaten the main lines of protectionist tariff policy. In the end, as so often seemed to be the case, the choice of leadership may have been the decisive question in the election. Quebec chose its native son by a wide margin — 75 per cent of the seats. Laurier also won a majority of seats in British Columbia and on the Prairies, still unorganized into provinces and still known as the Northwest Territories. Tupper's forces secured majorities in Manitoba, New Brunswick, and Prince Edward Island and split the seats in his home province, Nova Scotia. In Ontario six constituencies went to minor parties and the remaining eighty-six were divided evenly between the Liberals and the Conservatives. Overall, and largely as a result of the Quebec results, Laurier's Liberals had a comfort-

---

3. Paul Crunican, *Priests and Politicians: Manitoba Schools and the Election of 1896* (Toronto, 1974), is a detailed analysis of the Manitoba school question. David Hall gives another perspective on the schools issue in Manitoba in *Clifford Sifton*, Volume One: *The Young Napoleon, 1861–1900* (Vancouver, 1981). A useful collection of documents is Lovell Clark, *The Manitoba School Question: Majority Rule or Minority Rights?* (Toronto, 1968). A related issue is explored in Manoly R. Lupul, *The Roman Catholic Church and the North-West School Question: A Study in Church-State Relations in Western Canada, 1875–1905* (Toronto, 1974). See also W.L. Morton, "Manitoba Schools and Canadian Nationality, 1890–1923," *Canadian Historical Association Annual Report, 1951,* and Ramsay Cook, "Church, Schools and Politics in Manitoba, 1902–1912," *Canadian Historical Review,* XXXIX (1958).

able majority of thirty seats. The dominance of federal politics by the Conservative party since Confederation was broken. The Laurier era, the Liberal century, had begun.

Laurier in Power

Canadians greeted the Laurier years with a heady optimism stimulated by a new Government and by an impressive upturn in the economy. Conscientious government clerks in Ottawa and in the provincial capitals eagerly compiled mountains of statistics to illustrate the growth of productivity in every imaginable endeavour from the growing of grains and the husbandry of livestock to the mining of peat moss, the export of bicycles, and the number of telegraphic messages sent every year. Businessmen rivalled politicians in their glowing recitations of Canada's potential for greatness. Everyone, an English visitor observed, perhaps a little tired of constant boosterism, "is preaching, praising, prophesying."

Much was made of Canadian progress in education, "religious and moral interests," the arts and music, literature and journalism. But the focus of attention was on material development, and nowhere more so than in Ottawa. "Official Ottawa shows nothing of the sedate dignity of a Government capital," another visitor wrote. "Her clubs and offices are tense with the spirit of the 'boom'." With a keen appreciation of the political value of good times, Laurier boasted that "the twentieth century shall be the century of Canada and of Canadian development." Development was good politics. It contrasted sharply with the stalemate, confusion, and acrimony that marked the last years of Conservative rule. It caught the imagination of a newly confident nation yearning for self-realization.[4]

Six days after the election the new Prime Minister sent a reassuring letter to John Willison, editor of the Toronto *Globe*, who was worried about the reaction of businessmen to the new Government. "The tariff should not be reformed," Laurier wrote, "until there has been ample discussion with the businessmen. ... " He was already preparing an even stronger signal to the manufacturers, whose interests had been so assiduously protected by the National Policy, that they would be kindly treated by the new Government. Sir Richard Cartwright, the long-time Liberal financial critic and an ardent advocate of unrestricted reciprocity, was

4. The most comprehensive survey of the Laurier years is Robert Craig Brown and Ramsay Cook, *Canada, 1896-1921: A Nation Transformed* (Toronto, 1974). A major study of developments in Quebec is Paul André Linteau, René Durocher, and Jean-Claude Robert, *Histoire du Québec Contemporain: De la Confederation à la crise, 1867-1929* (Québec, 1979).

relegated to the secondary Ministry of Trade and Commerce in the Government. And Laurier's "Cabinet of all talents" included many new faces sympathetic to the protectionist principles of the National Policy. Most important was the new Minister of Finance, William S. Fielding who, as Premier of Nova Scotia, had courted American financial interests to develop the coal resources of his province. The Quebec delegation included Joseph Israel Tarte, a former Tory with strong protectionist sympathies, and Richard Dobell, a Quebec City conservative who had been elected with Tory support. Ontario's members included Sir Oliver Mowat, who had had a long and distinguished career as Premier, and William Paterson, a manufacturer who became Controller of Customs. They would soon be joined by Clifford Sifton, the Manitoba attorney general, as the new Minister of the Interior. Sifton shared the Prime Minister's shrewd respect for the political force of entrenched economic policies. He knew that for Westerners free trade was second only to the Gospels as a sacred principle of life. But, as he bluntly told a constituent:

> I not only would not retire from the Government because they refused to eliminate the principle of protection from the tariff, but I would not remain in the Government if they did eliminate the principle of protection from the tariff. I would consider that to so construct the tariff as to wantonly destroy the industries that have been built up under it, would be utterly unjustifiable from any standpoint of reason.

During the winter of 1896–97 Fielding, Paterson, and Cartwright travelled from city to city, listening carefully to the detailed tariff briefs of manufacturers and boards of trade, hearing few representations from the farmers who had been the backbone of the Liberal party and the staunchest advocates of free trade. Then, in April, 1897, Fielding announced the new tariff. Agrarians found some satisfaction in the reduction of duties on implements, binder twine, and a few other goods essential to agricultural production. There was also some prospect of freer trade in the most innovative feature of Fielding's policy, the adoption of a two-tier tariff. Canada would offer a 12½ per cent preference immediately, to be raised to 25 per cent in the next year, to any nation which lowered its duties against Canadian goods by an equivalent rate. Because of Britain's free trade policy, the United Kingdom, a major market for agricultural exports, would automatically qualify for the preference; British goods, as a result, would be allowed into Canada more cheaply than American products.

But, behind the preference, the solid structure of protection remained intact. Laurier's quiet assurances to the business community had been fulfilled. Apart from Britain, the onus to proceed further in the direction of freer trade had shifted from Ottawa to Canada's trading partners.

Ten years later, in 1907, after another round of tariff hearings, the tariff was again modified. A third, "intermediate" schedule of duties, between the general tariff and what had become the "British Preference," was introduced. This quickly led to limited reciprocal trade agreements at the intermediate level with France, Japan, and Italy. Protectionism, the keystone of Macdonald's National Policy, remained the fundamental principle of the tariff, as it would for decades to come. The significance of the modifications the Laurier Government made in the tariff was less in policy innovation than in administrative adaption to changing patterns of international trade. The multi-tiered tariffs of the Laurier Government modernized Macdonald's National Policy. The protective principle was retained but the additional schedules gave the Government flexibility in its efforts to encourage foreign customers to buy an ever-increasing flow of Canadian products for export.

The other great issue of the 1896 election, the schools question, was addressed with the same circumspection that marked Laurier's approach to the tariff. Manitoba might have to be coerced. But Laurier knew that compulsion could only intensify distrust between French and English Canadians on this most sensitive of Canadian problems. A face-saving compromise, quietly arranged between the Liberal Governments in Ottawa and Winnipeg, was a much better solution. By November, 1896, it was in place. Manitoba's public school system would remain intact and Catholics would have to support it with their tax dollars. But religious instruction by clergy could take place during the last half-hour of the school day and public school trustees would have to provide a Catholic teacher for every twenty-five Catholic pupils in rural districts and every forty Catholic students in urban areas. Moreover, in schools where ten or more students spoke French or any other language than English, instruction had to be provided in French or such other language, as well as in English.

The Laurier-Greenway compromise did not satisfy the clerical leadership in Manitoba and Quebec. The hierarchy had always been suspicious of Laurier, of his *rouge* background, of his unwavering espousal of the principles of English Liberalism. Laurier always seemed too ready to yield to English-Canadian arguments that separate schools perpetuated religious prejudice and prevented the social homogeneity essential in a democracy. However, for the churchmen Catholic schools were a matter of survival, survival of the race and its rich cultural heritage in and outside Quebec, survival of the religious convictions that were the foundation of a Christian society. The clerics appealed to Rome for intervention against

Laurier's compromise with Manitoba's "godless" school system. When, in December, 1897, the papal encyclical *Affari Vos* advised acceptance of the Manitoba settlement, the clergy obeyed. But very reluctantly.

Still, opposition to Laurier's policy continued to smoulder among his clerical critics. For his part, the Prime Minister remained an enthusiastic champion of school systems "where the young children of the land are taught Christian morals and Christian dogmas." But it was not enough. The Roman Catholic clergy correctly perceived that the Prime Minister was charting a new course, trying to accommodate the traditional role of the Catholic school in French-Canadian society, so deeply rooted in the history of Quebec and embodied in the Manitoba Act of 1870, to the demographic and political realities of the emerging West that had been crystallized in the Manitoba Schools Act of 1890. Unlike his critics, Laurier did not believe that the survival of French-Canadian culture rested upon the preservation of entrenched guarantees for separate schools. He had a more optimistic faith in his people, in their talent of survival. "The salvation of the French race is not in isolation," he told a member of his caucus, "but in struggle. Give our children the best education possible, put them on equal footing with those of the other race, and give them the legitimate pride which they will have in such a struggle. There is salvation. There is autonomy."

Immigrants Are Welcome

It was Clifford Sifton, the Minister of the Interior, who provided the innovative spark to the new Laurier administration. The astonishing success of his aggressive programs to promote immigration laid the foundations for the Government's breathtaking national development policies. The goal of his immigration policy was to attract experienced farmers to Canada to exploit the rich soil of the prairie West, and the improved economic conditions of the Laurier era made Sifton's policies all the more attractive to prospective immigrants. Prices for food products rose rapidly, the price of wheat in the British market increasing by 35 per cent between 1896 and 1913. At the same time cost increases for new, labour-saving farm implements like the chilled steel plow, the improved harrow and seed-driller, and the threshing machine were more moderate. Transportation costs, both ocean freight rates and railway rates, dropped in Canada. In 1897, for example, the Government negotiated the Crow's Nest Pass Agreement with the Canadian Pacific Railway. The agreement stipulated that in return for government assistance in building a branch line through the difficult terrain of the Crow's Nest Pass, the railway would reduce its freight rates for westbound articles necessary for agricultural production and for eastbound shipments of grain. In addition, federal government scientists and technicians promoted improved farming techniques, such as dry farming, and experimented with new strains of wheat, such as Marquis, developed by Dominion cerealist C.E. Saunders, which would mature more rapidly in the short growing season of the prairie West. Taken together, these developments transformed the Canadian prairies into a land of promise for future settlers.[5]

The chief impediments to immigration had hitherto been erected by the Government of Canada. Railway construction had been assisted by the grant of huge blocks of land to the railways, tieing up many of the most fertile areas in the Prairies. Sifton persuaded the Government to abandon that policy and pressured the holders of grants to select their land and put it on the market. Administration of lands policy under the Dominion Lands Act of 1872 was simplified and centralized in Ottawa. Most important, the Department of the Interior embarked upon an unprecedented promotion of Canada as a land of opportunity, not just in the United Kingdom, the traditional focus of Canada's immigration effort, but also in the United States and in Europe.

Sifton's immigration policy was selective: Canada wanted farmers accustomed to working the grainlands of Europe and the United States where conditions were similar to those of the Prairies. "Labouring men and mechanics," Sifton repeatedly said, were to be discouraged. And, after 1905, when Frank Oliver succeeded Sifton as Minister of Interior, immigration policy became increasingly restrictive. By then men of lesser vision than Sifton had begun to worry whether Canada could absorb and make loyal citizens of the hordes of "strangers" who had responded to the challenge of his policy. Between 1896 and 1905, 58 000 immigrants had arrived

5. For Sifton's immigration policy see Hall, *Clifford Sifton*, vol I. Other studies include M.F. Timlin, "Canada's Immigration Policy, 1896–1910," *Canadian Journal of Economics and Political Science*, XXVI (1960); George Woodcock and Ivan Avakumovic, *The Doukhobors* (Toronto, 1968); Robin Winks, *The Blacks in Canada* (New Haven, 1971); Peter Ward, *White Canada Forever: Popular Attitudes and Public Policy toward Orientals in British Columbia* (Montreal, 1978); and Donald Avery, *"Dangerous Foreigners": European Immigrant Workers and Labour Radicalism in Canada, 1896–1932* (Toronto, 1979).

On the opening of the West see J.B. Hedges, *Building the Canadian West* (New York, 1939); A.S. Morton and Chester Martin, *History of Prairie Settlement and Dominion Lands Policy* (Toronto, 1938); W.L. Morton, *Manitoba, A History* (Toronto, 1967); and Margaret Ormsby, *British Columbia, A History* (Toronto, 1958). See also Donald Swainson, ed., *Historical Essays on the Prairie Provinces* (Toronto, 1970); and Carl Berger and Ramsay Cook, eds., *The West and the Nation, Essays in Honour of W.L. Morton* (Toronto, 1976).

from Austria-Hungary, 32 000 from Russia, 8000 from Italy, and almost 12 000 from China. The question of restricting Asiatic immigration had become a prominent political issue and Oliver, who shared the growing disquiet, broadened his ministerial powers to reject and deport immigrants from Asia. In 1907, in the wake of rioting against Asiatic immigration in Vancouver, the Government concluded a gentlemen's agreement with Japan to limit sharply Japanese migration to Canada. The following year the Immigration Act was amended to require immigrants to come to Canada by direct passage from their home country. This further curtailed the prospect of Asiatic immigration. By the end of the Laurier years the full force of the Department of the Interior's administrative machinery was also being applied to discourage further immigration of blacks, who had made up 9 per cent of the 303 680 immigrants from the United States who had come to Canada by 1911.

Public concern over the accommodation to Canadian life of "Sifton's pets," as European immigrants were being called, was also a fundamental factor in a new schools issue in national politics. Between 1891 and 1901 the population of the Northwest Territories had increased by 66 per cent. In response to demands from politicians from the Territories for provincial

Conditions for entry into Canada were not stringent, but some unfortunates — including the boy on crutches — were deported because they failed various physical, mental, and moral requirements. (PA-20910/Public Archives Canada)

Inaugural ceremonies of the province of Saskatchewan were held on September 4, 1905. Laurier is fifth from the left, and others in the group include the Governor General and his wife and William Paterson, Minister of Customs. (C-21896/Public Archives Canada)

THE PROTEST OF THE WEST.

The bull: — "You may coerce me into it, but it's another thing to make me drink."

status, Laurier promised to create new provinces in his 1904 election campaign. In February, 1905, bills creating the provinces of Saskatchewan and Alberta were introduced in the House of Commons.

When the Territories were organized by the Dominion Government in 1875, separate and equal Catholic and Protestant school systems had been established. Over the years Territorial Ordinances had dramatically altered the educational system, partly in response to need for greater efficiency and partly to meet the need to "Canadianize" the growing foreign-born population which, by 1900, was more than 27 per cent of the populace. All schools had become public schools, with the same regulations and curriculum. Religious instruction was permitted only at the end of the school day, and the majority in each district determined whether Catholic or Protestant teachers were hired.

Conscious of the lingering distrust of the administration by the Catholic clergy, and of a growing concern among French Canadians that Sifton's immigration policy was excluding them from their rightful share in western development, Laurier gave the task of drafting the education clauses of the autonomy bills to his Minister of Justice, Charles Fitzpatrick from Quebec, and to the M.P. from Labelle, Henri Bourassa. Sifton, who remained adamantly opposed to separate schools, was excluded. When the bills were introduced, the ambiguously worded education clauses conveyed the impression that the Government was going to restore the separate school system of 1875 and impose it on the new provinces.

The clauses provoked a heated debate in the House of Commons, one which threatened to split both parties on religious and racial lines. Robert Borden, who had become leader of the Conservative Opposition in 1901, was forced to allow his caucus a free vote on the issue. For his own part, Borden firmly argued that the education clauses would deny the new provinces the right to determine their own education policies. It was a telling constitutional and political point. Liberals, after all, had long prided themselves on their respect for provincial autonomy. And what province had more to fear from the precedent of Dominion interference in its educational system than Quebec?

Far more damaging to the Government was the resignation of Sifton as Minister of Interior and the threatened resignation of Fielding. Laurier, taken aback, denied that his purpose had been to present Sifton, as the key spokesman for the West in the Cabinet, with a fait accompli. But he did not urge Sifton to rejoin the Cabinet. He did however, entrust him with the responsibility for redrafting the education clauses. The new version, accepted by Parliament, recognized only the minority rights that remained in the 1901 Territorial Ordinances.

Laurier had kept his election promise to create the new provinces, but at great cost. Once again, in the eyes of the more militant clergy and of a small but growing number of French-Canadian nationalists such as Henri Bourassa, the Prime Minister had backed down and sacrificed sacred principles in the face of an entrenched English-Canadian majority. "In constituting the French Canadian, who has lived in this country since its discovery, the equal in rights and privileges to the Dukobor [sic] or the Galician who has just embarked," one critic said, "we have opened a gulf between eastern and western Canadians which nothing will fill." The speaker, Armand Lavergne, would soon join forces with an even more outspoken proponent of *nationalisme*, Bourassa. And though Sifton continued to sit on the Liberal side of the Commons, he never trusted Laurier again. With diametrically opposite visions of the nature and the future of Canada, these men all would play prominent roles in Laurier's defeat in 1911.

For the immigrants, arguments in Parliament about the nation's destiny could be of only passing interest. But, if the acquisition of citizenship is a guide, the vast majority quickly sought formal identity with their new homeland. By 1911, 45 per cent of the foreign-born had become British subjects. If the 360 000 immigrants who arrived after 1905 (most of whom

These homesteaders lived in a partially sodded hut south of Estevan, Saskatchewan in 1911. The difficulties of raising three preschool children — and keeping them clean! — in such surroundings must have taken the patience of Job. (Glenbow Archives, NA 1405-1)

had still not completed the three-year period of naturalization) are excluded, more than 70 per cent of the foreign-born became naturalized. Beyond that their daily concerns were more prosaic: finding a piece of land, erecting a dwelling, making provisions for the families who had accompanied them or would soon arrive, coping with a strange language, different customs and, not least of all, the elements. The Government's terms of settlement were generous. On Dominion lands, as distinct from land granted to the railways or the Hudson's Bay Company, the settler was entitled to a free quarter-section if he lived on it and "proved it up" over a period of three years. He was also allowed a preemption to purchase an additional 160 acres. Lastly, and this obviously influenced the rate of naturalization, the settler had to become a British subject before he was given the final patent to his land.

Still, though the terms were generous, the process of settlement was costly. This was true whether the settler came from Britain, Europe, the grainlands of the American Midwest, or an Ontario or Nova Scotia farmstead to strike out anew in the prairie West. Estimates varied from $250 to as much as $1500 as start-up costs, depending upon the degree of deprivation a settler would tolerate for a new life in the West. Cash was only a part of the cost. There was the back-breaking labour of breaking sod or clearing parkland, the risk of hailstorms and early frost that could destroy a year's work in a matter of minutes, and the lonely isolation and privation of a sod hut. But the settlers came and most of them told immigration officials that they were bound for the West.

Every province except Prince Edward Island experienced a growth in population between 1901 and 1911, but the increases in the West were astonishing.

A massive internal migration in Canada supplemented immigration from abroad. Also spurred by better times and new economic opportunities, patterns of internal migration varied from region to region. Some Maritimers sought better jobs close to home in another province in the region. Tens of thousands of French Canadians moved into eastern and northern Ontario to work in the lumber camps and mines of that rapidly developing area. In general, however, the flow of migration was clearly from east to west. Large numbers from the Maritimes and Quebec joined Ontarians in the flood into the western provinces.

By 1911 more than 12 per cent of all native-born Ontarians lived between the Red River and the Pacific Ocean, exerting their heavy influence upon the developing institutions and cultural attitudes of Sifton's "New Canada."

INTENDED DESTINATION OF IMMIGRANTS TO CANADA, 1901–1911

	Maritime Provinces	Quebec	Ontario	Manitoba	Saskatchewan and Alberta	British Columbia and Yukon Territories	CANADA
Total number 1901–1911	73 501	258 820	403 899	309 623	516 832	188 571	1 751 246
%	4.3	14.8	23.0	17.7	29.5	10.7	100.0

Source: *Canada Year Book*, 1913.

POPULATION OF CANADA AND THE PROVINCES, 1901-1911

	1901	1911	% change
Nova Scotia	459 574	492 338	7.1
New Brunswick	331 120	351 889	6.3
Prince Edward Island	103 259	93 728	−9.2
Quebec	1 648 898	2 003 232	21.5
Ontario	2 182 947	2 523 274	15.6
Manitoba	255 211	455 614	78.5
Saskatchewan	91 279	492 432	439.5
Alberta	73 022	374 663	413.1
British Columbia	178 657	392 480	119.7
CANADA	5 371 315	7 206 643	34.2

Source: *Canada Year Book*, 1913, p. 51

BIRTHPLACES OF POPULATION BY PROVINCE IN 1911 (PERCENTAGES)

	Canadian Born		Immigrants	
	Born in Province	Born in another Province	British-Born	Foreign-Born
Nova Scotia	90.2	2.5	5.1	2.2
New Brunswick	90.7	4.1	2.9	2.3
Prince Edward Island	95.4	1.8	1.8	1.0
Quebec	91.1	1.6	3.6	3.7
Ontario	76.6	3.3	14.2	5.9
Manitoba	37.5	20.6	20.9	21.0
Saskatchewan	20.7	29.8	16.5	33.0
Alberta	19.7	23.6	18.6	38.1
British Columbia	21.5	21.6	30.1	26.8
CANADA	70.2	7.8	11.6	10.4

Source: *Canada Year Book*, 1913.

The Peoples' Lives

It would be a mistake to assume that all of the migrants were or even intended to be agriculturalists. Thousands of Canadians and immigrants found new jobs in the forest industries of northern Ontario, Quebec, and British Columbia, in the hardrock mines of Ontario and British Columbia, and in the newly opened coal shafts in the Rocky Mountains. The number employed in those occupations increased by 156 per cent and 119 per cent, respectively, between 1901 and 1911. And, among the gainfully employed, the proportion of farmers, despite the emphasis in immigration policy, steadily declined from 45 per cent in 1891 to 40.2 per cent in 1901 and 34.3 per cent in 1911. No less significant, whatever Sifton wished, was the growth of the cities, which was as pronounced in the Laurier years as the development of the West. Thousands of "labourers and mechanics" were assiduously sought out by the owners of factories and mills, by railways and building contractors. Sometimes the immigrants were encouraged to come to Canada because they had special skills required in the industrialization of Canada; more often they were hired because they were willing to accept lower wages than Canadian workers. They were joined by an army of girls and young women who were exploited even more in the sweatshops of the cities, or who were in great demand as domestic servants for the rapidly increasing numbers of businessmen and professionals in the work force. Along with the large number of migrants who failed as homesteaders, they all sought a fresh start in newly crowded cities from Halifax to Victoria.

For most, life was at least as harsh as it could be on a quarter-section. Basic services in the cities lagged far behind the growth of population. Urban governments focussed their attention on the costly business of giving tax concessions and bonuses to industries and neglected the expansion and up-grading of water and sewer systems. The enforcement of public health regulations, where they existed, was shockingly deficient. Hydro-electricity and telephone lines spread quickly through middle- and upper-class areas and industrial and business districts. They seldom penetrated the working class wards of Halifax, Montreal, Toronto, Winnipeg, and Vancouver. A shortage of low-cost housing forced thousands of people to live in the deplorable conditions described by a Toronto civil servant in 1904, "in stables, tents, old cars, sheds (others in damp cellars), where we would not place a valued animal, let alone a human being."[6]

6. Contemporary accounts of urban life include Herbert Brown Ames, *The City Below the Hill* (Toronto, 1972); C.S. Clark, *Of Toronto the Good: A Social Study* (Montreal, 1898); and J.S. Woodsworth, *My Neighbour* (Toronto, 1972). A.F.J. Artibise and Gilbert A. Stelter have edited the valuable collection, *The Canadian City: Essays in Urban History* (Toronto, 1977). Artibise is also the author of a major urban history, *Winnipeg: A Social History of Urban Growth, 1874–1914* (Montreal, 1975).

Major studies of industrial development include H.V. Nelles, *The Politics of Development: Forests, Mines, and Hydro-Electric Power in Ontario, 1849–1941* (Toronto, 1974); J.H. Dales, *Hydroelectricity and Industrial Development, Quebec, 1898–1940* (Cambridge, 1957); W.J. Ryan, *The Clergy and Economic Growth in Quebec, 1896–1914* (Quebec, 1966); H.G.J. Aitken, *American Capital and Canadian Resources* (Cambridge, 1961); and K. Buckley, *Capital Formation in Canada, 1896–1930* (Toronto, 1955).

POPULATION OF SELECTED CITIES, 1901-1911

	1901	1911	% change
Halifax	40 832	46 619	14.2
Saint John	40 711	42 511	4.4
Charlottetown	12 080	11 203	-7.3
Quebec	68 840	78 710	14.3
Montreal	328 172	490 504	49.5
Ottawa	59 928	87 062	45.3
Toronto	209 892	381 833	81.9
Hamilton	52 634	81 969	55.7
Winnipeg	42 340	136 035	221.3
Regina	2 249	30 213	1 243.4
Saskatoon	113	12 004	10 523.0
Edmonton	4 176	31 064	643.9
Calgary	4 392	43 704	895.1
Vancouver	27 010	100 401	271.7
Victoria	20 919	31 660	51.3

Source: *Canada Year Book*, 1922–23, p. 171

In time governments at all levels responded to the social and economic pressures of urban growth and the opening of virgin territory. In the cities welfare services, traditionally the responsibility of the churches and private charities, were gradually taken over by municipal governments. To control the "diseases" of urban life, prostitution, drunkenness, vagrancy, and juvenile delinquency, cities modernized their police forces and passed hefty lists of more restrictive bylaws. (As a result, between 1901 and 1911 the number of convictions for offences by juveniles and other minor crimes skyrocketed from thirty-two thousand to ninety-four thousand per annum.) By the end of the Laurier years some cities had begun to experiment with commission government and other formulas which, urban reformers promised, would wipe out ward politics and corruption and bring efficient administration and balanced budgets to city governments.

At the provincial level new departments, bureaus, and branches of provincial administration multiplied as the provinces tried to cope with growing demands for public services. Particular attention was paid to education where both educators and social reformers demanded tighter regulations for school attendance and substantial revisions to the curriculum to make it more "practical" and responsive to the needs of a complex society and diversified economy. Domestic science and technical and agricultural education were but three of the new subjects being taught in public and secondary schools by the end of the Laurier years. Similarly, increasing emphasis on pure science, engineering, social science, forestry, and agriculture was evident in university faculties across the land. But the universities, whether privately funded or provincially supported, remained small, elite institutions open only to the few. Only 7437 students were enrolled in universities in 1904, and graduating classes ranged in size from 25 at the University of New Brunswick and 65 at Dalhousie to 210 at McGill and 424 at Toronto. Among the few, women were fewer still. As late as 1921, a decade after Laurier's defeat, females accounted for less than 30 per cent of the university students in Canada.

At the national level the Laurier Government tinkered with the great social issues of the day. A referendum on the prohibition question in 1898 revealed a decisive split between French and English Canada, reason enough to bury the issue. After a divisive debate, the Government passed the Lord's Day Act in 1906, but delegated the responsibility for enforcement of the Sunday legislation to the provincial governments. In part the Dominion response was dictated by the British North America Act. Like education, jurisdiction for most of the pressing social questions of the period was assigned to the provinces. But the hesitant response of the Liberals was also a measure of their very conservative attitude on all social issues, especially women's rights, and of the explosive potential of federal initiatives in areas where English- and French-Canadian attitudes were so different.

Far safer, and much more popular with the voters, was the heavy investment by every level of government in transportation and public utilities. City governments recklessly expanded their street railway systems. Provinces like Ontario and Alberta chartered railways to frontier areas to promote resource development and joined other provinces in offering land grants and bond guarantees for the construction of branch lines. Responding to pressure from municipalities in southern Ontario, the Conservative Whitney Government took the first steps towards the creation of a publicly owned hydro-electric system in 1908. In Manitoba and Alberta the telephone systems were already publicly owned.

The most spectacular plunge was taken by the Dominion Government. As soon as large numbers of settlers began to spread out across the prairie and parkland of Manitoba and the Territories it became obvious that the C.P.R. system would not be adequate to service the transportation needs of the new homesteaders. By 1901, the owners of the Canadian Northern Railway, William Mackenzie and Donald Mann, who already had a line to the Lakehead and were building westward from Manitoba,

Living conditions in the mining and lumber camps of the frontier were far from luxurious at the turn of the century. In addition, working conditions were often extremely dangerous. (C-38620/Public Archives Canada)

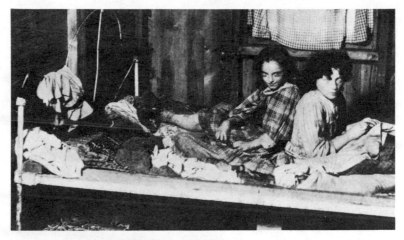

Social problems abounded amidst the prosperity of Edwardian Canada. This photograph, taken in Winnipeg in 1912, was entitled "The One-Room Home" and carried the apt caption, "The Shame of Large Cities . . ." (C-30936/Public Archives of Canada)

These workmen were building a railway trestle for the Canadian Northern near Ernsted, Alberta in late 1912. (Mr. and Mrs. Percy Hitchcock collection)

announced their ambition to construct another transcontinental line. The Grand Trunk, long established in the East, also was interested in building a new railway to the Pacific. Here were the obvious elements of a partnership in a new transcontinental railway. But the two companies could never agree to terms, and Laurier shied away from the role of honest broker. Instead, he cast his lot with the Grand Trunk while refusing to discourage the plans of Mackenzie and Mann. In effect, and over the opposition of his Minister of Railways, A.G. Blair, who wanted one new publicly owned transcontinental line, Laurier sanctioned two new railways from coast to coast.[7]

The Grand Trunk drove a very hard and advantageous bargain. A subsidiary company, the Grand Trunk Pacific, would build the line (in many places parallel to and in sight of the Canadian Northern) from Winnipeg to Prince Rupert, British Columbia. In return, the Government would guarantee 75 per cent of the company's bonds. But the Grand Trunk wanted no part of the construction of the politically rewarding but unprofitable link from Winnipeg across northern Ontario and Quebec, through Quebec City to Moncton. Instead, that 3000 km line, called the National Transcontinental, would be built by the Government of Canada and, when completed, leased to the G.T.P. at 3 per cent of its cost per annum. Blair resigned when the scheme was announced in Parliament. (Laurier quickly appointed him to the Board of Railway Commissioners.) The leader of the Conservative Opposition, Robert Borden, argued for a publicly owned line, making it the chief issue in his unsuccessful 1904 election campaign. Laurier dismissed charges of extravagance and, with Finance Minister Fielding, pooh-poohed the potential costs of the plan. The future was limitless, the Government was accumulating unprecedented surpluses in its public accounts ($14 million in 1903, $15 million in 1904) and such concerns could be harboured only by the faint-hearted. "This plan may scare the timid and frighten the irresolute," Laurier said. "But I may claim that every man who has in his bosom a stout Canadian heart will welcome it as worthy of this young nation, for which a heavy task has no terrors, which has strength to face grave duties and grave responsibilities." That was magnificent, but it was most imprudent; by 1911 neither

---

7. The pioneering history of the C.P.R. is H.A. Innis, *A History of the Canadian Pacific Railway* (Toronto, 1971), which can be supplemented by the more colourful books of Pierre Berton, *The National Dream* and *The Last Spike* (Toronto, 1970 and 1971). G.R. Stevens, *Canadian National Railways*, 2 vols. (Toronto, 1960 and 1962), and T.D. Regehr, *The Canadian Northern Railway: Pioneer Road of the Northern Prairies, 1895–1915* (Toronto, 1976), are impressive studies.

of the new railways was finished and both were in financial trouble. Borden, the new Prime Minister, was eventually forced to take them over as major components of the publicly owned and operated Canadian National Railways system.

Railway schemes were especially attractive to politicians. The costs were distant and indirect, tucked away in long-term bond guarantees. The benefits were widespread and immediately apparent. Farmers and land speculators, often one in the same person, reaped the rewards of the railway boom in rising land prices and improved access to foreign markets. So too did the railway contractors and, in a very different way, the immigrant and native labourers who found steady but hard and often dangerous employment constructing the new railways. The manufacturers of iron and steel products, of the components of railway cars and the hundreds of other goods necessary to build a modern railway were also major benefactors. And the payoffs spread still wider to the producers of the thousands of items pictured in the retail store catalogues so popular at the turn of the century. Orders for boots and corsets and tools and stoves and pianos could be sped over the new lines from big city warehouses to distant customers.

By 1910 the amount of capital invested in manufacturing and the value of manufactured products produced had both exceeded one billion dollars. The value added by manufacturing, a more exact indicator of the contribution of manufacturing to the economy, increased by 163 per cent between 1900 and 1910. The growth of the number of employees by product groups within the manufacturing sector gives one indication of the fastest growing areas of manufacturing. Vehicles for land transport, which by 1910 included an expanding automobile industry, led the list, and developments in iron, steel, other metals, and chemicals all pointed towards a quickly maturing industrial economy.

The growth of investment in manufacturing, 179 per cent between 1900 and 1910, was marked at the end of the Laurier years by a very substantial consolidation movement. Financiers in Montreal and Toronto promoted vertical or horizontal integrations of major areas of manufacturing from iron and steel to cement, bakery products, and canned foods. The returns were usually handsome for investors and promoters alike. Industrial workers, however, predictably did less well. The approximate annual wage in manufacturing rose 44.5 per cent between 1900 and 1910, but this figure must be put in a broader perspective. Wage increases varied significantly from group to group. Groups such as textiles, food, and tobacco, which employed significant numbers of women, paid their female

NUMBER OF WAGE EARNERS AND APPROXIMATE ANNUAL WAGE BY MANUFACTURING GROUP 1900 and 1910

Manufacturing Group	Employees			Approximate Annual Wage		
	1900	1910	% change	1900	1910	% change
Food Products	42 401	52 730	24.2	189	275	45.5
Textiles	59 324	72 672	22.5	258	368	42.6
Iron & Steel	24 766	48 558	96.0	397	531	33.8
Timber, Lumber & Wood Products	75 704	110 049	45.4	250	358	43.2
Leather & Products	19 204	22 742	18.4	315	425	34.9
Paper & Printing	15 413	22 894	48.6	369	474	28.5
Liquor & Beverage	3 208	4 688	46.1	397	563	41.8
Chemicals & Allied Products	2 868	5 274	83.9	357	452	26.6
Clay, Glass & Stone Products	10 765	17 699	64.4	256	435	69.9
Other Metals & Products	9 358	17 502	87.0	414	559	35.0
Tobacco & Products	6 329	8 763	38.5	306	378	23.5
Vehicles for Land Transport	14 866	35 778	140.7	424	546	28.8
Vehicles for Water Transport	2 587	4 414	70.6	324	530	63.6
Miscellaneous	21 084	38 537	82.8	356	480	34.8
Hand Trades	605	8 826	1358.8	413	466	12.8
All Manufacturing	308 482	471 126	52.7	290	419	44.5

Source: *Canada Year Book*, 1913.

workers substantially lower wages than males earned. In addition, employment in many manufacturing groups was seasonal, ranging from a few months to three-quarters of the year. Year-round employment in a factory was the exception in the Laurier era.

The Dominion Department of Labour calculated that the cost of food, laundry starch, fuel, lighting, and rent of a six-room dwelling was $9.38 per week ($490 per annum) in 1900. By 1910 these selected items in a family budget had increased more than 31 per cent to $640 per annum. In neither year did approximate annual wages match these costs, much less afford the industrial worker any surplus for the other necessities and incidentals of family life. These estimates of the costs of bare essentials in a budget for a family of four, based on departmental surveys in sixty cities, strongly suggest that at least two and often more members of a working-class family had to work for as many weeks a year as they could to make ends meet. In short, while wages for industrial workers rose significantly during the first decade of the twentieth century, there appears to be little evidence that wages increased enough for most workers to improve their living standard.

Beyond that, the work environment was invariably harsh and often deadly. The ten- or twelve-hour day and sixty-hour week was normal; the "eight-hour-day" movement was just beginning to attract attention at the end of the Laurier years. Factories were dirty, noisy, and dangerous places. Owners provided little protection for workers from heavy, fast-moving machinery. Provinces like Ontario, which did have rudimentary safety regulations for the workplace, employed too few factory inspectors to ensure that the rules were enforced.

Exploitive and dangerous working conditions invited the intervention of the trade union movement. Even though workers lacked governmental recognition of such elemental rights as collective bargaining, trade unionism had deep roots in ninteenth century Canada. The trade union movement was tiny in 1900, claiming only some 20 000 organized workers. Over the next decade it experienced phenomenal growth. By 1911 about 130 000 workers were members of union locals. Lists of union locals compiled by the Department of Labour strongly suggest that most unionists worked in traditional crafts in the building trades and printing, and in transportation, mining, and lumbering. The expansion of trade unionism in the first years of the new century was remarkable, but organization of the industrial workplace had barely begun.

Moreover, the union movement was deeply divided both regionally and culturally in 1911. Almost 90 per cent of Canadian trade unionists were members of international unions affiliated with Samuel Gomper's conservatively oriented American Federation of Labor in the United States. Equally conservative was the Provincial Workman's Association, the major trade union force in Nova Scotia, though its influence was waning under the challenge of American miners' unions. Yet another American union, the radical Western Federation of Miners, had established a foothold in British Columbia. At the beginning of the century the American-based Knights of Labour had a relatively strong base in Quebec, but over the decade a growing number of workers came to support an emerging French-speaking Catholic union movement in the province.[8]

Industrial warfare was rampant in the mines, in factories, and on the railways. More than a thousand disputes were recorded between 1901 and 1911. In most strikes the basic issue was wages, frequently supplemented by the fundamental issue of union recognition. Often the response of government was to call out the militia in aid of the civil power to suppress violence between strikers and scab labour. Administratively, the problem of strikes and lockouts was complex. Except in a few industries under Dominion jurisdiction such as the major railways, labour questions were the responsibility of the provinces and very few provinces had the administrative capacity or the political inclination to deal with them adequately. In 1900 the Laurier Government created a Department of Labour under the authority of the Conciliation Act. The department was charged to provide assistance in the prevention and settlement of strikes and to enforce a fair wages policy — within Dominion jurisdiction. Seven years later Parliament passed the Industrial Disputes Investigation Act, the brain child of the then-Deputy Minister of Labour, William Lyon Mackenzie King. A tiny element of compulsion was included in the act: strikes and lockouts in the mines or public utilities were prohibited until the dispute had been investigated by a three-man board. But conciliation remained the essence of Ottawa's labour policy. Thorough investigation and public revelation of grievances, King believed, should be enough to bring reasonable men to their senses.

Even this hint of government intervention caused alarm among some businessmen. However, the more tough-minded accepted the I.D.I.A.

---

8. Robert Babcock, *Gompers in Canada: A Study in American Continentalism Before the First World War* (Toronto, 1974), examines the relationship of Canadian unions to the American Federation of Labor. Two excellent studies of labour and working class life in Quebec are Jacques Rouillard, *Les travailleurs du coton au Quebec, 1900-1915* (Montréal, 1974), and T.J. Copp, *Anatomy of Poverty: The Condition of the Working Class in Montréal, 1896-1929* (Toronto, 1974). *Women at Work: Ontario, 1850-1930* (Toronto, 1974), is valuable.

for what it was, a potentially useful device to persuade the parties in an industrial dispute to reach a settlement. Of course, because neither party was compelled to accept the recommendations of the board of investigation, management's prerogatives remained unchallenged and the rights demanded by workers unrecognized. Owners and managers remained confident of public — or at least political — support. Neither the Laurier Government nor its provincial counterparts displayed any desire to interfere with business. After all, aided by incentives and development policies at every level of government, businessmen were as much nation builders as the politicians. And so they saw themselves. Left to their own devices, they argued, they were exploiting neither workers nor consumers. Instead, theirs was a noble mission. The President of the Canadian Manufacturers Association put it best in 1903:

> We are not manufacturers merely of articles of wood and stone, and iron and cotton and wool, and so on; we manufacture enthusiasms; we manufacturer Canadian sentiment; . . . we manufacture a spirit of independence, a spirit of national pride.

The Life of the Mind

With a confidence spurred on by prosperity, it seemed as if everyone was in the business of manufacturing the Canadian identity during the Laurier years. Some Protestants toyed with the idea of church unification as an expression of a uniquely Canadian Protestantism. When the idea came to flower in the postwar years, one of its proponents explained that "the heritage of the Gospel we have in common with fellow-Christians the world over, but we have also the heritage of the Canadian spirit and this will find in the new Church an expression and an instrument peculiarly its own." In Quebec the Catholic Church, intensely concerned over the growing secular influences in French-Canadian society and the increasing Americanization of the economy, gave enthusiastic support to a traditionalist and nationalist student movement, the Association Catholique de la Jeunesse Canadienne-Française. A founder of the movement summarized its tenets as:

> . . . l'amour de la race canadienne-française et de la mission spéciale que la Providence lui destine; c'est aussi l'amour du sol que lui est échu, avec ses ressources suffisantes à la formation d'une grande nation.

The militia, with broad support in English Canada and rather less influence in Quebec, actively promoted the cadet movement in schools to encourage preparedness and patriotism, and laboured mightily to Canadianize — and mythologize — the history of Canadian arms. Their patrons in Ottawa, led by Sir Frederick Borden, Laurier's Minister of Militia and Defence, struggled to revitalize the militia and wrest its control away from British-appointed commanding officers.

Among the most interesting efforts of self-discovery was the experimentation by writers and artists with subject matter and techniques which would reveal distinctively Canadian art forms. In Winnipeg, for example, the Reverend Charles W. Gordon, as Ralph Connor, used the challenging environment of the Prairies as the setting for most of his melodramatic novels. A fascination with the Canadian landscape, with its uniqueness and its challenging harshness, was even more evident in the work of Montreal painters J.W. Morrice, Maurice Cullen, and Clarence Gagnon. The trend was more self-conscious in Toronto where the artist Charles Jefferys observed that "it is inevitable that a country with such marked physical characteristics as Canada should impress itself forcefully upon our artists."

If the land was one source of inspiration, the past was another. In the academies the first serious efforts at research in Canadian history were underway, and before the Laurier years were over an impressive list of multi-volume projects had been launched. At l'Université Laval Thomas Chapais completed his studies of Talon and Montcalm and began work on his eight-volume *Cours d'histoire du Canada; 1760-1867*. Lionel Groulx returned to Valleyfield Seminary from studies in Europe and started his research on a history of French Canada that would contrast sharply with Chapais's in its nationalist interpretation. In 1897 a University of Toronto historian, George M. Wrong, started the *Review of Historical Publications Relating to Canada*. He was also one of the founders of the Champlain Society in 1905, and with H.H. Langton, the university librarian, Wrong organized the thirty-two-volume *Chronicles of Canada*. Pelham Edgar of Victoria College and Duncan Campbell Scott, poet and Dominion civil servant, launched the biographical series, *The Makers of Canada*. Most impressive as a monument to sound scholarship was the majestic twenty-three-volume *Canada and its Provinces: a History of the Canadian People and Their Institutions*, edited by Adam Shortt of the Civil Service Commission and A.G. Doughty, the Dominion archivist. Doughty's archival work was equally important. He collected documents in London and Paris, provided scholars with ready access to historical records, and intiated a series of Archives publications which began in 1907 with *Documents Relating to the Constitutional History of Canada: 1758-1828*.

The search for the meaning of Canada by artists, writers, and historians added authenticity and perspective to the maturing Canadian nationalism of the Laurier years. It sharpened the awareness of Canada's dual cultural heritage and documented the role Canada had played in the British Empire. It also defined the very significant differences in culture, attitudes, and political systems between Canada and the United States. But this heady exercise created its own problems. Foremost among them was the revelation that there were many different realities in the Canadian identity. For many English Canadians in the older provinces the nation's destiny rested squarely upon its imperial foundations. As Principal Grant of Queen's University put it, "We are Canadian, and in order to be Canadian we must be British." Most French Canadians were no less attached to Canada's inherited British political institutions but took a much more detached attitude to the Empire and the aggressive imperialism of late Victorian Britain. "All our patriotism, all our love, all our aspirations, all our memories, all our soul attaches us to the Canadian land," the newspaper *La Patrie* proclaimed. "It is our only Fatherland." If eastern Canadians found their identities in the past, western Canadians posited their destiny on buoyant assumptions about the future. "In western Canada there is seen today that most fascinating of all human phenomena, the making of a nation out of breeds diverse in traditions, in ideals, in speech, and in manner of life, Saxon and Slav, Teuton, Celt and Gaul, one people is being made," Ralph Connor wrote in his immensely popular novel, *The Foreigner*. "The blood strains of great races will mingle in the blood of a race greater than the greatest of them all."[9]

The Imperial Tie

Each perspective and its several variations informed arguments and shaped decisions on the domestic issues of the day, great and small. Each perspective also had to be recognized and accommodated in the Laurier Government's approach to external relations. Canada's relations with foreign states, in law and in practice, were the responsibility of the Foreign

9. Carl Berger, *The Sense of Power: Studies in the Ideas of Canadian Imperialism, 1867–1914* (Toronto, 1970), is a brilliant analysis of imperialist and nationalist ideologies. The perspective of the foremost French-Canadian nationalist, Henri Bourassa, is examined in Joseph Levitt, *Henri Bourassa and the Golden Calf* (Ottawa, 1969), and in Robert Rumilly, *Henri Bourassa* (Montreal, 1953). For an incisive analysis of French-Canadian nationalism see Ramsay Cook, *Canada and the French-Canadian Question* (Toronto, 1966), which can be supplemented by his *French-Canadian Nationalism: An Anthology* (Toronto, 1970).

Office in London. Only gradually was the Government of Canada acquiring self-government in external relations, and Laurier was in no particular hurry to hasten the process of autonomy. In part, he correctly reasoned that it would continue to evolve through precedent and circumstance as it had in the Macdonald years with the appointment in 1880 of a High Commissioner as Canada's quasi-diplomatic representative in London. In part, recognizing how potentially explosive issues in external relations could be, given the contrasting perspectives of English and French Canadians, retention of responsibility in London provided a convenient focus for blame when Canadians believed (as they very often did) that their interests in imperial and foreign affairs had been mishandled. In consequence, serious, systematic analysis of external problems had a secondary priority in the Laurier Government. Foreign affairs were seen as something to be considered when occasion demanded, and even then policies were governed more by abstract perceptions of Canada's place in the Empire than by tough-minded scrutiny of practical issues.[10]

A clear example was Laurier's cautious and circumspect approach to the Colonial Conferences in London in 1897 and 1902, where delegates from the self-governing colonies gathered under the chairmanship of the Colonial Secretary, Joseph Chamberlain, to discuss a wide range of imperial problems. Chamberlain was an ambitious champion of the aggressive imperialism that characterized late Victorian Britain and he had set himself the goal of efficient management of imperial affairs by encouraging participation of the colonies in the policy-making process in London. Chamberlain was thoroughly confused and frustrated by Laurier's ardent declarations of faith in British political institutions and his eloquent praise of the British connection. To Laurier these were the bedrock of Canada's freedom of action and absence of prior commitment in external affairs. Chamberlain, however, misinterpreted Laurier's rhetoric as an indication of sympathy with his own centralizing vision. Laurier acknowledged, as he told the House of Commons in 1900, that *if* Canada were compelled to share all

10. The best survey of Canadian external affairs is C.P. Stacey, *Canada and the Age of Conflict*, vol. 1, *1867-1921* (Toronto, 1977). Carl Berger, *Imperial Relations in the Age of Laurier* (Toronto, 1969), is an important collection of essays. Political relations are studied in J.E. Kendle, *The Colonial and Imperial Conferences, 1887-1911* (London, 1967). Military aspects are surveyed in Desmond Morton, *Ministers and Generals* (Toronto, 1970), and in Richard Preston, *Canada and "Imperial Defence"* (Toronto, 1969). Norman Penlington, *Canada and Imperialism 1896-1899* (Toronto, 1965), is important for the South African War as is the introduction to Paul Stevens and John T. Saywell eds., *Lord Minto's Canadian Papers*, vol. 1, *1898-1900*, (Toronto, 1982). The naval question is exploded in G.N. Tucker, *The Naval Service of Canada*, 2 vols. (Ottawa, 1952), and in Robert Craig Brown, *Robert Laird Borden: A Biography*, vol. 1, *1854-1914* (Toronto, 1975).

"HOME, SWEET HOME."

This cartoon by J.W. Bengough was prepared to celebrate Laurier's return home from the Colonial Conference of 1897. (C-8427/Public Archives Canada)

of the burdens of empire, then Canada would have the right to say to the imperial Government, "Call us to your councils." But such was not the case. And Laurier would have none of Chamberlain's centralizing schemes. His stance, as he put it in 1902, was that imperial relations "are generally satisfactory under the existing condition of things." At the 1902 conference, Laurier adroitly sidestepped a proposal of colonial contributions to an imperial naval force with a vague promise to establish in due course a

Canadian navy. This elusive approach angered Chamberlain and other centralists. "That dam' dancing-master," a South African representative remarked, "bitched the whole show." So he did, deliberately. Laurier did so because he believed that for Canada the maintenance of the imperial connection depended not on contrived centralization but upon the silken bond of sentiment and freedom of choice.

When the Laurier Government came to power the area of immediate concern in external affairs was relations with the United States. They were not in good repair and, shortly after Laurier returned from the 1897 Colonial Conference, he secretly slipped off to Washington to propose negotiations on all outstanding questions. An Anglo-American Joint Commission, the last of a series that had begun before Confederation, finally met over the fall and winter of 1898–99. It was in this realm, where Canadians could convincingly argue that they knew their own problems far better than British diplomats, that Canada's developing autonomy in external affairs was most evident. For example, in 1871 Sir John A. Macdonald was one of three British representatives on a similar commission, taking his instructions from London. In 1898–99 there were four Canadians and one British member, and all took their instructions from Ottawa.[11]

The list of problems on the Joint Commission's agenda was long. Included were a number of minor problems characteristic of neighbouring states with close commercial, financial, social, and cultural links to each other. The major items included trade relations and disputes about fishing rights on both the Atlantic and Pacific coasts. Most immediate and contentious was the argument over the delineation of the boundary in the Alaskan panhandle. Here Canada pinned its ambition to control the exploitation of the gold fields of the Yukon upon claims for access across the panhandle to the sea. When the Canadians, led by Laurier, could not win the diplomatic concessions to overcome their shaky legal claims, they held out for an all-or-nothing settlement and the Joint Commission collapsed. Looking back, it is clear that the commissioners tried to do too much, to balance too many delicate trade-offs and compromises in one negotiating package. Laurier, however, explained the diplomatic failure

11. Robert Craig Brown, *Canada's National Policy, 1883-1900: A Study in Canadian-American Relations* (Princeton, 1964), is an analysis of the relationship of external policies to domestic politics. C.S. Campbell, *Anglo-American Understanding, 1898-1903* (Baltimore, 1957), and A.E. Campbell, *Great Britain and the United States, 1895-1903* (London, 1960), look at Canadian-American relations in the context of Anglo-American diplomacy. An important essay is A.C. Gluek, Jr., "Pilgrimages to Ottawa: Canadian-American Diplomacy, 1903–1913," *Historical Papers, 1968*. A standard account of the reciprocity agreement of 1911 is L.E. Ellis, *Reciprocity, 1911* (New Haven, 1939).

in strongly nationalistic terms. A mature Canada, he explained, no longer had to make diplomatic concessions to senior partners in the North Atlantic triangle.

Laurier's argument, as appealing as it was, ignored the very real limits on Canada's freedom of action in external relations. By 1903 the Foreign Office and the State Department had agreed that the boundary question would be resolved by a tribunal which would meet in London. As the tribunal waded through the contending legal arguments, President Theodore Roosevelt's administration in Washington pointedly informed the Foreign Office in Whitehall that it would not tolerate a decision contrary to its claims. The tribunal award, with the two Canadian members dissenting, generally concurred with the United States' case. And, in the bargain, at the last moment, the British member of the tribunal, Lord Alverstone, changed his mind and sided with the Americans on the drawing of the boundary around a group of tiny islands at the southernmost tip of the panhandle. Lord Alverstone's decision touched off a furious reaction in Ottawa, rekindling old charges that the British always sacrificed Canadian interests when they dealt with the untrustworthy Yankees.

Even before the Alaskan award some thoughtful Canadians argued that Laurier's ambiguous status quo stance in imperial relations was endangering Canadian interests. If Canada expected firmer support from the British at the negotiating table, then Ottawa had to be prepared to take a more active role in imperial affairs. Moreover, involvement in the empire had become a matter of national honour. Canada was no longer a weak, struggling, self-governing colony. The Dominion, imperial nationalists believed, was a rapidly industrializing, powerful nation, fully capable of participating in the development and execution of imperial policy. This argument gave substance to the clamourous demand, in the fall in 1899, for Canadian participation in the South African War.

Laurier was fully prepared to give his moral support to the British effort to suppress the Boers who were alleged to have persecuted British subjects in the Transvaal. "To me," he wrote some months later, "it is clearly and manifestly a war for religious liberty, political equality and civil rights." But sending troops — that was another matter. His initial response to a call from Chamberlain for soldiers was to temporize, arguing that no action could be taken without summoning Parliament into session. Within a matter of days, however, Laurier was forced to reconcile the English-Canadian demands for troops with an obvious reluctance in the French-language press and the opposition of his French-speaking ministers to a conribution. His policy of necessity became a carefully constructed compromise. Canada would raise a volunteer contingent of one thousand men and transport it to South Africa where the British Government would assume financial support for the soldiers. To placate French-Canadian critics, Laurier resorted to legal contrivances. The order-in-council authorizing the contingent firmly declared that the policy would not be "construed as a precedent for future action." Another contingent went forward in December, 1899, and still more Canadians fought in South Africa in unofficial contingents. In all, some seven thousand Canadians eventually saw service in South Africa.

Neither English- nor French-Canadian nationalists were satisfied with Laurier's policy. The English believed that the Prime Minister's voluntarist compromise was a clever but unworthy evasion of responsibility. The French argued that he had made a binding commitment to participation in all of the empire's military adventures in the future. "The precedent," Henri Bourassa observed with impeccable logic, "is the accomplished fact." Nevertheless, Laurier kept the overwhelming support of his caucus throughout the conflict. He believed that the South African War clearly illustrated the danger of prior commitments in imperial relations, and the necessity to have freedom to act or not to act, depending upon the circumstances of the moment. Of course, the extremists were not satisfied. They never were with compromises. But compromise was the essence of Canada, the glue of national unity. "If we had refused our Imperial duty," Laurier observed, "the most dangerous agitation would have arisen, an agitation which, according to all human probability, would have ended in a cleavage in the population of this country upon racial lines. A greater calamity could never take place in Canada."

Steering a cautious middle course between the demands of his critics remained the foundation of Laurier's imperial policy. After 1905, when the Liberals came to power in Great Britain, much of the agitation for colonial participation in the administration of the empire abated. The British Government was as reluctant to share the responsibility as Laurier was to have a share in it. Then the agitation was revived in the winter of 1908–09 when an apparent acceleration in the rate of construction of German capital ships threatened the margin of superiority the Royal Navy maintained in dreadnaughts. The "naval scare," like the South African War a decade earlier, aroused the English-Canadian press to demand a Canadian contribution.

But of what kind? Should Laurier be forced to make good his long-delayed promise to create a Canadian navy? If so, what aid could a Canadian force provide? Was not a financial contribution to the Admiralty's

In 1902, after the South African War, men of the Second Battalion of the Canadian Mounted Rifles embarked for home at Durban. (PA-16388/Public Archives Canada)

dreadnaught construction program the most obvious and effective solution? In the spring of 1909 Liberals and Conservatives in the House of Commons joined together to pass a resolution favouring the building of a Canadian navy and rejecting *regular* financial contributions to the Admiralty. What was left out of the text was as important as what was included. In the eyes of some an unmentioned *emergency* contribution remained an option for the Laurier Government.

Laurier's policy was announced in January, 1910. The Canadian navy would have a complement of five cruisers and six destroyers, manned by a volunteer force. A naval college would be established to train officers.

The navy would be under Canadian command but, in the event of war, it could, with the consent of Parliament, be placed under imperial control. It was another compromise: a major step towards autonomous responsibility in external policy coupled with a recognition that in time of war unified command of the Empire's naval resources was a necessity.

Robert Borden's Conservative Opposition, pushed hard by the imperially minded Tory premiers of British Columbia, Manitoba, and Ontario, had two major objections. Laurier's navy would take years to build, especially with the meagre annual appropriations being proposed by the penny-pinching Minister of Finance. The Opposition supported the building of a Canadian navy, but it was no contribution at all in the present crisis. Therefore, an emergency contribution was also in order. In addition, the arm's-length relationship between the Canadian and the Royal navies, dictated by the provision that Parliament would decide the extent and mode of participation in the event of war, made Laurier's force an "order-in-council" navy. That was doubly dangerous; it was tantamount to a declaration of independence from the Empire, and it left open the possibility that Parliament, especially a Laurier Parliament, would decide not to participate at all!

That last charge was a deliberate misreading of Laurier's intentions. The consent of Parliament was a formality, but it was also an important assertion of Canada's autonomy *within* the British Empire. As Laurier explained to a Montreal audience, if a major war broke out, his Government would not hesitate to come to Britain's aid.

> Nous ne sommes obligés de prendre part à aucune guerre, mais cependant je déclare que, s'il y avait des guerres ... s'il y avait une guerre dans laquelle la suprématie navale de l'Empire serait mise en péril, je serais d'opinion moi-même, — et je ne veux pas que d'autres en soient blâmés, parce que j'en prends la responsabilité — je crois que nous devions aider l'Angleterre de toutes nos forces.

After fierce and fractious debate Laurier mustered his majority and the Naval Service bill was passed. A short while later two old British cruisers, the *Niobe* and the *Rainbow*, were acquired as training ships for the new Canadian Naval Service.

Again the Quebec nationalists complained. Since the South African War, their forces had grown considerably. They now posed a much greater threat to the leaders of both political parties. On the Conservative side, Borden's small contingent of French-Canadian M.P.s, led by Frederick Monk, and deeply influenced by the growing *nationaliste* sentiment in Quebec, had bolted from party ranks and demanded a referendum before

Sir Wilfrid Laurier addressing a crowd gathered in Wetaskiwin, Saskatchewan in 1910 during his tour of the West. (Glenbow Archives, NA3592-6)

Henri Bourassa was Laurier's greatest foe in Quebec. This photo dates from 1898 and was inset into the first issue of Bourassa's Le Devoir. *(C-27495/Public Archives Canada)*

any naval policy was adopted. Borden's challenge paralleled Laurier's — to find some middle ground between them and the contributionist Tory premiers. He argued that, in addition to a Canadian navy and an emergency contribution, any contribution to imperial defence had to be matched by a Canadian voice in the determination of imperial foreign policy.

Many strong-minded imperialists in the Liberal camp also grumbled that Laurier's policy did not go far enough. But a more immediate threat came from his former protegé, Henri Bourassa. In 1907 Bourassa had resigned his House of Commons seat to begin an angry campaign against Laurier Liberalism, all its works, and all its hangers-on in Quebec City and Ottawa. By 1910 his creed was being expounded in an influential new journal, *Le Devoir*. In the fall a by-election was called in the Drummond-Arthabaska riding, once Laurier's own seat. While the Quebec Tories watched from the sidelines, all of Bourassa's followers rallied to the support of a *nationaliste* candidate who narrowly beat out the Liberal party candidate. For Laurier, the result, in one of the safest Liberal seats in Quebec, was an ominous warning. For Borden, it was a delicate and dangerous opportunity. If Laurier's stranglehold on Quebec could be broken, if an alliance could be cemented between Monk and Bourassa, and if the imperial extremists among the English Tories could be kept in check, Laurier's long reign of power would be threatened as never before.

The political consequences of Laurier's external policies had begun to accumulate. Since 1907, in a broadly based effort to "clean the slate" of unresolved problems with the United States, the several issues left in dispute by the Anglo-American Joint Commission were separately and successfully resolved. In addition, in 1909 a Boundary Waters Treaty was signed, establishing the Canada-United States International Joint Commission to deal with future problems in the sharing of boundary water resources. And in the same year the Laurier Government took a significant step towards formalizing the administration of its external policies when it established the Department of External Affairs.

The most contentious and sensitive problem in Canadian-American relations, trade policy, remained a divisive political issue. Canadian farmers had not been satisfied with the minor concessions they had been given in the 1907 tariff. Especially in the West, where agrarians had formed powerful farmers' organizations, the tariff was the potent symbol of the "new feudalism," of the class bias and regional favouritism of the Laurier Government's economic policies, of its toadying to the monopolists, the banks, and the railways, and of its abject subservience to the political strength of Quebec and Ontario. On a three-month-long whistle-stop tour of the West in the summer of 1910 Laurier discovered that the demand for free trade was stronger than ever. Then, in December, an angry delegation of farmers besieged Ottawa, pressing its case for relief from the oppression of protectionism.

In fact, reciprocity negotiations with the United States were far advanced. In January, 1911, Finance Minister Fielding astonished the House of Commons when he announced a comprehensive trade agreement with the United States. Ottawa and Washington had agreed to free trade in the natural products of either country. In addition, other schedules lowered the duties on selected lists of manufactured goods originating in one or the other nation. Equally important, the agreement was not in the form of a treaty. Rather, it would come into force only after it had been approved by the legislatures of both nations. By the summer the sanction of Congress was in place.

At first, as Robert Borden later recalled in his *Memoirs*, the Tories were utterly dismayed. Here was the trade agreement with the United States that Canadian governments, Conservative and Liberal, had sought in one form or another since Confederation. On the face of it, reciprocity, with so many obvious benefits to Canadian consumers — and voters — was hard to oppose. The wily old fox of Canadian Liberalism seemed assured of another term in office. And it was, in fact, only a disastrous split among Laurier's followers which soon brought the Opposition to its senses. Clifford Sifton and an influential group of eighteen Liberal Toronto businessmen — "certain hysterical women of the male sex," Sir Richard Cartwright called them — discovered a traitorous continentalist drift in Laurier's policy. They joined the Ottawa Conservatives to denounce the inner meaning of reciprocity. So encouraged, Borden's men filibustered the reciprocity bill in the House until July when Laurier finally accepted the challenge, prorogued Parliament, and called a general election.

Like the Liberal businessmen, who threw the full weight of their dollars and their organizational and promotional skills into the campaign, the Tory premiers rallied behind Borden. Both groups professed strong imperialist loyalties, agreed with Borden that the issue was "continentalism or Canadianism," and regarded Laurier as dangerously equivocal on the imperial connection. For them the defeat of reciprocity was a matter of both the pocketbook and the heart, and an opportunity to punish Laurier for his Naval Service Act. For French-Canadian *nationalistes* the election was also an opportunity to seek revenge for the Naval Service Act, for the long list of other sellouts of French-Canadian interests the Laurier Government had accumulated, and for the cynical manipulation and callous patronage that, they believed, was the secret to Laurier's power.

Laurier's power, in fact, was by no means as great as it appeared. Behind the facade of incalculable influence every governing party carried into an election, the Liberals' organization, in the hands of smugly confident but used-up party chieftains, was a shambles. By contrast, over the ten years of Borden's leadership, the Opposition Conservatives had slowly but steadily strengthened their local and provincial party machines. Now the last bit of strategy fell into place, and a quiet, effective arrangement was made with Bourassa.

On election day, September 21, 1911, the unthinkable happened. The popular vote was very close: 666 074 for the Tories, 623 554 for the Grits. But it was seats in the House of Commons which counted. "Follow my white plume!" Laurier had said in the campaign. In too many constituencies too few Liberals were still listening. The Conservatives scored a stunning triumph, winning 134 seats to 87 for the Liberals. In Quebec the *nationaliste* alliance yielded a gain of sixteen seats for Borden. In Tory Ontario, the Liberals won only 13 of 86 seats. The Laurier years were over. Robert Borden, the shy, earnest lawyer from Halifax, awaited a summons from the Governor General.

Sir Wilfrid Laurier was the political architect of modern Canada, the eloquent spokesman and gallant defender of the transformation of the Dominion into a twentieth-century industrial state. Paradoxically the success of Laurier's policies proved his undoing. The pride and confidence in the reawakening of Canada that took place during his term of office were the prerequisites of the nationalist challenges to his policies that grew in both French and English Canada. The settlers who came by the thousands to build the West forced his Government into the fatal pact with Washington.

There is another paradox. Laurier, the champion of twentieth-century Canada, was the last of the great nineteenth-century politicians to serve as prime minister. He had scant sympathy for many of the political reforms, bureaucratic procedures and regulatory practices that his policies stimulated. His beliefs, his political style, and his solutions to political problems were deeply rooted in an earlier day, in the laissez faire Liberalism of his long term as Opposition leader, in the comfortable hierarchical society of Victorian Canada, and most of all, in the subtle compromises between the aspirations of French and English Canadians that had made Confederation possible in 1867. Most of the great political issues of the Laurier years were old issues, perennial problems with schools, tariffs, railways, and imperial relations. And so were Sir Wilfrid's solutions to them.

Chapter III

Parties
Are Not
Perfect
Organizations

The top storey of the old Marché St-Pierre in Quebec City was poorly lit, full of shadows, gloomy. It was here that Laurier came with friends and followers on the evening of September 21, 1911, to await the results of the general election. Like the humblest junior member of the House of Commons, on election day the political fortunes of the Prime Minister of Canada rested in the hands of his constituents. Not that anyone in the cheerful crowd doubted the result. Laurier had first won the favour of the voters of Quebec East in a by-election in November, 1877, after accepting Cabinet office in Alexander Mackenzie's Government. They had returned him to Ottawa ever since and would do so again this night. Early results from other constituencies were equally promising.

Then came the news that Labelle, long a Liberal seat, had fallen to the Opposition. Then Brome, the seat of Sydney Fisher, Laurier's Minister of Agriculture since 1896. In Nova Scotia the seats of two other Cabinet ministers, William S. Fielding and Frederick Borden, were captured by the Tories. In all, seven of Laurier's Cabinet colleagues, including William Paterson, George Graham, and the young, ambitious William Lyon Mackenzie King from Ontario, were beaten. Now the shadows seemed ominous, the room, a journalist recorded, "full of fear." The hangers-on had drifted away. Laurier was alone with his loyal followers. In the gloom they raised their voices in a brave cheer to their leader and moved close to the platform where he stood. "Sir Wilfrid spoke briefly," the journalist wrote, "perhaps being unwilling to trust himself too far, then sat down at the table with the look of a man who has said good-bye."[1]

The Electoral System

Looking back on it, the 1911 election was a classic political confrontation, illustrating the assets and liabilities that both parties carried into the contest. On the Liberal side, Wilfrid Laurier had devoted his whole life to the Liberal party. And, more than any other person, he had shaped and defined the party's principles. He was a disciple of the great British liberal reformers, of Fox, of Russell, of Gladstone. He was, he said in the Manitoba schools debate, "a Liberal of the English school. ... I believe in that school which has all along claimed that it is the privilege of all subjects, whether high or low, whether rich or poor, whether ecclesiastics or layman, to participate in the administration of public affairs, to discuss, to influence, to persuade, to convince — but which has always denied even to the highest the right to dictate even to the lowest." Canadians, he had remarked shortly before entering Mackenzie's Cabinet, "are a free and happy people, and we are so owing to the liberal institutions by which we are governed, institutions which we owe to the exertions of our forefathers and the wisdom of the mother country." It was the policy of the Liberal party to protect, defend, and extend those institutions: "It has no other."

Laurier recognized that in the electoral process some ways of influencing and persuading voters were more legitimate than others and that parties were as prone to human frailty as individuals. "Parties are not perfect organizations," he once told a friend, "but after all, constitutional government founded on the existence of parties is still the best system which has been invented by man."

Parties at the turn of the century were complex, delicately balanced

1. The books cited in note 1, Chapter II, contain a wealth of information on Laurier's political career. Also valuable are Paul Stevens, "Wilfrid Laurier, Politician," in Marcel Hamelin, ed., *Les Idées Politiques des Premiers Ministres du Canada* (Ottawa, 1969); the essays by John T. Saywell, "The 1890s," and H. Blair Neatby, "The 1900s," in Robert Craig Brown and J.M.S. Careless, eds., *The Canadians, 1867-1967* (Toronto, 1967); the appropriate chapters of P.-A. Linteau, R. Durocher and J.-C. Robert, *Histoire du Québec Contemporain* (Montréal, 1979); and J.S. Willison, *Reminiscences, Political and Personal* (Toronto, 1919). More generally, all students of Canadian political history must consult *Morang's Annual Register of Canadian Affairs, 1901*, edited by J. Castell Hopkins, and Hopkins' series of volumes of *The Canadian Annual Review, 1902-1937*. The Conservative bias of Hopkins' volumes is more than balanced by the mine of information in his annual accounts of national and provincial political events and personalities.

machines, ever needful of attention and care. At the top, the party leader was chosen by the caucus, the members of the party sitting in the House of Commons or the Senate. He was at once expected to represent their views and to be the spokesman and leader for the whole of the party. For their part, as representatives of their party in Parliament, members of the party caucus jealously guarded their right to speak for the interest of their constituents on all public matters great and small. At the same time they were expected to adhere to party policy in Parliament and on the hustings. They were also expected to keep the faithful in the constituencies organized and ready to destroy the enemy at any moment. And in the constituencies the same delicate balances had to be maintained. A Member of Parliament who casually neglected his constituents' interests could expect decisive retribution at the next election.

The task of influencing and convincing the electors had become increasingly difficult since Confederation. One reason was that the number of potential voters grew steadily with the growth of population. At the time of the second Dominion general election in 1872, there was one representative in the House of Commons for every 18 500 Canadians. By 1891 each M.P. represented about 22 500 Canadians. By 1911 there was one representative for every 30 800 Canadians.

That did not mean that each constituency had the same, or even approximately the same, population. The relationship between the number of members in the House of Commons and the population was much more complicated than that. Generally speaking, the process of distribution of seats began with the assignment of sixty-five seats to the Province of Quebec in the British North America Act. The ratio of seats to population in Quebec then was used to determine the number of seats relative to the population of each of the other provinces. Within each province the distribution of seats and the size and boundaries of each constituency were quite literally the object of the partisan manipulation of the governing party at the redistribution following each decennial census.

At no time was the ratio of seats to population in Quebec more than a rough guide to the population of each constituency represented in the House of Commons. For example, after the 1892 redistribution of seats, which established the constituencies for the elections of 1896 and 1900, 46.6 per cent of the constituencies had populations greater than the Quebec standard. Similarly, after the 1903 redistribution, only 32 of the 208 constituencies had populations equal to the Quebec standard. There were many reasons for this. Most important was the agreement among the politicians that urban seats should have larger, in some cases much larger, populations than rural constituencies. In short, rural Canada should be overrepresented in the House of Commons. Thus, in 1904, Brome, Quebec, Sydney Fisher's rural seat, had a population of 13 400, while Laurier's Quebec City seat had a population of 40 000 people.[2]

In addition, the number of people eligible to vote in each constituency grew rapidly as the population increased and the election laws became more liberal. The first general elections after Confederation used the various provincial franchise laws to determine voter eligibility, and each provincial franchise contained some kind of property or other qualification for a man to become a voter. In 1885 Sir John A. Macdonald's Government enacted a separate federal franchise which governed the eligibility of voters in the 1887, 1891, and 1896 elections. It also contained a property qualification — $300 in cities and towns and $150 in rural areas — and a host of other provisions that, as one scholar put it, was "an astonishing hodge-podge that discriminated between provinces, social classes and racial groups." Laurier was determined to do away with the 1885 federal franchise, and in 1898 the Franchise Act returned control of the franchise to the provinces. By no coincidence, Liberal regimes were in power in every province but British Columbia at the time. (The first party government in Victoria came to power in 1903 and was Conservative.) The result was a culling of the swollen federal lists in Nova Scotia, Quebec, Manitoba, and most dramatically, in Ontario. At Queen's Park the friendly, i.e., Liberal, Ross Government reduced the number of eligible voters from 650 000 in 1896 to 482 000 in the 1900 general election!

At the same time, the more general effect of returning control of the franchise to the provinces was to eliminate property qualifications for voter eligibility and establish the principle of universal male suffrage, paving the way for universal suffrage in the next decade.

During the Laurier years the number of eligible voters grew by 34 per cent and the number of voters who cast ballots rose by 45 per cent from the 1896 to the 1911 election. Naturally enough, the largest increases in the number of eligible voters occurred in the western provinces where population growth was so rapid in the Laurier years.

The number of eligible voters participating in elections varied from election to election and province to province. On election day voter participation was affected by a huge number of variables including weather, ease of access to the local poll, party organization and strength within the

2. Norman Ward, *The House of Commons: Representation* (Toronto, 1950), is an indispensible guide to the history of representation.

This election advertising card for a Conservative candidate was distributed in 1902 by-election. Note that there is no party specified, although the reverse of the card sets out Wallace's platform — One Policy, One Country, One Empire, One Flag — and identifies him implicitly. Wallace lost to the Liberal.

constituency, treating, impersonation, intimidation, and other forms of illegal electoral manipulation. Party bosses, acutely aware of these variables, recognized that elections were risky ventures. An election, therefore, was seldom called without the most thorough preparation to convince the voters, by fair means or foul, to vote for the governing party. For all that, participation in the five general elections between 1896 and 1911 was remarkably high, averaging 75 per cent across the nation.

The governing party (the Liberals throughout this period), with an infinite range of patronage at its disposal, was usually thought to have the upper hand in the contest. The battle in the British Columbia constituency of Yale-Cariboo in 1900 illustrates how a government could come to the aid of a local candidate. The Liberals feared they might lose the seat and the candidate was desperately short of funds. Cash always seemed to be in short supply everywhere in an election but the Minister of the Interior, Clifford Sifton, himself a strict prohibitionist, did control the issuance of liquor permits in the Yukon area. The candidate was promised a permit and agreed to contribute one dollar per gallon from the proceeds to the party treasury. A permit for five thousand gallons was issued and the support of another Liberal back-bencher in the next Parliament was secured.

The Party Press

Sifton illustrated the advantages of personal wealth for a political career in these years. Members of Parliament received a sessional indemnity of $1500 ($2500 after 1905), a handsome sum for the day. But their expenses for travel, accommodation in Ottawa, constituency services, and other demands were correspondingly high. That, in part, accounts for the very substantial proportion of financiers, lawyers, manufacturers, and merchants in the Parliaments of the Laurier years. These men were better able to afford to spend several months each year in Ottawa attending to the public's business, they were not solely dependent upon the indemnity paid to members of Parliament, and they were better able to bear the risks of the insecurity of political careers. They also could afford the expense of elections. Time and again throughout Sifton's long political career a multitude of election expenses were borne by his ample pocketbook. And, being one of the most skilful managers of the art of politics in the Laurier era, he left nothing to chance. It was said that Sifton made a practice of knowing the political leaning of every voter in his Brandon constituency. But this was not enough. When he learned that far more Brandon families were reading the Opposition's newspaper than his own *Free Press*, he quickly arranged for 1000 copies of his paper to be distributed to homes in his constituency for several months prior to the election of 1900.

The support of a vigorous party press was thought to be a key to the survival of the political parties in the Laurier years. As historian Paul Rutherford put it, "The typical politician saw newspapers as essential vehicles of publicity, indeed a surrogate for organization, which could confound foes, strengthen party discipline and morale, and educate electors." The educative process was subject to formidable manipulation. Even editorial support could never be taken for granted. Throughout his long career, Laurier continually had to remind the editors of party journals to adhere to the party policy on every issue. But, as Sifton recognized, management of the news was even more important. A properly written news story, extolling the insight and propriety of the Liberal party and eliminating or belittling the view of the Opposition, could have the desired impact on the reader. A journalist of those years recalled that "the government news, official announcements and what not was exclusive to the Liberal correspondents ... no correspondent in the confidence of the Government had anything like the latitude which was open to his competitors. He could not indulge in intelligent anticipation or, indeed, in any kind of anticipation, but was bound and gagged by the responsibilities of a partisan journalist connection."

The symbiotic relationship between the party and its party press waxed and waned with the fortunes of the party. At the heart of the matter was patronage, government advertising and printing contracts upon which many small party journals partly depended for survival. A change in Government was the dispair of many a publisher. For example, between 1891 and 1896, when there was a Conservative Government in Ottawa, the Tory Halifax *Herald* received $33 951.75 in government business, and the Liberal Halifax *Chronicle* received $38. Between 1896 and 1901, with a Liberal Govenment in Ottawa, the *Chronicle* received $27 811.31 and the *Herald* $1152.73. Likewise in Montreal, the Liberal *Herald* received $105.83 between 1891 and 1896 and $97 796.57 between 1896 and 1901.

An ominous warning to both parties of changing times was the growing popularity of the independent press, especially in urban Canada. By 1900 independent dailies and weeklies accounted for 46 per cent of the circulation of Canadian newspapers. The independents threatened traditional modes of influencing the voter in two ways: they could not be relied upon for partisan support and, equally damaging, the whole thrust of their treatment of information was towards local issues, problems, and happenings and away from partisan politics and national issues. At the very time that the number of voters was growing, so too was the probability that more and more electors were acquiring their news and views of the world from independent newspapers. The role of the party press as a surrogate for party organization was slipping away.[3]

Two other well-established ways to influence the voter were elaborate and expensive programs for economic development and extensive use of government patronage. As we have seen in the preceding chapter, the Laurier Government was especially adept at the former. Investigations of the Departments of Marine and Fisheries, Interior, Militia and Defence, and Railways and Canals between 1906 and 1909 revealed that it was equally skilled at the latter. Marine and Fisheries, for example, had paid $10 000 for $2800 worth of pemmican for the exploratory voyage of the *Arctic* to Hudson's Bay. Some other items purchased for Captain Bernier's expedition had been acquired in quantities sufficient for a thirty-year voy-

3. A classic analysis of electoral politics in Canada, published in 1906, is André Siegfried, *Le Canada, les deux races: problèmes politiques contemporains*; a recent English edition is Siegfried, *The Race Question in Canada* (Toronto, 1966). Normal Ward, ed., *A Party Politician, The Memoirs of Chubby Power* (Toronto, 1966), gives a glimpse of politics in Quebec in the Laurier years. Paul Rutherford, *A Victorian Authority: the Daily Press in Late Nineteenth-Century Canada* (Toronto, 1982), contains a superb analysis of the party press. The same subject is discussed in Norman Ward, "The Press and Patronage: An Exploratory Operation," in J.H. Aitchison, ed., *The Political Process in Canada* (Toronto, 1963).

age. The whole issue of corruption in government was argued out in bitter debates engineered by the Conservative Opposition in the parliamentary sessions of 1906, 1907, and 1908, and scandal charges were the centrepiece of the Tory campaign in the 1908 election.[4]

The net effect was to discredit the party system as much as the Liberal Government in the minds of many voters. "There is no more any difference between the two so-called parties in the House," wrote a young Montreal lawyer.

> They are alike in the scandals in which members of them participate. They are alike in the maxims by which they are content to be guided. They are alike in their utter contempt of arguments that are founded not upon expediency but upon right. They are alike, therefore, through and through, in their political barrenness; and in need of a complete new birth, if they are not to become an absolute danger to the country.

J. Catell Hopkins, editor of the *Canadian Annual Review*, agreed. "The great principles of the past have died out," he observed after the 1908 election, "and been replaced by political organizations whose distinctive features are those of the ins and outs."

The Opposition

Robert Borden, the Conservative party leader, was much more receptive to this kind of critique than Laurier. He could afford to be. As Laurier observed with steely realism, "Reforms are for Oppositions. It is the business of governments to stay in office." Staying in office, as we have seen, involved alliances with provincial governments of the same political stripe at election time, the widespread distribution of patronage, the initiation of development projects that had a beneficial impact on large numbers of voters, and the nourishment and manipulation of the party press.

The Leader of the Opposition possessed none of this heavy weaponry of political warfare. Only in the last years of Borden's Opposition leadership did powerful Conservative Governments reign in a number of the provincial capitals. Only then could they exercise their influence over voters' lists or distribute largesse in favour of the federal Tories as well as of their own machines. Borden had no policies to implement, only promises

4. John English, *The Decline of Politics: The Conservatives and the Party System, 1901-1920* (Toronto, 1977), includes an incisive analysis of patronage and political corruption in the Laurier years. See also Robert Craig Brown, "The Politics of Billingsgate," in Carl Berger and Ramsay Cook, eds., *The West and The Nation*, and Norman Ward, "The Bristol Papers: A Note on Patronage," *Canadian Journal of Economics and Political Science*, XII (1946).

This is a splendid photograph of Laurier mainstreeting during the 1908 election campaign. (C-932/Public Archives Canada)

— some vague, others remarkably like the Laurier Government's programs — of what his party would do if called to power. He had to rely
upon party loyalty and his own powers of persuasion to keep the Conservative press faithful. Neither paid the bills for editors' and correspondents' loyalty or for the tons of newsprint required by a big city daily.

Party loyalty, in the absence of constant nourishment, could be unreliable indeed. Like many politicians who assume leadership in Opposition, Borden had a dual challenge: to retain and consolidate his support
within the party and to shape its policies to attract enough additional
voters to supply the margin of victory. Support within the party began
with the parliamentary caucus which elected him leader, and the Conservative caucus, in Borden's day, was an especially fractious body representing Protestant Orangemen, a small group of French Canadians with
growing *nationaliste* sympathies, veteran Tory members wedded to the
ideas and practices of the Conservatism of Macdonald, and young bloods
demanding new approaches to both policy and party organization.

Borden himself was a remarkably successful and extraordinarily ambi-
tious self-made man who had risen from very modest beginnings on an
Annapolis Valley farm to wealth and a distinguished reputation at the
Nova Scotia bar. He had entered politics at the personal request of Sir
Charles Tupper in 1896. Five years later Tupper and his son, Sir Charles
Hibbert Tupper (Borden's former law partner), had engineered his selection as party leader. Naturally enough, many of the veteran members of
the caucus regarded Borden both as a novice and as a mouthpiece for the
Tuppers. The French-Canadian members viewed him, correctly, as a moderate on the sensitive issues of English-French relations but also as a man
who had less understanding of and sympathy for their special role in Canadian politics than they desired. Although Borden was also distrusted by
many militant Protestants in the party and by old-style Conservative loy-
alists steeped in Macdonald's National policy, the newer men welcomed
his fresh approaches to policy, such as his advocacy of government ownership of the new transcontinental railway in 1904, and his desire to build
a new organizational structure for the Conservative party. As he established himself as a leader, Borden challenged the view that the Conservative caucus was the repository of all wisdom on party policy, the mediator
between the leader and the voters, and the centrepiece of party organization.[5]

5. The standard biography of Borden is Robert Craig Brown, *Robert Laird Borden, A Biography,
1854-1937*, 2 vols. (Toronto, 1975 and 1980). Borden's own account is Henry Borden, ed.,
Robert Laird Borden: His Memoirs, 2 vols. (Toronto, 1938). Another collection of Borden's
views, Henry Borden, ed., *Letters to Limbo* (Toronto, 1971), contains many insights on
Borden's life and career. See also Robert Craig Brown, "The Political Ideas of Robert Borden,"

A characteristic example of Borden's style of leadership was his announce-ment of the "progressive" Halifax platform in 1907. It attacked the prob-lem of corruption in government by promising the honest appropriation and expenditure of public monies and the more advanced proposition of a thorough overhaul of the civil service, as well as the appointment of pub-lic officials on the merit principle. In its tariff plank Borden eliminated the cherished term "protection" and suggested a more systematic and efficient tariff policy to promote the production of Canadian goods. Bor-den also called for government regulation of telephones and express compa-nies as well as railways and for the eventual establishment of a system of national telegraphs and telephones. Defending his platform, Borden argued that natural resources, national franchises, and public utilities had to be seen as "the property of the State, and they must be administered and exploited for the public benefit." That could best be done, he said, by "Government ownership or operation."

Heady stuff for Premier Rodmond Roblin, whose recently elected Con-servative Government in Winnipeg administered a public telephone sys-tem; also, in some measure, for Premier James Pliny Whitney in Ontario, whose Government was moving towards the establishment of Ontario Hydro. But Borden's views were dangerous and frightening to party con-tributors on Montreal's St. James Street and to many veteran members of the caucus. Caucus members also thought the way Borden inaugurated the Halifax platform still more threatening. After elaborate consultation with a selected group of Conservative M.P.s, with some prominent busi-nessmen, and with the Conservative provincial premiers, Borden simply announced the platform in a major address in Halifax. The parliamentary party was not consulted, nor was it given the opportunity to debate and endorse the platform. Borden, in short, had by-passed party structures, courted and received advice beyond the parliamentary party, and taken a major step towards building an independent power base in the party. Sig-nificantly, in the 1908 general election the Halifax platform was given far less prominence than the charges of scandal in the Laurier Government. It is probable that discontented M.P.s were sending a signal to the leader from the hustings that consultation and cooperation between Borden and his parliamentary colleagues was a two-way street.

---

in Hamelin, *Les Idées Politiques des Premiers Ministres du Canada*. An interesting perspective on Borden's problems as a party leader in the early years may be gained by comparing the above with Lovell Clark, "Macdonald's Conservative Successors, 1891–1896," in John Moir, ed., *Character and Circumstance: Essays in Honour of Donald Grant Creighton* (Toronto, 1970). English, *The Decline of Politics*, is an excellent analysis of Borden's party, and Arthur Ford, *As the World Wags On* (Toronto, 1950), is a delightful reminiscence of the era.

Borden's attitudes and actions indicated his dissatisfaction with the Conservative party's traditional procedures and practices. But that did not mean that Borden questioned either the principle or the efficacy of party government. He echoed Laurier in his commitment to government by party: "Government by party is more in the interest of the great mass of the people than any other system which has been devised by human wisdom up to the present time." Critics of his Halifax platform had raised the spectre of incompetent or corrupt administration against his advocacy of government ownership. But, Borden countered, should private enterprise be condemned for insurance frauds or business failures? "The principle of state ownership is no more to be condemned for its defects or errors of administration than is the general principle of responsible government. The remedy is to amend the methods." The defence of the party system was exactly the same. Like many other institutions, it was noble in purpose and replete with faults in administration. "The remedy is to amend the methods."

Borden's attitude towards party business differed from that of many of his colleagues. This was neatly illustrated by his acceptance of the new special allowance to the Leader of the Opposition of $7000 per session, the equivalent of a Cabinet minister's payment, which was introduced by the Laurier Government in 1905. Borden recognized that party leadership was expensive. That limited the party's choice of leader to the wealthy who were willing to make a personal financial sacrifice to the cause, or required a subscription to a fund by the rich men in the party to support the leader, as had been done for Macdonald and many other party leaders before and since. When the special allowance came into effect, disgruntled Tories suggested Borden had become "a payee of the Government of the day" or "an unattached member of the Administration." They believed that the party should fund the leader. Not so, Borden replied. The expenses of leadership:

> ... should come as a provision from the country for public service [rather] than as a contribution from party funds. In the latter case the leader is in effect a pensioner of a few men of wealth within the ranks of the party. This condition is obviously not a desirable one. It does not seem to me that the independence of a leader is in any way affected by a special indemnity payable out of the Exchequer. The independence of members in Opposition is surely not affected by an indemnity paid in the same way.

Remedying the method of party government went far beyond the payment of Borden's leadership expenses. A prominent Montreal businessman and Conservative M.P., Herbert Brown Ames, argued that critics of partyism and corruption were firing at the wrong target when they trained their guns on the party machine. The way to clean up politics, he proclaimed, was to impose the principles of business efficiency and business management upon the party's organization, thus relieving the party of the baneful influences of special interests and allowing it to "claim the services of the noblest men" who would give Canada "pure and honest administration." That idea, which confidently identified the business and industrial elite as the leaders in the modernization of Canada, was the most popular cliché of the day, as much a cure-all for the sickness of party politics as it was for the building of city sewers, the growing of wheat, or the education of young Canadians. But Borden and other progressively inclined politicians firmly believed it. And they had a point. Just as efficient methods and skillful management were enabling industry to produce more and better products for an expanding market, the time had come to apply the same principles to an ever-expanding electorate. Properly organized and properly administered, the party machine could be made to run for the people rather than for the business and industrial interests.

The problem was that a parallel party structure, elaborate in organization, with elected party officials at every level from the constituency district to the national committee of advisors to the leader, could impair the influence and authority of the member of Parliament both in his constituency and with the party leader. Borden never resolved this, and his attempts to build a tightly controlled, carefully managed organization for the Conservative party received only lukewarm support in the caucus and in the growing provincial party organizations across the country.

The focus of party attention upon systematic organization, however, did have its rewards. Party organizations appropriate to local conditions and designed in close cooperation with provincial leaders were created or revived and given a new sense of purpose. The total Conservative vote increased steadily during Borden's leadership. It increased by 7.2 per cent from 1900 to 1904, another 14.3 per cent from 1904 to 1908, and another 21.3 per cent from 1908 to 1911. Overall, the Conservative vote increased by almost 61 per cent from 1896 to 1911, the Liberal vote by 54 per cent.

The Reciprocity Election

Nonetheless, the Liberals approached the 1911 election with supreme confidence. They had much to be confident about. The party, after all, had compiled a remarkable string of victories under Laurier's guidance and Laurier was widely acknowledged as a masterful leader. As the architect of the social and economic changes that had transformed Canada in the past fifteen years, Laurier was immensely proud of his accomplishments. More than that, there was, as his biographer put it, "an indefinable touch of authority" about Laurier that had proved compelling to voters in the past. The party counted on that image of mastery and statesmanship to work its magic on the voters again in 1911. So did Laurier.

Confidence also rested upon the fact of power. Properly managed, the power of the governing party could be decisive in an election. Liberal principles were important, and a commitment to Liberalism was deep in the hearts of generations of Canadian voters. But, as Laurier, ever the realist, once remarked, "It is always more easy to govern if, besides appealing to their best nature, we can also show them some substantial advantage." Never was the axiom more true than at election time. Then a wharf, a bridge, a post office, a few judiciously placed printing contracts, or a new customs shed with its attendant jobs more often than not provided the margin of victory in a host of constituencies. Some studies of elections even suggest that these substantial advantages and the constituency organizations are more important than great issues in persuading a majority of electors to vote for a governing party's candidate. But in 1911 the great issue for the governing party itself promised a substantial advantage to electors: cheaper binder twine would cut farmers' production costs; cheaper food would benefit urban workers. That, as the Liberals saw it, was the issue and the compelling promise of the 1911 election.

So attractive was the package that there was more than a hint of complacency in the Liberal ranks. Always more comfortable with proven formulas than with untried experiments, Laurier seemed wedded to the approaches and appeals that had worked in previous elections: a winning record, his own reputation, an attractive issue, the support of Liberal Governments in the provinces, and the distribution of largesse. The turning point may well have come in late April when Borden announced the "uncompromising hostility" of the Tories to the reciprocity bill and Laurier countered with his party's "uncompromising support" and determination to see it through Parliament. Borden was threatening to use the procedures of the House of Commons to tie up the bill indefinitely while Laurier was anxious to bring it to a final vote so that he could leave for an Imperial Conference in London. Unwilling to compromise with Borden on any point, Laurier refused his offer of a two- or three-month adjournment and the vote of interim supply. A deadlock had been reached. Then, early in May, the Government did decide to adjourn Parliament, with the reciprocity bill in limbo, for two months. Laurier left for England. Borden rushed off to western Canada to try to convince prairie farmers that reciprocity was not the panacea that many of them believed it to be. The threat to tie the House of Commons in procedural knots earned Borden a precious two months of time to campaign while Laurier was out of the country.

The day before the party leaders exchanged challenges in the House of Commons, Hartley Dewart, a worried young Toronto Liberal, published an ominous letter in the Toronto *Globe*. To ritual denunciations of the Conservative party he added the warning that "the Liberal party in Ontario today, while strong in its constructive policy, is lamentably weak in the matter of organization." The blame rested with Laurier's Ontario ministers and especially with Allen Aylesworth, the Minister of Justice, who was senior among them. "A Commander-in-Chief," Dewart wrote, "even if he be as brilliant and skillful as Sir Wilfrid Laurier undoubtedly is, cannot be expected to achieve the success that he should without able tacticians between himself and the men in the ranks." Whatever the other talents of Laurier's lieutenants, they had neglected their crucial organizational roles in the province with the largest number of seats in the House of Commons. And Dewart was not a lone complainer. Long before his letter appeared, Laurier had been told that Liberals would not follow his cadre of Ontario ministers. As one correspondent put it, "With the present organization it would be impossible to elect St. Peter to any one of our seats." It added up to this: while no election had been called, the Conservatives had offered the Government a choice of a vote or a filibuster and still the Liberal election machine was in storage, its gears awaiting grease, its fixtures needing polish, its drivers unpopular.

Not so the Conservative side. In mid-April J.D. "Doc" Reid, a veteran Ontario M.P. and sometime discontented member of Borden's caucus, prepared a long memorandum for the leader reporting the results of the most recent meeting of Ontario organizers. By then the Ontario Tory machine was moving into high gear and it may be safely assumed that the same was also true in the Conservative provinces of British Columbia and Manitoba. (New Brunswick's Conservative Government, led by lethargic Douglas Hazen, plagued by uncertainty, and short of cash, lagged behind.) Reid reported that thirty-six of the present fifty Conservative seats were "absolutely sure"; the remainder would be fiercely contested by the Liberals. Of the thirty-six Grit seats in Ontario, the Conservatives would concede only fourteen. In the remaining twenty-two a "vicious attack" was planned. "A good man" or "the best available man" had already been nominated or was slated for nomination in half of the seats. The Tories were ready.[6]

When first announced in January, the reciprocity agreement with the United States had thrown Borden and his colleagues into despair. But Borden, by nature a cautious and deliberative leader, slowly but surely discovered the fatal flaws in the Government's policy. From Winnipeg and Queen's Park came signals that reciprocity had struck a severe blow at "Canadian national development" (the protective tariff policy) and "sane imperialism" (the imperial connection). That was the theme of Borden's response in the House of Commons in early February and it was echoed in the anti-reciprocity manifesto of eighteen Toronto entrepreneurs a few days later. The components of Borden's election strategy were falling into place.

The first part of the plan was to capitalize on the outrage of the business community and especially to hold out a welcoming hand to Liberal capitalists whose imperialist sentiments had been offended by the Naval Service Act and who viewed reciprocity as yet another blow to national dignity and purpose — and their own financial holdings. Borden had always believed that a successful party leader had two equally important duties. One was to retain, consolidate, and strengthen his electoral support among voters who were loyal to the party through thick and thin. The other, and this was the key to victory, was to "seek to reach and influence men of moderate opinion who vote now with one and now with the other party." For election purposes the businessmen fit neatly into this category. Most businessmen had probably supported Macdonald in his day and it was certain that most had rallied behind Laurier's revamped and more successful National Policy since 1896. Now they might be moved again, but nothing could be left to chance. If businessmen believed that reciprocity could be turned back by a few meetings and a manifesto, they were "living in a fool's paradise," Borden told Premier Whitney. They had to be brought into active partnership in the Tory campaign.

The businessmen agreed. Very quietly — at first not even Borden was privy to what was afoot in "another organization" — the "nonpartisan"

6. Many of the political and organizational factors in the 1911 election are covered in R.D. Cuff, "The Conservative Party Machine and the Election of 1911 in Ontario," and "The Toronto Eighteen and the Election of 1911," *Ontario History*, LVII (1965); W.M. Baker, "A Case Study of Anti-Americanism in English-speaking Canada: The Election Campaign of 1911," *Canadian Historical Review*, LI, 1970; and in Paul Steven's valuable collection of documents and readings, *The 1911 General Election: A Study in Canadian Politics* (Toronto, 1970).

Canadian Manufacturers Association set up the Canadian Home Market Association with headquarters in Toronto and branch operations in Montreal and Winnipeg. Lavishly funded by annual subscriptions from its member firms, the C.H.M.A. was in fact a huge propaganda machine organizing the preparation of anti-reciprocity pamphlets distributed by a front organization, the Canadian National League, and of editorials and "news stories" sent in boiler plate for regular printing in hundreds of country dailies and weeklies from Nova Scotia to British Columbia. By late August the C.H.M.A. had sent out 9.5 million pieces of its material and was despatching another twenty thousand each day.

The blitz of the country papers was not a substitute for, but a potent supplement to, party organization. Here, in the absence of a strong national party structure, the key was wholehearted cooperation between the Ottawa Tories and the four provincial Conservative Governments. Borden had courted the Tory premiers for years and had won their support. Imperialists to a man, the affront of reciprocity now added fervour to their support. In Manitoba Robert "Hon. Bob" Rogers, Roblin's Minister of Public Works and unofficial "Minister of Elections," quickly put the provincial civil service on combat status as Conservative soldiers. Roblin also assigned Rogers, who had close ties to most French-Canadian Conservatives and Montreal financiers, to part-time duty as bagman for the national party.

Similarly, Rogers' counterpart in Ontario, "Silent Frank" Cochrane, the Minister of Mines, was brought into the Ontario campaign. He was a key figure in the organizational meetings Doc Reid was attending. Reid's memorandum to Borden revealed the fullness of Premier Whitney's commitment. Several of the nominees chosen to contest tough Liberal seats were members of Whitney's caucus, M.P.P.s who had been "given" to Borden by Whitney because they were the most likely candidates to capture the Liberal constituencies. Beyond that, Whitney had played a critical role in negotiating the alliance between the Borden Conservatives and the Toronto businessmen, and Borden relied upon Whitney for advice on matters great and small throughout the campaign.

Another alliance, unofficial, unannounced and, as Liberals charged, unholy, was at work in Quebec. William Price, lumberman and member for Quebec West, was given major organizational responsibilities in Quebec and New Brunswick. He soon discovered that he was not completely in charge in his own province. Frederick Monk, sometime leader of the Quebec Conservatives in Parliament, "has again put us into a most horrible mess," Price wrote in alarm. "He has made a definite alliance with Bourassa and the Nationalists, and this new combination is calling itself an Independent Conservative Party, under the leadership of Monk. They will not be able to obtain much funds for organization, but they will, at any rate, take several seats from the Liberals."

An arrangement between Borden, Monk, and Bourassa was not as strange as it seemed at first sight. During the last year of Borden's first term as M.P. he had boarded with Bourassa in Ottawa and each had developed a strong respect for the intelligence and integrity of the other. Their views on English-French relations and, to a large extent, on imperial questions were poles apart. But on other major issues, especially on questions of political reform and progressive approaches to the relations between the state and private enterprise, they were at one. In 1908, when Bourassa campaigned on a reform platform against the Liberal Government of Lomer Gouin in Quebec, he received support from important Quebec Conservatives and proposed an "alliance — not open, but real" with Borden's party. Then, as in 1911, the heart of the matter was Bourassa's detestation of Laurier and Laurier Liberalism in Quebec City and in Ottawa, detestation of its endless compromises, its scruffy deals and cynical politics. If Monk and Bourassa could take seats away from Laurier in his own fortress, Borden was more than willing to give his silent consent to their arrangement.

Winning the support of disenchanted Liberal capitalists, working closely with the Conservative provincial premiers, and encouraging the independent campaign of Monk and Bourassa in Quebec were, then, the components of Borden's election strategy. Slowly and carefully developed, they were all in place long before July when Laurier finally called the general election. They were specially significant because each of the elements was an arrangement with a group outside the caucus, a manifestation of Borden's belief that the road to victory was paved with alliances with political forces not represented in the parliamentary party. That made some members of caucus very, very nervous. In 1910 Borden's neglect of the tender sensibilities of caucus had led to an abortive but widely publicized revolt. In March, 1911, the discontent resurfaced over Borden's courting of his new allies. Even though it was quickly squashed by Borden the revolt left some of the dissidents — among them were Reid, Price, and Monk — "very frightened." That within weeks each of these three men was playing a major role in the Conservative campaign revealed much about the fevered intensity of Opposition politics and the astute leadership of the party by Borden. In the end he put together a powerful combination of political forces which exploited the negative responses to the Laurier Government's policies and marched to battle in carefully organized formation.

The effectiveness of Borden's strategy was obvious on election night. There were minor increases in the Conservative popular vote in Prince Edward Island and Nova Scotia but more than an 11 per cent increase in Hazen's New Brunswick. The "horrible mess" in Quebec paid handsome dividends. Whether interpreted as a Conservative vote, a Conservative-*nationaliste* vote, or simply as an anti-Laurier vote, the Opposition candidates in Quebec tallied 37.8 per cent more votes in 1911 than they had in 1908. And the close working relationships with the provincial governments in Ontario, Manitoba, and British Columbia yielded 13 per cent, 15 per cent, and 46 per cent gains in Tory support in those provinces. For the Liberals, the largest gains came in Saskatchewan, with a 56 per cent increase, and in Alberta, with 61 per cent. There Liberal provincial governments reigned and farmers' support for reciprocity was most intense. Fractional increases in the Liberal popular vote in Quebec and Nova Scotia were offset by minor losses in Prince Edward Island and New Brunswick and a significant 5 per cent drop in Ontario. The Liberals also won major gains in the popular vote in Manitoba and British Columbia, but it was not enough to influence the results in either province. As elsewhere, the popular vote in those provinces provided one gauge of the people's support for the Liberal party.

What really counted, however, was the contest for seats constituency by constituency. There the provincial control of electoral lists and the strengths and weaknesses of local party organization came into play. The Liberals lost seats in six of the nine provinces: Prince Edward Island – one; Nova Scotia – three; New Brunswick – three; Quebec – sixteen; Ontario – twenty-five; and British Columbia – two. Their only gain was in Alberta, where they picked up two seats. Clearly, the close cooperation between Borden and his provincial colleagues had paid off most handsomely in Ontario, and the Conservative-*nationaliste* arrangement in Quebec had cut deeply into Laurier's support in his home province.

A Liberal candidate from a constituency which included a large manufacturing town in Ontario reflected upon his losing campaign after the election:

> I fought a good fight on a cause I did not believe in and which I will never do again. Fighting for the "full dinner pail" and the "farmer" is poor policy — neither appreciate your efforts on their behalf, and are controlled by their employer when it comes down to the finally final.

"I am neither laughing nor weeping," he concluded. "I am just thinking — what damn fools we were." The Liberals in 1911 relied too much on past accomplishments, too much on their leader's personal prestige and popular appeal, too much on a seemingly attractive policy. The problem with reciprocity was that it undercut the carefully modulated but solid support for protectionism that had characterized Liberal policy since 1896. It threatened, or seemed to threaten, too many economic interests that had flourished under that tariff policy. And, in the eyes of too many Canadians, it challenged the very essence of Canada's identity and future. The Liberal leadership, smugly satisfied with the reciprocity agreement Fielding had engineered in Washington and convinced that this panacea from the past was the magic formula for retaining power, was much too slow off the mark in the campaign of persuasion. The Liberals never did marshal enough force to turn back the assault of Conservative propaganda against the "inner meaning" of reciprocity.

It was equally significant that in the latter years of the Laurier regime the party's organizational talent, so evident in earlier elections, had been allowed to wither away. That was the point of Hartley Dewart's outburst in April, 1911. But by then it was much too late to act; many of Laurier's Cabinet colleagues who were charged with organizational responsibilities were old and tired, but they could not be replaced on the eve of an election. The ossification of the Liberal machine had already become evident in the 1908 election, but the Prime Minister, intensely loyal to long-time, trusted colleagues like Aylesworth, refused to replace them. Alexander Smith, veteran party organizer in Ontario, made the point in a letter to Laurier after the 1911 election. "Warnings, suggestions, directions and offers of assistance were all resented," he wrote, "and the result was that you had not the support of the lineal descendants of those who were proud to see you elected in 1896 and followed you until old age denied their ardour."

Laurier received the letter in November, two months after the election. Smith, who had been at the centre of electoral organization in Ontario since 1896, was sorting and burning correspondence that contained the deeper secrets of party activity in federal and provincial elections over fifteen years. The exercise stirred many memories and gave Smith a unique perspective on the state of the Liberal party in 1911. Two sentences from his letter were a telling epitaph on the death of Laurier Liberalism:

> We had nobody in charge. It was like playing marbles with marbles made out of ordinary roadside mud.

The Keys to Political Success

A general election is the beginning- and the end-point of the Canadian political system. Each election, federal or provincial, is fixed in time and place, conditioned by the circumstances of the day, and shaped by the personalities and activities of all the actors from the party leader to the local poll captain. But many factors which were important in the 1911 election are constant and worth remembering as we continue our study of twentieth century Canada.

The foundation stones of the political process are deeply imbedded in the past. The parliamentary system, which confounds facile comparison between Canadian and American politics, grew out of the earliest European colonies in British North America and evolved alongside the "mother of Parliaments" in London. Party government grew out of the rebellions in the Canadas in 1837 and the gradual establishment of responsible government in the 1840s. Together, the parliamentary system and party government created the liberal-democratic political institutions that were as much the beacon for Robert Borden's "progressive" Conservatism as they were for Sir Wilfrid Laurier's Liberalism.

Later twentieth century political parties faced many of the same difficulties and challenges that confronted Laurier's Liberals and Borden's Conservatives. The number of potential voters to be influenced and persuaded grew, especially with the adoption of female suffrage — which began in the English-speaking provinces in the years of the Great War and ended in federal female suffrage — and the return of the control of the federal franchise to Ottawa in 1918. So too did the average size of each constituency grow, to 34 500 by 1958 when John Diefenbaker's Progressive Conservative party swept the nation and captured 208 (79 per cent!) of the 265 seats in the House of Commons. Over the decades the rules governing the conduct of elections were tightened. In time regulations affecting party funding were adopted, in part by legislation, in part by codes formulated by the parties themselves. Both tended to curb the more imaginative schemes to manipulate the electoral process so freely used by men like Sifton, Rogers, Reid, and Cochrane — or at least to make their application more discreet. For all the changes, however, the party leaders of the 1930s or the 1970s faced the same fundamental challenge as Laurier and Borden — to persuade more voters in each constituency to vote for their party than for their opponents'.

The most significant change was the gradual acceptance by electors of third parties. The effect in some provinces was practically to displace one or the other of the traditional parties. Alberta from the 1920s to the 1970s and Quebec since the 1930s are examples of this process. At the federal level the Social Credit party was a significant factor in electoral politics for almost three decades, and the Cooperative Commonwealth Federation/New Democratic party has become a permanent fixture deeply

◄ *Sir Robert Borden, soon after he had been elected to power in 1911. (C-18632/ Pubic Archives Canada)*

influencing the development of policy by the governing parties and adding yet another complexity to their electoral strategies.

The role of the media in elections has also changed dramatically, partly in response to a growing electorate but even more as the result of remarkable innovations in communications technology, from radio broadcasting to television's hourly transmission of news and information to a mass audience. The party press, as it was known and used by Laurier, has been eclipsed. Generally, "kept" editors and journalists are few in number, and parties have developed more elaborate strategies, from constituency newsletters and the use of advertising agencies to televised national press conferences, to get their news and views directly to the voter. The communications blitz organized by the Canadian Home Market Association in 1911 has been taken over by the parties themselves and developed into a higher art. If the party press is no longer a surrogate for party organization, the management of information and the dissemination of publicity has certainly come to be among the most important and costly activities of the late twentieth century Canadian political party.

All of these changes have made the need for broadly based, vital, party organizational structures more imperative. In a sense the process had begun before 1896, with the first national party convention staged by the Laurier Liberals in 1893. Borden has also toyed with the convention idea but held back, arguing that a well-organized party structure in each province was a necessary antecedent to a national convention. The Conservatives did not convene a convention until 1927. For their part, the Liberals called another convention in 1919.[7] It was most significant because that convention not only charted future party policy but also elected the party leader, William Lyon Mackenzie King. The transfer of the selection of the party leader from the caucus to a national party convention was a fundamental step in the democratization of the political party, and it set the pattern for regularly scheduled party conventions, leadership elections, and even leadership reviews that today characterize the business of all political parties in Canada.

The gloom in the Marché St-Pierre contrasted sharply with the scene

---

7. On the Liberal party conventions of 1893 and 1919 see J.W. Lederle, "The Liberal Convention of 1893," *Canadian Journal of Economics and Political Science*, XVI, (1950), and "The Liberal Convention of 1919 and the Selection of Mackenzie King," *Dalhousie Review*, XXVII (1948).

in the Union Bank Building in Halifax on the night of September 21, 1911. Borden arrived at his constituency headquarters early. The initial results were not encouraging and for a time Borden wondered if his carefully planned election strategy had backfired. By the time the news of the triumph in Ontario was announced it was late, and later still when the sweep of British Columbia was known. By then the rooms were crowded with shouting, cheering, backslapping party workers. Borden, among old friends and acquaintances, was joyful and confident. The decade-long test of party leadership in Opposition was over; his policies and his political strategy had been vindicated. He planned to spend a day or so at the family homestead in Grand Pré. Then he would go back to Ottawa to test the opportunities, and the limits, of power.

As party organization developed into an elaborate operation with its own leadership figures and councils and committees, the opportunities for disagreement and tension between the party and the caucus multiplied. Borden's problems in this area pale into insignificance compared to those of Mackenzie King, John Diefenbaker, Joe Clark, and Pierre Elliott Trudeau. As the chief of both the party and the caucus, the party leader, as Borden's career illustrated, must walk a fine line. Unlike Borden or Laurier, the modern political leader is the creature of his party, not his caucus. But, as John Diefenbaker's leadership demonstrated, a party leader who loses the loyalty and daily support of his caucus is in very great trouble.

Finally, leadership is perhaps the determining factor in the health of each political party and hence, of the vitality of the political process in Canada. Obviously, the style and tone of the party will be influenced by the leader's personality and character. But successful party leaders have had several common attributes: a deep commitment to the integrity of the democratic political process, an ability to follow as well as to command, patience, a keen instinct for compromise, and a high level of ambition. Laurier put it best in his analysis of the reason why Alexander Mackenzie was a notably lacklustre leader: "He has no zest to carry a party on." Laurier, Borden, R.B. Bennett, King, M.J. Coldwell, and Diefenbaker, among others, had zest in abundance. Their party members responded to it. So too did that body of electors Borden thought so significant — citizens "of moderate opinion who vote now with one and now with the other party."

Chapter IV

*1911–1919:
The
Road
to and from
Vimy Ridge*

By the spring of 1915 the men of the Canadian Division were getting used to the routine and drudgery of trench warfare — it was a world of mud, filth, stink, bad food, little sleep, and sheer boredom. This was quite a contrast to the glory, colour, and excitement many had expected when they crowded into the recruiting offices back home in those hectic days of August and September, 1914. If any of the Canadians remembered that excitement as they lolled in the warm sun in their trenches near Ypres, Belgium, on the afternoon of April 22, 1915, it must have brought a smile of bitter irony to their lips.

At a nearby airfield, a reconnaissance pilot rolled his biplane to a stop and jumped from the cockpit with a report that he had spotted a large cloud of yellowish smoke drifting towards the Allied trenches from the German lines. At about the same time, French colonial troops on the left flank of the Canadians saw a wall of smoke rising about a metre from the ground and behind it, higher than a man's head, a greenish-yellow cloud drifting towards them. In their positions the Canadians noticed a quick intensification of German shell fire directed towards the trenches on their left and heard, soon after, the replies from the French guns. Soon German shells were falling near the Canadian positions and the men began to notice a greenish tinge around the sun. They began to cough and choke, their lungs filling with chlorine, their eyes tearing from the stinging gas.

They grabbed their rifles and prepared to try to defend their trenches in the greenish murk. For the Canadians the boredom of trench life was over. They and the French colonial troops to their left had been picked by the Germans to suffer the first gas attack of the war.

The war, which Canada had entered as part of the British Empire at midnight on August 4, 1914, was the greatest struggle in the short history of the young country; when it finally ended, over four years later, sixty thousand Canadians had been killed in action and tens of thousands more had been wounded, many badly maimed and scarred for life. It was the supreme test that marked Canada's coming of age, and it challenged Canada's leaders with political, social, ecomomic, and moral problems that dwarfed the troubles of times gone by. It brought Canada's Prime Minister, Robert Laird Borden, to the pinnacle of his career at home and abroad while, at the same time, it brought him close to resignation and placed burdens on him which no Canadian leader up to that time had ever had to bear. He had been elected leader of his country in days of optimism and peaceful expansion, but he was destined to lead Canada through dark days of division, despair, and death.

Borden in Power

Borden and his Conservative party had been swept into office on September 21, 1911, in the eleventh general election since Confederation. The new Prime Minister was the antithesis of an ideal war leader. He was neither colourful nor flamboyant nor charismatic, and his speeches, even on the most dramatic of occasions, were uninspiring. He was a lawyer by occupation and temperament, a careful, honest man, loyal to his friends and reluctant to make the hard decisions sometimes demanded of a leader. Borden's watchwords were duty and sacrifice, and both qualities would be essential in the years ahead.[1]

In the weeks following the election victory Borden busied himself with the difficult and delicate work of sorting out claims to positions in the new Conservative Government. There were many seekers after Cabinet

1. On Borden as a political leader and the Conservative party after 1911, see Robert Craig Brown's *Robert Laird Borden*, vol. I (Toronto, 1975), and vol. II (Toronto, 1980). Conservative politics are covered in John English, *The Decline of Politics: The Conservatives and the Party System* (Toronto, 1977). The stories of two leading Liberal politicians during this period are told in Margaret Prang, *N.W. Rowell, Ontario Nationalist* (Toronto, 1975), and O.D. Skelton, *The Life and Letters of Sir Wilfrid Laurier* (Toronto, 1921), which is dated, but still the best work on Laurier. W.R. Graham, *Arthur Meighen*, vol. I (Toronto, 1921), is the biography of an important Conservative minister and Borden's successor as leader and Prime Minister.

posts and Borden was forced to weigh ability against political muscle. He had many political debts to pay. Borden also had to follow the time-honoured tradition of including in the Cabinet representatives of the French and the English, of Catholics and Protestants, and of all the regions in Canada. Sometimes it may have seemed to him that ability was not a very important factor in building a Cabinet. While Borden was in the process of selecting his ministers, Conservative party leaders were beginning to hand out government jobs. In every riding people who had supported the Conservatives clamoured for positions from postmasterships to judgeships as rewards for faithful service: patronage was normal in Canadian politics at that time and many governments jobs were ordinarily filled by political appointments.

Borden took more than two weeks to construct his Cabinet. It was sworn in on October 9, 1911, a mixture of old party supporters and some recent converts with a more progressive outlook, such as W.T. White, a former Liberal closely associated with Clifford Sifton and the "Toronto Eighteen." One appointment that was to haunt Borden was his selection of Colonel Sam Hughes as Minister of Militia and Defence. Hughes had been a loyal supporter of Borden through thick and thin, but he had the potential to cause trouble for his leader. He was cantankerous, arrogant, and opinionated. He thought little of the professional officers in the army and did not hesitate to tell them so. On the other hand he considered himself a genuine military hero, demanding at least one and possibly two V.C.s for his feats in the South African War, and a logistical and organizational genius. As long as Canada was at peace Hughes, leading a small peacetime militia and an even smaller professional army, was harmless. Once the war began, however, he would prove a serious obstacle to the operation of the war effort.

Hughes was not the only weak spot in Borden's Cabinet. Another was Frederick D. Monk, the Minister of Public Works and the acknowledged leader of the Conservative party in Quebec. Borden had little choice but to appoint Monk, but if he expected him to be a source of strength and leadership in Quebec, his hopes were misplaced. Monk was a weak and hesitant man and he was often incapable of making important decisions and sticking by them. His support for Borden's external policies was never more than lukewarm and he failed entirely to keep Borden in close touch with Quebec opinion or to act as a bridge between Ottawa and his native province as other leading French-Canadian Conservatives had done before him since the days of Georges-Etienne Cartier. Monk was simply not cut from the same sort of cloth as his predecessors.

Borden and his Cabinet soon turned their attention to the business of government. As far back as 1907 Borden had advocated government intervention in and regulation of many commercial and economic activities such as railway transportation and had allied himself with others who appeared to share his views. He had also pledged to reform the federal bureaucracy by replacing the patronage system with a merit system. This would mean setting up an independent commission to hire civil servants and to decide questions of pay, promotion, and advancement.

Borden did not forget his reform promises and in December, 1911, his Government appointed a royal commission to make a thorough investigation of the public service. Sir George Murray, a former permanent secretary to the British Treasury, was appointed to come up with the answers. He recommended that ministers no longer involve themselves with the day-to-day operation of their departments but instead give their ministries broad political direction. He also recommended competitive examinations to fill civil service posts and urged tighter control over appointments and promotions. Murray's report, if implemented, would have resulted in a vastly improved and more efficient civil service, but aside from some minor changes to the Civil Service Act in 1912, the Borden Government did little until the spring of 1918 because there was too much opposition to change within the Cabinet and the Conservative party. The Tories had been out of power for fifteen years while the Liberals took every opportunity to reward their faithful followers with jobs in almost every area of government service. Now the Conservatives had their chance, and they were not to be denied. Patronage was too deeply rooted in the Canadian party system to be eradicated overnight, especially as many politicans were convinced that patronage attracted and kept the allegiance of party supporters.

As this example suggests, Borden's reform record in the prewar period was uneven. His Government also failed to reform the machinery for setting and regulating tariffs, and it did nothing to bring the railways under public control in the first years of his administration. The Government did pass the Canada Grain Act in 1912, which established a Board of Grain Commissioners to supervise grain inspection and to regulate the grain trade. The act also gave the Government the authority to own and operate terminal elevators and went far to meet farmers' complaints about elevator monopolies, shoddy grain grading, and inspection practices that robbed them of a fair return for their labour. Other measures were introduced to aid farmers, including federal assistance to the provinces for the upgrading of agricultural education, rural free delivery of mail, and federal funds for provincial highway construction.

Borden's attempts at reform suffered from opposition within his own party and Government and from the Liberal majority in the Senate, which did not hesitate on several occasions to reject bills passed by the Conservative majority in the Commons. At the same time, growing tensions in Europe forced Borden to pay less attention to domestic affairs and more to imperial defence questions, particularly the naval issue. The naval debates of 1909 and 1910 had been bitter. They had not resulted in a Canadian navy but rather in a "Laurier navy," and soon after taking office in March, 1912, Borden announced that he would submit a new naval policy to Parliament. He believed that Canadian participation in British naval expansion ought to bring a greater Canadian role in the shaping of imperial defence and foreign policy, and he was convinced that if Canada and the other dominions had a duty to help Great Britain defend the Empire, then they must also share in making those decisions that would determine peace or war.

Borden had little time to plan his new naval policy because almost as soon as he had made his announcement, word came from the British Government that their naval building program was going to be stepped up to match an accelerated German fleet expansion. The British wanted an emergency contribution from Canada. Borden was thus forced to postpone his own plans, devote his attention to the British request and, at the same time, try to keep the Government united on the issue. In June, 1912, he led a Canadian delegation to England to study the naval emergency. The party left in late June and spent two months in England examining the problems of the Empire's defence and other imperial issues. While there, Borden was able to convince British Prime Minister Herbert Asquith to agree that the dominions should be allowed representation on the Imperial Defence Committee when dominion defence matters were being discussed. This was far short of the overall consultation Borden had aimed for, but it was all he could get.

Borden returned to Canada at the end of August and waited for secret Admiralty reports to spell out, in detail, the extent of the naval crisis. When they finally arrived at the end of September, Borden revealed them to the Cabinet and sought support for an immediate cash contribution to Britain. Monk refused to agree and insisted that the Government hold a plebiscite before aid was extended to the British, a position he had taken as far back as 1909 when the Laurier naval bills were being discussed. Borden, fearing an angry reaction from English Canada, refused, and in mid-October Monk resigned. These serious divisions were likely to split the Government, and Borden tried to secure the backing of other French Conservatives and *nationalistes* by stressing the concessions he claimed to have won from the British on consultation. He gained some French support, but a significant number of his Quebec members still refused to go along.

In early December, 1912, Borden introduced his emergency naval aid bill into the House of Commons. Canada would give the British an immediate contribution of $35 million for the construction of dreadnaughts to be placed at the disposal of the British for the common defence of the Empire. Borden stressed the emergency nature of the contribution and claimed, incorrectly, that the British had agreed to consult with Canada and the other dominions on imperial foreign policy in future. In fact, the British had made no such promise and had only pledged to consult with the dominions on matters that directly concerned them. Borden's attempts to placate the Opposition were a total failure, and a bitter five-month debate followed which ended only in May, 1913, when the Conservatives invoked closure. Borden's naval bill finally passed on May 15, but by the end of the month it had been defeated in the Liberal-dominated Senate.

Borden's attention was soon diverted. Canada's apparently endless economic expansion ended abruptly in the fall of 1913 as the worst depression in two decades gripped the country. The most direct cause was a sudden decline in the British investment capital which had largely financed the commercial, industrial, and real estate expansion of the previous decade. Wars in the Balkans prompted many British investors to believe that a major European war was just around the corner and to begin to withdraw their funds from Canada. Many had also lost confidence in the Canadian economy, and Canada, with little surplus capital of its own to invest, was caught short. By early 1914 tens of thousands of Canadians were out of work, and trade unions began to demand an immediate end to immigration and the establishment of government measures to help the unemployed. But the federal government did little to help, while immigration continued at an accelerated rate — four hundred thousand immigrants entered Canada in 1913.

The bulk of the problems generated by the depression was borne by the cities. Many farmers, in debt and cut off by their banks, abandoned their farms to move to the cities. There they competed for work with the urban unemployed, whose ranks were further swollen by newly arrived immigrants. Some city governments, like the one in Toronto, did all they could to help the unemployed with the few resources available. Others showed little or no sympathy: the mayor of Winnipeg told the jobless there to "hit the trail." The prevailing social and political thinking of the day dictated that periodic depressions were actually to be expected and that little could, or should, be done to help those who suffered. Social welfare was a matter for private charity, not for governments.

The most immediate cause of the economic recovery that ended the depression was an assassin's bullet in far-off Serbia. On the morning of June 28, 1914, a young Serbian nationalist shot and killed the Archduke Ferdinand, heir apparent to the Austrian throne, in Sarajevo. The killing sparked off a chain of events that soon led to war. Austria attacked Serbia, which was allied to Russia, while Germany, allied to Austria, prepared to attack both Russia and its ally, France. The intrigues of European diplomacy had created a net of secret alliances and agreements that quickly dragged millions into what was, up to that time, the most murderous war in history. Britain and its empire were not to be spared because Britain had ties to France and had, for at least a century, taken upon itself the task of guaranteeing the neutrality of Belgium. When German forces crossed the Belgian border in preparation for a sweeping attack into France, Britain declared war on Germany.

The British declaration of war was made by King George V on behalf of all his subjects. Canada was bound by this declaration because it was still a colony, with almost no control over its own foreign affairs and no autonomous status within the empire. Few worried about this lack of status in 1914, and Canadians threw themselves into the war in a great burst of enthusiasm. Canada may have had no choice as to its participation, but Canada alone would decide the degree of its involvement, and in this most people undoubtedly agreed with Liberal leader Sir Wilfrid Laurier that their country should give "assistance to the fullest extent of [its] power." For one thing, most believed that the war would be short and glorious and would afford a good opportunity to demonstrate what the young dominion could accomplish on the battlefield. For another, a majority of Canadians were still either British-born or of British origin, and the sentimental and emotional ties to the mother country, as well as the economic and constitutional ones, were strong. As the oldest self-governing dominion, therefore, Canada was bound to do its duty. To this end Laurier pledged that the Opposition would do everything possible to assist the Government in the smooth operation of the war effort. Laurier was in every respect a British Liberal, and it should have come as no surprise that he would rally to the side of his philosophical homeland.

Canada at War

In the first weeks of war the Government moved quickly to give itself extraordinary powers to govern in this time of national crisis. A War Measures Act was drawn up and passed into law, giving sweeping powers to the Government to be used to meet the war emergency. There had never been anything quite like it in Canadian history. The W.M.A. gave the federal government the power to use orders-in-council in a broader and more sweeping fashion than during peacetime, even, in some cases, to bypass the normal legislative process which required passage of bills through the Commons and Senate and the approval of the Governor General. It effectively suspended the right of habeas corpus by allowing government officers to order arrests and detentions without having to bring specific charges before a judge. It gave the Government power to deport without trial and power to regulate or interfere in any area of society or the economy that was considered necessary for the prosecution of the war. Matters that were defined by the constitution as provincial areas during peacetime could pass under federal jurisdiction during times of war. The act, in the words of one political scientist, made Canada into a "democratic dictatorship."

At first few of these emergency powers were used except for those which allowed the government to control the movements of "enemy aliens." These were immigrants — roughly a half million — who had come to Canada from Germany or Austria-Hungary and who had not yet become British subjects. There was substantial fear that they might work secretly for a British defeat and sabotage the war effort, even though very few of them harboured pro-German or pro-Austrian sympathies. Enemy aliens were required to carry special identity cards and to register at regular intervals, and 8300 of them were interned in four special camps in isolated parts of the country. The Government also established a Chief Press Censor, whose job it was to examine magazines and newspapers and order the deletion of articles and stories that he judged harmful to the war effort. Most of the Canadian press cooperated fully with him because the editors were, as a rule, solidly behind the war effort and refused to print material they believed would be damaging.

When the war began Canada's army was too small, too ill-equipped, and too poorly trained to make an immediate contribution to the Allied cause. Canada's mobilization plans had been drawn up in 1911, but they were scrapped almost immediately by the Minister of Militia, Sam Hughes, who called instead on existing militia units to launch a direct recruiting drive that soon brought in tens of thousands of volunteers. A very large number of those men who rushed to join up were British immigrants who felt strong ties to the British cause; many others were unemployed workers who needed a roof over their heads, clothing, and three meals a day.

The men were brought to a new army camp at Valcartier, Quebec, where thousands of tents were quickly set up while mess halls, latrines, rifle ranges, and drill fields were laid out. Hughes had an office built on a hill overlooking the camp so that he could survey the scene like some medi-aeval lord.

On October 3, 1914, thirty thousand Canadian troops sailed for England from Gaspé Basin in the largest convoy to that time. They arrived less than two weeks later and were soon encamped on Salisbury Plain where they spent a cold, wet winter in training, fighting mud, discomfort, and disease before being transferred to France. By the middle of February the Canadian Division, as it was designated by the British War Office, had taken its place in the lines on the western front near the Belgian town of Ypres. There Canadians found a war that few were prepared for. The initial German assault into France in August, 1914, had been stopped by the French and British armies, and the fighting had settled down to the deadly stalemate of trench warfare. Both sides dug complex defences, usually consisting of three or more parallel lines of trenches connected by other trenches dug at right angles to the main lines. The defence systems combined trenches, tunnels, dugouts, and deep underground shelters with minefields, barbed wire, and sandbags. At carefully sited key positions machine guns with sweeping fields of fire were emplaced, and behind the lines the artillery was positioned to allow each side to pound the enemy's front line with continuous and deadly barrages. There was little drama in this, just a steady toll of lives.

The trenches were like some dark, subterranean hell, and the men in them endured a cramped existence. Water from rains or from the seeping ground water of Flanders flooded the bottoms, creating a thick mud, col-lapsing the trench walls, and making life one long, soggy battle to stay clean, warm, and dry. Rats were everywhere, growing fat on the flesh of dead horses and dead men and scurrying over the living during the nights as a constant reminder of the fate that seemed to await them all. The stench of rotting flesh mixed with the stink of sweat, filthy bodies, and latrines. By day all movement was careful and crouched — a head above the trench line was too good a target for enemy snipers. By night men stumbled down ragged trenches with no light to guide their way. There were diseases — from trench foot to pneumonia — and boredom, there were lice and nits, and there developed, under these conditions, a gal-lows humour that summed up the bitter irony of the men. In one section of trenches the hand of a corpse stuck out from the mud and each new man joining the unit was obliged to shake it. But perhaps nothing expressed the aimless cruelty of it all as much as the soldiers' ditty sung to the tune of *Auld Lang Syne*, which gave their view of the lofty purposes for which they were suffering and dying:

> We're here because we're here because
> We're here because we're here
> We're here because we're here because
> We're here because we're here. . . .[2]

In April, 1915, the Germans began to mount limited offensives on the western front to hold the British and French at bay while they devoted their attention to defeating the Russians. One of these assaults was the gas attack at Ypres on April 22. Although the Allied High Command had received indications that the Germans were about to unleash this new and terrible weapon, the staff had failed to warn the front lines or to provide for an adequate defence, and when the choking, green clouds were carried by the wind over the French colonial troops in the trenches, the men panicked and ran. The Canadians did not receive the full brunt of the gas and this combined with the quick reaction of Canadian officers under the command of Lt. Gen. E.A.H. Alderson, the British officer in command of the division, enabled them to send troops northward to try to fill the gap in the line while they prepared for a counterattack. For the next three days the Canadians and the British fought tenaciously to restore the Allied lines, but casualties were heavy because of repeated German assaults supported by massive artillery fire and more chlorine gas. The Germans were eventually pushed back, but at a high cost. When the Canadian troops were withdrawn from the battle on April 25, few were left. Out of a front-line strength of ten thousand men when the Germans attacked, 1850 Canadians had been killed, 3411 had been wounded, and 776 had been taken prisoner. The division had lost more than six out of every ten of its combat troops.

While the Canadian Division was receiving its introduction to battle,

2. For life and death on the western front from a soldier's perspective, see John Keegan, *The Face of Battle* (New York, 1976), which describes the Somme campaign, and John Ellis, *Eye Deep in Hell: The Trenches, 1914-1918* (London, 1975). The effect of the war on the psyche of those who fought in it is analyzed in Paul Fussell, *The Great War and Modern Memory* (New York, 1975). There are many memoirs of those who were there. A Canadian work is Charles Yale Harrison, *Generals Die in Bed* (Hamilton, 1975). Three new books which relate experiences of Canadians at home and at the front are William B. Mathieson (ed.), *My Grandfather's War: Canadians Remember The First World War 1914-1918* (Toronto 1981); Grace Morris Craig, *But This Is Our War* (Toronto, 1981); and Gordon Reid (ed.), *Poor Bloody Murder: Personal Memoirs of the First World War* (Oakville, 1980).

tens of thousands back home continued to volunteer for army service. The recruiting was carried out with a flourish of patriotic propaganda exhorting Canada's young men to heed the call of honour as clergymen, prominent politicians, and leaders of women's organizations took part in the drive. Despite the growing realization that the war would not be short, an increasing number of volunteers joined up during 1915, and a monthly peak of thirty thousand was reached in March, 1916. Prime Minister Borden continued to raise the authorized force levels until early 1916, when the size of the army was set at half a million men. As each new division was formed and despatched to Europe it joined the others there to form a four-division corps by August, 1916.

The Home Front

For the first time in Canadian history a massed army of citizen-soldiers was taking to the field. And for the first time they were leaving behind tens of thousands of wives, mothers, and children who depended on them for food, rent, and clothing. With the men gone who would now take care of their families? The problem was recognized early by the Governments and private charitable organizations that took up the task of providing a basic income for the immediate families of men overseas. Most of the work was voluntary, supported by private and corporate donations to charities such as the Canadian Patriotic Fund, incorporated by the federal government in August, 1914. The fund undertook to pay as much as $30 per month to the families of soldiers living in eastern Canada, with $10 more for those living in the West, where the cost of living was recognized to be higher. Later in the war the basic payment was raised to $50 per month and was supplemented by federal widows' and dependents' pensions. The fund's work was assisted by other organizations that distributed food, cigarettes, and clothing to the men in Europe, and by service groups such as the Y.M.C.A., which maintained gathering places for men on leave in Great Britain and Canada. These activities were supported by the time and money contributed by thousands of Canadians, and particularly in the first years of the war, when the expeditionary force was still small and enthusiasm great, they helped considerably to ease the burden on soldiers' families.

Canada's contributions on the field of battle were considerable but they were only part of the total Canadian war effort, which also included the supply of millions of tons of foodstuffs to the Allied cause as well as the production of hundreds of millions of dollars in munitions and other war supplies. In this area as in others, Canada started virtually from scratch. When war broke out there was only one factory in the country capable of producing artillery shells, and its capacity was limited to about seventy-five shells per day. In the trench fighting of the Great War artillery was particularly important, and the guns could fire hundreds of thousands of shells per day. Britain produced much of this but Canada, far from the front, was also called upon to help. The war production effort was initially directed by the Shell Committee, an arm of the British Ministry of Munitions headed by a Canadian officer, Lt. Col. Alexander Bertram. The Shell Committee included several prominent Canadian manufacturers and was responsible for placing contracts for the production of shells with Canadian manufacturers on behalf of the British Government. At the start of the war the Committee offered lucrative contracts to induce Canadian factories to change to war production. Contracts to make shells went to companies with experience in metal manufacturing, such as railway repair shops, farm implement factories, bed-spring manufacturers, and structural iron works, all across Canada. The companies were forced to learn new methods of organizing production and new and more exacting techniques for manufacturing according to strict specifications in order for the system to work smoothly. When the fuse that was manufactured in Winnipeg was mated with the shell casing from Hamilton and the explosive charge from Toronto, all components had to fit perfectly. This was a new challenge for managers and workers alike.

The manufacturing process went smoothly enough but the operation of the Shell Committee did not, and by the fall of 1915 considerable evidence had piled up that Committee members were making fat profits through shady deals. After consultations between the British and Canadian Governments, the Shell Committee was disbanded and replaced by the Imperial Munitions Board, headed by the Toronto pork-packing magnate, Joseph Wesley Flavelle. Flavelle was rather conservative in his outlook, unfriendly towards trade unions, and a superb organizer and businessman. There was never a whiff of scandal in the I.M.B. after his takeover, though there was considerable controversy over working conditions and industrial relations questions in factories working on I.M.B.-awarded contracts.

Flavelle was soon the virtual czar of Canadian munitions manufacture, which by the third year of the war continued to set new production records in terms of quantity and variety. It started with the manufacture of shells but expanded to include production of explosives, guns, ships, aircraft, aircraft engines, and many other implements of war. By 1917 the I.M.B.

was establishing "national factories," directly owned and controlled by the Board, to produce war equipment that private corporations were unwilling or unable to handle. Tens of thousands of Canadians from coast to coast were engaged in war work and were, in effect, working directly or indirectly for the I.M.B.

The Canadian munitions industry expanded at the same time that the authorized force levels for the Canadian army were being raised and recruiting was being stepped up. As a result, industry and the army were competing for manpower, and the unemployment that had marked the prewar depression began to decline until it was replaced in late 1915 by a labour shortage. For the first time in many years Canadian workers, especially those in the munitions industry, were in a good position to demand better wages and working conditions and to organize into trade unions to defend and advance their interests. The labour shortage made it increasingly difficult for employers to dismiss workers who organized unions or demanded higher wages, although in some industries not directly related to the war effort, such as construction, this labour shortage was not so acute or never developed at all.

Workers faced tremendous problems during the war, but their leaders were rarely consulted by the federal government when solutions were sought to problems directly affecting them, such as increases in the cost of living, the establishment of minimum wages in war industries, and the maintenance of decent working conditions in munitions plants. There were many complaints from workers that employers were reluctant to improve plant conditions or raise wages, but the thorniest problems arose when workers organized unions only to have employers refuse to bargain or sign contracts with them. Many strikes during the war were caused directly by this refusal to recognize unions. Even though workers in war industries enjoyed higher wages and better working conditions than many other industrial workers in Canada, they lived in constant fear that employers were only waiting for a good chance to destroy their unions and roll back their wages.

Employers tried to end the labour shortage by hiring unskilled workers to take the place of skilled men who had joined the army and by opening the doors of heavy industry to women for the first time. Women were not new to the industrial work force — thousands had been employed in the textile and other light industries at least as far back as the 1880s — but they traditionally had been barred from work in heavy industries and from jobs that demanded special skills, such as those in machine shops and metal foundries. This had changed by 1916, when industries desperate for labour hired some thirty thousand women for the munitions plants, shipyards, and agricultural implements factories. At first the labour movement protested, but eventually the unions began to consider a special campaign to organize these new workers into unions.

It became easier for women to enter the industrial labour force in the Great War, but it was never simple. No special efforts were made to open day-care centres to allow married women to work, and their pay was almost always considerably lower than that given male workers. In most factories they found poor sanitary facilities, and in many cases no special toilets had been set aside for women. It was made clear to them from the start that they would not be wanted after the war and that their work was a special departure, made necessary by the war, from their traditional tasks of child-rearing and taking care of their husbands' needs.

Despite this bias, women played an active and vigorous role in the war effort. They filled jobs traditionally held by men. They participated actively in recruiting leagues, the Patriotic Fund, and in organizations such as the Y.M.C.A. to give aid and comfort to soldiers far from home. Housewives determined to provide wholesome and nutritious meals on reduced family budgets, with the prices of food climbing ever higher and some products not available at all, may have contributed as much to the war effort as did single girls labouring in shell plants. Women also played leading roles in movements to introduce reform to Canadian society during wartime as they continued their drive for full political rights. At first women's special contributions to the war effort were rarely acknowledged — except in war propaganda that exhorted mothers to send their sons to the field of battle — and women's rights received little attention. By the end of the war, however, women were admitted to full political equality in federal politics, even though the cause of female emancipation in industry and the professions benefited little from the war experience.

Making an Army

The rapid expansion of the munitions industry and the growth of the industrial work force created many difficulties on the domestic front. At the same time problems arising from poor administration of the Department of Militia and Defence were beginning to undermine the morale of the troops abroad. The trouble was due, in no small measure, to Sir Sam Hughes and was exemplified by the scandal over the Ross rifle, a Canadian-designed-and-built weapon primarily used for hunting and target shooting which had been tried and rejected for service use by the Royal North

West Mounted Police before the war because of its unreliability in field conditions. This did not bother Hughes, who considered it superior to other available weapons and who decided that it must be used by the Canadian army. Soldiers going overseas in the first years of the war were thus armed with an unreliable weapon and soon learned this after they had entered the front lines. They began to throw the Ross rifle away by the thousands and unofficially re-equipped themselves with the British-manufactured Lee-Enfield rifle by raiding British arms dumps or stripping weapons from British dead on the battlefield. Complaints to Ottawa about the Ross produced no results until the Battle of the St. Eloi Craters in the spring of 1916, when large numbers of Ross rifles jammed during the fighting. An official British War Office investigation followed, and the Canadian Cabinet finally stepped in to overrule Hughes and order the re-equipping of the troops with the Lee-Enfield.

As the war dragged on Borden became increasingly aware that Hughes was a public embarrassment, but he continued to stand by him — Hughes had often supported Borden in the past. Instead of sacking the Minister, he took important areas of responsibility from him and placed them under the control of other ministers. The most important move in this direction came in the fall of 1916 when Borden created the Ministry of Overseas Military Forces, located in London and headed by Sir George Perley. Perley assumed control of the army in Europe, thereby stripping Hughes of much of his authority. By the time Hughes resigned from the Cabinet in November, 1916, his departure had little effect on the management of the war.

The Canadian Government was responsible for recruiting, training, transporting, equipping, and paying for the Canadian troops overseas, but it had almost no control over the deployment and use of its own soldiers. The commander of the imperial forces was Sir Douglas Haig, who showed little imagination or originality in his tactics and strategy and even less compassion. The lives of tens of thousands of Canadians and other imperial troops were thrown away in massive battles such as those of the Somme campaign, which began July 1, 1916. This was intended to be a coordinated assault of the British and French armies aimed at smashing through the German defences, but it was badly planned and poorly executed. The initial focus of the assault was a position which the Germans had strongly fortified and which they defended in great depth. It was chosen only because it faced the point in the Allied lines where the British and French armies joined. Allied guns bombarded the German lines for days before the attack, but when the barrage lifted the German

This quite extraordinary photograph was taken during the capture of Vimy. A party of Germans, overrun in the initial advance, are surrendering to soldiers of the second wave. (P.A.-1123/Public Archives Canada)

*Sir Sam Hughes.
(C-20240/Public
Archives Canada)*

This famous cartoon appeared in Punch *to celebrate the Canadian capture of Vimy. Five years later it made a fine cover for the program of a reunion dinner.*
(Toronto Telegram *Collection, York University Archives)*

General Sir Arthur Currie. (Toronto Telegram *Collection, York University Archives)*

soldiers reappeared from deep bunkers to take their places in their trenches and gun-pits. They opened fire with a hail of machine-gun bullets that tore up the ranks of the British attacks. In the *first day* of fighting twenty thousand British soldiers were killed, with thirty-seven thousand more wounded. The Newfoundland regiment, caught in a crossfire in front of the village of Beaumont Hamel, lost seven hundred men in about thirty minutes. Despite the heavy losses Haig continued to throw fresh troops, including the Canadian divisions, into the attack for several more months. The Canadians went into action in September, capturing the village of Courcellette and suffering 7230 casualties in one week's fighting. By the time the offensive was called off in November, British and French troops had advanced 13 km over a 20 km front at a cost of six hundred thousand casualties. The Canadian divisions, pulled out of the line in October, had suffered eight thousand killed and sixteen thousand wounded for a total gain of 2800 m.

The Somme fighting exemplified the Great War. An entire generation of young men from all the countries involved were moulded by the horrific experiences of trench warfare, traumatized by murderous meat-grinder battles, like the Somme campaign, that wasted an appalling number of lives. Entire villages, neighbourhoods, counties, and parishes lost a generation of young men to the shells or the choking, burning chlorine gas. Men became resigned to death and almost stoic in its presence. The war thrust millions of them into a subterranean world where their horizons were the muddy walls of their trenches. For these human moles, forests were replaced by twisted and gnarled nightmare trees, shorn of leaves by the whistling shrapnel. Grass gave way to mud, and sunrise and sunset became nothing more than times for renewed attack and killing. Many staff officers were incompetent bumblers whose mistakes, perhaps confined to columns of numbers in a balance book during peacetime, now cost thousands of lives. They seemed to forget everything and learn nothing while they tested their theories of battle with real soldiers. A generation of cynics climbed from the trenches after the war, men whose faith in faith itself had been eroded, men who no longer took anything for granted or trusted as readily as before. For millions, it was a war against idealism, and it marked the end of naiveté and innocence.

There was, however, still a place for pride in the accomplishments of arms. And for the Canadians, the testing ground was to be Vimy Ridge, a German-held salient that poked into the British lines between Lens and Arras. The ridge was used by enemy observers to keep watch over a large area and call down deadly artillery fire on troop movements. It had been assaulted repeatedly by the French since 1914 with no result except the loss of two hundred thousand men. The Canadians, strengthened by the fourth Canadian division in late 1916, were transferred to the lines opposite Vimy after the Somme battle. There they would fight together as a corps under the command of British General Julian Byng in yet another attack on the ridge and as the left flank of a larger British offensive aimed at the German lines south of Arras.

The British and the Canadians had learned much from their failures in the Somme campaign, but the German general commanding the troops in Vimy, General von Falkenhausen, had learned little. His defences were based on the tried and, he thought, still true concepts of wire, trenches, and artillery support. The Germans were well dug in on the ridge and had placed their artillery on the far side, out of sight of the British and the Canadians, with reserves held well back. The four Canadian divisions were assigned to attack this force with a total of 120 000 men. The preparations for the assault were painstaking in detail. A large clay model of the ridge was built and carefully studied by the officers, while a full scale mock-up, with German defensive positions well marked, was used to familiarize the troops with their objective. Royal Flying Corps surveillance photographs were studied to determine shifts in the German positions that might necessitate changes in the assault plans. The German guns were located using new sounding devices and were systematically destroyed by British and Canadian counterbattery fire. Tunnels were dug from rearward positions to the front lines to enable the Canadians to move forward out of sight of German observers. Huge mines were placed under the German positions, to be detonated as the attack began. Plans were laid for a creeping artillery barrage that would lay a curtain of fire ahead of the attacking troops and be moved forward at 92 m intervals every five minutes.

In the early morning hours of Easter Monday, April 9, 1917, the explosive charges under the German lines were blown and the artillery began a massive barrage that was concentrated on specific German targets — guns, fortified positions, and wire entanglements were levelled as the first line of German trenches disappeared in a rain of shellfire. Then the creeping barrage began and the Canadian attackers moved out of their forward positions and began to assault on the ridge. The German defenders were stunned. The communications to their artillery were cut, and there were too few guns left to give them much support. The attack rolled forward, and only on the extreme left flank did the Fourth Division run into difficulties in an assault on Hill 145, where many Canadian soldiers were cut

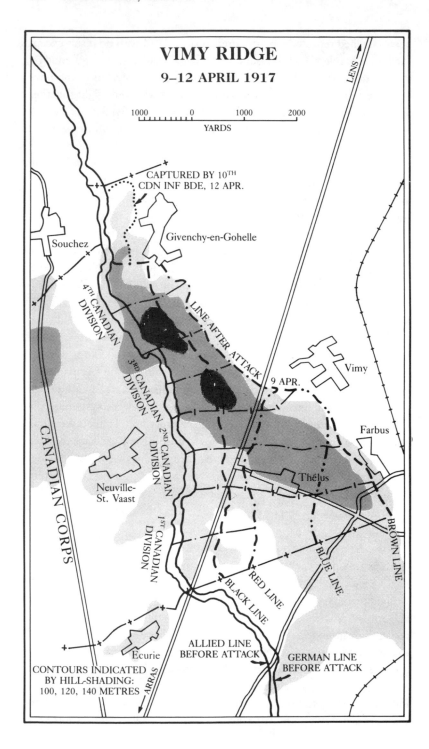

VIMY RIDGE
9–12 APRIL 1917

1000   0   1000   2000

YARDS

LENS

CAPTURED BY 10ᵀᴴ
CDN INF BDE, 12 APR.

Souchez

Givenchy-en-Gohelle

4ᵀᴴ CANADIAN DIVISION

LINE AFTER ATTACK

3ᴿᴰ CANADIAN DIVISION

2ᴺᴰ CANADIAN DIVISION

Vimy

9 APR.

Farbus

CANADIAN CORPS

Neuville-
St. Vaast

1ˢᵀ CANADIAN DIVISION

Thélus

BROWN LINE

BLUE LINE

RED LINE

BLACK LINE

Ecurie

ARRAS

ALLIED LINE
BEFORE ATTACK

GERMAN LINE
BEFORE ATTACK

CONTOURS INDICATED
BY HILL-SHADING:
100, 120, 140 METRES

Vimy Ridge Map
◀ *The great Canadian victory of the Great War was at Vimy Ridge in April, 1917. Some historians have even argued that Canadian nationalism was born in the pride felt over the achievement of the Canadian Corps. Note the small scale of the action with the best gains amounting only to 1800 m or so, an illustration of the terrible cost paid in the First World War for victories, large or small. (Adapted from* Canada's Soldiers *by George F.G. Stanley, published by Macmillan of Canada, p. 324.)*

down by massed machine-gun fire. Elsewhere the attack was a brilliant success, and before long the Canadian soldiers were standing on the heights of Vimy Ridge looking down at thousands of German troops in headlong retreat. Some German guns had been left behind and were turned against their former owners by specially trained troops. The sight was one few Canadian soldiers had ever seen because the land which lay before them, once behind the front lines, was almost untouched by war. It was as if a stake had been driven through hell which, when removed, revealed the peace of heaven on the far side.

The victory of Vimy Ridge had been costly — 10 602 Canadian casualties, 3598 of them fatal — but for once that cost had returned positive results. The German lines had been pierced and an important enemy position had been captured. Fighting as a unit for the first time, the Canadian Corps had proved itself second to none, and Canadian officers, particularly General Arthur Currie, commander of the First Division, had demonstrated that they were capable of planning and carrying out a well-coordinated attack. Less tangible, but perhaps more important, was the turning point the victory marked in the attitude of many Canadians about themselves and about the war. Canada, the oldest self-governing dominion, was rapidly passing from colony to new nation, and the pride of the Vimy victory speeded that process. Canadians were already coming to believe that this was not a British or imperial war alone, but also a Canadian one in which the entire resources of the country had to be mobilized at home and at the front. Vimy strengthened that belief and represented a renewed Canadian commitment to the war. When the campaign ended Byng was promoted and General Currie was placed in command of the corps at the behest of the British and with the solid approval of the Canadian Government.

Currie was the epitome of the citizen-soldier. At the time of his promotion to lieutenant-general and to command of the corps, he was forty-one and had received no formal officer's training. Before the war, he had been a businessman in Victoria, making a good living in insurance and real estate until he was almost wiped out in the 1913 depression. He might have remained an unknown failure but for his continuing interest in soldiering. He was active in the militia, where he soon gained a reputation as an able organizer, respected for his fairness and strength of character and for his ability to generate loyalty among his troops. He rose rapidly through the ranks and was appointed commanding officer of the Fiftieth Victoria Regiment in January, 1914. When war broke out he was offered command of a brigade in the Canadian contingent. Currie's appointment as corps commander, coming after the Vimy battle, also marked Canada's achievement of a new maturity. His quiet strength, great popularity, and obvious ability soon turned him into a popular hero.

The victories of the Canadian divisions naturally commanded enormous attention at home and swelled national pride (most particularly among English-speaking Canadians) but so too did the exploits of those individual knights of the air who flew into battle with the Royal Flying Corps or Royal Navy and captured the imagination of a generation. By the end of the war almost every schoolboy could recite the stories of Canadian flyers such as Raymond Collishaw, "Wop" May, Billy Barker, Roy Brown, and the most famous of all, Billy Bishop, a dashing, former cavalryman from Owen Sound, Ontario. Bishop shot down seventy-two German fighters before the war ended, but his most famous exploit was undoubtedly his attack on a German airfield near Cambrai on June 2, 1917, which won him the Victoria Cross.

On that cold and drizzly morning Billy Bishop awoke in the dark at 3 a.m., pulled his flying suit on over his pajamas, gulped a quick cup of tea, and climbed into the cockpit of his waiting Nieuport fighter. He gunned his motor and was soon climbing through the fog and rain in the general direction of the German lines. The cloud and darkness made navigation almost impossible, but when Bishop descended he found himself over a German airfield at Estourmel, where the day's flying activities had not yet begun. Bishop dropped low, to perhaps 15 m or less, and roared over the field firing at parked enemy planes, their pilots and mechanics, and dodging anti-aircraft fire. Two German fighters struggled into the air, but Bishop swung behind them and shot them down in quick order. A third and fourth German fighter then came after the Canadian flyer, and Bishop shot one of these down before running out of ammunition. He was then forced to change his ammunition drum while keeping his plane level and evading the other German fighter. With his gun reloaded he fought off his attacker by firing his full drum of ninety-nine rounds in one long burst and then dove down and headed for home. This was the first low-level raid of its type in the war. Bishop had bagged at least three German fighters and pioneered a new type of aerial tactic.[3]

The war not only stimulated national feeling in Canada, it also gave that feeling a shape and a direction in the impact it had on Canadian culture. Several famous Canadian painters — Frederick Varley and A.Y. Jackson of the Group of Seven and David Milne among them — were war artists participating in a program to record the exploits of Canada's troops on canvas. The experience left deep impressions in each case. Varley, for example, developed a sombre style that reflected the tragedy and decay of the battlefield. At one point he wrote to Arthur Lismer, another member of the Group of Seven, to describe the horror of the western front. "You pass over swamps on rotting duck boards, past bleached bones of horses with their harness still on, past isolated crude crosses sticking up from the filth, and the stink of decay is flung all over." His painting ever after reflected his war experiences.

Literature too was changed by the war and came to reflect the cynicism of the soldiers in the trenches. One of the great, but generally unknown, Canadian novels to come out of the war was *Generals Die in Bed*, by Charles Yale Harrison, a Philadelphia-born newspaper reporter who served with the Royal Montreal Regiment. His book, first published in 1930 when the public was beginning to read novels such as *All Quiet on the Western Front* and *A Farewell to Arms*, was hailed by the *New York Evening Post* as "the best of the war books." In deliberately simple prose, it told the story of a group of Canadian soldiers on the western front in a powerful portrayal of the brutalizing impact of war. Harrison's soldiers were far removed from the glories of a spit-and polish war fought for king and empire:

3. The story of the Canadian army in the war is told in several works, including G.W.L. Nicholson, *The Canadian Expeditionary Force: 1914-1919* (Ottawa, 1962), which is the official history, and D.J. Goodspeed, *The Road Past Vimy: The Canadian Corps, 1914-1918* (Toronto, 1969), a short popular account. Another popular version is John Swettenham, *To Seize the Victory* (Toronto, 1965). The Vimy battle is highlighted in Kenneth Macksey, *Vimy Ridge* (New York, 1972). The Currie biography is H.M. Urquhart, *Arthur Currie: The Biography of a Great Canadian* (Toronto, 1950). The exploits of Canadian pilots are related in Edmund Cosgrove, *Canada's Fighting Pilots* (Toronto, 1965), a short, popular account, and S.F. Wise, *Canadian Airmen and the First World War* (Toronto, 1980), which is the official history. The story of Billy Bishop is told in his son's *The Courage of the Early Morning* (Toronto, 1965). The manner in which the government coped with mobilization (or did not) and built an administrative framework to support its troops overseas is described by Desmond Morton in *A Peculiar Kind of Politics: Canada's Overseas Ministry in the First World War* (Toronto, 1982).

*The war sparked terrific interest at home in
the boys overseas. This card was one of a
series distributed by a cocoa manufacturer.*

We have advanced about a hundred yards. There is no enemy fire. It is
nearly dawn. A blue grey light appears. Renaud walks by my side. His face
is red with excitement now. To my left Anderson and Fry walk together.
Legs and arms in grey rags lie here and there. The trenches are almost
flattened. In the smoke-murk I step on something. It is soft. I look down.
It is the ripped open stomach of a German. We walk on.

In a later period, pacifists such as F.R. Scott would draw on wartime
memories to explain their antiwar views. In "Lest We Forget," Scott wrote:

The British troops at the Dardanelles
Were blown to bits by British shells
   Sold to the Turks by Vickers.
And many a brave Canadian youth
Will shed his blood on foreign shores,
And die for democracy, freedom, truth,
With his body full of Canadian ores ...

(Reprinted by permission of McClelland & Stewart Ltd., the Canadian Publishers.)

The Hothouse of War

Canadian society also had begun to come of age in meeting the challenges of this most terrible conflict. In British Columbia the demand for ores and ships kept the mines and smelters of the interior working at full tilt and stimulated a rapid expansion of local shipyards. In some coastal communities a high rate of enlistment created acute manpower shortages that could only be filled by women and hitherto unskilled immigrants, though the rate of female participation in the work force was low compared to that of central Canada because of the relative lack of heavy war industry.

Billy Bishop. (P.A.-1654/Public Archives Canada)

On the Prairies high rates of enlistment, especially in Manitoba, also produced labour shortages, although communities with substantial numbers of eastern European immigrants in their populations did not experience the same problem. Farmers expanded their production and turned increasingly to mechanization to take advantage of high grain prices, but the horse remained the chief motive power for farm equipment for at least two decades after the war. While the farmers busied themselves with the land, many middle-class reformers in the cities pushed ahead with their demands for change and linked those demands to the war. This was, they claimed, a just war to defeat a cruel enemy and bring about a better world. What better time was there to reform Canadian society at home? Men and women crusaded for votes for women, for temperance and prohibition, a fair system of taxation, and greater government regulation and ownership. One tangible result was the election of an unabashedly reformist Liberal Government in Manitoba in 1916 under the leadership of T.C. Norris. Norris introduced prohibition, the female franchise, laws to improve working conditions, a minimum wage law for women, and an industrial conciliation and collective bargaining law for the trade unions.

Manitoba's move towards reform was strongly influenced by the active and vigorous women's movement, which had been developing in the province for several years before the war and which was linked to the women's movement across the country. Organizations such as the Women's Christian Temperance Union, the National Council of Women of Canada, the Canadian Suffrage Association and, in Manitoba, the Manitoba Political Equality League, had first appeared on the stage in the 1870s dedicated to the enlightenment of women and to the improvement of their place in society. Many of these organizations quickly concluded that women's emancipation was directly linked to general social improvement and began to advocate a range of reforms from temperance to universal suffrage. Some female reformers believed that women were more moral and upright than men and that granting the vote to women somehow would produce a more moral and pacifist society. Others had no such illusions, however, and campaigned for the vote using the argument that governments could scarcely govern in the interests of women and their families if only men cast ballots. In that campaign, the fight was pressed by a broad coalition of reformers — male and female — who also wanted to use the powers of the state to remedy the myriad ills of the nation. But it was the women who led the suffrage struggle, as Nellie McClung, Frances

Maryon Beynon, Flora Macdonald Denison, and hundreds of others demanded women's just rights. By September, 1917, the fight had begun to pay off: women had been granted the right to vote in provincial elections in Ontario, Manitoba, Saskatchewan, Alberta, and British Columbia.

The campaign for women's right to vote was part of the rise of the progressivism that was directly related to the war's significant social impact on the entire country. The effects were felt most strongly in Ontario and Quebec. Both provinces were heavily industrialized and both experienced rapid growth in war-related industries and the towns and cities that contained them. There were increased demands for electricity and municipal services as well as for political and social reforms. The process of rural depopulation — the move of young men and women away from the farms and small country towns and villages to the big cities — accelerated, adding to fears that already existed in both provinces that the rural values that had dominated social and political mores for so long would be undermined and perhaps even destroyed.

In Atlantic Canada, coal mining and ship building were the industries most directly affected by the war, and production in both increased by leaps and bounds, creating new demands for skilled labour and stimulating rapid increases in wages. Warring union factions in the Nova Scotia coal industry finally united under the banner of the Amalgamated Mineworkers of Nova Scotia, the forerunner of the United Mine Workers of America's District 26, which was established in the coalfields by 1919. Halifax, always a busy port town, became the chief eastern terminus of the Atlantic convoys organized by the Royal Navy to protect shipping from German submarines, and local businesses thrived on the demands for goods and services created by the merchant ships that stopped here before joining eastbound convoys to Britain. Halifax also suffered terribly because of this role. On the morning of December 6, 1917, the French ship *Mont Blanc*, carrying more than two thousand tons of explosives and explosive chemicals, was steaming slowly into Halifax harbour towards Bedford Basin when it was struck by the Belgian vessel *Imo* in the narrows opposite the northwest portion of the city. Fire broke out on the ammunition ship and the crew hastily abandoned the vessel and made for shore. The *Mont Blanc* then drifted towards the docks. At 9:05 a.m. the French ship blew up with a roar heard 320 km away and Halifax was devastated. Close to two thousand people were killed, nine thousand were injured, and thousands more were left homeless. Food, medicine, building materials, and other relief supplies began to pour into Halifax from across the

The Halifax explosion on December 6, 1917, caused extensive devastation.
(C-19945/Public Archives Canada)

country and from the northeastern United States while rescue parties searched among the smouldering ruins for the dead and the living. It was the worst single disaster ever to befall a Canadian city.[4]

Becoming a Nation

The cruel blow of the Halifax explosion and the charge under fire at Vimy Ridge were dramatic examples of the high cost Canadians were paying

4. The Halifax explosion is documented in Graham Metson, ed., *The Halifax Explosion: December 6, 1917* (Toronto, 1978), and a fictional account is presented in Hugh MacLennan, *Barometer Rising* (Toronto, 1941). Up to now not much has been published specifically on the effect of the war on Canadian society. Available works include Barbara M. Wilson, ed., *Ontario and the First World War* (Toronto, 1977), and Leslie Frost, *Fighting Men* (Toronto, 1967), as well as Ceta Ramkhalawansingh, "Women During the Great War," in *Women at Work: Ontario, 1850-1930* (Toronto, 1974), and Catherine L. Cleverdon, *The Woman Suffrage Movement in Canada* (Toronto, 1950). On the reform movement see also Robert Craig Brown and Ramsay Cook, *Canada: 1896-1921: A Nation Transformed* (Toronto, 1974), and John H. Thompson, "The Beginning of our Regeneration: The Great War and Western Canadian Reform Movements," in *Historical Papers, 1972*. For the effect of the war on one large immigrant group, see Myrna Kostash, *All of Baba's Children* (Edmonton, 1977). The impact of the war on one aspect of Canadian culture is found in Maria Tippett, *Art at the Service of War: Canada, Art and the Great War* (Toronto, 1984).

for the country's new maturity and self-confidence. However, it was obvious even before the Vimy assault that Canada was making an important contribution to the war effort and was paying a heavy price to do it. This contribution was recognized in late 1916 when British Prime Minister David Lloyd George invited Borden and the other dominion premiers to London to sit as members of the newly constituted Imperial War Cabinet. Borden arrived in London in late February, 1917, and immediately busied himself studying the vast documentation compiled by the British War Cabinet — a smaller inner group of the United Kingdom Cabinet that was responsible for directing the British war effort. For the first time Borden had access to the whole picture of Britain's war effort and its foreign relations. At last he and the other prime ministers were about to achieve the consultation in foreign and defence matters that Borden had sought at least as far back as the 1910 naval crisis.

The Imperial War Conference opened on March 20, 1917, and it was soon evident that the dominions were being asked to pay a further price for the new equality that the British were apparently about to extend to them: they would have to contribute more men. Lloyd George wasted no time with facile predictions of imminent victory but told the dominion leaders that Germany was strong and growing stronger, that a renewed effort was needed for victory. Borden supported this and backed the British leader in his belief that the whole Empire must bring its total military power to bear in the struggle.

The prime ministers learned much at the meetings of the Imperial War Cabinet, although their opinions on military matters counted for little with the Imperial General Staff who were directing the military operations in Europe. Nevertheless, the meetings were more than just a sop to the increased national feelings so much in evidence in Canada and the other self-governing dominions: the basis of the modern commonwealth was built there. At the Imperial War Conference, held at the same time as the I.W.C. meetings, a resolution was adopted that was "the brainchild of Borden and [his advisor] Loring Christie." It declared that the constitutional status of "the component parts of the Empire" should be discussed at a special imperial conference to be held immediately after the war. Until the end of hostilities the British and dominion Governments placed on record their belief that this new constitutional status "should be based upon a full recognition of the Dominions as autonomous nations of an Imperial Commonwealth" with the right to "an adequate voice in foreign policy and in foreign relations" and with "effective arrangements for continuous consultation" in imperial questions of common concern. It was obvious that the dominions would no longer be mere self-governing colonies in the British Empire but would, instead, become partners in a newly structured empire-commonwealth. This rapid elevation of Canada's status was unquestionably rooted in the Canadian war effort and the list of Canadian dead and wounded that grew with each passing day.[5]

Borden stayed in England until early May, 1917, and took every spare moment to visit as many Canadian soldiers as he could at the front and in the barracks and hospitals in England. He had done this on an earlier trip to England in 1915, and he was again deeply moved by the sacrifice of these citizen-soldiers. He was more convinced than ever that Canadians must do all in their power, make any necessary sacrifice, to support these men. He knew that voluntary enlistment was falling off rapidly from the peak it had reached in the spring of 1916; he knew that losses were now outstripping replacements in the Canadian corps; and he was all too sensitive to Lloyd George's plea for more men from the dominions to shore up the forces of the empire already in the field. He was buoyed by the thought that the recent entry of the United States into the war against Germany would add tremendous new resources of military and industrial power to the struggle, but he worried about a total collapse on the Russian front. A new constitutional Government, headed by Alexander Kerensky, had overthrown the Czar in February, 1917. Although it had chosen to continue the war against Germany, the decision was not popular in Russia, and some of Kerensky's left-wing opponents were loudly demanding peace with Germany. On the passage back to Canada Borden made up his mind to propose conscription to his Cabinet in order to raise an additional one hundred thousand men. He also decided to try to create a coalition government to bring this about.

5. There is much work, mostly in article form, on Canada's imperial and foreign relations during and after the war. Two document collections that are particularly useful are R.M. Dawson, *The Development of Dominion Status: 1900-1931* (Hamden, Conn., 1967), and *Documents on Canadian External Relations*, published by the Department of External Affairs. Volume I covers the period 1909–1918, and volume II is devoted solely to the Paris Peace Conference of 1919. The Borden biography by Brown gives the best overview. See also R.C. Brown, "Sir Robert Borden, the Great War and Anglo-Canadian Relations," in J.S. Moir, ed., *Character and Circumstance* (Toronto, 1970); Brown and Robert Bothwell, "The 'Canadian Resolution'," in M. Cross and R. Bothwell, eds., *Policy by Other Means* (Toronto, 1972); L.F. Fitzhardinge, "Hughes, Borden and Dominion Representation at the Paris Peace Conference," *Canadian Historical Review, 1968*; G.P. de T. Glazebrook, *Canada at the Paris Peace Conference* (Toronto, 1942), and C.P. Stacey, *Canada and the Age of Conflict*, vol. I (Toronto, 1977).

Regulation 17 and Conscription

Borden and many other Canadians had been thinking about conscription, the compulsory draft of men for overseas military service, since early in the war. Borden's first inclination was to reject it, and he publicly declared against conscription in 1914. The political cost, especially in Quebec, where most French Canadians were dead-set against being forced to serve in foreign wars, was too high to justify it, particularly when voluntary recruiting was producing more men than were immediately needed. However, as the war dragged on and the manpower shortage became more acute, more and more voices in the country were raised to demand an end to voluntary recruiting and the introduction of the draft. This reflected the growing belief that voluntary enlistment was not sufficient to carry Canada through a conflict of this magnitude and the frustration of recruiters, particularly those civilians organized into local recruiting leagues, who were having increasing difficulty attracting young men to the army as the manpower shortage worsened. There was also a growing awareness that French Canadians were not enlisting at anywhere near the rate that characterized Canadians elsewhere, and this factor exacerbated other English-French tensions that were already boiling to the surface.

The fight over Ontario Department of Education Instruction 17 — it was popularly referred to as Regulation 17 — symbolized the deepening chasm between the English and the French. It had been issued by Ontario's Conservative Government in 1912 to restrict French severely as a language of instruction in the province's schools, including those in regions with large French populations. The move was a response to fears that the rapidly expanding Franco-Ontarian population might one day become the majority of Ontario. These fears were unreasonable, but they were fed by the claims of some Francophone leaders that the high French-Canadian birth rate would constitute a "revenge of the cradle." Regulation 17 had provoked an angry reaction from Franco-Ontarians who were forced to turn to the federal Liberal party for aid because the provincial Liberal opposition, headed by Newton W. Rowell, refused to take up their cause. In 1916 Ernest Lapointe introduced the matter into Parliament with a motion that Ottawa "respectfully suggest to the Legislative Assembly of Ontario the wisdom of making it clear that the privilege of the children of French parentage being taught in their mother tongue be not interfered with."

Though there was some sympathy for the Franco-Ontarian cause among French members of Borden's Cabinet, the Prime Minister refused to touch this political hot potato. Borden was convinced there was nothing he or his Government could do, and he was not willing to risk a split with the Ontario Government in the midst of a war. Once again, as on the emergency naval contribution issue, Borden showed a decided lack of understanding of, or sympathy with, French Canada and placed other matters higher on his list of priorities, and once again French-English antagonism increased as a result. For many Quebeckers, particularly those of a *nationaliste* bent, the fight over Regulation 17 was every bit as important as, and perhaps more important than, the war in Europe. Ontario's restriction of French in its schools was denounced as "Prussianism" at home.

It is hard to know what effect Regulation 17 had on recruiting in Quebec because there were other important factors which discouraged a higher rate of voluntary enlistment there. Much of the recruiting was done by the English elites of Montreal and Quebec City who traditionally had little contact with French Canadians, and who tended to look down on them. Indeed, Protestant clergymen sometimes acted as recruiters in predominantly French-Catholic areas when no curé could be found to do the job. Those French Canadians who did sign up were often shunted to garrison duty in quiet backwaters of the war while others were placed in English-speaking units. Few completely French-speaking battalions were formed, and so French-Canadian soldiers were denied the right to communicate with their fellows in times of danger on the battlefield. To French Canadians the war was not an emotional struggle in support of a mother country as it was to many English Canadians, especially those who had recently arrived, or who were one generation removed, from Britain. There were few, if any, emotional ties to bind French Canadians to a France that had abandoned Quebec in the 1760s and had then turned republican and anticlerical after the French Revolution. Many Quebec Catholics believed, in fact, that the Church was oppressed in France while liberals, socialists, and other anti-Christian groups were allowed to run rampant. After so many years of physical and spiritual separation from the land of their ancestors, it was hard to generate much enthusiasm in Quebec for a crusade designed to save France from German aggression, even though the Church in Quebec formally supported the war effort. For French Canada the war was not an affair of the heart.

However, French Canadians were not alone in their opposition to conscription. Many workers and farmers in all parts of Canada opposed compulsory military service. Workers feared that conscription for military service would soon lead to conscription for industrial service as well, forcing them to stay at one job in one plant for the duration of the war. This would give tremendous power to employers and rob the trade unions of virtually all their leverage. They joined with the farmers in demanding that the Government consider "conscription of wealth" — the nationalization of banks and industries for the duration of the war — if it conscripted manpower. Many immigrants, especially in western Canada, also opposed conscription because they did not feel as emotionally involved in the war effort as Canadians of British background.

Despite this opposition to conscription, Borden had been moving closer to such a change in recruiting policy since the fall of 1916. In August his Government had established the National Service Board to survey manpower distribution and to try to increase recruiting while, at the same time, avoiding the withdrawal of much-needed skilled labour from war industries. There was at first some difficulty in finding a chairman for the Board, but the Prime Minister eventually settled on R.B. Bennett, a Calgary lawyer and fellow Conservative M.P. In January, 1917, the Board launched a national registration drive by sending a registration card to every male of military age in Canada, asking for information on age, health, job status, and other factors to help the Board determine how many men eligible for military service remained in the country. At the time, Borden insisted that registration was not intended as a first step towards conscription, but he refused to give assurances to labour leaders that conscription would never be used. In fact, he made it quite plain that conscription would be resorted to if other means of increasing the number of recruits failed. By the time he had returned from England in May, he had decided that the first priority of his Government was to reinforce the army in the field and to ensure that the flow of men to the front was sufficient to maintain the strength of the four divisions there; this could only be done with conscription. Nothing else — French-Canadian anger, the resentment of the workers and farmers, the survival of the Conservative party — would be allowed to take a higher priority. Borden now was determined to do whatever was necessary to ensure the introduction of conscription.[6]

The Prime Minister announced his Government's new policy to the House of Commons on May 18, 1917, and then prepared to approach Laurier with a proposal to establish a coalition government. Coalition, the temporary joining together of the Liberal and Conservative parties

6. Conscription is covered in J.L. Granatstein and J.M. Hitsman, *Broken Promises: A History of Conscription in Canada* (Toronto, 1977). An older but still valuable work is Elizabeth Armstrong, *The Crisis of Quebec: 1914–1918* (New York, 1937). Several good articles on the subject can be found in Carl Berger, ed., *Conscription 1917* (Toronto, n.d.).

inside the government, had been suggested in some quarters since early in the war as a move to ensure a united, nonpartisan war effort, though both the Liberals and the Conservatives had shied away from it, thinking they would lose much and gain little from a coalition. However, in 1916, when Lloyd George assumed power in Great Britain, he forged a coalition that included all the major political parties. This spurred many Canadians to renew their call for a national coalition, and when Borden decided to introduce conscription, he attempted to forge a union of his party with the Liberals to provide bipartisan support for the contentious measure.

The approach to Laurier was made on May 25, one day after rioting in Montreal underlined the implacable opposition of French Canada to conscription. Borden proposed that the Liberals join a new government with half the Cabinet positions reserved for Liberal ministers. Borden was to remain Prime Minister. Laurier did not reject the proposal but instead asked for time to consult with his political advisors. This was undoubtedly only a delaying tactic because he knew that any French Canadian who agreed to support conscription was sounding his own political death knell. Laurier may have stood for Quebec in the House of Commons in Ottawa, but he knew well that Henri Bourassa and the *nationalistes* were waiting in the wings, and that they would profit from the destruction of the Quebec Liberals that would follow if Laurier joined a conscriptionist coalition. Although Borden approached Laurier a second time less than a week later to sweeten the post by promising to hold back on conscription until after it was confirmed by a general election, Laurier refused to give in. If there was to be a coalition, therefore, the leader of the Liberal party and his followers would have to be left out of it.

The Military Service Act was debated and passed in the House of Commons in July, and many English-speaking Liberal M.P.s bolted party lines to support it, proof that a considerable number of Liberals outside Quebec might be willing to break with Laurier and join Borden in a coalition. Some acted purely out of support for the war, but others, particularly those from Ontario and western Canada, believed in "progressivism," the idea that government ownership or regulation of the economy, combined with government support for basic social services, was absolutely necessary in a modern, industrialized society, and they were eager for a chance to undermine Laurier's reactionary power in the Liberal party. They knew he had little sympathy for progressivism and were all too aware of the power of Laurier and the Quebec Liberals. They reasoned that if they could join with Borden, their survival in the next general election would be ensured because of their support for conscription. They

Suicide? *Forrester*

Quebec's attitude to conscription never wavered, as the cover of this pamphlet, published by Le Devoir *in 1917, demonstrates.*

could break with the Conservatives after the war to re-create a more progressive Liberal party that was not as dependent on Quebec.

Managing the War

Though Borden spent most of his time in the spring and summer of 1917 on the fight for conscription and coalition, his Government was also moving to come to grips with growing social and economic problems.[7] It was becoming more apparent all the time that economic voluntarism was not working and that government intervention in and regulation of broad areas of social and economic activity were crucial. In a sense, conscription set the tone because once compulsion was brought to army recruiting there could be little philosophical reason for opposing the extension of compulsion to other areas of the daily lives of Canadians. The process started slowly and hesitantly, but the turning point was not reached until 1917, when government control in Canada was extended through direct taxation of incomes and the control of supplies of food and fuel.

Inflation was one of the most pressing problems. When war broke out in August, 1914, the country was in the midst of a depression and wages and prices had been falling steadily since late 1913. The war brought with it munitions production and the beginning of recruiting and, by the end of 1915, a labour shortage that forced wages up in industries most closely connected with the war. At the same time, shortages began to show up in supplies of food and raw materials because a large army had to be fed, food was needed by Canada's European allies, and war factories demanded massive amounts of metals, textiles, wood, chemicals, and other materials. The shortages, combined with a rise in labour costs caused by a growing labour shortage, created inflation, but the Government's fiscal policies made it worse. Ottawa spent hundreds of millions of dollars on the war effort, far more than it raised through taxation, and it had to

7. There are few works which focus directly on government intervention and regulation during the war. A good overview is Robert Cuff, "Organizing for War: Canada and the United States During World War I," *Canadian Historical Association Report, 1969*, which should be supplemented with reading from the Borden biography by R.C. Brown, and Brown and Cook's *Canada: 1896-1921*. On the Imperial Munitions Board see Michael Bliss, *A Canadian Millionaire: The Life and Business Times of Sir Joseph Flavelle, Bart, 1858-1939* (Toronto, 1978). There are several works which cover railway nationalization, including the Graham biography of Meighen. The most complete account is found in T.D. Regehr, *The Canadian Northern Railway* (Toronto, 1976). A good analysis of business attitudes is Tom Traves, *The State and Enterprise: Canadian Manufacturers and the Federal Government, 1917-1931* (Toronto, 1979).

TO WIN THE WAR

THIS HOUSEHOLD IS PLEDGED

TO CARRY OUT CONSCIENTIOUSLY THE ADVICE AND DIRECTIONS OF THE

FOOD CONTROLLER

By 1918 Canada was increasingly well organized for the war as government extended its controls into the public sector. These cards were put in the windows of houses or displayed in restaurants.

ALL persons in ordering their food ought to consider the needs of Great Britain, the Allies and the armies for wheat, beef and bacon. The Food Controller requires the public to do everything in their power to make these commodities available for export by eating as little as possible of them, by using substitutes and by avoiding waste.

borrow vast sums at home and abroad to pay the bills. This borrowing added to inflation by driving up interest rates, which in turn increased production costs. The rise of living costs began in the last months of 1915 and became noticeable by early 1916. By 1917 many Canadians were complaining bitterly about inflation, pointing out that their living standard was dropping because wage increases were not, in most cases, keeping up with rising prices. Soon there were charges that "food pirates and price manipulators" were gouging Canadian consumers. The Government first took action in 1916, when a cost-of-living commissioner was appointed to investigate complaints about increasing prices. He found no conspiracies. In 1917 food and fuel controllers were appointed to attack inflation in these two basic commodities, while a Board of Grain Supervisors was formed with total control over wheat sales in Canada and abroad. Thus the free market system for buying and selling wheat was suspended and compulsion put in its place for the duration of the war.

One of the most revolutionary means of government intervention in the economy was direct taxation, which began in 1916 with the establishment of a business profits tax, a direct tax levied on businesses by the federal government to raise revenue and decrease the enormous profits which many businesses were making from the war. The Minister of Finance summed up the Government's approach by declaring that since some businesses were doing so well compared to other Canadians, it was only "just that a portion of their advantage should be appropriated to the benefit of the state." One year later, in July, 1917, income taxes were introduced. Now there was direct taxation on the incomes of all Canadians (still relatively few in number) who earned more than $2000 per year.

The Government's new activism was obvious in its solution to the deepening financial troubles that plagued several large Canadian railways which, because of the war, could not borrow the money needed to keep them running. The Canadian Northern Railway was in the worst shape and had approached the federal government for loans several times in the early stages of the war. Finance Minister White was forced to warn the Cabinet that failure to extend aid would force the railway into bankruptcy and possibly cause it to be dismembered by its receivers. This would be a heavy blow to the confidence of foreign investors — and to the war effort. When the railway came to the Government again in 1916, White proposed an extension of government aid coupled with the appointment of a commission of experts to examine the situation of the major Canadian railways and report to the Government on suggested courses of action for a future railway policy. In July a royal commission of three was appointed

THE CANADIAN LIBERAL MONTHLY

VOL. V. No. 1.   OTTAWA, SEPTEMBER, 1917.   TWO CENTS

ON THE ROCKS, OR

' SAFETY FIRST FOR SOME,

By 1917 the Liberals were convinced that Borden's Government was mired in corruption and waste, as this cartoon from the Liberals' monthly magazine illustrates.

— A.H. Smith, President of the New York Central Railroad, W.H. Acworth, an expert on British railways, and Sir Henry L. Drayton, Chief Commissioner of the Canadian Board of Railway Commissioners. The three spent months studying the structures, finances, and prospects of Canada's major railways and reported to the Government in the spring of 1917.

The commissioners were divided in their recommendations. Smith proposed that in future the Grand Trunk Railway operate the eastern section of its own and the Canadian Northern tracks, while the Canadian Northern operate its own western section together with the entire Grand Trunk Pacific network. The Government would then operate the section connecting the two systems or turn it over to a private company. He admitted that the railways were overbuilt but was optimistic that a solution could be found within the existing system. Drayton and Acworth, on the other hand, recommended that the Canadian Northern, Grand Trunk, and Grand Trunk Pacific Railways be consolidated into a single corporation managed by a board to be appointed by the Government. This was to be a private company managed by a self-perpetuating board. Neither plan was fully acceptable to the Government, which instead presented a plan to Parliament to begin nationalizing all of the major railways, except the C.P.R., by the purchase of the Canadian Northern. The nationalization was but the first step in a process that eventually resulted in the formation of Canadian National Railways. This issue, involving vast sums of money, remained a political crisis of the first rank for years.

The Conscription Election

While the Government made significant headway in its efforts to bring major areas of the economy under its direct control, it made little initial progress on the coalition question. Laurier's refusal to join the Cabinet meant that overtures had to be made over Laurier's head to other Liberals who supported conscription and who were unhappy with his leadership. Nevertheless, many believed that their party stood a good chance of winning a federal election because of the scandals, the rising cost of living, growing social unrest, and the unwavering support of French Canadians and others opposed to conscription. There was little doubt about how the soldiers would vote, but Liberals believed that it would be extremely difficult to collect and count the soldiers' ballots while the fighting raged.

The normal parliamentary term of five years had expired long before, but in 1915 and again in 1916 Laurier and Borden agreed to one-year extensions to avoid a wartime vote. However, in 1917 the Liberals (and many Conservatives) were opposed to another extension. There was also a possibility that the war, which had lasted far longer than most had ever expected, would continue indefinitely. Borden was unwilling to push for another extension without the consent of the Opposition and was forced to schedule the election for December 17, 1917. As the date neared, the political maneuvring over the coalition intensified.

Borden was determined to win the election at any cost because losing would mean the downfall of conscription. He had made his pledge to the troops — he was deeply committed to them — and he was willing to resort to almost any measure to guarantee victory, despite the political consequences. This reasoning led to the Military Voters Act, proposed to the House of Commons in mid-August, and the Wartime Elections Act, brought down in mid-September. The first gave the vote to all members of the armed forces, male or female, no matter how long they had lived in Canada, and stipulated that they were to vote for or against the Government and not for individual candidates in their home ridings. If military personnel could not name their home riding, their votes could be allo-

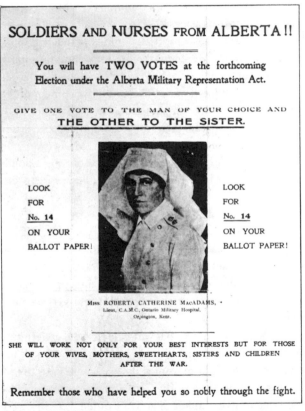

Women on the Prairies got the vote as early as 1916 for provincial elections. And with the vote came the right of election. Nursing Sister MacAdams, helped by her clever campaign slogan, won election to the Alberta legislature in 1917. (Glenbow Archives, NA1404-3)

cated to whatever riding the electoral officer saw fit. The second bill gave the vote to all Canadian women who were mothers, wives, sisters, or daughters of servicemen and took the vote away from all immigrants from enemy countries who had settled in Canada after 1902, as well as all conscientious objectors.

The two bills were drawn up by Arthur Meighen, a Portage la Prairie lawyer who was appointed Solicitor General, an office without a Cabinet seat, in 1913, and who entered the Cabinet two years later. Meighen possessed a brilliant mind, a sharp tongue, and considerable oratorical powers. He was didactic and sharply logical in his reasoning, and though he was conservative in both philosophy and temperament, he did not allow his ideological proclivities to stand in the way of his duty, as he interpreted it, to party, country, and empire. He was, for example, also the author of the controversial legislation to nationalize the Canadian Northern Railway, thus earning for himself the enmity of much of the Montreal business establishment. Meighen was openly contemptuous of wishy-washy politicians and seemed to thrive on destroying their arguments in the parry and thrust of Commons debate. He was a man of great skill, little warmth, and even less compassion, at least in public.

When added together, Meighen's bills assured the Government of a distinct advantage in the forthcoming election. Many immigrants, who traditionally voted Liberal because they had settled in Canada during Laurier's time as Prime Minister, would not be able to vote, while women who were close to men at the front and who could, therefore, be depended upon to vote in favour of the Government and its conscription policy, were to be allowed to vote for the first time. A large bloc of Liberal votes had been cancelled and a large bloc of Government votes had been created. In addition, the soldiers' vote, which could also be counted on to favour the Government, could be divided up and apportioned to those constituencies where close battles between Conservatives and Liberals were expected.

The women's movement was badly divided by the government's decision to grant the vote to some women but not to others. The Borden administration had worked with women pro-conscriptionists to try to determine the reaction of women to the partial grant of the franchise, and it had decided that a large number of active women were more concerned about the fate of conscription than about discrimination against non-Anglo Saxon women. This reflected the earlier view, uttered by Nellie McClung, the Manitoba reformer, that even a "partial franchise" was "better than none" because it opened the door to a full franchise later on. McClung was chastised for this by Frances Maryon Beynon, another Manitoba leader, who believed that a grave injustice would be done if foreign-born women were denied the vote.

The vast majority of leaders of women's organizations in 1917 were Canadian- or British-born and strongly supported the Wartime Elections Act. Mrs. A.E. Gooderham, President of the Independent Order of the Daughters of the Empire, Mrs. L.A. Hamilton, President of the National Equal Franchise Union, and Mrs. F.H. Torrington, President of the National Council of Women, along with many other women's leaders, endorsed the measure. But voices were raised in opposition. At the Ontario Women's Christian Temperance Union annual convention in 1917, for example, a blunt motion was passed stating that "we resent the action of the government in creating an arbitrary distinction among the women of Canada by placing on the books the war-time elections act."

The division in the ranks was not closed until March, 1918, when the Borden government extended voting rights to all women in Canada on the same basis as men.

The Wartime Elections Act and the Military Voters Act weighted the vote in favour of the Government, but there was still significant opposition to conscription outside Quebec among workers and farmers who thought it unfair of the Government to conscript a man's very body while so many businesses in Canada were thriving on war-generated profits. Some labour leaders, particularly in western Canada, wanted to organize a national general strike in opposition to conscription, but the national convention of the Trades and Labour Congress of Canada in September, 1917, decided instead to launch a political campaign and to support labour candidates who wished to take the field against the Government. Farmers were already angry with the Government because of the ceilings imposed on the prices of farm products and resisted any notion that their sons and farm hands should be forced to join the army. How could they produce the food the Government wanted without help? But in a shrewd move to undermine this opposition the Government issued an order-in-council two weeks before the election to exempt agricultural labourers from compulsory military duty.

By late September the conscriptionist Liberals were ready to make a deal with Borden. Most of those willing to enter the coalition were connected to provincial Liberal parties, for Laurier's hold on federal M.P.s was still strong, and in two conventions of federal Liberals, in Toronto in July and Winnipeg in August, support for him was reaffirmed. Nevertheless, by early October Borden had succeeded in enticing a number of

Liberals to enter his Cabinet under a coalition agreement. The most prominent of these were Alberta Premier Arthur Sifton and the leader of the
Liberal Opposition in the Ontario legislature, Newton W. Rowell. The
new Union Government, as it was called, was sworn in on October 12.

*The Union Government of 1917, here pictured in an
election advertisement, contained only two French Canadians, and neither survived the election. (Crerar Papers,
Queen's University)*

There was little doubt about the outcome of the election when the
effect of the new coalition was added to the Wartime Elections Act and
the Military Voters Act, but the country was deeply divided nonetheless.
Government election propaganda claimed that a vote for Laurier was a
vote for the Kaiser and against the boys in the trenches. Even though the

Double jeu des
Chefs Libéraux

Dans Québec, ils sont contre le service militaire.

Dans les autres provinces, ils sont pour le service militaire.

Aux Canadiens-français ils disent que la conscription vise la Province de Québec.

Aux Canadiens-anglais ils affirment que la conscription sauvegardera les intéréts de la province de Québec.

The Union Government campaign in Quebec, while doomed from the start, was vigorous nonetheless. This pamphlet accused the Liberals of talking one way in Quebec and another elsewhere in the country and was one effort to stem the anticonscriptionist tide.

new Union Government was armed with a broad platform of progressive campaign promises — temperance, votes for all women, civil service and tariff reform — most of the electioneering centred on conscription. Traditional Conservatives concentrated on conscription as the one issue sure to bring victory while Unionist Liberals concentrated on it because they feared that many of their traditional supporters would not otherwise follow them into the Government camp. Laurier and his followers were, ironically, also preoccupied with conscription. They concentrated on the issue not because they thought they could win on it — it was clear by late October that they would not — but to avoid coming to grips with the Union Government's progressive and state-interventionist policies to which Laurier was opposed. Campaigning on conscription was good, old-fashioned politics, and it allowed Laurier to keep his loyal Liberals together to await the end of the war and the collapse of the Unionist coalition. It seems hardly possible, but on election night all three groups were proved

In Flanders' Fields

by

Colonel John McCrea

of Guelph, Canada

Now serving in France

IN Flanders' fields the poppies blow
Between the crosses, row on row,
That mark our place, and in the sky
The larks still bravely singing fly,
Scarce heard amidst the guns below.
We are the dead. Short days ago
We lived, felt dawn, saw sunset glow,
Loved and were loved, and now we lie
In Flanders' fields.

Take up our quarrel with the foe,
To you from falling hands we throw
The Torch—be yours to hold it high;
If ye break faith with us who die,
We shall not sleep though poppies grow
In Flanders' fields.

VOTE UNION GOVERNMENT

Issued by the Union Government Publicity Bureau, 47 Slater St., Ottawa
Modern Press Print.

Union Government election propaganda worked very hard to equate a vote for Borden with patriotism. This flyer was more restrained than most.

correct. The Unionist coalition swept the country outside of Quebec (when the military vote was taken into account), while Laurier captured all of French Canada. Within the coalition, the Unionist Liberals did well, capturing 39 of the Government's 152 seats — 25.6 per cent of the total.

Union Government in Power

Following the election the Government settled in to fulfill its campaign pledges and oversee the operation of conscription. One of the first reform measures it enacted was prohibition. Many progressives viewed alcohol as an evil almost as great as the Kaiser himself and used the opportunity created by the war to claim that drink undermined the war effort and should be prohibited. Borden responded by imposing a prohibition on the manufacture, import, and transportation of almost all alcoholic beverages within a week of the election. In February, 1918, the War Trade Board was set up as a subcommittee of the Cabinet in response to the desire of many businessmen that more government direction of the war economy be introduced to cut down on "wasteful" competition and to promote cooperation between government and business. The Board had power to supervise imports and exports, prevent wastage of labour and raw materials, direct the distribution of fuel, electricity and raw materials, and encourage economic cooperation between Canada and the United States. The Board could negotiate contracts for the Government and, before the war ended, started to regulate the production of pig iron, an essential component in the manufacture of steel.

In the six-week session of Parliament that opened on March 18 the Government revealed the full extent of its reform program. A Civil Service Act was passed which placed almost all civil service jobs under the control of the Civil Service Commission, thus taking a large patronage plum out of the hands of the Government. This fulfilled Borden's 1911 election pledge. The vote was granted to all Canadian women. The Department of Soldiers' Civil Re-Establishment was set up, belatedly, to begin planning for the day when the soldiers would return to Canada to be reintegrated into civilian life. The Government was moving quickly now, but it was not quick enough for western farmers or organized labour.

The West had played an important role in the triumph of the Union Government and had placed great store in the Unionist promises for sweeping reforms. One area that concerned farmers was the tariff, and they believed they had a good case for the abolition of tariffs on farm machinery during the war as essential to the war effort. But the protectionist faction in the Government was strong, and no tariff relief was offered. When this was coupled with the Government's sudden cancellation of conscription exemptions for all classes of labourers aged twenty to twenty-two — the result, Borden claimed, of a need for rapid reinforcement of Canadian troops because of a massive German offensive on the western front in March — farmers in the West believed themselves betrayed.

For organized labour the reforms were too little too late. Labour leaders had warned Borden in 1916 that his Government had an obligation to "prevent employers from taking advantage of the war to increase the exploitation of their employees," and, by the spring of 1917, they had put together a long list of complaints about wages and working conditions in war industries. The Government did little other than extend the Industrial Disputes Investigation Act, a measure unpopular with Canadian trade unionists, to war plants. Labour leaders, unlike business leaders, were not called upon to help the war effort and were rarely, if ever, taken into the Government's confidence. The unions had been thwarted in an attempt, launched early in the war, to have fair-wage clauses inserted into war contracts to protect the wages of war workers, and they had been defeated over conscription. By 1918 they were less willing to compromise and more prone to strike than ever before.

Work time lost from industrial disputes climbed steadily from a low in 1915 and reached a new peak during 1917 with strikes in many major war industries. But 1917 was peaceful compared with 1918. During that year strikes broke out in West Coast shipyards, Winnipeg metal working shops, and the postal service. A strike of Winnipeg city employees in May spread to become almost general before it was ended by the intervention of Senator Gideon Robertson, a vice-president of the railway telegraphers union, who was sent to restore peace as the personal representative of Prime Minister Borden. A dispute between the major Canadian railways and their repair and maintenance workers threatened to paralyze the Canadian rail transport system in July and was averted only when the Borden Government threatened to conscript the workers and force them to work under army supervision on army pay.

Although these disputes were caused by workers trying to force their employers to recognize their unions or by demands for higher pay to keep up with increases in the cost of living, the Government did little or nothing to solve the basic problems affecting Canadian workers. Instead it issued orders-in-council banning strikes and lockouts, forbidding the public use of "enemy" languages such as German, Ukrainian, and Czech,

Canadian soldiers ended the war at Mons, Belgium, the very place where the British first met the Germans in 1914. When this photograph was published fifteen years later, the Toronto Evening Telegram *carefully air-brushed out the signboard pointing to the latrine. (*Toronto Telegram *Collection, York University Archives)*

and declaring fourteen radical unions and left-wing political parties illegal. The Government had become convinced that radicals and revolutionaries were behind the strikes and were trying to undermine the war effort. There was little evidence to support this, and much to suggest that inflation, thwarted worker aspirations, and the irresponsible actions of some employers were at fault; nevertheless, the Government chose to believe that the unrest was connected with foreign movements such as the Bolshevik revolution that broke out in Russia, toppling Kerensky, in November, 1917.

When the Bolsheviks seized power in Russia, they sued for peace with Germany, and the Germans were able to concentrate their resources on the western front. The Kaiser's officers decided to deal the Allies one massive knockout blow before the full strength of the United States, still mobilizing a vast army, could be brought to bear, and in March, 1918, Germany launched a massive attack in the west. The attack nearly succeeded but was eventually thwarted by stubborn British resistance. This offensive, together with the heavy Allied losses in the Battle of Passchendaele in late 1917, became the chief topic of discussion at the meeting of the Imperial War Cabinet in the summer of 1918. Borden was appalled at the casualty rate, accused the Imperial General Staff of incompetence, and backed a strenuous effort by Lloyd George to bring the military under the direct control of civilian authorities, represented by the Imperial War Cabinet. The year before, Canada and the other dominions had finally won British agreement, in theory, to consult them on foreign policy and defence matters; at the 1918 meeting the dominions won that agreement in practice by taking part in the determination of future war strategy for the combined imperial forces.

In early August, 1918, a massive combined offensive was launched by American, British, and French forces with the Canadian Corps and the Australians taking the British lead and acting as shock troops. The offensive, using new artillery and infantry tactics and backed by the use of tanks and aircraft, rolled forward, recapturing much of the French and Belgian territory taken by the Germans in the first months of the war. The German armies were on the verge of collapse, and the Kaiser was forced to abdicate in favour of a republican administration headed by the Social Democrats. As the Allied armies neared the borders of Germany itself, the new German Government pressed for an armistice. The Allies agreed, and all fighting on the western front ended at 11 a.m. on November 11, 1918. The bloodbath was over and the peacemaking was about to begin.

Once the fighting ended Borden was determined to keep the political gains that had been made during the war, while Lloyd George appeared determined to undo much that had been done. It was not that he wanted the dominions to revert to their strictly colonial prewar status: far from it. But he was determined to guard jealously the prerogative of the major Allies — Britain, France, the United States, and, to a lesser degree, Italy — to shape the peace without the interference of the lesser powers. Thus, to placate the Imperial War Cabinet without offering them any substantial representation among the ranks of the Allied peace negotiators, Lloyd George proposed that Borden represent the dominions as one of the five imperial delegates at the peace conference in Paris.

Borden refused. He wanted nothing less than full representation for each dominion as part of the British delegation; he had no right or desire to speak for the others. Borden had to contend not only with the British but also with the Americans, who initially balked at the idea that the dominions should be separately represented at the peace negotiations, even though it was clear that they would also be part of the British delegation. American Secretary of State Robert Lansing wondered aloud what business Canada had in the settlement of European affairs, ignoring the large Canadian contribution to the war and the sixty thousand Canadian dead. However, in mid-January President Woodrow Wilson proposed a compromise to allow two delegates each from Canada, South Africa, Australia, and India, and one from New Zealand (but none from Newfoundland) to take part in the peace conference. But the dominions contributed little to the actual formation of the peace treaty, which was moulded almost exclusively by the major powers.

The Paris Peace Conference set the terms of the peace settlement and established the foundation of the League of Nations, an organization of countries to guard the peace and punish aggressor nations. Borden was able to secure separate Canadian representation in the League and eligibility for membership on the League's governing council, as well as separate Canadian representation on the League's International Labour Organization. However, he was decidedly unhappy over the League's collective security arrangements as outlined in Article 10 of its charter. This stipulated that the League's governing council had the power to tell League members what action to take in case of a threat to peace. Borden thought the article imposed unreasonable obligations upon League members, and he had, in any case, more faith in a British-American alliance to keep peace than in any action the League might take. Borden stayed in Paris until mid-May but took little real part in the deliberations, except for a brief stint on a commission established to set the boundaries of the Balkan countries.

While Borden was trying to help forge a new international peace in Paris, the home front in Canada was deteriorating into class and sectional warfare. Canadians in all walks of life had made sacrifices to win the war, but none matched that of Canada's 650 000 men and women who had served in the armed forces. Deaths had totalled 60 000 and there had been 173 000 wounded. Some of the survivors had been returned to Canada even before the war ended, but the coming of peace brought a virtual flood of veterans eager to take their places in civilian life again. The Government's Department of Soldiers' Civil Re-Establishment orchestrated efforts to reintegrate the veterans into society by spearheading a campaign to urge private businesses to hire returned soldiers, while the Government gave them preference in hiring for the civil service. In addition, a limited pension scheme was set up, homestead land was made available, and veterans' hospitals were built at government expense to care for the critically wounded and sick. But these measures did little to meet veterans' demands for tangible rewards for their long and faithful service, and in the winter and spring of 1919 veterans across the country staged brief riots and attacked aliens, leftist political organizations (both seen as "slackers" and anti-British), and businesses that employed foreigners. On January 26, 1919, an angry crowd of veterans attacked the headquarters of the Socialist Party of Canada in Winnipeg. They stormed up the stairs, broke through the door, and smashed up the furniture, pushing a piano through the window to crash to the street below. They showered books, leaflets, and pamphlets down on the shattered piano and then set the whole pile ablaze. For the next two days they demonstrated against employers who hired aliens rather than returned soldiers. In the spring, veterans attacked socialist and labour organizers in British Columbia's interior, throwing several out of mining towns such as Trail, Silverton, and Cranbrook. One union organizer thought that "the time [had] arrived when a working man [needed] a bodyguard as well as a King." Probably the worst incident took place in Drumheller, a small Alberta coal-mining town, in early August, when crowds of veterans attacked the homes of striking miners and forced many of them to flee with their families into the hills for safety.

The unrest among the veterans paralleled the growing unrest among Canadian workers. Many had suffered a decline in their living standard because of inflation, while others feared a return to the prewar depression once war-related prosperity disappeared. Although some had resorted to strikes during wartime, many had not, out of a sense of patriotism, and they expected matters to improve after the war. They, like other Canadians, had been promised a better society after the killing was over, and now they waited, impatiently, for the Government to make good.[8]

8. Labour unrest during and after the war is covered in David J. Bercuson, *Confrontation at Winnipeg: Labour, Industrial Relations and the General Strike* (Montreal, 1974), and *Fools and Wise Men: The Rise and Fall of the One Big Union* (Toronto, 1978). On radicalism see A.R. McCormack, *Reformers, Rebels and Revolutionaries: The Western Canadian Radical Movement, 1899-1919* (Toronto, 1977), and Martin Robin, *Radical Politics and Canadian Labour: 1880-1930* (Kingston, 1968).

Chapter V

The
Years of
Labour
Radicalism

The streetcar moved slowly as it proceeded south through a milling crowd of several hundred angry demonstrators on the city's main street. Two or three men climbed atop the moving car and pulled its trolley off the wires, depriving it of electricity and stopping it dead, while others smashed in the windows. Soon the sound of shouting men filled the air as hundreds of strikers pushed at the side of the car to tip it over. They almost succeeded, but the car was too heavy, and its swaying slowly stopped. One man then ran into the car, slashed several seats and set the interior ablaze. While the crowd's attention was focussed on the streetcar, a squad of mounted police galloped on to the main street from a connecting avenue. There were as many as fifty by some accounts, their revolvers in their holsters and their batons in their hands. They galloped through the jeering crowd and stopped to regroup. For a few moments the police and the crowd, led by returned soldiers, watched each other uneasily over a distance of several blocks. Then the police charged again, and this time the crowd reacted by throwing bricks, stones, and bottles. None of the mounted men was seriously hurt. They completed their charge through the crowd, wheeled about, and charged back again. Again they rode through a rain of missiles, and again they turned to the charge. This time they did not escape unharmed. One horse stumbled over a piece of streetcar fender that had been torn off and left lying in the street. The rider was thrown from the saddle, but his foot caught in the stirrup, and he was dragged along the street until a man leaped from the crowd, freed him, and started to beat him. When the other police saw this they stopped, turned around quickly, and rode towards the crowd with "revolvers cocked in their hands." Their commander gave the order to "fire a volley into the crowd," and gunfire crackled out. Bullets ricocheted off brick and concrete as the crowd broke up in panic. One man was killed instantly, shot through the heart, and another was mortally wounded, while others sustained less serious injuries. Hundreds ducked down side streets and alleys trying to escape the deadly fusillade and were met by cordons of club-wielding police who beat them back and arrested scores. Within minutes, trucks carrying soldiers armed with rifles and bayonets, and with heavy machine guns bolted to their flatbeds, began to roll into the heart of the city as a short-lived army occupation of the downtown core began.

This did not happen in some strike-torn foreign capital; the city is not Petrograd in the fall of 1917 or Gdansk in the summer of 1980. This confrontation between strikers and the Royal North West Mounted Police took place in Winnipeg, then Canada's third largest city, on June 21, 1919 — "Bloody Saturday" — and was the climax of the Winnipeg General Strike, which paralyzed the city for six long weeks in that hot summer of 1919. Though Canadians like to think of themselves as a peaceful people, settling their disputes with discussions and arbitrating their differences in law courts and legislatures, in the twentieth century they have had, as one historian noted, "a record of labour unrest and industrial conflict, with illegal and violent overtones, second only to the United States, and far greater than that of most west European countries."[1] If this is true of the twentieth century in general, it is certainly true of the period from 1911 to 1921. During this decade the Canadian working class was afflicted with runaway inflation, rampant unemployment, the ravages of war, repression by the government, and the bitter disappointment of a peace which did not bring the better world working men and women thought had been promised them.

When the Great War ended, Canadian workers from coast to coast revolted, turning to strikes, political action, and revolutionary unionism to show their anger at the existing social, economic, and industrial sys-

1. The statement comes from S. M. Jamieson, *Times of Trouble: Labour Unrest and Industrial Conflict in Canada, 1900-1966* (Ottawa, 1971). Several violent strikes are described in I.M. Abella, ed., *On Strike: Six Key Labour Struggles in Canada 1919-1949* (Toronto, 1974). A good overview of the violent Nova Scotia coal strikes of the 1920s is presented in Paul MacEwan, *Miners and Steelworkers: Labour in Cape Breton* (Toronto, 1976), while violent strikes in British Columbia are covered by Paul Phillips, *No Power Greater: A Century of Labour in B.C.* (Vancouver, 1967).

tem and to demand immediate and drastic change. The six-week strike in Winnipeg was, in many ways, the climax of that revolt. Workers used the power of their unions to paralyze the city in an effort to force a small group of stubborn employers to recognize their unions and raise their wages to keep up with the cost of living. The strikers were supported by thousands of other working-class men and women in Winnipeg who did not belong to unions but who shared the anger and frustration of their unionized neighbours. Across the country thousands raised money, marched, and staged sympathetic strikes to show support for the strikers in Winnipeg. Ranged against them were the manufacturers, shopkeepers, grain exchange merchants, lawyers, and other members of Winnipeg's upper crust, allied with the city, provincial, and federal governments. It was Canada's first general strike, the first test of an awesome tactic designed to bring employers and their allies to their knees, and it came after years of increasing bitterness, despair, and class division. When the great test of strength was over, little had been resolved except that the federal government, with its army and police, was still the ultimate power in the country. The workers had been drained of their strength, and a long decline of trade union power, lasting well into the 1930s, began.

The Rise of Unionism

Before the Great War, Canada was still primarily an agricultural country and more Canadians lived on farms and in small country towns than in the cities. The 1911 census showed that more than three out of ten working Canadians were farmers or farm labourers, the largest single group in the country's labour force. Other Canadians worked in manufacturing (18 per cent of the labour force), trade and commerce (10 per cent), transportation (10 per cent), building and construction (9 per cent), domestic and personal service (8 per cent), and a large variety of other occupations such as mining, fishing, and government service. Although many were highly skilled craftsmen who had served long apprenticeships and who earned good, steady wages, a very large number were unskilled labourers who earned little. Men dominated the working places in manufacturing, transportation, and mining, but large numbers of women worked as domestic servants, laundresses, housekeepers, and hotel and restaurant workers. Large numbers could also be found in cotton and woolen mills and in tailoring shops. Women, in fact, made up slightly more than 20 per cent of the nonagricultural work force. Their children, too, were often forced to work.

Family economic necessity and a blind eye turned by employers combined to let young children like this boy of fourteen do hard and dangerous jobs in 1912. The child was working in a coal mine. (C-30945/Public Archives Canada)

For many Canadian workers — men and women — work places were unsafe and unhealthy. In July, 1911, a typical month, ninety-two Canadian workers were killed on the job. An iron worker in Davenport, Ontario, was crushed by iron rails; a brakeman in Saskatoon was crushed between two box cars; a coal miner in Sydney Mines, Nova Scotia, was buried by falling rock; a lock tender in Montreal was drowned. The toll was always heavy among railway workers, sailors, and miners, as well as farmers and farm labourers. For every one killed there were others who survived industrial accidents with mangled limbs, pain-wracked bodies, or sightless eyes. Friends, relatives, fellow union members, or private charities supported many of these victims of industrial accidents for the rest of their lives because there was no government-operated compensation plan anywhere in Canada, and provincial laws were almost entirely ineffective in forcing employers to pay compensation.

When physical survival was not directly threatened, economic survival was still a basic question for Canadian workers. Few unskilled workers in factories, on construction sites, or in track-laying gangs earned enough to support themselves in anything but a hand-to-mouth existence. An unskilled Hamilton factory worker, for example, had to work two hours to earn enough to buy a pound of coffee and eighty hours to pay for one month's rent. Skilled workers, such as bricklayers or carpenters, earned enough to raise families and sustain a relatively high standard of living, but others were much worse off. However, even the skilled had much to worry about because work was often seasonal, and carpenters, for example, could expect many months of unemployment during the winter. There was no unemployment insurance in 1911. The skilled too could suffer drastically if their working days were cut by sickness, accident, or prolonged unemployment.[2]

Trade unions helped improve the wages and working conditions of Canadian workers and aided them in times of distress with a variety of union-financed insurance schemes to cover sickness, accident, and death.

2. Conditions of work and life for the Canadian working class in this period can be found in several books, including Terry Copp, *The Anatomy of Poverty: The Condition of the Working Class in Montreal, 1897-1929* (Toronto, 1974); Michael J. Piva, *The Condition of the Working Class in Toronto: 1900-1921* (Ottawa, 1979); and Alan F.J. Artibise, *Winnipeg: A Social History of Urban Growth, 1874-1914* (Montreal, 1975). MacEwan's *Miners and Steelworkers* presents a good overview of the situation in Cape Breton, while David J. Bercuson, *Fools and Wise Men: The Rise and Fall of the One Big Union*, (Toronto, 1978), contains descriptions of working-class life in western Canada. Canadian attitudes towards the unemployed are detailed in James Struthers, *No Fault of Their Own: Unemployment and the Canadian Welfare State, 1914-1941* (Toronto, 1983).

But few Canadian workers were members of unions. In 1911, 1 560 000 Canadians worked for wages as part of the nonagricultural work force, but only 133 000 of them, roughly 8.5 per cent, carried union membership cards. Most union members were skilled workers who could not easily be replaced by an employer who ordinarily might have fired them for joining a union. In 1911 there were no laws protecting workers from harassment for union activity, and unskilled workers who were easily replaced in shop or factory were usually fired on the spot for joining a union. Some employers insisted that their workers, skilled or not, sign contracts stipulating that they would never join a union.

Most unions in Canada were affiliated with the Trades and Labour Congress of Canada (T.L.C.), which was itself affiliated with and dominated by the American Federation of Labor (A.F.L.) and its president, Samuel Gompers. Gompers was born in Britain in 1850 to immigrant Jewish parents and in 1863 came to the United States, where he took up the trade of cigar maker. He joined the Cigar Makers Union and soon began to play an active part in local and then national union politics. He took part in the founding of the American Federation of Labor and became president of that organization in 1886. The A.F.L. was a loose federation of unions, most of which were craft unions uniting workers of one particular skill. (A small number of industrial unions such as the United Mine Workers of America, which brought together all workers within one industry, were also affiliated.) Gompers came to personify the A.F.L. and espoused its philosophy in government hearings, at labour conventions, and in the pages of the *American Federationist*. This philosophy was based on the notion that workers should use their economic power — strikes and boycotts — to lever more wealth out of the capitalists in the form of higher wages, lower hours, and better fringe benefits and working conditions. In this way a slow but steady redistribution of wealth in society would take place until the workers achieved their rightful place in the industrial and economic hierarchy. The highly skilled were to be organized first as the vanguard of the working class, and they were to be organized in craft unions wherever possible. Unions were to stay away from partisan political activities that could divide the workers along party lines, and they were to concentrate on the immediate improvement of working and living standards rather than wasting their time and energy on foolish notions such as fomenting revolutions or building utopian workers' societies.

Although many Canadian union members agreed with Gompers' philosophy, others did not. James Watters, elected to the presidency of the T.L.C. in 1911, was a mild socialist and former miner from British

Columbia who believed that the craft unions should actively involve themselves in the fight to create a democratic socialist society in Canada and that industrial unionism was an effective organizational form for workers in certain industries such as mining, logging, and transportation. The man he succeeded, Alphonse Verville, was a Montreal plumber more prepared to follow Gompers' line on organizational questions but opposed to the A.F.L.'s antipolitical philosophy. He was, in fact, elected to the House of Commons in a 1906 by-election on a Labour ticket to represent a Montreal constituency. However, both men were rather weak and indecisive and were reluctant to lead the T.L.C. in a more independent direction. Besides, they had to contend with P.M. Draper, T.L.C. secretary, throughout this period. He believed staunchly in the basic philosophy of the American Federation of Labor, though he wanted the Canadian labour movement to have more autonomy. Draper's views were close to those of John A. Flett, A.F.L. organizer and former T.L.C. president, who strongly backed Gompers and the A.F.L. and worked hard for the subordination of the Canadian labour movement to that of the United States. Flett, from Hamilton, was a forceful speaker, effective organizer, and hard worker and remained very influential in the Trades Congress after his presidential term ended in 1904.[3]

There were other Canadian workers who scorned the A.F.L. altogether and supported instead organizations such as the Industrial Workers of the World, a United States-based revolutionary industrial union. The I.W.W. aimed to organize all workers in society into one highly centralized union and then, once this was accomplished, it intended to call a massive general strike which would bring capitalism crashing down. The I.W.W. in Canada attracted few skilled workers and concentrated on the unskilled labourers in the harvest fields, lumber camps, and track-laying gangs. Its most spectacular efforts were concentrated in Alberta and British Columbia where it organized free speech demonstrations, unemployment marches, and bush workers' and track-layers' strikes. In the spring

3. Much has been written on Samuel Gompers, including a memoir in two volumes, *Seventy Years of Life and Labor* (New York, 1925). A short introduction to Gompers' effect on the labour movement is contained in Harold C. Livesay, *Samuel Gompers and Organized Labor in America* (Boston, 1978). Gompers' ideas can be analyzed in William Dick, *Labor and Socialism in America: The Gompers Years* (Port Washington, 1972). For a good overview of Gompers' social thought see Fred Greenbaum, "The Social Ideas of Samuel Gompers," *Labor History* (Winter, 1966). The American Federation of Labor's takeover of the Trades and Labour Congress of Canada is analyzed and described in Robert H. Babcock, *Gompers in Canada: A Study in American Continentalism Before the First World War* (Toronto, 1974).

and summer of 1912 close to nine thousand railway construction workers employed by the Canadian Northern and Grand Trunk Pacific Railways in British Columbia's interior took part in I.W.W.-organized strikes for higher wages and better working conditions. The strikes were eventually broken by the railways with the help of the federal government, which allowed immigrant strike-breakers to enter the area, and by the provincial government, which used the provincial police to arrest strike leaders.

The opposition of employers was by no means limited to radical union organizations such as the I.W.W. Few employers willingly recognized or bargained with any unions, and even those that did rarely agreed to the wage demands of their workers. Strikes to force employers to recognize unions and strikes for higher wages and better economic conditions were frequent in all industries. Moreover, in the early part of the century many employers had begun to reorganize their factories to make them more efficient, and to this end they embarked on a campaign to break the stranglehold skilled workers had on important parts of the production process. The workers reacted by striking to defend their position in industry.

In the labour newspapers of the day, employers — the bosses — were almost always pictured in cartoons wearing top hats and tail coats, with money spilling out of their pockets, evil grins on their faces, and their white gloved hands clutching instruments of torture to crush, flay, or otherwise destroy the workers. This was too simple. Employers were also human beings whose attitudes and motives varied greatly. Some of the large employers of the late nineteenth and early twentieth centuries were self-made men who had, through intelligence, skill, daring, and luck, risen from the lower ranks of society. They had a special talent for organizing and mobilizing capital; they were artists who created corporations instead of paintings or sculpture. The accumulation of money was often unimportant to them as an end in itself; it was the creation of giant corporations, smoothly efficient factories, or continent-spanning merchandizing establishments that posed the real challenge.

These men tended to judge their fellow human beings as harshly as they judged themselves and their colleagues. Only weak and incapable men and women needed to unite to advance themselves, while those of real talent had no need for trade unions or collective action. As a rule then, unions were scorned by entrepreneurs such as Robert Dunsmuir, a British Columbia mine owner, who proclaimed his beliefs to a royal commission in 1903: "[The workers] can belong to a union if they like — I don't care . . . I have my rights. I can hire them if I like and they can work if they like." Other employers across the country, from Thomas Russell

Deacon of the Manitoba Bridge and Iron Works in Winnipeg to Joseph W. Flavelle of the William Davies Company in Toronto, could readily agree with Dunsmuir's views, though perhaps not with his willingness to proclaim them to the public. Given the determination of the trade unions to expand and increase their economic power, clashes between the unions and employers such as Dunsmuir were inevitable.

Some of the longest and most violent strikes in the prewar era involved coal miners who were members of the United Mine Workers of America (U.M.W.). In Alberta and eastern British Columbia the U.M.W. had succeeded in winning recognition from the Western Canada Coal Operators Association in 1907, but this did not smooth the way for an easy relationship between the operators and miners. Strikes over wages were called in 1909 and 1911, and unresolved grievances and bitterness continued to sour the air in the coalfields.

On Vancouver Island employer-employee relations were even worse. There, miners had been trying without success to win union recognition since the 1880s, and a legacy of violence and hatred continued to poison any attempts at conciliation. In September, 1912, Canadian Collieries (Dunsmuir) Limited at Cumberland and Ladysmith was struck. Three thousand miners left work for a variety of reasons, including the issue of union recognition and fears that the company was negligent in enforcing mine safety regulations. The strike spread in the following months, but the company, using strike-breakers, succeeded in restoring production to two-thirds of the prestrike level. The union reacted with a general strike of all Vancouver Island miners, but this made little impact on coal production. Union members then launched a series of attacks on strike-breakers' houses and mine entrances, and in one night of violence, gunfire and dynamite punctuated the darkness at South Wellington, Nanaimo, Ladysmith, and Extension. The provincial government sent in the militia, which quickly arrested 250 miners to break the strike. That sequence of events was not untypical.

Strikes were usually a mark of boom times, when there were accompanying labour shortages and inflation; Canada experienced plenty of these starting in the mid-1890s. However, in the fall of 1913 the economy ran out of steam, and a severe depression began. The effect on Canadian working people was immediate and dramatic. Trade union membership dropped from approximately 176 000 in 1913 to 143 000 in 1915, or more than 18 per cent. Unemployment rose quickly as construction slowed and heavy industry laid off thousands of workers. In the pre-unemployment insurance days, a worker without work received no money for the basics of life. Without a job, there might not be food, clothing, or shelter. Private charities provided a patchwork system of soup-kitchen relief, and city governments opened employment agencies to try to steer workers to available jobs, but such measures were far from adequate. Everywhere in Canada unemployment grew, despair deepened, and economic disaster stared hundreds of thousands in the face.

The War and Labour

The outbreak of war in Europe in August, 1914, signalled a rapid shift in the nature of Canadian manufacturing and better economic times for many Canadian workers. The voracious Allied war machine needed armaments, particularly artillery shells, and the British Ministry of Munitions was soon enquiring if Canadian manufacturers could help fill that demand. A Shell Committee was established to place war orders in Canada, and soon structural steel companies, railway repair shops, and metalworking establishments of all kinds were in the shell-making business. Canada produced barely three thousands shells in 1914 but almost twenty million in 1916, along with an ever-expanding range of other munitions products. Munitions factories expanded rapidly, and the war labour force grew apace. By 1916, 185 000 Canadians were directly employed in munitions manufacturing. The expansion of the munitions industry and the demand for munitions workers helped ease the job shortage and banish the depression while, at the same time, hundreds of thousands of young men joined the Canadian Expeditionary Force. By the end of 1915 unemployment seemed a thing of the past.

The manpower shortage gave the unions their best opportunity in years to recruit new members, and trade union membership began to grow significantly from a low of 143 000 in 1915 to 249 000 by 1918. The organizing drives which brought these new members into the union fold tended to increase worker militancy, but this was tempered in the first years of the war by a conviction that workers and their unions should not disrupt the war effort with strikes. Patriotism muffled militancy. Union leaders were themselves partly responsible for this because many strongly supported the war effort and were determined not to let their rank-and-file members hold the country to ransom during wartime.

The patriotic approach was soon undermined by the rapidly rising cost of living that quickly surpassed the inflation rate of the predepression period. The country's need to feed, clothe, and equip a large army, the pressure to export food to European allies, and the ever-increasing requirements for raw materials for Canadian munitions plants created new demands on the Canadian economy that the economy could not meet. Demand outstripped supply, and prices rose accordingly. In the period from 1915 to 1918 the average family budget in Canada rose by 50 per cent, while the average hourly wage in Canada increased by only 44 per cent, thus causing a decline in real wages of about 2 per cent per year. However, these figures are averages, and in some parts of Canada, particularly the West, the increase in prices was usually higher than in the rest of the country, while wages of workers in nonmunitions industries, such as construction and urban transportation, rose much more slowly than the national average. The unions complained bitterly about inflation and flung charges of price manipulation and food profiteering about, but in fact, there was little evidence that scheming was behind the inflation. It was, quite simply, a case of the federal government's unwillingness and inability to take the strong measures, such as rationing, that might have cured the problem.

Very simply, the federal government was trying to manage a major war effort for the first time in Canadian history and did not know how to go about the task. Borden and his colleagues learned much, but they learned slowly and often by trial and error that the total mobilization of society and of the economy needed to sustain the war effort could not be done on a voluntary basis. It was simply not enough to trust to the good intentions and patriotic feelings of the majority of Canadians. It was only towards the end of the war that the Government began to move more quickly to enact compulsory measures to guide the war effort.

The Government also failed to treat the labour movement as an important partner in the war effort. Businessmen, from the very start of the war, had been treated as part of the war management team, while organized labour was held at arm's length, almost as if the unions were considered an impediment to the war effort. There was little consultation between the Government and labour leaders on measures that would inevitably affect labour directly, and labour's most reasonable requests — for a fair-wage clause in war supply contracts, for example — were not granted. In fact, in March, 1916, the Government, in a surprise move, extended the Industrial Disputes Investigation Act — much hated by organized labour — to cover war industries. By this time it was beginning to dawn on labour leaders that although they were trying to cooperate with the Government, the Government was not cooperating with them.

Borden and his Cabinet were not entirely at fault for the growing disaffection of organized labour. Joseph Wesley Flavelle must surely share

AVERAGE WEEKLY BUDGET OF A FAMILY IN CANADA, 1914-1918

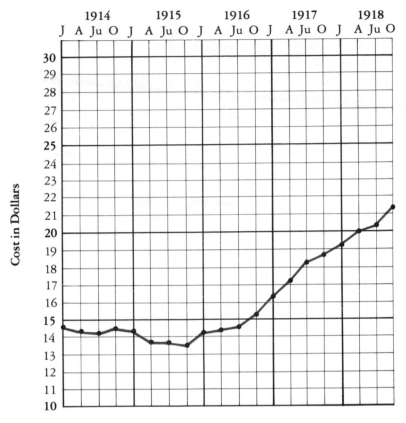

J = January   Ju = July
A = April   O = October

Source: Compiled from monthly figures in *Labour Gazette*, 1914–1918.

part of the blame. Flavelle, the Toronto pork-packing magnate who became chairman of the Imperial Munitions Board in late 1915, was a devout Methodist and a rugged individualist who was determined to run the I.M.B. as efficiently as possible with one goal in view — increased munitions production. He bristled at the idea that unions should be able to use the war to climb a few more rungs up the ladder of official recognition or that workers should use the labour shortage to better their economic position. That thousands of businessmen in Canada were doing just that either did not occur to him or did not bother him. In the final analysis, it was

Flavelle who blocked government action on fair-wage clauses in munitions contracts.[4]

In the spring of 1916 workers' growing frustrations finally sparked off strikes in munitions plants in Toronto and Hamilton. In both cities the International Association of Machinists had been active organizing munitions workers, and in March and April the I.A.M. presented wage demands to factory owners. Many Toronto plants agreed to the union's demands, but the Canada Foundry Company did not and was struck. The plant manager, Colonel Frederick Nichols, responded with a complete lock out and a declaration that he would never submit to organized labour. The I.A.M.'s answer was to threaten a general strike of all Toronto munitions workers. In Hamilton the employers, all members of the Canadian Manufacturers Association, organized a special committttee to oversee labour relations in the city and coordinate the campaign to block the I.A.M. The union demands for higher wages and shorter hours were met with accusations that the workers were "in the pay of the Kaiser" and declarations that unions had no right to exist inside the factories.

Faced with a serious disruption in the flow of shells, the federal government intervened and appointed a royal commission headed by Judge Colin Snyder to examine labour problems in the Toronto and Hamilton war plants. When the commission reported in May, it fully endorsed the demands of the I.A.M., but the Hamilton employers, including such major concerns as the Steel Company of Canada, Canadian Westinghouse, and the National Steel Car Company, refused to implement the royal commission's recommendations. Thus, on June 12, 1916, close to two thousand munitions workers at more than thirty Hamilton war plants went on strike. Although the munitions workers received the moral support of the Toronto machinists, it was not nearly enough to ensure victory. The federal government ordered the Chief Press Censor to ban news of the strike to stop it from spreading, and the employers brought in strikebreakers. The effectiveness of the strike was also undermined by the union leadership, which urged its own members to "act honourably" during the work stoppage. In a little over one month the strike petered out, a definite defeat for organized labour.

4. The difficulties encountered by organized labour during the war, and the response of the Imperial Munitions Board, are described in David Jay Bercuson, "Organized Labour and the Imperial Munitions Board," *Industrial Relations/Relations Industrielles*, XXVIII (1973); Myer Siemiatycki, "Munitions and Labour Militancy: The 1916 Hamilton Machinists' Strike," *Labour/Le Travailleur* (1978); Michael Bliss, *A Canadian Millionaire: The Life and Business Times of Sir Joseph Flavelle, Bart. 1858–1939* (Toronto, 1978); and Daphne Read, *et al.*, *The Great War and Canadian Society: An Oral History* (Toronto, 1978).

The strike in Hamilton should have provided a clear warning to the federal government and to Flavelle that war workers were absolutely determined to win significant improvements in their wages and working conditions and would disregard appeals to patriotism if necessary to bring pressure on the employers. But aside from pious appeals to reason, nothing was done. There were no bold, new initiatives to improve working conditions or invite labour into the Government's confidence, and there was no change of heart on the part of Flavelle or the country's war industry employers. Things continued as they were, and the unions grew more desperate and more angry. In the spring of 1917, the Trades and Labour Congress presented a list of complaints to the federal government concerning wages and working conditions in all I.M.B.-controlled war industries. The Congress charged that construction workers employed on I.M.B. jobs were living in unhealthy and unsanitary conditions and that wages in war plants were too low, while work days were too long — sixeen-hour days were not unusual. The I.M.B., it charged, deliberately snubbed union officials and allowed "the unnecessary dilution of labour by the introduction of female labour" and the "substitution of cheap semi-skilled labour . . . because of their willingness to accept less than trade union rates." Employers were replacing highly skilled workers going off to war with women, immigrants, and labourers from the country who knew little about metalworking but were perfectly able to perform the tasks of assembly-line shell production. The employers insisted on paying these unskilled workers less than the rate applicable to the skilled workers, a practice the unions bitterly resisted, fearing that established wage standards would be undermined and destroyed. In the case of female workers the unions were reluctant to attempt organizing drives until late in the war, even though an increasing number of women were entering heavy industry to work in munitions and other war-related production. This reluctance was undoubtedly due in part to prejudice against women working in factories and to the belief that the situation would, in the long run, be temporary and would not outlast the war.

T.L.C. warnings that the I.M.B. was forcing unions to "obtain reasonable conditions by use of their organized power" went unheeded, and 1917 turned out to be a year of strikes, as more than 1.1 million working-days were lost in work disruptions, an increase of 374 per cent over 1916. Almost every industry was affected including, once again, shell manufacturing, but the most serious disputes disrupted the coal mines of western Canada. The coal of British Columbia and Alberta was not only used to heat homes, it was vital to the operation of the railways and the smelters in the British Columbia interior, particularly at Trail, which did considerable business for the Imperial Munitions Board.

Inflation was the direct cause of the troubles in the western coalfields: miners' wages were not keeping up with the increasing cost of living. From the summer of 1916 until April, 1917, a number of short strikes for war bonuses or wage increases broke out, involving in each case from three to six thousand miners. Both the federal government and the international leaders of the miners union watched these events with growing alarm and intervened to get the men back to work. For several months they managed to maintain a shaky peace, but in April, 1917, seven thousand miners were locked out in a dispute with the coal operators, and a strike and lock out shut down the coalfields for three months. Once again the federal government intervened, this time by appointing a Director of Coal Operations for eastern British Columbia and Alberta. He was given power to determine wages, working conditions, and fuel prices, and he quickly intervened in the dispute to order the mines reopened and to impose an immediate wage increase. A commission was soon established under the Director's authority to examine the cost of living continually and to adjust wages every four months, in line with changes in the cost of living.

One of labour's biggest fights in 1917 was not against employers but against the conscription policies of the federal government. When the federal government announced a voluntary national registration in December, 1916, the Trades and Labour Congress sought assurances from the Prime Minister that this was not a prelude to conscription. Borden did not promise that he would not introduce conscription under any circumstances, but he did assure T.L.C. president James Watters that registration was not the first step towards conscription. Watters and the Congress then mildly endorsed the program, even though some labour leaders, particularly in western Canada, denounced the Congress and urged their followers not to cooperate.

Clearly, trade union leaders and their followers were not of one mind about the war. Some labour leaders opposed Canada's participation in the war, particularly if they were of a left-wing political persuasion, and many such leaders were to be found in western Canada. Others endorsed the war and publicly proclaimed their support for the war effort. In the spring of 1917, after the United States entered the war, they found a vocal leader and supporter in Samuel Gompers, who fervently threw himself behind the United States' war effort and urged his Canadian followers to do the same. But most labour leaders contented themselves with few or no public proclamations about the war, while they worked to ensure the cooperation of their unions in the war effort and to secure labour peace, sometimes at the sacrifice of the economic interests of their members.

However, whatever their views on the war almost all Canadian labour leaders opposed conscription. The draft represented compulsion and raised the prospect that it might be followed by industrial conscription that would tightly regulate workers' freedom to change jobs or to strike for improvements in wages or working conditions. This would not only put workers more directly under the thumb of employers, it would greatly undermine the unions' ability to protect their members' interests or attract new members. Conscription, in other words, was viewed as a grave and direct threat to the viability of the trade union movement.

Western Radicalism

When Borden announced the imminent introduction of conscription in May, 1917, the T.L.C., lulled by his earlier assurances on registration, was caught by surprise, and labour responded with a howl of protest. A campaign to take direct action to counter the draft gained momentum through the spring and summer of 1917, with union leaders in eastern and central Canada urging an electoral campaign, and those in the West advocating a national general strike. At the Congress convention in September, 1917, the advocates of political action won out, and a decision was taken to launch a coast-to-coast electoral effort in the forthcoming federal election campaign. This was done under the auspices of an umbrella organization known as the Dominion Labour party, which was a loose, poorly financed amalgam of socialists, labourites, pacifists, and even, in some cases, Laurier Liberals, all of whom had little in common except their opposition to the draft. It was an uphill battle against a Government which used the basest appeals to patriotism and which painted its opposition as advocates of the Kaiser's cause. The Dominion Labour party was certainly not helped by Samuel Gompers, who appeared in the fall of 1917 to strongly endorse the Government's conscriptionist course. Every labour candidate was defeated.[5]

5. There are many works describing and explaining the political activities of the Canadian labour movement before, during, and after this period. See, for example, Martin Robin, *Radical Politics and Canadian Labour: 1880-1930* (Kingston, 1968); Gad Horowitz, *Canadian Labour in Politics* (Toronto, 1968); Kenneth W. McNaught, *A Prophet in Politics: A Biography of J.S. Woodsworth* (Toronto, 1959); and A.R. McCormack, *Reformers, Rebels and Revolutionaries: The Western Canadian Radical Movement, 1899-1919* (Toronto, 1977).

The conscription fight nor only embittered the labour movement and further soured relations between it and the Borden Government, it also aggravated the continuing disagreements between the majority of organized workers, who lived in eastern and central Canada, and those in the West over the policies, direction, and fundamental nature of the labour movement. The West tended to be more radical, more oriented towards industrial unionism and more captivated by dreams of a socialist paradise than the East, which hewed more closely to Gompers' line. The divisions had been apparent for years prior to the war, and there were occasional flare-ups of secessionist fever in western Canada whenever workers there judged that the eastern majority at T.L.C. conventions was directly undermining the vital interests of western union members.

The West's lean towards radicalism is explained by a variety of factors. There were a larger number of immigrants in the West on a per capita basis than anywhere else in Canada, and many of these, particularly those from Great Britain or the United States, had strong labour and socialist backgrounds. Other immigrant groups such as the Finns, Ukrainians, Jews, and Italians, also brought strong leftist traditions. The backbone for many a socialist local in the West was provided by a mixture of immigrant radicals headed by British socialists who were, of course, far more articulate in the language of their adopted country.[6]

Working conditions also played a part. The coal and hardrock mines of the West were dangerous places where workers were regularly killed at rates that far surpassed those of mines in other parts of North America. Logging and railway construction camps were little better. Wages were usually higher in the West than elsewhere, but so too was the cost of living, and it was apparent to many of the industrial workers who had come to the West from homes far away that there was little immediate chance for them to improve their social or economic station in life. Thus, frustrated expectations also played a part in the western workers' growing commitment to radicalism.

Union structure itself contributed to western labour's lean towards radicalism. The Canadian labour movement was largely constructed in the

6. Several works have recently appeared describing the growth and development of immigrant radicalism. The only survey is Donald Avery, *"Dangerous Foreigners": European Immigrant Workers and Labour Radicalism in Canada, 1896-1932* (Toronto, 1979). The journal *Canadian Ethnic Studies* devoted an entire issue, No. 2 (1978), to ethnic radicals and includes articles on Finns, British, Norwegians, and Croatians. Some material on this subject can also be found in Ivan Avakumovic, *The Communist Party in Canada: A History* (Toronto, 1975).

image of the American Federation of Labor with its craft union base. There were more than one hundred unions affiliated with the A.F.L., but this was not so serious in the United States because the A.F.L., at the beginning of the Great War, counted more than two million members. Thus even the small unions had enough members to be viable. In Canada there were fewer unions — eighty-eight reported to the Department of Labour in 1913 — but there were also far fewer members (128 652 in 1913), and many of the craft unions here were small and ineffective. This was particularly true in western Canada, which was home to about one-third of Canada's union members in 1913. Many western union leaders concluded that their bargaining strength was seriously eroded by the craft union structure and opted instead for industrial unions. They were forced to push this notion against the bitter opposition of American and central Canadian union leaders who supported the policies of Samuel Gompers. However, at the same time, radical labour organizations such as the I.W.W. and the United Brotherhood of Railway Employees adopted the industrial union model.

The West's growing militancy and radicalism became all too apparent in the spring and summer of 1918. In April, 1918, several groups of employees of the City of Winnipeg approached the municipal government to demand wage increases. The city adminstration refused and offered instead to pay civic employees a war bonus to tide them over until peacetime, when a new schedule of wages could be negotiated. The unions rejected the proposal and called their members out on strike on May 7. The city government, backed by the press and the business community, took a hard line and threatened to remove its employees' right to strike. The Winnipeg Trades and Labour Council took a hard line of its own and called upon its member unions to support the strikers. Workers all over the city, in public service or private business, began to vote to strike in sympathy with the civic workers, and the civic strike was soon spreading into a general strike. After three weeks the federal government intervened out of fear that Canada's third largest city, a key rail junction and the commercial centre for all of western Canada, would be paralyzed. Senator Gideon Robertson, a vice-president of the Order of Railway Telegraphers (and described by Flavelle as a "sane, wise, labour leader"), was sent to Winnipeg by the Prime Minister to settle the dispute. Robertson was a staunch Conservative who subscribed to the basic principles of Samuel Gompers, even though his union was not affiliated with the A.F.L. He especially opposed strikes during wartime, but within three days of his arrival, he hammered out an agreement that represented a substantial victory for the unions in both increased wages and the confirmation of their right to collective bargaining.

Robertson had been largely responsible for the shape of the settlement, but it was the sympathetic strike that had given labour the power to force its demands upon the city. The lesson was not lost on labour radicals in Winnipeg and elsewhere who declared that the power of individual unions acting alone to "enforce their economic demands" was slipping aways as the "master class" united. The answer had now been demonstrated to be the general strike and industrial unionism. Militancy appeared to pay off in Winnipeg, and just a few weeks later, in West Coast shipyards as well. In May, five thousand shipyard workers employed by firms engaged in work for the Imperial Munitions Board went on strike for union recognition and higher wage despite appeals to their sense of patriotic duty. Pressures upon the workers from press and politicians alike mounted as the workers were accused of disloyalty. However, they stayed united and continued to support their leadership until Robertson arrived to bring an end to the strike. Although the unions did not score as clear-cut a victory as the civic workers in Winnipeg, they made obvious gains and appeared well satisfied with the final settlement. Once again strike action had paid off.

The strikes in Winnipeg and on the West Coast had been localized, but another dispute was brewing in the spring and summer of 1918 that had the potential of seriously threatening, if not paralyzing, the entire Canadian war effort from coast to coast. It began in late April, 1918, when unions representing fifty thousand shop-craft workers on all the major railways began negotiations for a new wage schedule with the Canadian Railway War Board, which had been formed by the major railways to promote more efficient rail transportation during the war. The shop-craft workers — they repaired and maintained the trains — had joined their different craft unions together in a bargaining federation known as Division 4 of the Railway Employees Department of the American Federation of Labor and had armed their representatives with a strike vote. When negotiations opened the workers demanded substantial wage increases; these were promptly rejected by the railways, which claimed they could not increase pay because their freight rates could not be raised during the war. As negotiations dragged on and the prospect of failure loomed, the federal government intervened to grant the railways a freight-rate increase and to force them to raise their wages to the same level as those paid for the same work by railways in the United States. The new Canadian shop-craft wages were a significant improvement over the old, but the unions were still not satisfied and threatened to strike.

The federal government was determined to prevent the unions from acting. Although a shop-craft strike would not immediately shut down rail service — engineers, firemen, and other running trades workers would still operate the trains — it would soon come to a complete standstill because maintenance and repair work could not be done. Nothing would move in Canada, and the economy, not to mention the war effort, would shortly be paralyzed. A strike was out of the question for the Borden Government, which announced that the shop-craft workers would be conscripted and ordered to work on army pay if they should carry through their threat to strike. At the same time the leadership of the shop-craft unions, based in the United States, cooperated with the Canadian Government and threatened to suspend or revoke the charters of union locals that quit work. At the negotiating table in Montreal, the Division 4 negotiators split as the eastern and central Canadian representatives caved in to accept the Government-imposed wage offer while the westerners walked out in disgust. But even though westerners attacked the "weak-kneed" retreat of their eastern brothers, the unions had clearly won a major victory in gaining wage parity with the United States. That victory had come, once again, from union militancy and worker resolve.

Both the growing East-West split and the tendency of workers to believe that militant action would invariably produce good results were reinforced by the July strike of letter carriers. They had been trying, since 1917, to win wage increases from the Government to match increases in the cost of living. When all else failed, the union called a strike and postal service was tied up throughout Canada. After a few days the federal government issued a vague promise to investigate the postal workers' grievances, and the predominantly eastern leadership of the union ordered its members back to work. Some complied, but the western members did not and stayed off the job until the Government announced that the Civil Service Commission would examine their grievances and promised them full pay for the time they had been on strike.

The strikes and threats of strikes of the spring and summer prompted Labour Minister T.W. Crothers, probably in conjunction with Gideon Robertson, to design a new war labour policy that was proclaimed to the nation in early July. It was, in many respects, an enlightened policy that represented a clear advance over the thinking of men such as J.W. Flavelle. It urged a number of principles and policies on workers and their employers, including a ban on work stoppages during the war, a recognition of the right of employees to organize trade unions without interference from their employers, and the right to "negotiate with employers concerning working conditions, rates of pay, or other grievances." Crothers' plan also suggested that workers had the right to a decent wage, reasonable hours of work, and safe and healthy working conditions. Women employed at jobs ordinarily performed by men should receive "equal pay for equal work." To ensure peace in industry workers and their employers were asked to use the machinery of the Industrial Disputes Investigation Act and a new Board of Appeal, composed of two representatives of organized labour, two representatives of the employers, and a neutral chairman. The Board would decide appeals against the findings of the conciliation boards normally established under the I.D.I.A.

The War Labour policy of July, 1918, might have gone far to restoring labour peace in Canada, but it suffered from one fatal flaw: it was, in the words of Senator Robertson, "permissive rather than compulsory as no penalty is provided for failure to comply." This made it a guideline which unions and employers were free to follow or disregard at will, and in the increasingly poisoned atmosphere of 1918, it was practically useless. One official of the Imperial Munitions Board considered it "spineless cowardice and double-faced action."

Robertson had assured union leaders that the Government was not in the process of imposing a compulsory ban on strikes, but trade unionists throughout Canada viewed the War Labour policy as a sure sign of things to come. Some took comfort in the Government's apparent support for trade unionism, collective bargaining, and a living wage, but others, especially in western Canada, were angered by the Government's interference with the right to strike. The militancy and radicalism that had been growing in western Canada throughout the war was, therefore, only intensified. Workers in Vancouver did not hesitate to conduct a short general strike in August to protest the killing — allegedly by accident — of labour leader and draft evader Albert "Ginger" Goodwin in the woods near Comox by a Dominion policeman. (The Dominion Police later merged with the Royal Canadian Mounted Police.) Many of the same union leaders were determined to force drastic changes in the policies and practices of the T.L.C., which they believed was betraying the true interests of Canadian workers.

The September, 1918, convention of the Trades and Labour Congress became a battleground between East and West. While the Congress leadership was busy congratulating itself for the new spirit of cooperation it had forged with the federal government, radicals, led by western delegates, issued a scathing condemnation of the executive's relations with the federal government and brought forward a long list of resolutions calling for a restructuring of the Congress and a redrafting of its policies. Every one of the resolutions, from those condemning the jailing of opponents of the war to those seeking the transformation of the Congress into an industrial union, were defeated. To add insult to injury, Congress president J.C. Watters, from British Columbia, was defeated in his bid for reelection by Thomas Moore, a Niagara Falls carpenter and a faithful follower of Samuel Gompers.

The Westerners were badly outnumbered at the Quebec City convention — they had forty-five delegates out of more than four hundred — and needed a new strategy. A caucus chaired by Dave Rees, an official of the United Mine Workers, decided to organize a meeting of western delegates prior to the 1919 Trades Congress convention to coordinate strategy and exchange views on policy and tactics. A commitee was formed, chaired by Rees and Vancouver Trades Council secretary Victor Midgley, to handle correspondence and organize the meeting. It was made clear that this was not intended to be a first step towards secession of western unions from the T.L.C. and the A.F.L.

The federal government was well aware of the increasing militancy and radicalism of organized labour and took steps to counter it. Montreal lawyer C.H. Cahan was appointed Director of Public Safety in the Department of Justice with a mandate to bring radicalism to heel. Cahan quickly concluded that radical and alien influences were behind the growing labour unrest, and in September, 1918, in response to his recommendations, the Cabinet issued orders-in-council which prohibited the public use of "enemy alien" languages and which banned ethnic associations, unions, and political parties, including the I.W.W. and the Social Democratic party, both of which had many immigrant members. Two weeks later another order-in-council was issued banning strikes and setting heavy penalties, including fines and imprisonment, for its violation. The Government also proclaimed that anyone violating the order would be immediately drafted and subject to military law for the duration of the war.

Organized labour reacted angrily to the orders-in-council; even T.L.C. president Moore cautioned the Government against taking labour for granted. But his reproaches were nothing compared to those of western union leaders who pledged to defy the strike ban. In fact, a strike of freight handlers in Calgary broke out five days after the ban was declared, and when several of the strikers were arrested for breaking the law, trades councils across the West began to poll their members on the question of whether or not to call a general strike to back the arrested men. However, before this strike was called the court inexplicably released the strikers without imposing either fines or imprisonment. The ban on strikes increased the atmosphere of hate and recriminations and accomplished nothing as the fighting in Europe stopped on November 11, and the strike ban was rescinded shortly after.

The Red Scare

The months following the armistic brought no relief from the rising cost of living, even though war production came to a quick halt. To make matters worse for Canadian workers, returned soldiers began to enter the job market in the winter of 1918/1919, causing a rapid increase in unemployment and spurring fears that the prewar depression was returning. It was also apparent that many employers were determined to erase labour's gains in increased wages and improved working conditions won during the war and roll matters back to the "bad old days." At the same time many workers had given their all to win the war in the plants and factories and at the battle front in the expectation that the war would usher in a new era of social justice and popular democracy. They had been promised as much by their political leaders, who had pledged to build a "new Jerusalem" after the "holocaust of blood." Instead of a new Jerusalem, there was a rising cost of living, increasing unemployment, and no significant changes in the social or economic status quo. The working class had been shortchanged.

For the returned soldiers, in particular, there was bitterness and despair. Politicians and the press initially showered the heroes of Vimy, Passchendaele, and Mons with praise and adulation, but old jobs were usually already filled, and new ones were hard to come by. The Department of Soldiers' Civil Re-Establishment urged private employers to hire veterans, and the Government gave them preference in filling civil service vacancies, but this produced little in the way of jobs over the hard winter of 1918/1919. The Government also set up a limited pension plan but refused veterans' demands for a large cash bonus based on length of service. Hospitals were built and homesteads were offered, but these measures served the needs of only a few. Many veterans tried to take matters into their own hands and roamed the streets of Canadian cities attacking people who looked like aliens and trying to force employers to fire immigrant workers to create vacancies for returned men. In several parts of Canada veterans vented their anger on those who had opposed the war and conscription. But many of these same veterans soon drifted towards the socialists in a search for leadership and a desire for social change. No less a figure than A. Bowen Perry, the commissioner of the Royal North West Mounted Police, worried about veterans throwing their support behind revolution and urged that their grievances be quickly resolved and that they be treated with sympathy and consideration to counter the "pernicious [socialist] propaganda" which was circulating among them.

Perry and other government officials were worried about both domestic and foreign radical influence. Even though no evidence has ever been revealed to confirm that foreign agents were attempting to foment revolution in Canada in early 1919, Perry and others thought that Canadian workers might be inspired by the example of foreign revolutionary movements. All over the world in the closing months of war and in the immediate postwar period the news was dominated by revolutions, attempted revolutions, general strikes, and worker uprisings.

The news from abroad strengthened a rising fear and uncertainty among many Canadians that was rooted in the belief that revolutionaries were capable of the most monstrous deeds. During the war Allied governments had perpetrated a propaganda campaign that aimed to convince their populations that the Germans were violating every code of decent human conduct. The Kaiser's troops were described as hordes, raping, murdering, and plundering their way across Europe. They were accused of the most unspeakable war crimes, from bayoneting babies to raping nuns to manufacturing soap from the bodies of their victims. When Lenin and the Bolsheviks came to power in Russia in 1917, these same governments, followed by the press and many religious groups, tarred him and his regime with the same brush. After all, he had been helped by the Germans, who knew that if he was successful he would end the war on the eastern front, freeing German troops for a final push against the Allies in the west. The Bolsheviks, therefore, were placed in the same camp as the Germans and accused of the same crimes. When the war ended, the Kaiser, who had abdicated, disappeared as an immediate object of hatred, but Lenin remained, and as country after country seemed to explode in Bolshevik-inspired revolutionary violence, many people in Canada and the United States panicked and concluded that the tide of revolution was about to sweep North America.

The growing "Red scare" formed a fitting backdrop for the work of the committee appointed by the western delegates to the T.L.C. convention of 1918. This committee, headed by Dave Rees and Victor Midgley, set to work contacting trades councils and union locals across the West to line up support for the western caucus, but their work was complicated by the growth of radicalism among western workers. Many western union members had concluded that T.L.C. reform was a lost cause and aimed to secede from the Congress prior to setting up a new revolutionary union organized along industrial lines. These workers were led by members of the Socialist Party of Canada, including fiery radicals such as Robert Boyd Russell, a Scottish-born machinist who headed the S.P.C. in Winnipeg and who was a power to be reckoned with among western shop-craft workers. Russell and his colleagues in the United Mine Workers and in the Alberta and British Columbia Federations of Labour worked behind the scenes to ensure the triumph of a radical platform at the forthcoming caucus. They eventually succeeded in having the very notion of a caucus set aside in favour of a full conference of western trade union representatives, and any others who wished to attend from the rest of Canada, to be held at Calgary in March, 1910.[7]

The General Strike

The Western Labour Conference that met on March 13, 1919, was one of the most radical labour conventions in Canadian history. Most of the delegates were fired by the rising tide of radical and revolutionary movements around the world and loudly proclaimed their belief that a new workers' paradise was at hand. They passed resolutions against political lobbying and in favour of the abolition of capitalism, secession from the T.L.C. and the A.F.L., and the formation of a new industrial union to be named the One Big Union, or O.B.U. The O.B.U. would organize all workers into one union which would be able to call general strikes to enforce workers' demands. The conference decided to hold two referenda, one on the question of conducting a general strike to back demands for a thirty-hour work week and the other to determine if Canadian workers favoured secession from the T.L.C. and the establishment of the O.B.U. The meeting also proclaimed its support for various European revolutionary movements, including Lenin's Bolshevik regime, and condemned the Borden Government. When the conference broke up, the work of conducting the votes on the general strike and secession began.

The Western Labour Conference further fueled the Red scare. Fol-

7. No book specifically on the Red scare has yet appeared in Canada, but a good survey of this phenomenon in the United States is Robert K. Murray, *Red Scare: A Study in National Hysteria, 1919-1920* (New York, 1964). There is a chapter on the Red scare in Canada in Bercuson, *Fools and Wise Men*, which presents a full account of the One Big Union. Other material on the Red scare and One Big Union is found in Robin, *Radical Politics and Canadian Labour*, and McCormack, *Reformers, Rebels and Revolutionaries*.

lowing the Calgary meeting, politicians, newspapers, and church leaders alike rallied Canadians against the forces of radicalism and revolution. Newspaper headlines proclaimed "Red Bolshevism Declares War On World At Large," while government reports warned that Bolsheviks might use new and secret weapons to cause blindness in their campaign for world domination. The Bolsheviks in Russia were accused of "nationalizing" women to provide sexual services for Red soldiers and of destroying the very foundations of civilization. Nothing was too evil to pin on the Reds.

Although some members of the federal government were all too ready to take part in the anti-Red hysteria and to blame labour unrest on Bolshevism, others were well aware that labour-management relations had taken a new turn since the start of the war and that the growth of unionism and the increased sophistication and strength of industrial capitalism were bound to bring greater antagonism between labour and capital. The task, as they saw it, was to create a new system of industrial cooperation that would make confrontation obsolete and that would increase productivity while bringing peace to the workplace. A middle ground was needed before it was too late.

The search began with the appointment in mid-April of a Royal Commission to Enquire into Industrial Relations in Canada, headed by Chief Justice Mathers of Manitoba. The Commission began its hearings in Victoria, B.C., on April 26 and completed its work in Ottawa on June 13, hearing 486 witnesses in twenty-eight communities. Many labour radicals chose to ignore the Commission, especially in western Canada, but other trade unionists, as well as employers and consumer groups, appeared or sent representatives. It was apparent from the hearings that the labour movement was in the throes of a reexamination of its traditional approaches to industrial relations and that it had many complaints about living costs, working conditions, and perhaps most significant of all, the tremendous difficulties unions encountered in winning recognition from employers. The employers, for the most part, claimed the right to operate their plants and shops without interference from organized labour, and it was clear that many of their attitudes had changed little from the early days of industrialization and laissez faire in Canada.

When the Commission issued its report in mid-June it confirmed the widespread labour unrest in the country, especially in western Canada, but it insisted, nevertheless, that the majority of workers and owners in Canada were interested in a middle way. That direction was outlined in the Commission's recommendations, which included a sweeping program of social welfare reforms such as minimum wage and maximum hours laws, state insurance against unemployment, sickness, disability, and old age, and the legalization of collective bargaining. To bring peace to the workplace the Commission recommended a system of joint plant and industrial councils, composed of representatives chosen by management and labour, to determine wages and working conditions, settle grievances and generally to regulate labour-management relations in the shop. Such councils already existed in Great Britain, where they were kown as Whitley councils, and in the United States where they were generally patterned after the industrial representation plan of the Colorado Fuel and Iron Company. This latter scheme had been established in 1914 by the former Canadian Minister of Labour, William Lyon Mackenzie King, while he was acting as a private consultant for the Rockefeller Foundation.

The Mathers commission's recommendations came too late for the city of Winnipeg, where trouble between labour and many local manufacturers and employers had been brewing for years. Winnipeg's spectacular growth since the 1880s had been based on the grain trade, the railways, and agricultural service industries. A vigorous group of businessmen took the city's growth in hand and worked, planned, and invested towards a golden future in which it would become the Chicago of western Canada. Only the unions seemed to stand in their way. Those unions derived most of their support from the thousands of railway workers who settled in Winnipeg after the 1890s to work in the city's repair shops, round houses, and marshalling yards. They were led mostly by British immigrants, veterans of the labour and socialists movements in their native land. They were determined to win a share of the power, influence, and wealth of the city and soon challenged the bosses and their allies in city government. Industrial unrest marked by violence was evident as far back as the street railway strike in 1906 and continued until the war. Labour's wartime grievances increased the unrest among Winnipeg's workers and led to the growth of militancy and radicalism. By the spring of 1919 the city was polarized into two camps and was ready for a major confrontation.[8]

8. There is much on the Winnipeg General Strike. Norman Penner, ed., *Winnipeg: 1919, The Strikers Own History of the Winnipeg General Strike* (Toronto, 1973), is a reprint of a book first published by the strikers just after the event. The first full scholarly treatment was D. C. Masters, *The Winnipeg General Strike* (Toronto, 1950), while a more recent account is D. J. Bercuson, *Confrontation at Winnipeg: Labour, Industrial Relations and the General Strike* (Montreal, 1974). A shorter overview which includes material on the One Big Union is Kenneth McNaught and D. J. Bercuson, *The Winnipeg Strike: 1919* (Toronto, 1974). The relationship of the Church and the strike is outlined in Richard Allen, *The Social Passion: Religion and Social Reform in Canada, 1914-1928* (Toronto, 1971), while the role of immi-

It came following two strikes in the metal and building trades over higher wages and union recognition which broke out May 1 and 2. The workers in these two industries soon approached the Winnipeg Trades and Labour Council seeking help, and the council responded by polling its members to see if they favoured a general strike. The membership was overwhelmingly in favour of action, and the strike was called for May 15. Within days every union local in the city was on strike, and private businesses, municipal offices, and even federal government services such as mail delivery were paralyzed. Only the city police stayed on the job. They had been asked to do so by the Strike Committee organized to run the strike by the Trades Council, which feared that the absence of police would lead to anarchy and bring government intervention. The Strike Committee was composed of radicals such as R.B. Russell and moderates like Ernie Robinson, a faithful craft unionist who had been secretary of the Winnipeg Trades and Labour Council for many years.

Almost from the beginning the strike was opposed by the federal government, represented by Senator Gideon Robertson, now Minister of Labour, and by the acting Justice Minister, Arthur Meighen, both of whom proclaimed that the strikers had no legitimate cause for the walkout but were aiming to build up the One Big Union, destroy craft unionism, and, at bottom, foment revolution. Robertson and Meighen were joined in this view by the Citizens' Committee of One Thousand, a body composed of business and industrial leaders and supported by Winnipeg's upper crust.

The Citizens' Committee cooperated with the militia, the federal, municipal, and provincial governments, and the employers, and coordinated strike-breaking activities. On the strikers' side the walk-out was supported by close to twenty thousand nonunion workers, many of whom were recent immigrants, who finally had a chance to vent the anger that had been building for years. It appears as if the general strike made Winnipeg a divided city, but in reality it had been divided for a long time, and the strike merely demonstrated this.

A city cannot live without essential services. Shortly after the strike began the Strike Committee, meeting with the Citizens' Committee and the city government, devised a plan to allow essential services to oper-

---

grants in the strike is explained in Donald Avery, "The Radical Alien and the Winnipeg General Strike of 1919," in Carl Berger and Ramsay Cook, eds., *The West and the Nation: Essays in Honour of W.L. Morton* (Toronto, 1976). A Marxist view of the labour revolt is presented by G.S. Kealey in "1919: The Canadian Labour Revolt," *Labour/Le Travail* (Spring, 1984).

ate. Placards were printed up which proclaimed that essential services, such as milk and bread delivery, were operating with the permission of the Strike Committee, thus informing striking workers that the services were not being run by strike-breakers. The wording was an error because the placards gave the impression that the Strike Committee was now running Winnipeg instead of the legally constituted city government. This confirmed fears in some quarters that Act I of the Canadian Bolshevik revolution was being played out on the banks of the Red and the Assiniboine Rivers.

As the strike began, the Twenty-seventh Battalion of the C.E.F., recruited in Winnipeg, arrived home from Europe and was demobilized. This added to the thousands of returned soldiers who were already roaming the streets of Winnipeg seeking work. The veterans began to involve themselves in the strike, with a minority, generally from the upper class of the city, opposing the strike, and a majority, with many former trade unionists among them, supporting it. They were an active lot and soon began to parade in the streets of Winnipeg to show solidarity with the strikers. The strike leaders did not want this — they begged their followers to sit tight, be quiet, and not provoke the authorities — but they had no control over the veterans. Once the prostrike veterans began to parade, the antistrike veterans took to the streets to oppose them. After a clash between the two groups was narrowly averted, Winnipeg's mayor, Charles F. Gray, issued a proclamation banning all public demonstrations. At first Gray had tried to stay neutral. He was different from most Winnipeg mayors in that he was not a wealthy member of the business establishment but had instead made a career in professional engineering. He was a moderate, mild man who had favoured liberal and progressive solutions to social problems, and like most progressives he had avoided taking sides during the growing confrontation between capital and labour. However, the strike which tied up his city appeared to challenge his authority and that of the constituted city government, and this led him to lean towards the employers. As the strike dragged on, that lean became more pronounced until he fell completely within the Citizens' Committee camp.

Gray's first ban on public demonstrations restored order for a time, but was defied on June 10 when a minor riot erupted between strike supporters and a band of Special Police in the centre of downtown Winnipeg. The Special Police had been recruited by the Citizens' Committee, acting in conjunction with the city council, mostly from students and returned soldiers at the suggestion of Major General H.D.B. Ketchem, commanding officer of Military District 10. Strike opponents had feared that the

*These mounted police were dispersing a crowd on Portage Avenue in Winnipeg.
(C-26782/Public Archives Canada)*

regular city police would not enforce the law against strikers because they
themselves were union members and had, indeed, voted to go on strike.
At one point city council ordered them to break their ties with the union
or be dismissed, but the ultimatum could not be enforced because doing
so would leave Winnipeg without a police force. The Special Police were
then recruited to replace them and were given clubs and white arm bands
for identification. A small mounted contingent was also set up, equipped
with draft horses donated by the T. Eaton Company. When there was a
sufficiently large force of Specials, the regular police were again told to
quit their union, and when many refused, they were fired. The Specials
took over the responsibility for keeping order in Winnipeg, but they had
no training, and when the mounted contingent tried to clear a small crowd
from the sidewalk on the afternoon of June 10, fighting broke out and
they were routed. Gray then issued his second ban on public demonstration, the mounted contingent was disbanded, and the city agreed to keep

the Specials as inconspicuous as possible so as not to provoke more trouble.

Although the Citizens' Committee was a formidable opponent, the federal government was far more powerful, and it threw its full weight against the strikers. Meighen and Robertson intervened from the beginning by ordering postal workers back to their jobs and then firing them when they refused to return within forty-eight hours. Robertson and Meighen also orchestrated the build up of militia and police forces in the city and worked in conjunction with the Minister of Immigration to ram an amendment through parliament in less than half a day giving the Government power to deport British subjects suspected of revolutionary activities. In the fifth week of the strike the Government arrested Russell and several other radical strike leaders in the hope that the moderates who remained in charge would end the strike on a conciliatory note. These arrests, and the return of Winnipeg's streetcars to the streets, led to the events of Bloody Saturday and the collapse of the strike.

On Friday evening, June 20, an angry crowd of strikers and prostrike veterans gathered in Market Square, near the city hall. Speaker after speaker reviewed the events of the preceding days, demanded that the veterans be allowed to meet in the Industrial Bureau's exposition building, and called for an end to streetcar service within forty-eight hours. The crowd then resolved to parade to the Royal Alexandra Hotel the next afternoon to have Senator Robertson address them. They were in an ugly mood. The strike had dragged on for almost six weeks with no break and no sign of a settlement. Savings had long since disappeared, cupboards were bare, nerves were frayed. The strike should have brought the bosses to their knees within days, but instead the opponents of the strike seemed to be growing stronger by the hour. Now popular strike leaders had been arrested, and the streetcars had returned to service, a highly visible symbol of the weakening resolve of some strikers and the growing strength of the city. Had this long, hot summer been wasted? The crowd was determined that it had not, and it would demonstrate this by mounting a parade in defiance of Mayor Gray's ban. The mayor, backed by Robertson, the Royal North West Mounted Police, and the militia, was equally determined to stop them.

The next morning Gray, Robertson, and representatives of the Citizens' Committee and the R.N.W.M.P. met a delegation of prostrike veterans to hear a recapitulation of the demands that had been voiced at Market Square the previous evening. Gray stood firm and told the veterans that he would stop the demonstration "peacefully if possible," but if not, "other measures would have to be taken." The militia and police were alerted. As the crowd began to gather in front of the city hall it stopped and attacked a southbound streetcar on Main Street, and Bloody Saturday moved to its inexorable and violent climax. After the shooting and rioting were over, the strikers' resolve collapsed completely, and the walkout was called off in return for a promise from the provincial government to appoint a royal commission to examine the causes of the strike.

The O.B.U.

The One Big Union had played no role in the Winnipeg General Strike despite the accusations of Senator Robertson, Arthur Meighen, and the Citizens' Committee. In fact, the O.B.U. had been born rather quietly in Calgary during the third week of the strike when a handful of O.B.U. representatives met to hammer out a constitution and proclaim the establishment of the new union. The referendum ordered by the Western Labour Conference in March had demonstrated overwhelming support for creation of the O.B.U. in western Canada, and the decision was consequently made to go ahead with the founding of the new organization despite the strike in Winnipeg.

The One Big Union grew rapidly in the following months, reaching a peak of perhaps seventy thousand members, concentrated mostly in western Canada, but with several thousand in Montreal, northern Ontario, Chicago, San Francisco, and the state of Washington. The leaders of the O.B.U. were dynamic, dedicated, and hardworking, and they had earned the respect of trade union members throughout the West because of their long and active involvement in the union and in socialist political parties. In Vancouver Victor Midgley, O.B.U. executive secretary, was a lathe operator by trade who had supported socialism and industrial unionism as far back as 1911. In his business correspondence, he showed the stiff formality that was so often a mark of self-educated union leaders. He was helped by William A. Pritchard, a fiery Socialist Party of Canada member who had arrived in Canada in 1911 to become one of the S.P.C.'s star attractions on the West Coast. Pritchard pushed the O.B.U. cause as far south as Seattle and as far east as Winnipeg. In Edmonton Carl Berg, a Swedish-born immigrant who had worked at everything from fruit picking to railway construction, carried the O.B.U. banner along with Joe and Sarah Knight. Joe was a carpenter, while Sarah seemed to spend most of her time speaking from S.P.C. platforms. She smoked in public — daring for a woman in those days — and stuck her hatpin in the cigarette butts to hold them when they burned too short. In Winnipeg R.B. Russell, the perennial radical, led the O.B.U. forces — after returning from his jail cell in Stoney Mountain Penitentiary in December, 1920.

These people were not short on ability, drive, or intelligence, but they were not united in their goals and aspirations, and this proved to be the fatal flaw for the One Big Union. Its demise was as rapid as its meteoric climb; by the end of 1922 there were five thousand members left in the entire country and most of these were in Winnipeg. The leaders of the O.B.U. could not agree on the kind of union they wanted or on basic issues of strategy and tactics. Some wanted true industrial unionism, others wanted revolutionary syndicalism. Some wanted the union to support political action, others were opposed to this. Some wanted all members to be members of the O.B.U. only, others wanted members to adhere to the O.B.U. through separate industrial unions such as the loggers union. The problems of internal disunity were made worse by the attacks upon the O.B.U. by employers and governments, usually in league with each other and sometimes in league with the craft unions. In Alberta and eastern British Columbia, for example, the Government was best man at the marriage of the coal operators and the United Mine Workers to keep the O.B.U. out of the coal fields. In the days before collective bargaining laws, it was perfectly legal for any employer to bargain with a craft union and ignore the O.B.U., even if a small minority of his workers supported the craft union and a heavy majority were O.B.U. members. Finally, after Winnipeg and after other sympathetic and general strikes that swept across Canada in the spring and summer of 1919, workers had little strength and few financial reserves left to use in a strike for recognition of the O.B.U. Since the O.B.U. gave little direction to the workers, and they gained little from it, they soon deserted it and caused its virtual collapse.

The 1919 strikes may have been failures in that they brought few tangible rewards and many crushing defeats to Canadian workers, but they definitely increased their political awareness of the need to elect labour representatives to all levels of government. In almost every province in Canada, labour representatives contested elections and scored greater successes than ever before in their history. In the 1919 Ontario election, eleven Independent Labour party members were elected to form a coalition Government with the forty-four members of the United Farmers of Ontario. In the following year, eleven labour members were elected to the Manitoba legislature, including three — William Ivens, John Queen, and George Armstrong — who were serving jail sentences after having been arrested during the Winnipeg General Strike. In other provincial elections held that year, four labour members were elected to the Nova Scotia legislature, three in British Columbia, and two in New Brunswick. In 1921 four were elected in Alberta and one in Saskatchewan. And in the federal election held in December, 1921, two labour men who had been connected with the Winnipeg General Strike, James Shaver Woodsworth and Abraham A. Heaps, were elected to represent two constituencies covering the north end and working-class districts of Winnipeg.

Labour's political offensive marked a new class awareness for workers across the country, but it did little to stall an employers' counteroffensive that began to roll towards the end of 1919. Spearheaded by groups such as the Canadian Manufacturers Association, the Canadian Reconstruction Association, and local employers' associations, management set out to roll back the gains that unions had won during the war in increased wages, better working conditions, and union recognition. Many employers' associations insisted their members sign pledges that bound employers to each other in establishing a common front against trade unions in their districts. Employers were aided in their campaign by a labour disunity that pitted craft unions against the O.B.U. and Catholic unions in Quebec against craft unions. Workers all over Canada had used up their meagre savings, and their unions had exhausted whatever financial resources they had in 1919 and were hard-pressed to defend themselves against the counteroffensive. All across Canada wages were cut, particularly in the mining and transportation industries; unemployment increased, and trade union membership, which had reached a peak of 378 000 in 1919, began to decline until it dropped to 260 000 by 1924, a loss of more than 30 per cent. Employers also resorted to the increased use of joint plant councils or industrial councils along the lines of those earlier designed by Mackenzie King. The anti-union campaign was ironically aided by the depression which began to grip the Canadian economy in the fall of 1920: it was the most severe economic downturn since 1913. Although many businesses suffered drastically while the depression ran its course until 1922, businessmen were able to take advantage of growing unemployment and falling prices to undermine union membership and cut wages.

In Quebec the employers' counteroffensive was given a tremendous boost by the founding of the Canadian and Catholic Confederation of Labour in December, 1920. This was a highly centralized federation of Catholic unions which had been growing in the province since the turn of the century. The unions were based on the ideas of social Catholicism first enunciated by Pope Leo XIII in the papal encyclical *Rerum Novarum* towards the end of the nineteenth century, which exhorted Catholics to strive for social justice within a general framework of Catholic human-ism. Catholics were warned not to forget that social harmony and Christian brotherhood, even between employers and workers, was more important than economic gain. Thus the Catholic union movement put protection of the Catholic ideals of its members ahead of economic advancement and condemned the use of strikes or other direct action methods. In Quebec the unions were largely led by priests who negotiated with the employers, kept the books, and guided the union in setting out strategy and tactics. The Catholic unions attacked the materialism of the craft unions and considered them little better than the communists. And although the craft unions continued to hold the allegiance of the better educated and more highly skilled Quebec workers, particularly in the construction trades, the Catholic unions were a direct threat, especially when employers, for obvious reasons, preferred to deal with them rather than with the strike-oriented craft unions.[9]

The Condition of Labour, 1920

By the end of the Borden era it must have appeared to many workers across Canada that the struggles and trials of the war period had brought little in the way of social advancement, economic improvement, or the acceptance of trade unions and collective bargaining as legitimate institutions in Canadian life. An examination of some cost-of-living and wage statistics collected by the Department of Labour in 1920 tends to bear this out. If a group of workers in Hamilton, Ontario, a leading industrial centre, can be taken as typical, the table on page 182 shows that there was little increase in their real wages between 1911 and 1920, and in some cases there was an actual decrease. The table gives the hourly wages for a cross section of workers in 1911 and 1920, and also shows how many hours of work were needed by each group of workers to pay for rent or basic commodities. If less work was required to buy a particular item in 1920 than in 1911, that worker's buying power had increased. If more work was required, buying power had been eroded. These Hamilton workers clearly paid less for rent in 1920 but almost as much, and sometimes more, for other items. After nine years, therefore, their living standard

9. Some background to the development of the Catholic union movement is contained in Babcock, *Gompers in Canada*. The most recent study is Jacques Rouillard, *Les Syndicats Nationaux au Québec de 1900 à 1930* (Québec, 1979). The memoir of an important leader of the Catholic union movement is Alfred Charpentier, *Ma conversion au syndicalisme catholique* (Montréal, 1946).

*Working conditions continued to be unsafe in many trades. These
workers, rebuilding a stretch of the Rideau Canal locks north of
Kingston, Ontario in the early 1920s, stood a good chance of
being hurt on the job. (Mr. and Mrs. Percy Hitchcock collection)*

was only slightly higher in spite of all the strikes and lockouts, the sacrifices of war, and the advances in industrial technology.

Similarly if industrial accidents can be taken as a general indicator of
working conditions in Canadian industry, there had been little improvement since 1911. In the last three months of 1920, 304 Canadians were
killed on the job, an average of 75 per month. Since the work force had

NUMBER OF HOURS OF WORK NEEDED TO PAY FOR BASIC COMMODITIES IN HAMILTON: 1911 AND 1920

| | Hourly Wage | | Month's Rent | | Ton Coal | | Hours of Work to Buy | | | | | | | |
| | | | | | | | 1 lb Coffee | | 1 lb Flour | | 1 lb Butter | | 1 lb Sirloin | |
	1911	1920	1911	1920	1911	1920	1911	1920	1911	1920	1911	1920	1911	1920
Bricklayers	.50	1.03	30	25	13.5	14	.7	.5	.06	.07	.5	.6	.4	.4
Carpenters	.40	.85	37.5	30	16.9	17	.9	.6	.07	.08	.6	.7	.5	.5
Sheet-Metal Workers	.35	.85	42.9	30	19.3	17	1	.6	.08	.08	.7	.7	.5	.5
Machinists	.32½	.73	46	36	20.8	20	1.1	.7	.09	.1	.7	.8	.6	.6
Bldg. Labourers	.27½	.55	54.5	47	24.5	26	1.3	.9	.11	.1	.9	1.0	.7	.7
Factory Labourers	.17	.41	88	63	40	35	2	1.2	.18	.13	1.4	1.1	1.1	.7

Source: Compiled from Monthly figures in *Labour Gazette*, 1911–1920, and in Canada Department of Labour, *Wages and Hours of Labour in Canada, 1902–1920* (Ottawa: 1921).

increased by roughly 17 per cent since 1911, and the death rate had dropped by about 24 per cent, matters were certainly improving, but not by much.

More Canadians were employed in 1921 than ten years before, reflecting the general increase in population, but their distribution in the different sectors of the economy had changed little since the war. The ratio of men to women had not changed much, and the distribution of women had also stayed about the same because the vast majority of women who entered heavy industry to work on munitions during the war went back to more traditional occupations afterwards. In many cases they had little choice, whatever their inclination. Men did not want to work with them, and the unions, for the most part, were interested in restoring their male members to their usual spots on the factory floor. Besides, government and society made it clear that women's place was in the home, raising and caring for the family, and nothing was done to make industry more hospitable to female workers.

Trade union membership reached a peak in 1919 but began to decline with the onset of the depression in 1920. Nevertheless, the ratio of organized to unorganized workers in the nonagricultural work force had changed over a ten-year period. Union members in 1921 accounted for roughly 17 per cent of nonagricultural workers, a doubling since 1911. However, it appears from an examination of the wage and price trends, as reflected by the preceding table, that the unions were able to do little to improve the living standards of the labour force over this period. Despite the sacrifices of war, little had changed for most Canadian workers in the basic struggle to eke out a living, raise a family, and provide a small cushion for old age. The 1920s have become known as the Roaring Twenties — an era of bathtub gin, fast cars, radio, daring fashions, and loose morals. This was the great blowout after the war, a return to the good life with a vengeance. The picture is true as far as it goes; a small number of middle- and upper-class Canadians did enjoy that Great Gatsby kind of life. However, for most Canadian workers there was a different reality to be faced every day — a reality of poor wages, periodic unemployment, unsafe and unhealthy living and working conditions, and a battle to rise above poverty. The war had made a nation of Canada, but most Canadian workers had still not found their place in the sun. The 1930s, just around the corner, were to be even worse for the vast majority.

Chapter VI

1919–1939:
The
Years of
Boom and Bust

The On-to-Ottawa trekkers clambered out of the boxcars and blinked in the early morning light. This was Regina in June, and there was still a chill in the morning air although the sun was already bright. The leaders formed the men into ragged ranks and marched them off through the streets to the Exhibition Grounds. To the suprise of some of the trekkers, the citizens of the city seemed friendly, and some of the major streets were actually lined with cheering crowds. For the unemployed, that was not the usual reception.

After some food — and after the issuance of relief vouchers — the trekkers settled back to wait on events. It did not take long before two Cabinet ministers arrived from Ottawa as emissaries of the Prime Minister, R.B. Bennett. Mr. Bennett would accept a delegation, the trekkers' leaders were informed, and the delegation of eight could proceed to Ottawa on first-class rail tickets with meals provided. That was a victory for the unemployed men — for five years they had been trying without success to get the Government to negotiate about their plight. At last, success.

But not for long. When the trekkers' representatives were ushered in to see the Prime Minister, his officials, and the Press, the meeting quickly blew up. Bennett began to attack the leaders of the trek as radicals and trouble-makers, and he singled out Slim Evans, one of the major organizers of the event. "We know you down here, Evans! You are a criminal and a thief!" Bennett's bluster had frightened many men, but Evans was not intimidated. "And you're a liar, Bennett," he shouted back at the portly, red-faced Prime Minister, "and what is more, you are not fit to run a Hottentot village, let alone a great country like Canada." The delegation was hustled out, and the negotiations were over.

Two days later, the Royal Canadian Mounted Police attacked the trekkers and broke up the On-to-Ottawa Trek. It was Dominion Day, July 1, 1935, the middle of the Great Depression.

Grievances

The social and political unrest and the personal dissatisfaction and frustration that followed the end of the Great War were not confined to industrial workers or returned soldiers. Among farmers there was bitter disappointment that Borden's Unionist colleagues had not produced the legislative results that they had believed would follow the 1917 election victory, especially in the area of lower tariffs. Some farmers had understood the Government's need to cancel military service exemptions in March, 1918, but all had hoped that this violation of a solemn pledge would be balanced by progressive measures in other areas; all felt betrayed when it was not. The one place where their demands were met was in the marketing of grain. When the war ended the demand dropped, and prices of wheat and other cereals fell accordingly. Many western farmers had overextended themselves during the war to produce as much as they could and had bought new machinery and new land, paying high prices and borrowing money at high interest rates. Now, left high and dry, they demanded government price supports. In response, in the summer of 1919 the Canadian Wheat Board was established to buy up all the grain and sell it at the highest possible price. After one year, it was disbanded.

Understandably, western farmers were angry; and so were farmers in Ontario, who faced different problems. They were worried about the growth of cities, the consequent shift of political power and influence from country to city, and about rural depopulation, the slow but steady movement of young people away from farming and agricultural communities into the big cities. A popular song of the time explained it all. It asked the unanswerable question about farm boys just returned from war: "How ya gonna keep 'em down on the farm, after they've seen Paree?" The shift brought with it a diminution of prestige and status. In the popular mind the once stalwart farmer, pillar of the community, was being reduced to a country bumpkin. Enraged and humiliated, the farmers demanded that the Ontario Government pay more attention to them and to their problems. They wanted ready and easy access to city markets via electrically powered railways and the maintenance and improvement of rural services such as schools and roads. The country was seething with unrest. Canadians had expected the war to change their lives, and instead all they received were the same old answers. New men and new ideas were needed.

Grits, Tories, and Progressives

In February, 1919, Sir Wilfrid Laurier died. By refusing to join a conscriptionist coalition, he had succeeded in preserving the Liberal party. Now the Liberals were faced with the dual task of finding a worthy successor and reuniting the party. Many Liberal supporters also wanted their party to branch out in new directions. They believed that a united and reinvigorated Liberal party would be able to find a solution to the labour problems that plagued the country and put forward new initiatives in social reform legislation.

In August, 1919, the Liberals met in convention and constructed a platform that placed the party solidly behind state intervention in social and economic affairs. They promised comprehensive pension legislation, a national health care insurance scheme, unemployment insurance, and in keeping with their new direction, elected a forty-four-year-old bachelor, William Lyon Mackenzie King, as party leader. During his years as deputy minister and then minister of labour in the Laurier Government, as consultant for the Rockefeller Foundation on the labour problems in Rockefeller's Colorado coalfields, and as the author of *Industry and Humanity*, published in 1918, King had become widely known as a labour expert and progressive thinker. This book outlined the need for a social welfare program much like that adopted at the Liberal party convention. King was a man of mixed motives. Highly religious and morally upright to the point of pompous stuffiness, he also projected, at least in his first years as leader, an image of youthful vigour and forward thinking. The power of public opinion, he believed, could do away with evils such as overcrowded factories or unsafe mines. At the same time, he had a keen appreciation of the ability of wealthy and powerful men, such as Rockefeller, to either speed up or block reform. He saw himself, always, as the great healer,

Laurier's death marked the end of a great era in Canadian politics. His successor ▶ at the Liberal helm would be a far different leader. (C-15874/Public Archives Canada)

divinely ordained to maintain Canadian unity across class, region, and ethnic and linguistic divisions, and this mission was always his first priority.[1]

Despite its new leader and new platform, the Liberal party made little headway with those, like the farmers, who were the most dissatisfied with the current social and economic state of affairs. In Ontario and throughout the West the agricultural leaders were arguing and debating political issues and organizing into political action groups. They had discussed direct political action for years and, in 1910, had first formulated a program which they called the Farmers' Platform or — pointedly, with a jab in the direction of the old one — the New National Policy. This demanded greater government intervention in the economy, public ownership of transportation and basic utilities, regulation of the grain trade, and lower tariffs. Abandoning the Liberal party, many farmers had supported the Unionist Government in 1917 because, unlike the Liberals, it promised change. But the Unionists had delivered little; worse, they had cancelled conscription exemptions in the bargain. Though reluctant to return to the Liberal fold, the farmers could no longer support the Unionists. Their answer was to launch their own parties, which, they believed, would most closely reflect their needs.[2]

The first break came in October, 1919, in Ontario, where farm candidates running under the banner of the United Farmers of Ontario captured the provincial government, a result that surprised them as much as

1. There is much material by and about King which gives a good picture of his career up to his assumption of the Liberal leadership in 1919. His own work, *Industry and Humanity*, had appeared in several editions, the most recent with an analysis and introduction by David J. Bercuson (Toronto, 1973). See also King's *The Secret of Heroism: A Memoir of Henry Albert Harper* (New York, 1906). Books on King include R.M. Dawson, *William Lyon Mackenzie King: A Political Biography, 1874-1923* (Toronto, 1953); H.S. Ferns and Bernard Ostry, *The Age of Mackenzie King: The Rise of the Leader* (London, 1955); and Paul Craven, *An Impartial Umpire: Industrial Relations and the Canadian State, 1900-1911* (Toronto, 1980), which details King's career as a labour arbitrator. A psychohistory is Joy E. Esberey, *Knight of the Holy Spirit: A Study of William Lyon Mackenzie King* (Toronto, 1980). A United States view of King's involvement with the Rockefellers is contained in George S. McGovern and Leonard F. Gittridge, *The Great Coalfield War* (Boston, 1972).
2. The farm protest movement has been well covered. Early works which are still useful include Paul F. Sharp, *The Agrarian Revolt in Western Canada: A Survey Showing American Parallels* (Minneapolis, 1948); W.L. Morton, *The Progressive Party in Canada* (Toronto, 1950); and W.K. Rolph, *Henry Wise Wood of Alberta*, (Toronto, 1950). For Ontario see E.C. Drury, *Farmer Premier: The Memoirs of E.C. Drury* (Toronto, 1966), and L.A. Wood, *A History of Farmers' Movements in Canada: The Origin and Development of Agrarian Protest, 1872-1924* (Toronto, 1975). Recent works on the subject include John H. Thompson, *The Harvests of War: The Prairie West, 1914-1918* (Toronto, 1978), John Kendle, *John Bracken: A Political Biography* (Toronto, 1979), and Gerald Friesen, *The Canadian Prairies* (Toronto, 1984).

anyone else. When the ballots were counted they had won forty-three seats to twenty-eight for the Liberals and twenty-six for the Conservatives. Although in a minority, they were able to form a Government with the help of members of the Independent Labour Party and took office under Premier E.C. Drury. In Canada's most urbanized and industrialized province, the farmers ruled.

Four months later a national farm party began to emerge out of the Unionist coalition. Under the leadership of the former Unionist agriculture minister, T.A. Crerar, a group of western M.P.s began to caucus together in Ottawa. This led to the birth of the National Progressive Party, which was fully endorsed by the Canadian Council of Agriculture in December, 1920. Crerar intended to unite progressive Canadians into one political organization that would not have to rely on the power of Montreal and Toronto bankers and businessmen or conservative voters in French Canada.

The rising political consciousness of the farmers was further reflected in the Manitoba provincial election at the end of June, 1920. The Liberal Government of Premier T.C. Norris, an administration which had passed much progressive legislation on such issues as temperance, votes for women, a minimum wage, and workers' compensation, sought a renewal of its mandate. Despite its reformism (or because of it, some said), the Norris Government lost considerable ground to farmer and labour candidates. The United Farmers of Manitoba elected twelve members to the legislature while labour candidates accounted for eleven seats, throwing the Norris Government into a minority and the legislature into a deadlock.

Farm support had been one of the major building blocks of the Unionist coalition, and it was obvious, by early 1920, that the farmers were turning away from the Borden Government. The coalition was in deep political trouble. In Quebec, it had no support outside the English-speaking community of Montreal. In the West, the Government's failure to lower tariffs and complete the nationalization of the railways cost it much support, and farmers were starting to back the Progressive party. In reality, the coalition had never truly united conscriptionist Liberals and Conservatives, as both had continued to maintain their identities and had rarely worked together. After Mackenzie King was elected leader and put a light in the window for all Unionist Liberals, no questions asked, many of them found it easy to abandon the coalition and return to the fold. Borden's long absences overseas and his apparent lack of interest in domestic political matters did not help Unionist fortunes. He had been in active politics as Leader of the Opposition and Prime Minister for nineteen years, and he was ill and tired. It seemed as if the greatest political triumph of his life — the election of 1917 and the successful introduction of conscription — had both exhausted him and soured him on politics. In early July, 1920, he resigned as party leader, and in elections among the Unionist caucus in the House of Commons and the Senate, Arthur Meighen was chosen to succeed him. At the same time, the party dropped the name Unionist and renamed itself the National Liberal and Conservative party, attempting with this cumbersome label to claim descent from the wartime coalition.

As the Unionist name passed from the scene, farm protest continued to rock the traditional party structure in the country. Farm candidates were elected to the Nova Scotia legislature in July and to the New Brunswick legislature in October; in the latter province they even held the balance of power. Another major victory for the farm parties was scored in the Alberta provincial election of June, 1921, when the United Farmers of Alberta swept to office with a majority, defeating the Liberals. Here, as in Ontario, the victory came as a surprise, and the U.F.A. was hard pressed to find a suitable candidate for premier. They eventually settled on Herbert Greenfield, vice-president of the U.F.A.

Now it was Meighen's turn to face the people — and the music. The election campaign began in September, 1921, amidst much popular grumbling. The depression that had been expected after the war had begun in earnest in late 1920 when the Government and the banks decided to put an end to inflation by calling in loans and tightening up on credit and borrowing. Once again unemployment lines grew while wages fell. The Government offered the people little except a promise that it would continue the National Policy and keep tariffs high. Meighen, with his didactic mind, tried to face the issue of conscription in Quebec and received a polite reception, but few votes. Nor was he much more successful in the West or in Ontario, where the back roads and concessions were still buzzing with talk of independent political action. Meanwhile, Mackenzie King and the Liberals ran on their reform platform and King's reputation as a conciliator, a man who could bind up the many wounds of the nation. When the voting was over Meighen's Government had been reduced to fifty seats while the Liberals won 116. Crerar's Progressive party scored the campaign's major upset by placing second with sixty-five seats — twenty-one in Ontario, one in New Brunswick, five in British Columbia, and thirty-eight on the Prairies. A decade of Conservative leadership had

Arthur Meighen, (C-5799/Public Archives Canada) ▶

Bringing Cheer to the Western Farmer

*T.A. Crerar, the
Progressive leader.
(PA-43102/Public
Archives Canada)*

ended, and the Liberal domination of Canadian political life in the twentieth century, begun by Laurier, was about to resume.

Mackenzie King in Power

The Canada that emerged from the election of 1921 seemed ungovernable. As the astute editor of the *Manitoba Free Press*, J.W. Dafoe, remarked at the time, ". . . any person who holds office . . . at any time during the next five years is entitled to a measure of sympathy." Never since Confederation had the country been so divided; never had the political map been in such shambles. Meighen's party had ceased to exist as a national party in any representative sense, for it had failed to elect a single member from six out of the nine provinces. The Liberals had won everything in Quebec, Nova Scotia, and Prince Edward Island but only three seats on the Prairies, while the newly created Progressives emerged as a new national threat, having elected members in six provinces (but tellingly, only one east of the Ottawa River).

It was a House of Commons unlike any other ever elected. Many of the members were in Ottawa for the first time, speaking for groups that had for too long been under-represented, if represented at all. Chief of these was, of course, the agricultural community, which now had some sixty-five members to voice its concerns. Among these was a young school teacher from Ontario, Agnes MacPhail, the country's first woman member of Parliament, elected, appropriately, in the first federal election in which women were officially distinguished from the insane and the imprisoned by being given the right to vote. Even the labour movement had its spokesmen in the House. As William Irvine informed the Speaker at the beginning of the session, "I wish to state that Mr. Woodsworth is the leader of the labour group . . . and I am the group." Then with a wicked nod at Prime Minister King, he added, "But even if we are small I would like to say without any presumption whatsoever that a small living seed, however small it may be, is greater than a dead trunk."

King was likely too concerned with other things to have noticed. After all, he was now the first prime minister in Canadian history elected without a majority in the House. He faced a double task, that of governing and reconstructing the country while rebuilding his own Liberal party which was, despite the election results, in ruins almost everywhere outside of Quebec. To remain in office he would be compelled to rely on the support of the Progressives.

And how ironic it was that just at the time the farmers were making their first concerted attack on the political system in 1921, the census takers were making their rounds. Their findings merely bore out what farmers had felt for some time: the rural and agricultural elements of Canadian society had had their day. They no longer made up the majority of the Canadian population. Canada was fast becoming an urban nation; about half those surveyed in the census lived in the rapidly expanding cities and towns of an increasingly industrial society. The hour of the farmer was fast passing and most of them knew it. This was their last chance to make the Canada they wanted.

The response to this challenge from the leader of the two old-line parties was typical of both men. To Meighen, the leader of the Conservatives, there were only two sides to every question: his own and the wrong one. He was a brilliant man who was seemingly aware of all facts but the facts of politics. Attack, to him, was the only legitimate form of defence. Deciding to confront the farmers head on, he told them that they were "backward" and "blazing madmen," and refused to listen to them. Mackenzie King, on the other hand, could not do enough for the farmers. He told them their policy was his and that he shared their objectives. Infinitely more shrewd than Meighen, at least in politics, King strove to defuse the farmers' rebellion by promising what they wanted and then wooing them back into the Liberal party from which many of them had come. Naturally, King succeeded. The revolt soon petered out, and many of the farmer-politicians soon headed back to the farm and the Liberal party.

Much of the problem was made by the Progressives themselves. They were hopelessly split on ideological issues. Some wished to rid the country of its party system and replace it with the innovation of an erratic American farmer, Henry Wise Wood, who had settled in Alberta and brought with him ideas taken from the Populists south of the border, blended with some thoughts he claimed to have got from the Russian Revolution. His was a theory of representation based on conflicting occupational and class groups. The larger section of the party, led by T. A. Crerar of Manitoba, simply wanted to reform the party system by lumping all the progressive groups in the country into one large political party that would exclude only the "big and powerful interests."

What united these two elements was their hostility to high tariffs and high freight rates and their feeling of being left behind; their complaints were often more psychological than material. But they could not agree on strategy, and their nominal leader, Crerar, refused to become the Leader of the Opposition. Instead, the Progressives chose to sit as independents, too divided amongst themselves to attempt the pretense of holding the

This farm near Delisle, Saskatchewan was a prosperous operation in the mid-1920s when the photograph was taken. But the owner, like so many others, went broke during the Depression. (Mr. and Mrs. Percy Hitchcock collection)

balance of power in the House. After a time, Crerar succumbed to the blandishments of King and rejoined the Liberal party he had left in 1917. In 1922 the United Farmer Government of Ontario came to an end, none too soon for the people of the province if the results of the 1923 provincial election were any reflection of the mood of the people: The party was savagely rebuffed, winning just a handful of seats.

Though the farmers hung on grittily to power in Alberta, by the mid-1920s the farm-power movement had lost its momentum in federal politics. It had blossomed almost overnight, but Progressivism had neither the leadership nor the program for a permanent place in the political spectrum. The movement was badly handicapped from the first by the individualism of the farmer and his suspicion, and even jealousy, of his own leaders. Above all, it came up against an obstacle it could not overcome: the political wizardry of a master of the craft, Mackenzie King.

By now in his late forties, shy, lonely, and dumpy-looking, King was already being recognized as the master tactician that he was. It was a disorganized and ambiguous country he had been elected to rule, and as an observer later remarked, his greatest talent was for dealing with the disorganized and the ambiguous. His was not simply the politics of opportunism. Though he was the perfect pragmatist and compromiser, there was more to King than that; there was more to his policies than simple expediency. The grandson of the great Canadian rebel whose name he bore so proudly, the son of a weak, inadequate father and a crushingly possessive mother, King was determined to make his mark on the country that had treated his grandfather so shabbily. And he would make his mark through his party. The Liberal party would provide, in King's mind, a home for all progressive Canadians; it would embody all their needs and concerns. It would be the party of national unity, regional interests, provincial rights, and French-Canadian nationalism, no matter how contradictory and antipathetic these were. "The whole farmers movement," he told a friend, "is a real liberal movement and . . . as such should be sympathetically viewed by the Liberals. . . . We should openly co-operate and . . . combine our forces in the face of the common enemy." The latter, of course, were the hated Tories, who had divided Canada, turned race against race and region against region.

Dale / Winnipeg Free Press

More important even than the farmers and the West in King's scheme were the French Canadians. Unity, he knew, depended on them. After the wrenching trauma of the conscription experience, their commitment to Confederation, he felt, was tenuous. Anything that would reassure them, that would strengthen their Canadianism, he would do. He was determined to preserve national unity at all costs. New *nationaliste* leaders were arising in Quebec who were promising to take their followers along new paths which would eventually lead out of Canada. Another false step, another crisis such as that of 1917, might forever sunder the delicate bonds tieing the sensitive French Canadians to the rest of Canada. In any case, over half of King's following in the House came from Quebec. It was the Quebeckers' support and allegiance which were crucial both to his leadership and his ability to govern; he could do nothing to offend them. In the hands of these members lay, in King's mind at least, the key to Quebec. Ernest Lapointe, a large, swarthy man with unmatched eloquence in both English and French, was given the responsibility of keeping Quebec happy. He could do anything he wished in the province, both in patronage and policy, so long as he strengthened the forces of federalism, and especially of Liberalism, in Quebec. For the next two decades King and Lapointe worked in tandem to retain the loyalty of the French Canadians. The Prime Minister rarely acted without the advice of his French-Canadian lieutenant, lest any of his policies alienate a substantial number of the people of Quebec.[3]

The Prosperous Twenties?

When King took office following the election of 1921, the surprising postwar boom had come to a sudden end. The Canadian economy was in a severe slump. In 1921 well over 15 per cent of the Canadian work force — about three hundred thousand men and women — found themselves without work. Many others were either underemployed or reduced to part-time labour at low wages. The haughty Canadian Manufacturers Association did not take the depression very seriously; however, it blamed the unemployment problem on the "large influx of labour to the cities who previously followed agriculture for a livelihood ... [and who were] attracted to the city by the hope of finding easier work at higher pay and enjoying the excitement of city life." But to the men and women looking for work, the problem was indeed serious. Many of these were veterans who expected — and certainly deserved — far better.

Unhappily, the new King Government, committed to appeasing the rural areas of the nation, did little for the unemployed. Both the Liberals and the Progressives were determined to slash government spending and to lower taxes. Any large-scale assistance to the victims of the depression would, in their eyes, only exacerbate the problems of rural depopulation by making the cities more attractive. The crisis to them was in any case rural in nature. With the end of the wartime boom, commodity prices moved steeply downward. As late as 1920, with wheat selling at the unheard-of price of three dollars a bushel, western farmers had confidently (and as it turned out, recklessly) expanded their productive capac-

3. There are a number of books on the politics of the 1920s. See Dawson's biography of King and also Roger Graham, *Arthur Meighen*, vol. II (Toronto, 1963). Other studies include Ramsay Cook, ed., *The Dafoe-Sifton Correspondence* (Altona, 1966); John Kendle, *John Bracken: A Political Biography* (Toronto, 1979); and Morton's study of the Progressives. An excellent overview of the interwar period is John H. Thompson with Allen Seager, *Canada 1922–39: Decades of Discord* (Toronto, 1985).

ity by borrowing heavily from the all-too-willing banks. The prairie West had become the world's bread-basket during the war, and few saw any reason why it should not remain so. However, the Government's decision to do away with the Wheat Board, which had stabilized the price of wheat, coupled with the decision of banks to call in loans and raise interest rates, brought about a collapse in the wheat economy. Prices plummeted as markets dried up, and wheat was soon selling for less than half of what it had brought only a few years before. Canadian export prices in general dropped almost as badly. And when the agricultural sector suffered, so did the manufacturing sector. Without funds, farmers made bad customers. The demand for consumer goods fell sharply, adding to the unemployment problems in Ontario and Quebec.

However, by the middle of the decade, the worst was over. Markets for Canadian goods reappeared, prices rose, and Canadian wheat was again king, its export far surpassing the record shipments of the war years. Investment was flowing in, and huge capital projects were being undertaken. New industries were being built to service what promised to be a growing and affluent population. The boom was back, or so it seemed. The world appeared to need Canada's wheat, lumber, and nickel. Large pulp and paper mills were springing up throughout northern Ontario and British Columbia. The completion of railway lines into the Precambrian Shield, where huge deposits of gold, copper, iron, zinc, and nickel had earlier been discovered, allowed an army of miners, prospectors, and businessmen to exploit the area. By 1928, over a billion dollars worth of metals and lumber products were being extracted from the shield alone. And to fuel the boom — while at the same time ensuring that wages would not skyrocket — the Government against adopted an open-door immigration policy. Nothing united Canadian industrialists and farmers more than their demand for more and cheaper immigrant labour. In response to cries from both farm and factory, the King Government accepted hundreds of thousands of immigrants. What was noteworthy about this economic upsurge, though few noted it at the time, was the growing importance of American markets and investments. The United States had, for the first time, displaced Great Britain as Canada's most important trading partner. Canadian trade was rapidly being redirected south from its historic trans-Atlantic flow. But perhaps of greater significance were the huge sums in United States dollars that were pouring into Canada to pay for businesses, factories, mines, and smelters. Much of the economic activity of the period, particularly in the mining sector, was dependent on these American funds. The Canadian patrimony was finding its way into the hands of American entrepreneurs. No one seemed to mind; in the heady 1920s there seemed to be plenty for everyone.

Prosperity in Canada was mostly the result of a spill-over of wealth from the United States. The introduction of new products into North American life was largely responsible for this boom. For example, between 1920 and 1930, more than a million cars and trucks were bought in Canada, and automobiles needed rubber and gasoline, roads and garages. For the first time North Americans were buying radios, telephones, electric appliances, and a host of other consumer products. Canadians alone acquired five hundred thousand telephones in these years. At the same time, to keep pace with the growing demand for energy, close to $700 million was spent on building new electrical power plants. According to many observers, for the middle and upper classes at least, the Roaring Twenties was an age of pleasure, with moving pictures, radio, the Model T Ford, and a more sophisticated amusement called the stock market. Everybody seemed to be playing it — and making huge profits. The rich seemed to be growing richer and some of the poor less poor. The symbols of the period, according to one historian, were the hip flask, the raccoon coat, short skirts, Ford roadster, and dollar sign.

There were, of course, many segments of society to whom the 1920s

Railway nationalization — and the costs involved — frightened many, as this cartoon from Bob Edwards' Summer Annual *of 1922 suggests. (Glenbow Archives, NA2920-9)*

were anything but golden. Most farmers did not share in the prosperity of the decade. Life for the farmer was still drab and unrewarding. And even worse, rubbing salt in his economic wounds, was his feeling of being unaccountably left out of the gay, carefree, and affluent life of the cities he heard and read about. Thousands packed their bags and left behind their dull lives on the farms and in the small towns of rural Canada for the glitter of life in the big cities. Most were disappointed. The jobs and money they thought readily available were hard to come by, and the conditions of life — and work, if they found any — were not much better than they had been on the farm.

Worst of all was the lot of the workers. The twenties hardly roared for them. These were lean years for the Canadian working class. Buffeted first by inflation at the beginning of the decade, and then by the sudden deflation that cost many of them their jobs, they soon found themselves competing for jobs with the thousands of hungry immigrants landing monthly in Canadian ports. These hapless newcomers found themselves in the most pitiable conditions of all. Promised jobs and security, they arrived in Canada and found neither. Many were penned up in company towns and slums and forced to work in horrific conditions for abysmally low wages. Threatened with deportation if they protested, most stayed at their jobs and said nothing. They had nowhere to turn for succour; the country's trade unions were both too weak and too insensitive to help.

No decade was more disappointing for the Canadian labour movement than the 1920s. Throughout the twenties union membership plummeted in the face of an unparalleled antilabour onslaught by business. Organizers were blacklisted and fired; strikes fell into disuse as companies had armies of strike-breakers on hand to deal with any disruptions. Taking their cue from their counterparts in the United States, Canadian employers began loudly demanding open shops and right-to-work laws which would bar unions from their plants. Others simply replaced unions with their own company unions. The crushing defeat of the Winnipeg General Strike had set a pattern for unholy alliances of business and government against unions all across Canada, but especially in the West. The labour movement was paralyzed, its leadership demoralized, its radicalism and vitality sapped.

There were some fresh initiatives, but their effect was limited. In Quebec a new labour federation, the Canadian and Catholic Federation of Labour, came into being in 1921 at the behest of the Church. Some years later, in 1927, a number of English-Canadian workers also broke with the internationals to form the All-Canadian Congress of Labour, an organization of unions committed to industrial and national unionism. Finally, at the end of the decade, the Communists, who since their founding meeting in Canada in 1921 had been determined to gain control of the labour movement and had failed abysmally, created the Workers' Unity League, an aggressive, militant organization, bent on organizing not only the unorganized, but the unemployed as well.

However, still dominating the Canadian labour scene in those years was the conservative, craft-dominated Trades and Labour Congress. It seemed totally unprepared to do anything for workers outside its fold. The rise of mass production industries called for different and more aggressive methods of organization. But organizing the unskilled was, to the T.L.C. leadership, anathema. Even though these new industries could not be accommodated within their existing craft structures, both the T.L.C. and its American parent organization, the A.F.L., were unwilling to adopt different structures. They were select organizations whose membership made up the elite of the labour movement; they wanted nothing else but to maintain their status and to be left alone.

Indeed the only labour militancy in the 1920s occurred among the miners of Cape Breton Island, where fully 50 per cent of Canada's strikes took place. Reacting to a series of pay cuts initiated by the new owners of the Sydney coal mines, the British Empire Steel Corporation, thousands of miners went out on strike. When half the cut was restored, they went back to work. But over the next few years violent strikes became a way of life among the steelworkers and miners of the island. Troops and police were permanently stationed around the mines and smelters. Shootings, beatings, and arrests were the order of the day. When a delegation of miners met with the Prime Minister to plead for pensions for their disabled colleagues, all they received from him was a copy of his book, *Industry and Humanity*. Miners and their families were eventually starved into submission. Twelve thousand survived only on rations provided by local relief committees. "Even the sparrows," reported one newspaper, "have a hard time to live in the Sydney Mines and Glace Bay districts." In the face of such adversity — even their own union, the United Mineworkers of America, disowned them — those miners who still had jobs went back to work, defeated but not humbled. Their leader, the fiery Scot, J.B. MacLachlan, was even sent to jail for "seditious libel." His crime? He had openly criticized the brutality of the provincial police in putting down the strike. Telling the truth, the stern Nova Scotian judge lectured MacLachlan, was no defence. "The truer the statement," said the province's attorney general, "the worse the libel." With such justice, could anyone wonder why the miners gave up their futile struggle and went back into the mines?[4]

The one industry that was thriving throughout this decade was smuggling. In the 1920s a large number of Canadians were making a living — and a very good one at that — by transporting liquor across the border. In the United States, the burning domestic political question of the times was whether or not people had the right to buy a drink. It turned out they did not: under the Eighteenth Amendment, the Volstead Act of 1919, all of America had suddenly gone dry. But with the help of Al Capone and his bootleggers, and the thousands of Canadian rumrunners, millions of Americans got drunk — unconstitutionally.

Prohibition forces were almost as potent in Canada. By the end of the war every single province had introduced some form of legislation prohibiting the consumption of alcohol. But because of various lobbies and pressure groups the provinces kept changing their regulations. As one wag put it, "Prohibition, semi-prohibition and the open bar raced back and forth through the statute books of the nine provinces like the lights on a busy switchboard." For example, to placate Niagara grape growers, the Government of Ontario allowed the production and sale of wine. Using this loophole, the province's wineries were soon producing wines which were up to 25 per cent proof, and this in a province which had just voted overwhelmingly to bar the sale of beer containing 2.5 per cent alcohol. As the forces of good fought with the forces of Demon Rum in each province, only one thing remained constant: no matter how dry a province was, it was still legal to produce and store alcoholic beverages for the export market. The returns from this enterprise were far too remunerative for any government to consider ordering it stopped. And in any case, the temperance groups were too concerned about saving their own citizens from drink to worry about foreigners. It was common knowledge that every night barges, schooners, launches, even canoes and sailboats left their berths in Halifax, Vancouver, Windsor, and scores of other tiny harbours for a quick trip across the border to unload cases of scotch, rye, gin, and whatever else the overworked distilleries of Canada were producing. In addition, on the Prairies, enterprising Canadians were cross-

---

4. On the economics of the 1920s, see W.L. Marr and D.G. Paterson, *Canada: An Economic History* (Toronto 1980); W.A. Mackintosh, *The Economic Background of Dominion-Provincial Relations* (Ottawa, 1939); and C.F. Wilson, *A Century of Canadian Grain* (Saskatoon, 1978). Dozens of additional studies can readily be found in the chapter by J.M. Bliss in J.L. Granatstein and P. Stevens, eds., *A Reader's Guide to Canadian History*, vol II (Toronto, 1982).

ing the border in cars, trucks, airplanes, and even on bicycles to unload their goods. This traffic, noted a Toronto newspaper, was helping give Canada a favourable trade balance. And even better, it was legal: the rumrunners were breaking no Canadian law. Though the Americans set up a so-called "dry navy" of motorboats to patrol the Great Lakes and the Atlantic and Pacific coasts, few Canadians were caught. Trade in spirits continued unabated.

Unfortunately, the fully loaded boats and vehicles which left Canada often did not return empty. Instead they smuggled back into Canada goods, especially textiles and tobacco products, worth millions of dollars annually. And only when manufacturers in these industries complained did the King Government attempt to put a halt to this illicit trade. But by then it was too late, at least for the Prime Minister. An investigation of the Customs Department and its Minister, the genial, ineffective Jacques Bureau, was begun and would eventually have very grave political and constitutional repercussions.

The King-Byng "Wing-Ding"

Presiding over all of these rapid changes and developments in the country and apparently oblivious to them all was Mackenzie King. He had taken office in 1921 with a limited but critical objective — to restore national unity. And by the end of his first term as Prime Minister in 1925 he had succeeded brilliantly. Not only was Quebec no longer isolated, but many English Canadians were again beginning to feel that that province, through its massive representation on the Government side of the House, had too much influence, that Lapointe, rather than King, was, in the words of one Toronto newspaper, "calling the shots on all important matters." Clearly, the conscription wounds, at least in French Canada, had been healed. Similarly, King's masterful and leisurely digestion of the rural protest movement seemed to have eased the crisis in the West. The Liberal party, so badly dispirited when King replaced Laurier, was again united. Normalcy, it seemed, had returned to Canada far sooner than most expected.

But if King expected the gratitude — and the votes — of the Canadian people for his achievements, he was to be sadly disappointed. Though he himself admitted that his Government's legislative record was not spectacular, he had given the country four years of calm and respite, and he certainly had provided adequate, though not spectacular, government. But events were not turning his way. The Conservatives had made a remarkable recovery from the 1921 election, which many had thought of as a fatal blow, and under the vigorous leadership of a renewed Arthur Meighen they were providing forceful opposition in the House.

On October 29, 1925, the people of Canada went to the polls. The campaign had been as dull as any in Canadian history. King ran on his record, Meighen on his eloquence. The people of Canada were not impressed with either. The Conservatives swept Ontario and the Maritimes; the Liberals, Quebec. Both shared the West with the Progressives. As a result of the vote, the Conservatives won 116 seats, the Liberals 99, the Progressives 24, with 6 going to independents, including Woodsworth and his labour group of one.

The election had been a personal disaster for the Prime Minister. Not only had his policies and his party been rejected at the polls, but he had suffered a personal defeat in his own York North riding. His once promising political career seemed over at fifty-two. But King's greatest political ally, Luck, did not desert him. The Progressives had lost two-thirds of their members but were now paradoxically in a stronger position. Their twenty-four seats put them in a commanding position in the next House. No government could be formed without their support. And on most issues of importance to them, they were far closer to King than to Meighen.

After many days of indecision, during which King consulted the Governor General, Baron Byng of Vimy, as well as his mother and father who had died years before ("The whole family in Heaven," he wrote in his diary, "are guiding and directing me."), the Prime Minister decided to stay in office until the Commons met. And he set about at once to get ready. He assured the Progressives of his support for their programs. To Woodsworth and his labour group he promised to introduce old-age pension legislation as soon as Parliament met. Meanwhile, Meighen, confidently expecting to become Prime Minister, sat tight, made no promises, courted no one, and played right into the Prime Minister's hands.

On January 7, 1926, with the Prime Minister of Canada looking on from the gallery, the House met. The fate of his Government now depended on the uncertain support of the Progressives, Woodsworth, and a handful of independents. He had made them promises. Would their gratitude be translated into enough votes to support the Government? Under the firm guidance of Ernest Lapointe, the Liberals and their allies held firm and beat back every Tory effort to defeat the Government. But a political time bomb was inexorably ticking away in the files of a former grocer who now sat as a Conservative member from Vancouver. H.H. Stevens had come into possession of the results of the investigation launched into the activities of the Customs Department and was waiting for the opportune moment to release its explosive contents to the House.

Finally the moment arrived. On February 2 Stevens rose and for the next few hours delivered his indictment of the Government's gross corruption and criminal behaviour. He charged that King, Lapointe, and various other ministers knew "that the grossest violations of customs laws were being perpetrated in this country," but did nothing. Officials involved in smuggling were kept in their jobs, or even worse, promoted. Known criminals had been kept out of jail in return for contributions to Liberal party war chests. There was hardly a crime, cried the enraged Stevens, of which this debauched government had not been guilty. What was necessary, he declared, was that a parliamentary committee be set up to investigate. The Liberals and the dazed Progressives had little choice but to go along. An all-party committee of nine was set up to look into Stevens's charges.

In June the committee reported. Its conclusions were not entirely what the Tories had expected. Instead of condemning the Government, the report simply stated that the Department of Customs was guilty of inefficiency, and its Minister had "failed to appreciate and properly discharge the responsibilities of his office." This was clearly inadequate for the Tories. At once, Stevens moved an amendment condemning the entire Government. Thus began one of the most crucial debates in Canadian parliamentary history. For four days the House argued whether to censure the King administration. If it did, the Government would fall and very likely King's own career would be destroyed. When it became evident to the Prime Minister that some of his Progressive supporters were deserting him, King played his trump card. Refusing to be the first prime minister to be censured by his colleagues, King decided to dissolve Parliament and call new elections. Since a request for dissolution had never before been rejected by a governor general, he expected no trouble from Lord Byng. He was in for a rude shock.

The Governor General had been convinced by the results of the election of 1925 that King should have resigned. After all, he pointed out to the Prime Minister, he "*had lost* seventeen seats, while the Leader of the Opposition had gained sixty-seven." In Byng's soldierly mind there was no moral justification for King remaining in office. Thus, when the Prime Minister approached him on a June weekend, without ever having suffered a major defeat in the House, to ask for a dissolution, Byng's sense of justice was outraged, and he refused. Three times the two men met, and each time King tried to convince the obdurate Byng that in a responsible

Mackenzie King spoke at Brampton, Ontario during the 1925 campaign. The two microphones suggest that some people were listening at home on their radios. (Ontario Archives, Accession 3117-2)

government the governor general had no legal right to reject the demands of a democratically elected prime minister. Each time Byng stood firm, convinced that King wanted dissolution simply for partisan reasons — so that he could go to the people as the Prime Minister, still not repudiated by the House, and could, for the purposes of the campaign, control the electoral and patronage machinery.

For the past two generations historians, politicians, lawyers, and constitutional experts have argued the merits of what one Canadian humourist has called "the King-Byng-wing-ding."[5] Who was right? Did the Governor General have the right arbitrarily to reject the request of the Prime

5. On the King-Byng affair, the starting point should be H.B. Neatby, *William Lyon Mackenzie King*, vol. II (Toronto, 1963), and Graham on Meighen, vol. II. Graham's collection of documents, *The King-Byng Affair, 1926* (Toronto, 1967), is very useful and recourse may be had to Eugene Forsey, *The Royal Power of Dissolution of Parliament in the British Commonwealth* (Toronto, 1943).

Viscount Byng, commander at Vimy Ridge and later Governor General of Canada.
(C-39555/Public Archives Canada)

Minister and refuse dissolution? Most scholars agree that Byng was right, although some argue that he made the right decision for the wrong reasons. In any case, under the Canadian system of government, the Governor General represented the Crown and the constitution, and even if what he did was wrong, it was, nonetheless, law. King had no choice but to return to the House, announce his resignation, and tell the country that Canada no longer had a government.

Within days, Byng called upon Meighen to form a new government. It was the biggest mistake in the Conservative leader's error-filled political life to accept the request. He probably had no choice. To refuse would have disgraced the Governor General, since Byng would then have been forced to call again on King to form a government. In any case, Meighen believed that the Governor General had acted correctly. Furthermore, Meighen had every confidence that as leader of the largest party in the House, he would have no problem in forming a viable government. And he might have succeeded, had it not been for some strange parliamentary procedures.

As the law stood then — it was changed several years later — a member of the House who accepted a Cabinet position was forced to resign to seek re-election. Thus, as soon as Meighen became Prime Minister, he lost his seat in the House. Like King at the beginning of the session, he was forced to conduct his Government's business from a parliamentary gallery. Even worse, to carry on the business of government and yet to keep enough members in the House, he was forced into the embarrassing position of appointing "acting" Cabinet ministers. But without the powerful presence of Meighen on the floor of the House, the Conservatives were hard put to withstand the Liberal onslaught. Concentrating on the appointment of an "acting ministry," King and his men charged that the new Government was illegal, that it had usurped the constitution and was making nonsense out of a thousand years of British history. If it was a legitimate Cabinet, he argued, its members had no right to sit in the House; if it was illegitimate, it had no right to transact business. Furious words were hurled across the House for three days and nights as both parties prepared for the ultimate test. Finally, in the early morning hours of July 2, the House was ready to vote on whether the new Government was legal. By one vote, ninety-six to ninety-five, the Commons decided it was not. Only after the roll call did a sheepish Progressive arise to inform the House that, so excited had he become during the debate, he had inadvertently voted against the Government. In fact he had been paired with a member who was absent and had committed himself to abstain. Thus the three-day-old Meighen Government collapsed because of a mischance. As one historian later commented, "Meighen's evil star had betrayed him again. King's infallible good luck had rescued him from the greatest gamble of his life — rescued him for two more decades of power."

The Governor General now had no alternative but to grant Meighen the dissolution he had refused King. For the second time in less than a year the Canadian people were required to go to the polls. Each side was convinced it had the winning issue. The Conservatives campaigned full-out on the corruption issue; the Liberals on the constitutional issue. King argued that what was at stake in this election was what his grandfather had fought for a century before — responsible government. The Conservative leader charged that the Liberals had provided the most corrupt government in Canadian history, and King's attempt to hang on to the premiership "like a lobster with lockjaw," had dealt a severe blow to Canadian democracy. In the end, nationalism won over corruption. But in fact neither issue caught fire. Though they lost seats, the Conservatives actually polled more votes than they had the year before. However, the Liberals again won most of Quebec as well as a substantial part of the Progressive vote in Ontario and the West and emerged decisive winners, 128 seats to the Conservatives' 91 and the Progressives' 20.

King had been vindicated. Through political ingenuity he had turned the greatest crisis of his political life into one of his greatest successes. He was now unchallenged as a political figure, the true heir of Wilfrid Laurier. Stable government had been restored and prosperity returned; the western protest movement had collapsed, and national unity had been regained. In the Prime Minister's mind all his major domestic objectives had been achieved. And even better, Arthur Meighen, his great nemesis, seemed to be finished as a major political figure. Shortly after the election of 1926, Meighen announced his resignation as Conservative leader and was replaced by a lesser man, but one who would prove to be a better political match for King, Calgary lawyer R.B. Bennett. However, for the foreseeable future King seemed unassailable. What could threaten his Government except some great national calamity? And who could imagine such a disaster as the affluent 1920s drew to a close?

"Parliament Will Decide"

Certainly not the Prime Minister, though if there were to be trouble, he believed it was most likely to come from Europe, its traditional source. King did not particularly dislike European statesmen; he just distrusted them. He had learned from the experiences of Wilfrid Laurier that nothing divided Canadians faster than foreign policy. The domestic impact of the Boer War and the Great War was not lost on him. An enterprising, aggressive foreign policy must be avoided at all costs since it seemed incompatible with national unity. He was a strong autonomist, but he also retained a close attachment to the British Commonwealth. He fought for a greater Canadian voice in the League of Nations; yet once he got it, he found he had nothing to say for fear he might say too much. Words preceded commitments; thus words should be shunned. For him it was important that Canada have a place among the nations of the world; but there was nothing he wished to do once he got there. He wanted recognition without obligation, status without responsibility, consultation without commitment. No one could decide for Canada, not the British Cabinet, not the Commonwealth, not the League of Nations. The Parliament of Canada alone could decide, but only after King and his Cabinet had handed down their decision. Parliament could always veto that decision, but King knew it never would.

In King's mind there was one overriding goal: full Canadian autonomy. Its achievement and extension were to be his greatest contributions to his country. Without autonomy, he knew, national unity was impossible; only with full autonomy was a national consensus on foreign policy possible. And only by standing up to the British and resisting their cajolery for a common imperial policy — obviously to be decided upon at Westminster rather than Ottawa, Canberra, or Pretoria — could autonomy be attained.[6]

It was not long after he had first taken office that the opportunity arose to show the British that a new day had dawned for the empire. On August 26, 1922, the Turks attacked the Greeks. It seemed that another of the interminable Balkan wars was about to break out. Few in Canada, including the Prime Minister, gave it a second thought. However, by the Treaty of Sèvres, one of the treaties that ended the Great War, the British had committed themselves to keeping the Straits of the Dardanelles demilitarized. Now only a tiny British garrison in the small Turkish village of Chanak stood between the Turkish army, led by the charismatic Mustapha Kemal, and the Straits. At once the British cabled the dominions for help. Unfortunately, on its arrival in Ottawa on September 15, the message was mislaid, and its contents were not made known to the Prime Minister until the following day, after King had read about the conflict in the morning newspapers. He also read that New Zealand had already agreed to send troops to the Balkans.

To the indignant King the affair reeked of imperial arrogance. He was convinced that the British were testing the waters to see how the dominions would respond. Now that the British had thrown down the gauntlet, King was anxious to fling it back in their faces. He was appalled at the bad

6. For foreign policy in the interwar years, see the King and Meighen biographies, J.L. Granatstein, *The Ottawa Men: The Civil Service Mandarins 1935-57* (Toronto, 1982), and Granatstein's *A Man of Influence: Norman A. Robertson and Canadian Statecraft, 1929-68* (Ottawa, 1981). See also Philip Wigley, *Canada and the Transition in Commonwealth: British-Canadian Relations 1917-26* (Cambridge, 1977), and Claude Bissell, *The Young Vincent Massey* (Toronto, 1981). On defence questions, see James Eayrs, *In Defence of Canada*, vols. I, II (Toronto, 1964, 1965).

manners of the British in publicly announcing a policy involving Canada before the Canadian Prime Minister had been informed. He was, as he wrote in his diary, annoyed, and he let the British Prime Minister, Lloyd George, know it. More significantly, after meeting his Cabinet he informed the British that he would not think of sending troops to Chanak without first consulting Parliament. And he had no intention, yet, of calling it into session. In effect, King was announcing that Canada's automatic commitment to fight at Britain's side anywhere and at any time the British demanded was finished for good. He was not going to ask Canadian boys who had just come home from four bloody years in Europe to go back and fight the Turks for reasons neither they, nor he, understood. "I am sure," he confided to his diary, "the people of Canada are against participation in this European war."

Arthur Meighen was less sure. To a Toronto audience, he stated categorically that he stood with the British. "When Britain's message came," he said, "then Canada should have said: 'Ready, aye Ready; we stand by you'." Nor was the Conservative leader alone. The Toronto *Globe* thundered, "If the Turk attacks Constantinople he attacks Canada." But before this "Oriental imbroglio," as it was described by Henri Bourassa, could blow up into a full-scale foreign crisis, cooler heads prevailed. A peace conference was hurriedly called to meet at Lausanne, Switzerland, and a settlement was reached which seemed to please everyone — including Mackenzie King since, to his great relief, Canada was not invited.

But the Prime Minister had only begun. At the Imperial Conference in London in 1923, King formally rejected the idea of a united Commonwealth policy determined by the British. Canada, he said, through its Parliament, would decide on its own course of action. And though this did not necessarily preclude Canada from joining with the British, it also did not obligate it to do so. King was less concerned with devising a distinctive Canadian foreign policy than he was with making sure that Britain did not devise one for Canada. Reluctantly the British accepted the new King formula; they had little choice. Already the Canadian Prime Minister had shown that he intended to push forward his country's new independent status at every opportunity. By signing a fishing agreement, the Halibut Treaty, with the United States in March, 1923, Canada had indicated that it was capable of negotiating its own treaties without British involvement.

The Imperial Conference of 1925 formally recognized that a new Commonwealth had emerged in which all members were autonomous, equal in status, and "in no way subordinate one to another in any aspect of their domestic or external affairs." Joined by the leaders of South Africa and Ireland, King would accept nothing less. Under his quiet prodding the structure of the Commonwealth was revamped, and the Statute of Westminster, in 1931, declared Canada's new status for all to see. Canada now had her own diplomatic identity within the Commonwealth. As befitted that new status, by 1929 Canadian legations were opened in Washington, Paris, and Tokyo, and a British High Commissioner had appeared in Ottawa. No longer would the Governor General act as a channel of communications between the British Government and the dominions. King had got his revenge on the hapless Byng.

If King's dealings with the empire were his greatest triumph, those with the League of Nations were his greatest failure. Though for a time he thought of the League as a symbol of civilized diplomacy, by the mid-1920s he saw it simply as a debating society. Even worse, he felt it was a harmful organization; there would have been no Second World War, he wrote much later, "if the League of Nations had never existed." He fully shared the sentiments of his representative to the League, Senator Raoul Dandurand, that Canada was "a fire-proof house, far from inflammable materials." Thus, from the beginning, the King administration (much like Borden's before it) strenuously opposed all efforts to strengthen the collective security arrangements of the League; it was not, in King's mind, a law enforcement agency. Without the security arrangements embodied in Article 10 of its Covenant the League of Nations was weak. If it could not deter aggression, then what could it do? It could debate. And the Canadian Government believed in these years that public debate would resolve disputes. Canada refused to sign any agreement which implied that it might be committed to come to the aid of any nation under attack. European disputes were essentially that: European. Canada did not wish to become involved. In this it shared the views of the United States, which had refused even to join the League. It was clear that, despite the efforts of Canadian leaders to achieve some sort of status on the world scene, they were not prepared to use that status in any positive way. All they were prepared to do was to join with those who were busily emasculating the League, so that when the crises of the 1930s arose, the League was impotent.

The Dirty Thirties

Few Canadians in the 1920s gave more than a passing thought to the League, to the imperial relationships, or even to the questions of status and autonomy. They had had their fill of Europe in the previous decade, and now they wished to be left alone to share in the prosperity of the decade. And indeed, at least in the latter years of the 1920s, rapid economic growth in both industry and agriculture led many to believe that at last Laurier's prediction was coming true: the twentieth century would be Canada's. Typically, there was only one foreign event that captured the imagination of the Canadian people. At the 1928 summer Olympic games in Amsterdam, Canadian women were competing for the first time. And what a debut they made! Not only did they win medals, but they captivated appreciative European fans with their new uniforms, which many considered *risqué.* For Canadian women this was not the sole triumph of the decade. Though women were beginning to make their mark in such professions as law and medicine, on the whole their conditions of work had improved little. Though more were being educated than ever before, and more were in the labour force, women were still largely restricted to traditional occupations. The workplace remained an area of great inequality. What had changed significantly was the legal status of women. On October 18, 1929, a Supreme Court decision that women were not persons and therefore not eligible for Senate appointments was overturned by the Judicial Committee of the Privy Council in Great Britain, then the highest court of appeal. Their lordships concluded that "the exclusion of women from all public offices is a relic of days more barbaric than ours.... To those who ask why the word [person] should include females the obvious answer is why should it not?" A few months later, the country's first woman senator, Cairine Wilson, was appointed by Mackenzie King.

Less than two weeks after the Privy Council decision, that triumph was almost forgotten in the general gloom. On October 29, Black Thursday, the great boom of the 1920s came to an end. On that day, after several false alarms, the New York Stock Market collapsed. "Playing the market" had been the national sport of the decade, but suddenly, for reasons economists are still debating, everybody lost confidence in the market at the same time. Everyone wanted to sell, and no one wanted to buy. Within days, thousands had lost their life savings and were destitute. Within weeks, the value of shares on the market had gone down by thirty billion dollars.

The collapse of the market was only the beginning. Consumer spending declined drastically, and without customers, stores and factories and banks were soon closing all over North America. Within a year, millions of middle-class Americans and Canadians were without work or money. The impact of the collapse of the American economic system on the rest of the world was devastating. The gigantic American market was closed off by punishing tariffs; American investment abroad ceased; and American bankers began recalling their loans. International trade slowed to a halt, dropping by 50 per cent within three years, and unemployment spread throughout the world.

Most desperately affected was Canada, which was so inextricably linked to the American market. The Canadian economy was geared to export markets in minerals, lumber, newsprint, fish, and especially wheat. As early as 1928, for those astute enough to see them, the warning signs abounded. Prices for Canada's most important exports, newsprint and wheat, had begun to sag, and there was a general oversupply of most products. But instead of cutting back, production actually increased. Even worse, expecting higher wheat prices, Canadian wheat pools kept much of their harvest off the market in 1929. By the time they realized their tragic miscalculation, it was too late: there was no market for their wheat anywhere. By the end of the year nearly two hundred millions of bushels remained unsold. Since Canada derived one-third of her national income directly from abroad, she was drastically affected by the decline in trade and foreign investment. Construction ground to a halt. There was no demand for new homes, stores, factories, or mines. Throughout the country, hundreds of thousands were on the street without jobs, without money, without security, and, even worse, without hope. For these hopeless men and women there was no relief, no social welfare, no unemployment insurance. Many men were forced to abandon their families to join the huge army of hoboes travelling by freight from place to place, looking for work, for food, indeed for anything to keep them alive.

Of course, not everyone suffered. Those on pensions or fixed salaries suddenly found their money would now buy much more. And it was a wonderful world for those who were still wealthy. As the young John David Eaton, scion of the affluent Eaton family, later recalled, the Depression for him was a grand time since he could spend an entire evening dining and dancing at a posh restaurant for less than ten dollars. Expressing the view of his class, Eaton added that the Depression was a worthwhile experience since it taught men the value of a job.

Though the Depression affected the whole country, some regions were hit harder than others. The worst by far was Saskatchewan. In the 1920s that province was among the most prosperous farming communities in the world; by the 1930s it was among the least, for the Depression there was aggravated by natural disaster — grasshoppers, rust, drought, and drifting soil. No province was so completely dependent on one sta-

The economic depression in Saskatchewan was compounded by a disastrous drought that produced dust storms and drifting soil. This 1936 photograph shows a typical scene near Ponteix. (Saskatchewan Archives, RA17005)

ple as Saskatchewan. And when the market for wheat collapsed, so did the entire economy of the province. In two years the total income of Saskatchewan's farmers fell by close to 90 per cent. Wheat sold for $1.65 a bushel in 1929 was, by 1931, selling for under 30 cents. Thousands of farmers left the province, and more would have followed had neighbouring provinces not warned indigent farmers from Saskatchewan to stay away. Others were forced to go on whatever relief existed; but so strapped for funds were relief agencies that they could not provide fruits or vegetables for the hungry. For the first time ever, scurvy appeared on the Prairies. And if that were not bad enough, swarms of grasshoppers, "so dense," in the words of one farmer, "that they obscured the sun," ate their way through large parts of the province. So terrible was their rampage that they stalled buses and trains, clogged car radiators, and almost choked a patient to death in a dentist's chair by lodging in his throat while he had his mouth open to have a tooth extracted. And what the grasshoppers left behind, windstorms blew away. Millions of acres of topsoil disappeared; much of southern Saskatchewan ended up in North Dakota and the American Midwest.

Though Saskatchewan was the most desperately affected by the Depression, her sister prairie provinces also suffered, though not as drastically. Neither relied so heavily on wheat, and neither experienced such ravages from natural forces. The most recently settled province, Alberta, was the least well prepared to cope with the problems of the Depression. Of all the farmers in Canada those in Alberta could least afford high interest rates; yet theirs were the country's highest. Thus, Alberta's major problem was one of debt rather than destitution. In Manitoba, the suffering was worst among the residents of Winnipeg. Because it was totally dependent on East-West trade, when that collapsed, the economy of the city went down with it. Not only were most of the city's workers unemployed, but they were joined by thousands of indigent farmers and labourers pouring in from rural areas looking for jobs that weren't there. The situation in British Columbia was not much better. Like its prairie neighbours, it depended largely on the export trade for its wealth. Unemployed miners and forestry workers poured into Vancouver from the interior of the province. They were joined by thousands of penniless prairie farmers searching for work and a milder climate; they found only the latter. In the words of one disgusted citizen, Vancouver had become "just a blamed summer resort for all the hoboes in Canada."

In the Maritime provinces the Depression made less of an impact only because these provinces had experienced an almost continuous depression since Confederation. Depression was also not new to Ontario and Quebec, but neither had ever known any so unrelenting and savage. Unemployment was particularly severe in southern Ontario and Montreal, both of which had relied heavily on western trade for their prosperity. The huge manufacturing complex of Canada's industrial heartland ground to a halt. Countless thousands were without jobs; many were evicted from their homes. They had nowhere to go and nothing to do.

Faced with such widespread destitution and hardship, the federal government was paralyzed. With the onset of the Depression even the usually unflappable Mackenzie King was shaken, though less, it seems, by the calamity itself than by his failure to correct the situation. He was a born conciliator, and he had no reason to doubt that he could negotiate his way out of this economic downturn. It was, he believed, only a "temporary seasonal slackness." His remedies were as useless as they were naive: balancing the budget and slashing government expenditures. These were typical Liberal solutions to a problem that had no solution; all they did was exacerbate the crisis. In any case, the Prime Minister was convinced that the Depression was a political rather than an economic problem. Thus, when he received desperate requests from provincial and municipal governments for financial assistance to cope with the horrendous difficulties confronting them, King passed them off as nothing more than a Tory plot to undermine his government. If these governments wanted to spend money, he told Parliament, they should collect it themselves. He would give them none. Why should he? As King told the House of Commons in April, 1930: "As far as giving moneys out of the federal treasury to any Tory government in this country for these alleged unemployment purposes . . . I would not give them a five cent piece."

Though later that evening he confided to his diary that he had gone too far and should never have made that statement since it made him appear "indifferent to the conditions of the unemployed," it was too late to do anything about it. Whatever he meant to say, the Tories did not let the country forget that the Prime Minister had publicly vowed not to give a five-cent piece for unemployment relief and to help only those who lived in provinces with Liberal administrations. This slip of the tongue would cost him dearly.

But the Prime Minister was totally oblivious to how unpopular he and his policies were with the Canadian people. Though he had another year in office to go, the supremely confident King decided to call an election. What he had not taken into account — and could not because he did not understand it — was the impact of the Depression on the Canadian electorate. As well, he seriously underestimated the abilities of the new Conservative leader, R.B. Bennett.

Bennett in Command

Born in New Brunswick of Loyalist stock, the ambitious Bennett went to Calgary at the age of twenty-six and began a lucrative career in law and business. Unlike the flabby Prime Minister, Bennett was tall, imposing, and immaculately groomed, though somewhat paunchy. In his later years he spent much time on the masseur's table in a vain attempt to control his weight. The alternative, to limit his voracious appetite to three meals a day, either never occurred to him or was unacceptable. He was a millionaire and he looked the part; he was rarely seen without his top hat or bowler, tail coat, striped trousers, expensive patent leather shoes, gloves, and cane. A fiery speaker — he was known as "Bonfire" Bennett, once having been clocked at 220 words per minute — he was more than King's match on the hustings.

Bennett's campaign was a classic. The less the Prime Minister talked about the Depression, the more Bennett emphasized it. And unlike King, he had a solution: he would "use tariffs to blast a way" for Canadian goods into world markets. The tariff was his panacea; it would restore prosperity to the businessman, the farmer, and the worker.

This was the first federal election fought on the issue of unemployment, and despite King's unstinting efforts to ignore it, he could not. Even though approximately 14 per cent of the work force was unemployed, King did not think it a serious political matter. "Men who are working," he said, "are not going to worry particularly over some of those who are not." Everywhere he went he became the target of wooden nickels or shouts of "Five-Cent Piece." And he received little help. With the Conservatives in control of most of the provinces, the Liberal election machine, which relied on provincial party support, was in total disarray. Liberals everywhere were overwhelmed by the Tory campaign. Bennett seemed to have all the answers; King had none. This was also the first federal campaign in which radio was extensively used by the candidates, and Bennett proved to be far superior to King as a communicator. However, neither was as popular as "Amos 'n Andy," an American comedy show which captured the vast bulk of the radio audience during the political broadcasts — and after.

Not surprisingly, in their desperation thousands turned to the new saviour. Bennett had promised to solve the economic problems or "perish in the attempt." By a landslide, Canadians voted to grant the Conservative leader his somewhat morbid wish. The Tories won 137 seats, including a remarkable 24 in Quebec; the Liberals won 91. The Depression would now be Bennett's problem to solve, and he threw himself into the task with enormous energy.

But even in defeat King's devoted political mistress, Lady Luck, had not deserted him. Aside from the stalemate in 1925, this was the only election he ever lost, and it was the only one worth losing. For now Bennett and the Conservatives would be saddled with the Depression. It was their unenviable task to find the appropriate nostrums. Defeat had saved the Liberals from disaster. As King noted in his diary on election night, "Bennett has promised impossible things and put himself in an impossible situation.... My guess is he will go to pieces under the strain."

As usual, King was right. There was no way that someone with Bennett's background and philosophy could solve the problems of the greatest economic crisis in Canadian history. He was a conservative who believed in a sound, hard currency and disliked spending money on massive public works or relief payments. A balanced budget, he was convinced, would protect Canada's credit rating, and this would ultimately help break the back of the Depression. He shared with his American counterpart, Herbert Hoover, the belief that the crisis was largely psychological. As the American President said, "What this country needs is a great big laugh. . . . If someone could get off a joke every ten days, I think our troubles would be over." Bennett was proud that the banks were bulging with money. "There is no shortage of currency," he reassured hungry, unemployed, homeless Canadians. Nor was unemployment a serious problem. "One of the greatest assets a man can have on entering life's struggle," he told a group of students, "is poverty." One of the few positive steps Bennett undertook in his first years in office was to raise the tariff. He did provide more than ten times the amount spent on relief in the entire previous decade to help those out of work, but he emphasized that unemployment was a provincial and municipal responsibility, and neither level of government could count on a continuous flow of funds from Ottawa. As under the previous regime, the provinces and municipalities would have to pay for the ravages of the Depression from their own rapidly dwindling treasuries.

There is no question that Bennett threw himself totally into his job. No prime minister worked harder or took on more responsibility. He was his own External Affairs Minister and, for a time, his own Finance Minister, and he delegated very little. In effect he was almost a one-man Government, causing one wit to remark that a Conservative Cabinet meeting was Bennett talking to himself. But he had only one policy, higher tariffs, and once that failed, he seemed to run out of ideas. He went to London to propose an imperial customs union against the rest of the world but was rebuffed by the British, who saw little in it for them. At the subsequent Imperial Economic Conference in Ottawa in 1932, the British were not much more forthcoming. Bennett did establish the Bank of Canada in 1934 to give greater stability to the country's finances, but he decreed that it would be privately owned and not controlled by the government.

The Depression worsened in the terrible winter of 1933, when about one-third of Canada's work force was unemployed, and nothing Bennett did worked. Canadians were now turning against their saviour, who had promised to get them out of the Depression but in fact, seemed to be immersing them even deeper. Soon the Prime Minister became the butt of their bitter humour. An abandoned prairie farm was now known as a Bennett barnyard; a Bennett blanket was a newspaper; and boiled wheat was Bennett coffee. Eggs Bennett? Boiled chestnuts. A Bennett buggy was a permanently out-of-gas automobile drawn by a horse.

And even when Bennett tried something new it boomeranged. The

Depression had spawned a new danger: thousands of homeless, jobless young men riding on freight cars, drifting from one place to another, and looking for work that was never there, were seen as a threat by many middle-class Canadians. The "menace of single men" spread across Canada almost like the Great Fear at the time of the French Revolution. They were hounded by police, arrested as vagrants, and then unceremoniously escorted out of town. In the words of Gideon Robertson, the Minister of Labour, who was asked to investigate the problem, "They are becoming a menace to the peace and even safety of many communities along the lines of railway... especially among the women folk."

In response to the demand that something be done about this army of the unemployed roaming throughout the land, "threatening everything in their path," in the words of one frightened matron, work camps were opened across the country. Most were run by the Department of National Defence under military control and law. They were supposed to help the single homeless persons, as they were euphemistically referred to on the official relief rolls, by providing them with work, food, and shelter. As a side benefit, the Chief of the General Staff, Major General A.G.L. McNaughton, reported that these camps were "directed to the breaking up of the congestion of single homeless men in the principal centres of population... otherwise we would have had no recourse [but to use] military forces to suppress disorder."

Whether the camps were used to benefit them or simply to keep them out of sight made little difference to the 175 000 inmates who at one time or another found themselves as guests of the Government. Though some camps were well run, comparatively comfortable, and treated the unemployed with respect, many were more like prisons or "slave camps," as they were known to the many who passed through them. The pay was an insulting 20 cents a day; the food was terrible; the bedbugs plentiful; the life depressing; the isolation unbearable. Most camps were deep in the bush, far from the cities. And the work was hard — clearing land for highways and airports in swampy, mosquito-infested areas. There was no entertainment: no books, no sports, and of course, no alcoholic beverages.

Frustrated beyond endurance by the conditions in the camps and by the federal government's adamant refusal — or inability — to provide work for real wages, these Royal Twenty-Centers, as they called themselves, eventually rebelled. Thousands left the camps in the interior of British Columbia and congregated in Vancouver to lobby for their cause. There they paraded through the streets, snake-danced down the city's main intersections, crowded in the aisles of department stores, pan-handled their way through the city, and eventually occupied the museum.

The Vancouver City Council did "donate" $1800 to recapture the museum, but when Ottawa failed to respond, the young men, led by their union, the Relief Camp Workers Union, decided to go directly to Parliament Hill to complain. As they headed across the Prairies by freight, the On-to-Ottawa Trek picked up hundreds of reinforcements.

After the collapse of the talks between Bennett and the march leaders, on July 1, Dominion Day, the order to clear the trekkers out of Regina was given. For two hours, Market Square was a mass of seething humanity as strikers battled both the Mounties and the city police. It was no contest. In short order, the trekkers were cowed. One man, a city detective, was killed, scores were injured, and 130 strikers were arrested. The rest dispersed quietly within a few weeks, some to their camps, others to their homes, but most to begin their lives as hoboes all over again.

To Bennett, these men were agitators and Communists, or at least the pawns of agitators and Communists. He was certain that Canada was on the verge of revolution and was determined to maintain law and order at all costs. In many instances the unemployed who organized were indeed led by Communists. Thus, under the infamous Section 98 of the Criminal Code, prominent Communists, including the party's leader, Tim Buck, were convicted of "seditious conspiracy, and belonging to an unlawful organization." Other alleged militants were also jailed and, when possible, deported. Troops were used to put down strikes and break up demonstrations. The Prime Minister even wanted to send a destroyer full of troops into Vancouver's harbour to prevent a May Day parade in that city in 1932. The R.C.M.P. was ordered to infiltrate trade unions, organizations of the unemployed, and other such "subversive" groups. Civil liberties were trampled; the right of thousands of hungry men and women to protest was forgotten in the frenzied atmosphere of the time. Teachers were fired for speaking their minds on the situation; foreigners were threatened with deportation if they went on strike or even took part in demonstrations; and union organizers were constantly harassed and always on the verge of being arrested.[7]

The Depression was even more desperately cruel and trying for Canadian women since neither government nor society in general took seri-

---

7. There is a large literature on the Depression. On the politics, see Neatby on King, vols. II, III. There is no good study of Bennett. A good survey is H.B. Neatby, *The Politics of Chaos* (Toronto, 1972), while the best economic study is A.E. Safarian, *The Canadian Economy in the Great Depression* (Toronto, 1959). See also Alvin Finkel, *Business and Social Reform in the Thirties* (Toronto, 1979), and Michiel Horn, *The Dirty Thirties* (Toronto, 1972), a good collection of documents. The best study of unemployment is James Struthers', *No Fault of their Own: Unemployment and the Canadian Welfare State* (Toronto, 1983).

ously their plight. After all, men were the breadwinners, the heads of families; it was their wages that provided sustenance to the family. And, as well, unlike women they were highly vocal, visible, and carried enormous political clout. How could the needs of women compare with those of men?

Or at least that was the predominant attitude of the period. For a woman to take a "man's job" simply was not done, no matter how desperate was her situation. How could she brazenly rob someone of his manhood and his family of an income? Every job held by a woman was perceived as one taken away from a man who needed it more. Society's priority was to find work for men, not for women. Thus, most school boards, professional organizations, governments, manufacturers, and retailers stopped hiring women.

In order to survive, many women were once again forced into domestic work, reversing the trend of the previous two decades in which women had been moving in increasing numbers into sales and clerical jobs, and even into the professions. Worse, the wages of domestics were abysmally low, even in a period in which all wages were low. Domestics in 1930, for example, averaged less than $300 a year, while employed males earned three or four times that amount. In some provinces domestics worked for less than $4 a week — and in some cases simply for room and board. According to a government study, between 1921 and 1936 the number of domestics in Canada doubled, while their wages decreased by half.

Ironically, working against women were the minimum wage laws that had been enacted in many provinces specifically to protect them. But since these laws did not apply to men, many companies simply fired the women and hired men and boys at a far lower wage, thus forcing women into occupations with no minimum wage protection, or worse, into unemployment. Two royal commissions of the period — on price spreads and the textile industry — uncovered much evidence of women being displaced by men because of the higher wage employers were required to pay their female workers. And in those industries not covered by legislation, women were paid 60 per cent less than men.

Nor were there any specific measures for unemployed women as there were for men — no work camps, no public work programs. Women were supposed to marry and be taken care of by their husbands; and if they were young and single, they were their father's responsibility. And if husbands and fathers could not provide the necessary support, there was always work as a char or a domestic. Sadly, many young women found they could only survive by selling their bodies. As a C.C.F. Member of

Parliament reported in the House in 1937, many of these single, unemployed women looking for work "ended up in questionable sections of cities [to be] taken advantage of by the touts of the underworld."[8]

New Ideas

Ironically, given the hardships and agonies endured by most Canadians, the number of civil disturbances in Canada were remarkably few. Perhaps the Canadian people were too hungry, too busy looking for work, too engrossed in mere survival to have time for rebellion. However, it is certain that the Bennett government overreacted. There was never a threat of revolution in Canada. But what did happen was perhaps as frightening to the Canadian establishment — the politicians, bankers, industrialists, businessmen, and senior civil servants who felt that they had the moral right to govern. For the first time Canadians began to examine the existing economic, social, and political systems and found them unsatisfactory. Throughout the country there was a clamour for change, culminating in a series of upheavals which changed the political topography of the nation.

Predictably, the most important of these disturbances occurred in western Canada, a region prone to political eruptions. For some time the various socialist and labour groups in the West had been chafing in frustration. It was clear that neither of the old-line parties had anything to offer the Canadian people except more of the same failed policies. Something new was needed. In the summer of 1932, in Calgary, something new was created. At a meeting of western labour parties, representatives appeared from various farm groups. It was decided to form a united socialist party with an imposing, if awkward, name: the Cooperative Commonwealth Federation (Farmer Labour Socialist). A year later these somewhat oddly assorted groups met again in Regina and accepted as their canon a manifesto written by members of the League for Social Reconstruction, a body of academics inclined to socialism. The manifesto called for the replacement of the capitalist system, with its inherent injustice and inhumanity, by "a social order from which domination and exploitation of one class by another will be eliminated"; it advocated public ownership of all financial institutions, public utilities, and transportation companies, especially that *bête noir* of all western farmers, the Canadian Pacific Railway.

8. For the role of women in the 1920s and 1930s, see V. Strong-Boag, "The Girl of the New Day," *Labour/Le Travailleur* (1979), as well as articles in S. Trofimenkoff and Alison Prentice, eds., *The Neglected Majority*, vols, I, II (Toronto, 1977, 1985), and J. Acton, *et al.*, eds., *Women at Work: Ontario 1850-1930* (Toronto, 1974).

Only one man could have united the several disparate farm, urban, labour, and socialist components that formed the C.C.F., and he was acclaimed the party's leader. James S. Woodsworth, the M.P. from Winnipeg, the House leader of the "Ginger Group" composed of Progressive and labour members, had provided much of the impetus for the Calgary and Regina meetings. He was comfortable with, and respected by, workers, farmers, and intellectuals. A former Methodist minister, he was steeped in the social gospel of an activist, caring Christianity and saw it, rather than Marxism, as the basis for socialism. Mild, gentle-mannered, extraordinarily patient and honest — his biographer not hyperbolically described him as "a prophet in politics," — he was able to convince many of the doubtful that, in spite of the fire and brimstone of its manifesto, the C.C.F. was actually a moderate reformist party, calling for changes "through orderly and peaceful means."

The C.C.F. made rapid headway, especially in the West. It soon became the official Opposition in British Columbia and Saskatchewan. And in the federal election of 1935 it polled about four hundred thousand votes and elected seven members. But even then the problems that would block its attempts to become a national force were readily apparent. The C.C.F. made little impact in either Quebec or the Maritime provinces, and it never would. It was shunned by many industrial workers, who preferred to continue voting the old family patterns of Tory or Grit. And to many, its philosophy, no matter how scented by Woodsworth, still reeked of Communism. Nonetheless, both as a party and a movement, the C.C.F. made an indelible mark on the Canadian scene, a mark far more enduring than its limited membership and electoral success seemed to warrant.[9]

At the other end of the ideological spectrum a movement arose in Alberta which would provide its own novel approach to the problems of the time. Social Credit was largely the work of one man, a fundamentalist lay preacher from Ontario, William Aberhart. Every Sunday afternoon throughout the early 1930s, a quarter of a million people in Alberta sat beside their radios listening to his fiery sermons. His, it was said, was the most

9. On the C.C.F., the basic book is Walter Young, *The Anatomy of a Party: the National CCF, 1932-61* (Toronto, 1969). This can now be supplemented by David Lewis, *The Good Fight: Political Memoirs 1909-58* (Toronto, 1981), Michiel Horn, *The League for Social Reconstruction: Intellectual Origins of the Democratic Left in Canada, 1930-42* (Toronto, 1980), and K. McNaught, *A Prophet in Politics* (Toronto, 1959). On Social Credit, the basic books can be found in the *Social Credit in Alberta* series, most notably the volumes by J.R. Mallory, John Irving, and C.B. Macpherson. The sole biography of Aberhart is by L.P.V. Johnson and Ola McNutt, *Aberhart of Alberta* (Edmonton, 1970). Useful documents are collected by Lewis Thomas in *William Aberhart and Social Credit in Alberta* (Toronto, 1977).

J.S. Woodsworth is at the centre of the first row of these delegates to the founding convention of the C.C.F., which was held in Regina in July, 1933. (C-29298/ Public Archives Canada)

R.B. Bennett. (C-7731/Public Archives Canada)

popular radio program in the province, next to Jack Benny's. And of course, Benny was not running for office; nor was Aberhart at first. He was interested only in spreading the word of the Lord, that is, until he read a book on Social Credit written by a peculiar Scottish engineer, Major C.H. Douglas. It was like a flash of revelation to Aberhart. Overnight he became a monetary as well as a religious fundamentalist and began preaching both the doctrines of Christ and of Social Credit. Taken together, to Aberhart they were the answer to all the world's moral and economic ills. The essence of Social Credit was that since there never was enough money available to buy the always available goods and services, governments should issue "social dividends," or cash payments, to everyone. This would keep the consumers' ability to buy in balance with the farmers' and manufacturers' ability to produce. Basically this was Social Credit's "A plus B theorem," which most economists dismiss as both semantic and financial nonsense. Nonetheless Aberhart was convinced, and he carried the message into every home with a radio.

It was an especially appealing doctrine in Alberta where there was an abundance of consumer goods but no money to buy them. Who could argue against a scheme that promised to provide funds to everyone, particularly when it was being sold by a man who was also busy saving souls? The new gospel of Social Credit spread like the ever-present prairie windstorms across the province. Aberhart set up study groups, circulated pamphlets, and made hundreds of speeches, preaching his inflationary message to anyone who would listen. It was only a matter of time before the religious crusade turned into a political one and Aberhart founded a party to contest the next provincial election.

The Alberta election of 1935 could not have come at a better time for Aberhart. The Premier of the province, John Brownlee, was in the process of losing a paternity suit brought by his housemaid. His Minister of Public Works was deeply involved in a messy divorce case. The Government was in a shambles, demoralized, scandal-ridden. With no viable opposition, the Social Credit party was merely filling a vacuum. It won a stunning victory, carrying sixty-three seats out of the seventy in the legislature. But as Premier Aberhart soon discovered, Social Credit was easier to preach than to practise. When, after some eighteen months in office, he eventually got around to introducing policies based on Social Credit theories, all were disallowed by the federal authorities or by the courts. Aberhart did pass major legislation to reduce debts and mortgages, but in the end, what happened was what Aberhart vowed never would: its fervour spent, Social Credit became just another political party. It would provide

J.S. Woodsworth, first leader of the C.C.F.
(C-34443/Public Archives Canada)

William Aberhart, Premier of Alberta.
(C-16476/Public Archives Canada)

Social Credit was viewed with scorn — outside of Alberta.

Dale's Social Crediters

Alberta with a solid, free-enterprise, conservative government for the next generation, but its theories were now only useful as campaign rhetoric. The eternal verities of Social Credit were never to be implemented.

The political ferment of these years was, surprisingly, matched by an unparalleled cultural activity. The 1920s and '30s were perhaps the golden years of Canadian art. The Group of Seven had come together, and such artists as David Milne, Emily Carr, and Fred Varley were winning an audience. In addition, more than seven hundred Canadian novels were published in these years. Publishing houses such as Ryerson, Gage, Macmillan, McClelland and Stewart, and Musson were actively searching for Canadian authors. Indeed, some of those authors, in particular Frederick Philip Grove, Mazo de la Roche, and Morley Callaghan, were already well known. Inspired by Ringuet's watershed novel *Thirty Acres*, the first full-scale, realistic treatment of the life of the Quebec farmer, a new generation of nationalistic French-Canadian writers came into being. The cauldron of the Depression was also forging a group of young writers who would soon revolutionize Canadian literature — Hugh MacLennan, A.M. Klein, Gabrielle Roy, and Frank Scott, to name but a few.

Ironically, though there was more ideological writing than ever before, the typical Canadian novel of the 1930s was escapist — an adventure, a historical romance, or a comedy. The grief of the decade, noted one commentator, was too overwhelming to write about. With the exception of *As For Me and My House* by Sinclair Ross, most of the good fiction about the Depression was written much later, by a younger generation. Clearly those living through it found it difficult to write about. When they could afford it, Canadians flocked to Hollywood movies; more often, they huddled around their radios listening to American comedy and variety shows. Even the formation of the Canadian Broadcasting Corporation could do little to stop the swamping effects of the American cultural juggernaut. In the depths of the Depression people wanted to forget, to be entertained; no one could do it better, it seemed, than the Americans.

With the economy worsening, western sectionalism on the rise again, new parties appearing all over, and with every Conservative provincial government gone, R.B. Bennett for the first time began to doubt his own policies. The champion of the status quo, the darling of the right, the man who advocated crushing Communists under "the iron heel of capitalism" suddenly, without warning, moved dramatically to the left. He had been disturbed by the allegations of his Minister of Trade and Commerce, H.H. Stevens, who claimed to have uncovered frightening evidence of price-fixing, starvation wages, barbaric working conditions, and stock fraud in the practices of large corporations. When Stevens went public with his indictment of the outrages of the capitalist system, he was forced out of the Cabinet and shortly thereafter set up his own Reconstruction party. Nonetheless, the Prime Minister could not ignore Stevens' popularity and the popular conviction that captains of industry, with whom he had for so long had a symbiotic relationship, were venal and corrupt. He now began to listen more intently to his brother-in-law, W.D. Herridge, the Canadian Minister to the United States, who was urging him to introduce into Canada some aspects of President Franklin Delano Roosevelt's New Deal.

Once convinced, the Prime Minister did not delay. Early in January, 1935, he stunned the public — as well as his Cabinet and caucus — with a series of five coast-to-coast radio broadcasts that called for nothing less than a new society. The old order, he announced, was gone and would never return. He advocated unemployment insurance, subsidized housing, and minimum wage legislation. The capitalist system was in desperate need of reform, he charged, and he was prepared to reform it. An unkind observer remarked that Bennett had discovered the evils of capitalism only after he had accumulated his millions. However, true to his word, within a matter of weeks the Prime Minister brought into the House the most far-reaching reform package ever introduced by any Canadian government. Legislation was passed to fix minimum wages and maximum hours, to establish unemployment insurance, and to give the government control over prices, business practices, and marketing conditions. Though not as radical as his radio talks, the legislation was still enough to frighten every Conservative in the country. "There could only be one explanation," said a prominent Tory. "The Prime Minister has gone mad."

Mad or not, Bennett knew he had to do something to save the country and his own political career. Elections were looming, and he could hardly go to the people on his record. After all, he had won an election five years before by promising to end unemployment. Now he was confronted with the worst unemployment in the country's history. His New Deal was a last, desperate attempt to salvage another term. Radio broadcasts had worked for Roosevelt; in Alberta they were performing miracles for Aberhart. Bennett was convinced they would do the same for him. But it was too late for what Woodsworth called "a deathbed conversion." Bennett had presided over the worst five years in Canadian history. The people of Canada were determined that he would not preside over another five.

On October 14, 1935, they got their chance. In a massive landslide vote the government of R.B. Bennett was swept away. Rarely has so unpopular a government faced an electorate; and it was a government badly divided. Many of his Cabinet ministers were opposed to Bennett's new economic and social policies. Tories throughout the country were confused and aghast at the new turn their party had taken. To them Bennett's policy was communistic. Many would stay home rather than vote. In truth, except for a slogan — "King or Chaos" — the Liberals had no platform; they did not need one. With Stevens' Reconstruction party successfully wooing away four hundred thousand potential Conservative voters, the Tories were nearly wiped out. They won only 40 seats, compared to the Liberals' 173. Not knowing what to expect from the suddenly unpredictable Bennett, the Canadian electorate took the safe path and opted for the dull, cautious, but eminently reliable Mackenzie King.

Five years in the Opposition seemed not to have changed Mackenzie King in the slightest. The magnitude of the Depression still escaped him. Campaigning in 1935, he sounded like the discredited Herbert Hoover: "What is needed more than a change of economic structure," he said, "is a change of heart." Unemployment was not the result of defects in the system, he claimed. Rather it was caused by human selfishness and greed. It was clear that King was far less likely to tamper with the system than was Bennett. Echoing the Bennett of 1930, he declared that balancing the budget and slashing government spending would start Canada back on the road to prosperity. All he would do to accelerate matters was to lower the tariff and to sign a trade agreement with the United States. To aid the unemployed who were still wandering around the country or sitting out the Depression in the work camps, he could think of nothing better than to close the camps, which he found too expensive. Predictably, an army of ten thousand homeless men were again soon on the march, looking for work and raising old fears of disorder. However, what disturbed him most was the crisis in federal-provincial financial relations. The four western provinces owed the federal government over $115 000 000 and could not pay back a penny. King vowed that they would be making no further raids on the federal treasury.

But how else could the provinces function unless they were funded from Ottawa? They had many responsibilities but no money. Under the British North America Act the provinces had very limited power to tax; yet it was they who bore the burden of the straitened times. The Depression had made it clear that the federal system was badly lopsided: the provinces had most of the pressing tasks — welfare services, relief payments, education, highway construction — but few sources of revenue, while the federal government had an almost unlimited taxing power but, under the constitution, could not infringe on the jurisdiction of the provinces. Indeed, much of Bennett's ill-fated New Deal legislation was rejected by the courts because it undertook activities in areas that were exclusively under provincial control. Thus Ottawa, even if it had the will, did not have the power to adopt measures which might alleviate the economic and social disasters that were crippling the nation. With the imminent possibility of some provinces going bankrupt, King was forced into action. He would not grant any more loans to the provinces, since to him it would be "simply sending good money after bad money"; furthermore, it would make it impossible for him to achieve his goal of balancing the federal budget. Instead he appointed a Royal Commission on Dominion-Provincial Relations under the Chief Justice of Ontario, Newton Rowell, to investigate and make recommendations concerning the constitutional and financial relations between Ottawa and the provinces. The Commission did not report until 1940.

Labour Organization

Rather than uniting Canada in a crusade against a common enemy, the Depression had exacerbated regional and provincial disparities. Emboldened by the acute conditions and their growing social responsibilities, the provinces rose up to challenge Ottawa. The provincial premiers of the 1930s were unique products of the Depression. For the most part bitter and resentful of their treatment at the hands of Ottawa, they were colourful, radical, and eccentric, and so were many of their policies. Some, such as Aberhart in Alberta and Maurice Duplessis in Quebec, founded new parties to express their discontent; others, such as T. Dufferin Pattullo in British Columbia and Mitchell Hepburn in Ontario, kept the old party names but undertook programs which had little in common with their traditional party platforms.

Born not too far from Mackenzie King's birthplace in southwestern Ontario, "Duff" Pattullo had made a name for himself in British Columbia as a dynamic entrepreneur. He was elected Premier in 1933 and at once attempted to introduce "a little New Deal" policy in British Columbia. "Work and Wages" was his slogan, and it swept the province. His was the most vigorous program of its kind in Canada. But it was dependent on federal funds, few of which were forthcoming from the tight-fisted administrators in Ottawa. Mackenzie King thought he could hoard his way out of the Depression; Pattullo wanted to spend his way out. His was a liberalism totally unrecognizable to the Prime Minister.

Even more unrecognizable, and much more dangerous, was the liber-

Mitch Hepburn (right) and Maurice Duplessis, Premiers of Ontario and Quebec in the late 1930s. (C-19518/Public Archives Canada)

alism of the Premier of Ontario, Mitch Hepburn. An onion farmer from the St. Thomas area, he had come to power on a radical program, promising "to swing to the left" and to fight for "the dispossessed and oppressed." However, it was not long after he took office that he began to fight against them. Under the influence of the industrial magnates of the province, he launched a crusade against a militant American industrial union, the Congress of Industrial Organizations (C.I.O.), which was threatening to organize the province's industries and mines. When King refused to send in the R.C.M.P. to help Hepburn put down a peaceful strike at the General Motors plant in Oshawa, the Ontario Premier declared war on the federal government. He organized his own antilabour police force — in Oshawa they were known as "Hepburn's Hussars," or the "Sons of Mitch's" — so he would not have to rely on "cowardly" federal authorities "when the security of Ontario is threatened." King, he said, was a "tin pot dictator" who was "living in a past age, a generation without any hope of betterment." He even thundered that he would push the Prime Minister through a washing-machine wringer.

Indeed, Hepburn had much to fear from the newly revivified labour movements that were threatening not only to organize workers under the nose of his wealthy cronies, but to turn the industrial relations system of his province — and perhaps of all Canada — upside down. For trade unions, as for everyone else, the Depression had been traumatic. Membership plummeted as jobs disappeared. Long-established locals vanished throughout the country. Never had the union movement been so immobilized. Indeed, only one union, the Workers Unity League, seemed to be functioning.

Created by the Communist Party, the W.U.L. consisted of industrial unions in the garment, lumber, mining, and textile industries. Its scores of devoted organizers provided the leadership for most of the important labour struggles of the period, including the bloody Estevan-Bienfait strike in which police killed three strikers, and the walkout of furniture workers and chicken-pluckers in Stratford, Ontario, which was put down only with the help of troops and armoured cars. By 1935, when it was disbanded on orders from the Soviet Union, it claimed a membership of some forty thousand, the majority of whom were not Communists.

In that same year, however, a year in which the Canadian labour movement was at its nadir with fewer members that at any time since the end of the war, a new labour organization was being created in the United States that would ultimately revolutionize trade unionism in Canada. Under the leadership of the fiery leader of the United Mine Workers, John L. Lewis, a new labour centre, the Committee for Industrial Organization, began a whirlwind campaign to organize industrial workers. In two short years it had enrolled millions of unskilled, previously unorganized workers in automobile, steel, meat packing, and other plants throughout America.

Enviously eyeing the C.I.O.'s success, Canadian workers — many of them one-time activists in the W.U.L. — began organizing C.I.O. unions north of the border without the permission, or knowledge, of the C.I.O. leadership. Within months, the C.I.O. had hundreds of new members and dozens of new unions it knew nothing about. Not one cent of C.I.O. money, not one C.I.O. organizer, not one note of C.I.O. encouragement had crossed the border to help in this campaign. Canadians were on their own.

The turning point for the C.I.O. in Canada, which changed its rather limited organizing campaign into a passionate crusade, occurred at Oshawa, Ontario, in April of 1937. There, four thousand workers of the huge General Motors plant went out on strike and asked the C.I.O. and its affiliate, the United Automobile Workers, for assistance. They received one organizer and no money. Despite the C.I.O.'s lack of support, and despite the desperate efforts of the Premier of Ontario to crush the strike and keep the C.I.O. out of Ontario, the strikers persevered and won a dramatic victory. Spurred on by this triumph, the C.I.O. began a vast organizational campaign largely in the industrial areas of Ontario, and within a year it had organized thousands of workers. A renewed sense of militancy and idealism permeated Canadian labour for the first time since the end of the Winnipeg Strike.

For the workers of Canada, C.I.O. was a magic name. Wherever they heard it they flocked; whoever used it, they trusted. Canadian workers obviously felt that the C.I.O. magic would rub off on them, that what the C.I.O. was achieving for its members in the United States it would also achieve for its members in Canada. For the first time unions were appearing in industries that were traditionally thought to be unorganizable: there were now unions for steel workers, automobile workers, electrical workers, rubber workers, packing-house workers, pulp and paper workers, lumber and sawmill workers, and mine and smelter workers. The C.I.O. had clearly revolutionized Canadian labour; it had created a powerful, aggressive and, most important, viable industrial union movement. It had, in effect, organized not only the unorganized but, as well, those thought to be unorganizable.[10]

It was largely to destroy the C.I.O. before it became a real threat that Hepburn began exploring the possibility of an alliance with the Premier of Quebec, Maurice Duplessis. Like Hepburn, Duplessis had come into office promising reform; once in power he conveniently forgot all his promises. The Depression had proved to be a boon for French-Canadian nationalism, for it brought home to the Québécois that the economy of their province was controlled by Americans and English Canadians. Taking advantage of the situation, Duplessis, the clever and opportunistic leader of the Conservative party of Quebec, formed an alliance with the *nationalistes* and created a new political party, the Union nationale. By advocating a wide range of economic, social, and political changes, and by holding out hope of restoring control of the province's economy to French Canadians, the Union nationale won a smashing victory in 1936. But Duplessis was soon collaborating with American and other foreign capitalists who wished to invest in his province, allowing them to exploit its

10. For an overview of the labour movement in the period, see Irving Abella, *Nationalism, Communism and Canadian Labour* (Toronto, 1973); Irving Abella, ed., *On Strike* (Toronto, 1974); and Gad Horowitz, *Canadian Labour in Politics* (Toronto, 1966).

resources and workers with little government interference. Reneging on his commitments for change, Duplessis exploited anti-Communist sentiment in his province by introducing such measures as the Padlock Law, which made it illegal to use a house "to propagate communism." Joining Hepburn in what one critic called "Canada's unholy alliance," he accused the federal government of undermining provincial autonomy and threatening the survival of French Canada.

For King, of all the political leaders in the country Duplessis was much the most frightening. As the leader of the forces of French-Canadian nationalism, he was the greatest threat to national unity and to the unity of the Liberal party; and in the late 1930s, with another European war in the offing, King could think of little else. If war was to come, then Canada must be united. Ironically, because of his concern for Canadian unity, King contributed to making it more likely that there would be a war.[11]

"Ready, Aye Ready" Again

With the rise of Nazism, the election of Adolf Hitler, the growing militarization of Germany, and its stated intent to expand into areas it thought should belong to the Reich, it was clear that trouble was once again brewing in Europe. Yet Mackenzie King publicly took little note of these events. To him foreign policy was divisive.

In October, 1935, Italy invaded Ethiopia. At the League the Canadian delegate, Dr. W.A. Riddell, took a lead in the attempt to apply sanctions against Mussolini's Government to force it to withdraw. At the height of the crisis, the Bennett Government was defeated. Caught without instructions, the Canadian delegation assumed that the policy would not change and thus proposed that oil be included in the materials under embargo. An oil embargo, as Mussolini later admitted, would have seriously hampered the invasion. If some other country had proposed these sanctions, Canada might have accepted them, but King did not intend to take the initiative. He told a reporter that Riddell deserved "a good spanking," and, when the League committee continued to debate the "Canadian resolution," the exasperated King finally told the press that Riddell had been acting on his own. King was prepared to follow, not to lead, since

11. On provincial politics, the material is varied and often thin. Conrad Black's *Duplessis* (Toronto, 1977), is a good, very opinionated study. Neil McKenty, *Mitch Hepburn* (Toronto, 1967), is entertaining, while Kendle's *Bracken* is thorough. There are no good studies of Maritime premiers for this period, and there is only article literature on the West. See *A Reader's Guide to Canadian History*, vol. II, for details.

leadership on such a sensitive matter might cause serious divisions within the country. The Italian dictator, King knew, had many admirers in Canada, especially in Quebec. In the end, the League never did agree to impose oil sanctions and Italy went on to conquer all of Ethiopia. Soon Hitler was taking over territories in Europe which he thought belonged to Germany.

In the Ethiopian crisis, King likely was a better reflection of Canadian opinion than Riddell. He knew most Canadians were not prepared to fight for the principle of collective security. They were in no mood to save either Ethiopia or the League. Nor were they in any mood to do anything about Hitler. The Primer Minister himself, after a visit with the Fuhrer, found him to be "a simple sort of peasant, not very intelligent and no serious danger to anyone."

A few Canadians thought differently. Led by John Dafoe of Winnipeg's *Free Press*, they urged the Prime Minister to take Hitler more seriously. Nazism, they warned, was a danger to world peace. Some Canadians were prepared to use more than words in their fight against fascism. Well over a thousand, many of them immigrants straight out of the relief camps, travelled to Spain in 1936 to fight for the Republican Government against the fascist insurgents of General Franco. The Spanish Civil War, to them and to countless others, was a veritable Armageddon, the ultimate confrontation between good and evil, light and darkness. Their fight was heroic but doomed. The bullets and bayonets of the Canadian Mackenzie-Papineau Battalion were no match for fascist bombs and tanks. More than a third of these Canadians never came back. One who did was Dr. Norman Bethune, a genuine war hero, who returned to warn an apathetic country of the evils of fascism. Few listened.

To the very end the Canadian Government supported the appeasement policies of the British Prime Minister, Neville Chamberlain; it was almost the only British policy with which King had agreed since he first became Prime Minister in 1921. Yet in 1938 he refused to allow the Royal Air Force to train its pilots in Canada lest this automatically involve Canada in any forthcoming war. King knew Duplessis and other French Canadians would have some choice words about British pilots training in Canada. In his battle for national unity, he could not risk Quebec's anger. In this he succeeded brilliantly. When war came in September, 1939, the Parliament of Canada — and the country itself — were united behind their Prime Minister. One week after Britain declared war a technically neutral Canada followed suit. Even though everyone knew that once Britain went to war Canada would go to war too, the formalities were observed to the very end. After a serious debate, Parliament, without a recorded vote, decided in favour of war. For the second time in a generation, the country was at war, and for much the same reason — the continuing sentimental link with Great Britain. Autonomous Canada might be, but when the mother country was in trouble, "ready, aye, ready" seemed the only possible response.

Chapter VII

A
Nation
of
Immigrants

In 1896, after twenty-five years of depression and gloom, prosperity
returned to Canada. The pessimism of the preceding generation was
replaced with an apparently boundless and hopelessly naive optimism.
As one breathless historian put it, "In the year in which Laurier Liberalism gained power, Canada was born again." Indeed the Prime Minister
himself was carried away; the twentieth century, he promised the nation,
would be Canada's. A speaker to the Canadian Club in Winnipeg reflected
the spirit of the times: "In forty/fifty years Canada will have a population
of forty/fifty millions and Saskatchewan and Alberta will be greater than
Ontario in population and Winnipeg will have surpassed Toronto and
Montreal." And why should they not have been optimistic? After two
decades of bust, the long-awaited boom had begun.

For many, it was too late. So many Canadians had lost hope that fortune would ever smile on Canada again that well over a million left their
farms and homes and made their way across the border to the United
States, so many, in fact, that a prominent Liberal politician, Sir Richard
Cartwright, was moved to remark that the Dominion of Canada that had
begun in Lamentations (the book of the Bible from which the word Dominion was taken) seemed to be ending in Exodus. And with reason. In the
twenty years before 1900 more people left Canada than came, 1 600 000
emigrating to the United States and only 1 225 000 arriving from overseas. Who could blame them for leaving? For farmers the great American

plains offered better land, to say nothing of a better climate and standard of living. And for thousands of penurious French Canadians unable to eke an existence out of their marginal lands, the factories and textile mills of New England gave new hope. So long as America remained hospitable, there seemed little reason for Canadians without jobs or with failing farms not to go, and even less reason for European immigrants to come.

However, by the dawn of the new century events outside of Canada began almost imperceptibly to alter the course of her history. Most of the fertile American land had been settled and the frontier was rapidly closing. The worldwide depression was lifting, and there were now new markets and higher prices for Canadian goods. With cheap land no longer available in the United States, prospective immigrants for the first time began to look at what Canada had to offer. Except for the criminal, the diseased, and the pauper, Canada was open to anyone — except, of course, for Chinese, who had to pay a $50 head tax. Aside from that, Canada had no immigration restrictions; until 1900 she scarcely needed any. What she needed, rather, were incentives.

Sifton and Immigration

The man appointed by Laurier to provide these incentives and to sell Canada to prospective immigrants was a forceful young businessman, the Minister of the Interior, Clifford Sifton. Indeed, Sifton saw his task as basically salesmanship. Immigrants, he said, had to be aggressively enticed. "In my judgement . . . the immigration work has to be carried out in the same manner as the sale of any commodity; just as soon as you stop advertising and missionary work, the movement is going to stop," he told the House of Commons. Born in Ontario, Sifton had moved to Manitoba in 1880 to make his fortune. Having done that, he returned to the East with a sense of mission. Determined to convince Ottawa that the future of the nation was dependent on the rapid development of the West, he agreed in 1896 to join the new Laurier administration. Above all, he was committed to bringing into the West the type of settler who could best adapt to the rigours of pioneer life. Like many transplanted Easterners, he had become a passionate Westerner, and he set about devising an immigration policy which was unashamedly designed to benefit western Canada. "Our desire," he told the Prime Minister, "is to promote the immigration of farmers and farm labourers." Urban immigrants, he said, were "undesirable from every standpoint," and would not contribute "in any way whatever to the . . . development of natural resources and the

Clifford Sifton, the man who encouraged immigrants to populate the West.
(PA-27942/Public Archives Canada)

increase of production of wealth from these resources." He specifically ordered Canadian immigration officials to try to prevent the influx of "labouring men and mechanics." The only good immigrant to Sifton was the homesteader. "Agriculture," he argued, was "the foundation of all real and enduring progress on the part of Canada." "Only farmers need apply" was the operating slogan of Sifton's immigration policy.[1]

As soon as he came into office Sifton galvanized the Immigration Branch, for years a backwater of government service. It was, he lamented, "a department of delay, a department of circumlocution, a department in which people could not get business done, a department which tried a man to death who undertook to get any business transacted with it." New blood replaced the stodgy time-watchers who had sat at their desks doing nothing under previous administrations. Seemingly limitless amounts of money were poured into the branch to pay for the new appointments, to launch massive advertising campaigns for immigrants in the United States, Great Britain, and continental Europe, and to subsidize tours of western Canada by foreign journalists. Each new settler was promised 160 acres of free land — though free did not necessarily mean arable, as many colonists were to discover — in western Canada. Agents were sent to nations with a large pool of potential immigrants to spread the word about opportunities in Canada and steamship passenger representatives were offered large bonuses for encouraging immigrants to choose Canada. Exhibitions throughout the world often contained large displays outlining the advantages of moving to Canada. There was hardly a method not tried by the creative Sifton to encourage immigrants from those countries he believed would provide western Canada with the young, hardy, aggressive pioneers she so desperately needed. Indeed, some of his arrangements were highly irregular, though extremely successful. The most notorious of these was the North American Trading Company.

Many European nations were incensed over the vigorous campaign for their citizens being mounted by the Canadian Government. Because many of the settlers Sifton wanted were precisely the ones these countries were loathe to lose, laws were passed to restrict emigration. Some governments even launched their own advertising campaigns to counter the activi-

1. See on immigration policy in the Sifton period, D.J. Hall, *Clifford Sifton*, vol. I (Vancouver, 1981), and vol. II (Vancouver, 1985); R.C. Brown and R. Cook, *Canada 1896-1921* (Toronto, 1974); K. Bicha, *The American Farmer and the Canadian West 1896-1914* (Lawrence, 1972); and H. Troper, *Only Farmers Need Apply (Toronto, 1972)*. General studies include *D.C. Corbett, Canada's Immigration Policy: A Critique* (Toronto, 1957), and Norman Macdonald, *Canada: Immigration and Colonization, 1841-1903* (Toronto, 1966).

ties of Canadian agents. In France, for example, all government officials, including school teachers and postal clerks, were ordered to warn potential immigrants of the dangers of emigrating to Canada. The greatest ally for most of these countries, the Canadian climate, was continuously used in the struggle to keep Europeans at home. Sifton had even seriously considered banning the publication of prairie temperatures lest they frighten off prospective immigrants. In order to overcome these obstacles, Canadian officials signed a secret agreement with a group of shipping agents calling themselves the North Atlantic Trading Company, who agreed to direct agricultural immigrants to Canada. In return the Canadian Government promised to pay a large bonus for each immigrant delivered. In the seven years of its existence, the company brought over seventy thousand immigrants to Canada. And much to Sifton's delight, it winnowed the pick of the immigrant crop for Canada, while in his words, sending the "riff-raff" elsewhere. A little bit of flim-flammery was a cheap price to pay for such a large number of high-quality immigrants.

Perhaps Sifton's greatest success was in reversing the tide of emigration to the United States. Prodded by an army of Canadian immigration agents, by a profusion of pamphlets describing the wonders of "The Last, Best West," and by offers of free trips and free land, hundreds of thousands of American farmers crossed the border and took up new homes in the Canadian West. These were, in Sifton's view, "of the finest quality and the most desirable settlers."

Much less successful was his attempt to recruit British agriculturalists. Though every farmer in the north of England and Scotland was sent a brochure graphically outlining the advantages of emigration to Canada, few responded. Rather, much to the Interior Minister's chagrin, large numbers of British labourers, artisans, and "city types," precisely the people he did not want, decided now was the opportune moment for them to move to the beckoning Dominion. To Sifton, these men, who knew nothing about farming, did not have the "fibre" to be successful pioneers; putting them on the frontier would be "a crime." Crime or not, they came by the hundreds of thousands. In 1907 alone, almost 125 000 Britons arrived, more than ten times the number who had come only eight years before.

However, undoubtedly the most innovative and radical of Sifton's schemes was his encouragement of continental European immigration. His ideal immigrant was "a stalwart peasant in a sheepskin coat, born of the soil, whose forefathers have been farmers for ten generations, with a stout wife and a half-dozen children." Sifton did not care whether he was

These Doukhobor women were hitched to a plow, twenty-four to the team.
(C-681/Public Archives Canada)

The Canadian Government Emigration Offices in London helped supply immi-
grants during the boom years of the century. (C-63257/Public Archives Canada)

of British stock, so long as he was hale, hardy, and ready to cultivate the soil. Nor did he care whether these immigrants could read or write; for the work he had in mind for them, it did not matter. These Poles, Ukrainians, Slavs, and Russians were slated to open up the vast, isolated, largely unsettled areas of the Canadian West. Sifton's orders were clear: immigration agents were to opt for brawn over brain, strong backs over strong minds. All the eastern European peasant asked for was *vilni zemli* — free land — and a place where, in the words of one, "we do not have to bow our heads to no one." In Canada he got both.

In return these immigrants not only cleared and cultivated huge areas of the Canadian West, but they also built the railways, constructed the roads, cut the timber, and mined the coal which allowed the great western boom to continue; though most of them came to Canada to take up land, they were more likely to take up picks and shovels. Despite Sifton's emphasis on agricultural immigrants, many who arrived were neither able nor willing to settle on the land. In order to build up a stake for homesteads, many were forced to become wage labourers; others found they could only survive the first few difficult years of farming by working on railway gangs or construction crews. These immigrants provided the cheap labour many industrialists and government officials thought was necessary for Canada's expanding industrial development.

The Open Door

Ironically, the most important determinant of immigration policy in these years was the business community. They lobbied incessantly and successfully for an open door policy. Anyone who wanted, so long as he was healthy, unskilled, and preferably illiterate, should be allowed to come to Canada. What industrialists wished above all else was to have a cheap, pliant labour force. And who could possibly be cheaper and more pliant than the hungry, confused, unlettered, docile southern and eastern European immigrants? This vast, apparently limitless source of manpower would assure the business community that labour costs would remain low and that the nascent Canadian trade union movement would be aborted.

In the minds of most Canadians these immigrants were both unassimilable and unorganizable. They would remain in Canada as long as their work was needed; when it no longer was, they could return home. And indeed, many immigrants shared this belief. They saw themseles as temporary sojourners coming to Canada to earn enough money to return home, in the words of one young Italian labourer, to "live like a prince"; they had arrived in Canada simply to improve their situation at home. So committed were they to returning that many had left their families behind in the old country. Unfortunately, most found their wages so low they could barely survive in Canada, let alone put some aside for the journey home. Many, perhaps most, in fact, became immigrants and eventually brought their families over to Canada.

And indeed, in the booming early years of the twentieth century the work of these migrants was essential. Two transcontinental railways were being rapidly pushed across the West. New mines and smelters were opening up all over the country. Factories were producing more than ever before. These were all labour-intensive industries which relied on low-paid workers. The large British immigration in this period could not satisfy this need. Most immigrants from the United Kingdom came with skills and a union background; both were anathema to Canadian employers. According to the president of the C.P.R., Canada needed men who were "accustomed to roughing it." It would be a huge mistake, he warned, to bring in British immigrants "who came here expecting to get high wages, a feather bed and a bath tub." They were not, he and his colleagues agreed, suited to frontier conditions. What Canada needed, the railway men stressed, were more Europeans, particularly Ukrainians. These had proven to be obedient and industrious workers who rarely complained about the admittedly deplorable work camp conditions, perhaps because they could not speak English.

Railway magnates were not alone in pushing for unlimited immigration. Eastern manufacturing interests saw a western hinterland full of immigrants as a growing market for their goods, as well as a source of valuable raw materials. Naturally they wanted their own low-cost labour force, particularly because of the inroads organized labour seemed to be making in industrial centres in Ontario and Quebec. But they were also in need of skilled workers, and in 1903 a group of them set up an unofficial Canadian Labour Bureau in London, ironically in the same building as the offices of the Immigration Branch. The latter took only agricultural workers, the former only industrial ones. A frustrated Sifton raged against the attempts to bring in "a lot of helpless people being lodged in cities and towns." Though he attempted to shut down the bureau, there was little he could do. The needs of an expanding capitalist labour market had to be met, and they could not be if Canada were to restrict itself to agricultural settlers.

So great was the demand for unskilled, transient labour — the so-called "navvies" — that some industrialists relied on subcontractors or *padroni* to supply the necessary bodies. These men, through connections overseas, brought over thousands of young Italians, directly from their homeland or from the United States, with promises of work at high wages. Once in Canada, the promises often dissipated, and the migrant workers found themselves at the mercy of callous employers. They were horribly exploited, their pay pitiable and their work back-breaking. But, particularly for railway contractors and mine operators, they were necessary, so long as they were in the bush or in the pits doing their jobs. However, in Canada's cities they were pariahs, totally unacceptable. Thus, when several hundred suddenly appeared without jobs in Montreal in 1904, popular opinion forced a royal commission enquiry into the entire *padrone* system. It achieved nothing; the exploitation continued. Nonetheless, many of the young Italian men who came over were able to return home with a substantial nest egg. All they left behind was their health.

Obviously not all Canadians endorsed an open door immigration policy. The Minister of the Interior, Frank Oliver, who took over in 1905 after Sifton's resignation, favoured a more restrictionist policy. Yet even he was unable to stop the flood of newcomers landing almost daily in Halifax, Quebec City, or Montreal. In Oliver's jaundiced view, these migrants were "the off-scourings and dregs of society." But with passenger agents still being paid to divert immigrants to Canada, and with industrialists still in need of workers, even the opposition of the Minister responsible for immigration could be overridden.

Most vociferous in its opposition to large-scale immigration was the Canadian labour movement. Though small in numbers it did have some influence which it desperately sought to use to limit the number of job-hungry foreigners coming to Canada's shores. Some of these had found themselves being used as strike-breakers; others replaced workers whose pay demands were too high; most were used as an ever-present threat to keep workers' expectations within limits. Frightened, penniless, hungry, they were mercilessly exploited by many employers. The protests of the trade union movement made little headway in Government circles. All the labour movement could do was send over representatives to England to warn potential immigrants of the deceptive activities of Canadian shipping and employment agencies.

Few paid them any attention. With the onset of a worldwide depression in 1907, thousands of unemployed British workers decided that the time had come to start their lives anew in Canada, especially since their passage overseas was being covered by local charities who wished to rid themselves of their heavy relief obligations. Many of these were, in the words of Frank Oliver, "a drag on the labour market from misfortune, incompetence or indifference." Indeed, not only did the British urban immigrant face much prejudice on his arrival in Canada — the *Edmonton Journal* warned in 1907 that "their presence [was] a mistake" — but as the depression deepened, the federal government had no hesitation in sending back over a thousand of these newcomers, who made up 70 per cent of those deported in 1908.

The labour movement had more success in restricting the flow of an even more worrisome stream of immigrants, the Orientals. No one worked harder and for less than did the Chinese, and no group of immigrants was more in demand by the railway, mining, lumber, and fishing interests of the country, particularly in British Columbia. By 1900 almost 11 per cent of that province's population was Asiatic. Legislative efforts to keep Orientals out had proved futile. In 1885 Chinese immigrants were compelled to pay a head tax of $50; fifteen years later it was increased to $100; in 1903 it was raised to a staggering $500. But still they came, lured by the promise of good fortune in the "Land of the Golden Mountains." There was a ferocious anti-Oriental sentiment throughout the province, fueled by those who feared that British Columbia would soon be taken over by the Chinese. "The yellow hordes," one newspaper warned, would take over "this great big province — a land virtually flowing with milk and honey" and push out the "white British subjects."

More rancorous was the labour press. Not only did the trade unions fear that the Chinese would create a "mongrelized nation," but they worried as well that Orientals would totally undermine the labour movement. "They are . . . fitted to become all too dangerous competitors in the labour market," warned one labour leader. Their "docile servility . . . renders them doubly dangerous as the willing tools whereby grasping and tyrannical employers grind down all labour to the lowest living point." A labour newspaper rhetorically asked, "What is in store for us as an Anglo-Saxon community? With the mongols in our mines, workshops, forests and on railroads and tilling our farms, what is to become of our white labourers, miners, and mechanics?" Most of the province's white population, with the significant exception of its industrialists, regarded the Orientals as an economic and cultural challenge, as unassimilable, and as severe obstructions to both national unity and a homogeneous society.

These sentiments were fully supported by a royal commission set up by the Laurier Government in 1902. The Chinese, it reported, were:

> . . . drawn from the poorer classes, reared in poverty where a few cents a day represent the earnings which must suffice for a family; accustomed to

crowd together in small tenements or huts, close, unhealthy and filthy, . . . with no desire to conform to Western ideas. They form . . . a foreign substance within, but not of our body politic, with no love for our laws and institutions; a people that will not assimilate or become an integral part of our race and nation . . . they are a continual menace to health . . . their effect on the rest of the community is bad. They pay no fair proportion of the taxes of the country. They keep out immigrants who would become permanent citizens, and create conditions inimical to labour and dangerous to the industrial peace of the community. . . . They are unfit for full citizenship. . . . They . . . are obnoxious to a free community and dangerous to the state.

As a result of the furor, the Laurier Government clamped down on Chinese immigration. Not to be outflanked, the province's business leaders, led by the C.P.R., began bringing in large numbers of Japanese and East Indians to do the heavy labour once done by the Chinese workers. Labour regarded the Japanese as an even more serious threat since they were more aggressive in going after skilled jobs and were supported by a home government whose good will was being courted by both Canadian and British officials. The arrival of so many Japanese and "Hindoos" (though most of the Indian immigrants were, in fact, Sikhs) offended nativist feeling in the province. Led by the chauvinistic Asiatic Exclusion League, a series of vast demonstrations and parades were held in Vancouver in 1907 to protest the steadily increasing flow of "brown and yellow" immigrants. Sparked by a series of demagogic speeches, a rally on June 7 turned into a full-scale riot as mobs descended on the Chinese and Japanese parts of the city, attacking any helpless Oriental who fell into their hands, breaking windows and destroying property. As a result of this uprising, the Laurier Government reluctantly placed severe restrictions on the entry of Oriental immigrants into Canada.

The most severe challenge to these restrictions arose in May, 1914, when a boatload of 376 East Indians arrived in Vancouver demanding to be admitted. Should these be accepted, warned a Vancouver newspaper, then the remaining three hundred million "natives of India . . . who have the same rights as these . . . would have the same claim." Again British Columbia was aflame. For over two months the ship, the *Komagata Maru*, lay in the harbour unable to dock while government officials decided what to do. For the people of British Columbia there was no question what should be done: the East Indians should be sent back home. To allow Orientals in, H.H. Stevens, a Conservative M.P. and later a key minister in the Bennett Government, told a large rally, would leave "not a vestige of the civilization of which we are so proud." Canada must go as far as possible, he urged his receptive audience, "to keep [itself] pure and free from the taint of other peoples." Attempts to deport some of the East Indians were foiled when the passengers seized control of the ship and repulsed Vancouver police and immigration officers who tried to board it. As tensions rose on the mainland, the Canadian navy went into action. The training ship *Rainbow*, which had just been acquired for Laurier's navy, pulled alongside the boat and escorted it out to sea while cheering thousands lined the waterfront. Just days before the outbreak of World War I, Canada had been saved from an invasion more dangerous than any the Germans could mount. British Columbia once again had made it clear that it was going to remain just that — British.

The citizens of Canada's westernmost province were not alone in their concern for their Anglo-Saxon heritage. Throughout the country questions were being asked about the impact on Canada of the large immigration movements that Sifton had initiated. A Calgary newspaper accused him of trying to build a nation "on the lines of the Tower of Babel, where the Lord confounded the language so that people might not understand one another's speech." To the Canadian economist and humourist Stephen Leacock, European immigrants "were herds of the proletariat of Europe, the lowest classes of industrial society . . . indifferent material from which to build the commonwealth of the future." These voices were not alone. Under Laurier and Sifton, they cried, Canada's ethnic priorities were askew. From the beginning Canadian Governments had divided the world into two categories, at least for purposes of immigration: preferred nations, such as the United States, Great Britain, and, to lesser extents, France, Scandinavia, the Low Countries, and Germany, whose immigrants were always welcome; and the nonpreferred peoples, such as southern and eastern Europeans, Asiatics, and Jews, whose arrival in Canada was officially discouraged. To many Canadians it seemed that under Sifton, the categories had been reversed; to them the country seemed to be teeming with Italians, Ukrainians, Jews, Poles, and Chinese. And even the new British arrivals were of the "wrong type." Many were children sent over by British orphanages, among them, of course, the famous Barnardo boys. In addition, in the eyes of a number of Canadians, there were far too many "assisted immigrants," those whose way was paid by charitable organizations or the Salvation Army. Canada, they feared, was being turned into a vast workhouse for the world's poor, a dumping ground for the social casualties of Europe.

Between 1900 and 1914, when immigration was shut off because of the war, more than one million Britons arrived. In addition, 110 000 Italians, 65 000 Jews, 95 000 Poles, 85 000 Russians, and 50 000 Ukrainians, as well as tens of thousands of Germans, Chinese, Finns, Hungarians,

Japanese, Swedes, Slavs, and others settled in various parts of the country. Thousands more appeared for short periods of time, laying track, mining coal, or clearing bush before returning to the old country with some money in their pockets. Many who came as settlers found that there was little arable land left, and forced to colonize isolated areas far from transportation or markets, they also decided to go back home or to the United States. Indeed, since the Canadian Government emphasized recruitment at the expense of settlement, most immigrants were forced to fend for themselves. There was little thought given to the foreigner once he arrived and even less assistance. As a result, a high percentage of those who came to Canada in these years eventually returned to Europe or sought entry to the United States. Those who did stay were more likely to become industrial workers than farmers. While the Government wanted them hidden away in the bush, on homesteads, in work camps or company towns, many tended to congregate in teeming, slum-ridden sections of Canada's few large cities, there to become objects of curiosity, often of hostility, and always of prejudice. An editorial in a prominent medical journal referred to the ethnic neighbourhoods as " . . . riff-raff from Europe, colonies of immigrants spreading crime, disease and ignorance." Yet they still continued to arrive. Even the downturn in the economy which began in 1912 dissuaded few. Indeed, in 1913, the worst year of the depression, more immigrants arrived in Canada than in any year in our history.

Canada had become home to newcomers many thought were both inferior and unassimilable.[2] By 1914 almost a quarter of the Canadian population was foreign-born. The impact of the huge migrations was profound. The population of the country increased by some 40 per cent in the years between 1900 and 1914, the fastest rate of increase of any major country at that time. Both the production of wheat and the gross national product more than doubled in these years; millions of acres of new land were cleared and settled; more than four hundred thousand

2. Responses to the influx at and after the turn of the century include Donald Avery, *Dangerous Foreigners: European Immigrant Workers and Labour Radicalism in Canada, 1896-1932* (Toronto, 1979); Robert Harney and V. Scarpaci, eds., *Little Italies in North America* (Toronto, 1981); Robert Harney and Harold Troper, *Immigrants* (Toronto, 1977); Jorgen Dahlie and Tissa Fernando, eds., *Ethnicity, Power and Politics in Canada* (Toronto, 1981); J.S. Woodsworth, *Strangers within our Gates* (Toronto, 1972); Robert England, *The Central European Immigrant in Canada* (Toronto, 1929); and England's *The Colonization of Western Canada* (London, 1936), Also interesting is J. Burgon Bickersteth, *The Land of Open Doors* (Toronto, 1976). More recent studies are numerous: K. Adachi, *The Enemy that Never Was: A History of the Japanese Canadians* (Toronto, 1976); Howard Palmer, *Patterns of Prejudice: A History of Nativism in Alberta* (Toronto, 1982) and *Immigration and the Rise of Multiculturalism* (Toronto, 1975); Stephen Speisman, *The Jews of Toronto* (Toronto, 1979); Hugh Johnston, *The Voyage*

new homestead applications were approved. Though real wages changed little, hundreds of thousands of new jobs were created. Yet what concerned most Canadians were not the economic results but the social consequences of the arrival of so many immigrants. Could the country absorb and assimilate such large numbers of people with alien ideas, cultures, religions, and languages? How were these foreigners to be "Canadianized"? These became the burning issues of the time. For many the only hope lay in the public school system. "If Canada is to become in any real sense a nation, if our people are to become one people, we must have one language," argued J.S. Woodsworth in 1905. "The public school is the most important factor in transforming the foreigners into Canadians."

To people like Woodsworth and John W. Dafoe, the influential editor of Winnipeg's *Free Press*, what was at stake was the future of western Canada. To them it was still a new, fluid, and insecure society which could hardly be expected to withstand successfully the shock of a huge immigration of people alien in language, religion, and culture. "We must Canadianize this generation of foreign-born settlers," said Dafoe, "or this will cease to be a Canadian country in any real sense of the term.... In a country like ours," he added, "where so many nationalities are settling in our midst, it is imperative that the children of these different nationalities should be taught the same language, the same aspirations, the same ideals of citizenship as our natural-born Canadians."

Others felt that the Protestant churches could play a key role in Canadianization by providing these immigrants with proper religious training and by introducing them to the Canadian way of life. Nonetheless, in spite of the unremitting efforts of dedicated teachers and ministers, many still clung to their European traditions, insisting on using their mother tongue and attending their Old World churches. Assimilation, it was clear, would not come quickly, if at all.

Urban Ghettos?

What concerned substantial numbers of Canadians as well was the problem of the urban immigrants. The ethnic ghettos of Toronto, Montreal, Winnipeg, and various smaller cities across the country were, in the eyes of respectable Canadians, breeding grounds for crime and disease. Over-

---

of the Komagata Maru (Delhi, 1979); Peter Ward, *White Canada Forever* (Montreal, 1978); James Morton, *In the Sea of Sterile Mountains: The Chinese in British Columbia* (Vancouver, 1974); Frank Epp, *Mennonites in Canada 1920–40* (Toronto, 1982); and Myrna Kostash, *All of Baba's Children* (Edmonton, 1977). There are also numerous histories of immigrant groups in the *Generations* series, published by McClelland and Stewart with the assistance of the federal government.

crowding, unsanitary conditions, hunger, and privation were common in many of these slums. Rather than blaming the system which exploited immigrants to the fullest, Canadians tended to blame the immigrants themselves. They were seen as ignorant, dirty, violent, constantly drunk, and a threat both to individual Canadians and to society as a whole. According to one prominent politician, Canada had become "the dumping ground for the refuse of every country in the world." Some newspapers were warning that Canada faced a future of lawlessness and revolution unless a better class of immigrant replaced those already in the country. Even British arrivals were disparaged as "sparrows," that ubiquitous city pest imported from Europe, or as "broncos" liable to kick over Canadian traditions. "Help wanted" signs reading "No English Need Apply" were common sights in many stores and factories in the years before the Great War.

What most observers ignored in their contempt for the Little Italies, Slavtowns, and Chinatowns that were the hallmark of many Canadian cities, was the incredible vitality of these immigrant communities. Where the Anglo social worker saw slums, disease, and poverty, there actually existed a richness of life far beyond his or her experience and understanding. The crowded tenements, the busy street life, the noise were all alien

To English and French Canadians the recent immigrants, with their colourful street life, seemed almost completely alien. This is a scene from the Toronto Jewish market in 1922. (PA-84811/Public Archives Canada)

and frightening to native-born Canadians, yet they were all necessary for the integration of the newcomers into Canadian society. To them, the ethnic ghettos were reminders of life in the old country. The streets were full of all sorts of hawkers, stalls, peddlers, street musicians, and promoters. Each area had its own national churches or synagogues to serve the spiritual needs of the immigrants; to meet their other needs there were the local "fixers," usually well-established members of the community, with political connections, who served as a liaison with government officials. There were also fraternal and mutual benefit societies. These offered some protection to the immigrants and provided them with a familiar milieu while they were overcoming the trauma of dealing with alien institutions, a new language, and a vastly different way of life.

For many migrants, especially the countless thousands who landed in Canada alone (in 1908, for example, forty-five hundred Italian men arrived in Toronto, and only four hundred women), the boarding house took the place of their far-away families, offering both moral and physical sustenance and camaraderie to ease the pain of loneliness. Most of these homes took in immigrants from the same country — and even from the same region or village back home — thus easing cultural shock. In addition, because there were often seven or eight men sharing one room, the beds occasionally being alternated between those on day shifts and those working at nights, costs were low. In Toronto, for example, in 1909, the cost per week for room, board, and laundry was just over a dollar; the average weekly wage was about ten dollars. Since most of the migrant workers were in Canada only to send home as much money as possible, these arrangements were quite satisfactory.[3]

Perhaps the most exploited of all the immigrants were the women. Responsible for the home and the children, they were also expected to bring in an outside income. In many households, only the wife's earnings saved the family from total destitution. Swarms of immigrant women and girls filled the sweatshops, factories, and textile mills of the country; others earned their keep as domestics and charwomen; still others were forced into prostitution. And when a woman could not leave the house because she had small children or because she was widowed, the home

3. For the urban immigrant experience, see Robert Harney, ed., *Gathering Place: Peoples and Neighbourhoods of Toronto 1834–1945* (Toronto, 1985); Robert Harney, "Boarding and Belonging: Thoughts on Sojourner Institutions," *Urban History Review*, 1978; Robert Harney and V. Scarpici, eds., *Little Italies in North America* (Toronto, 1981); Bruno Ramirez and M. Del Balso, *The Italians of Montreal: From Sojourning to Settlement* (Montreal, 1980); and V. Lindstrom-Best, *The Finnish Immigrant Community of Toronto 1887-1913* (Toronto, 1979).

became a boarding house. Thus, even those women who were not in the paid work force were still crucially important. As one historian put it, "The ability of these women to operate meagre family budgets success- fully was often the condition of survival itself."

Even worse was the life of the immigrant woman homesteading in the West. Often she worked side by side with her husband, clearing the land, removing stumps, building fences, seeding, threshing, or milking, while she alone was responsible for the children and the household chores. And when her husband was away at another job, at a political meeting, or visiting with friends (an opportunity most women got only on Sunday at church) she was on her own. As one Ukrainian woman later plaintively described her life to her children:

> Your crazy father was often at crazy meetings. I had to cut the ice, bring in water, cut wood, chop wood, bring it in. Who was supposed to do all that? I milked the cows, fed them, cleaned the barn and the chicken coop, gathered eggs. . . .[4]

Because of their inhuman working conditions and abysmally low wages, many immigrant workers became actively involved in radical political activ- ity and union organization. Often isolated in far-away railroad, mining, and lumber camps, these men were easy prey for callous bosses. Reluc- tant to interfere in the private sector, neither federal nor provincial gov- ernments provided any protection for the immigrant; alienated and defenceless, he was on his own. Many reacted by joining a union. By far the majority of the members of the revolutionary Industrial Workers of the World, the notorious Wobblies, were immigrant navvies or miners. Many of the largest strikes in this period, affecting key sectors of the Canadian economy, involved foreigners. However, most employers con- tinued to regard immigrants as a docile, helpless work force. "They are our strength and the weakness of the union," said one mine operator, and he and his ilk often arranged for shifts to include labourers of various nationalities in order to encourage competition and to keep the shifts fragmented. But in fact, many of these immigrants, particularly in the mining towns, displayed a real class consciousness and provided the back- bone of much of the militant union activity in western Canada in this period. Nor should this have surprised the bosses, since large numbers of these immigrants brought to their new home as part of their cultural bag-

---

4. On immigrant women, see Rolf Knight, *A Very Ordinary Life* (Vancouver, 1974); B. Caroli *et al.*, eds., *The Italian Immigrant Woman in North America* (Toronto, 1978); and Joan Sangster, "Finnish Women in Ontario," *Polyphony* (Fall, 1981).

gage a long-standing struggle against the state, the landlord, and occasionally even the Church. Once in Canada a small number, particularly Finns, Ukrainians, Russians, and Jews, joined various socialist political parties.

The presence of so many newcomers in the most militant labour and political organization in the country simply reinforced the fears of the Canadian gentry about the aliens in their midst. "These people know absolutely nothing of representative government," wrote a leading minister. "Anglo-Saxon institutions are meaningless to them." So concerned were government authorities that in 1910 the Immigration Act was amended to provide for the exclusion and deportation of those harbouring subversive and anarchistic views. However, that did not prevent massive strikes among immigrant workers throughout 1912 and 1913. So serious were they that troops were called out because, in the words of one commanding officer, "aliens [are] people without any sense of responsibility or respect for life or property."

The War's Impact

A year later Canadian soldiers were called upon for a more serious struggle. In August, 1914, Canada went to war against Germany and the Austrian Empire. The outbreak of war presented the Government with a potentially dangerous domestic problem: Canada was now host to some five hundred thousand enemy aliens. These included most of Sifton's "men in sheepskin coats" who were born in those parts of the Ukraine ruled by Austria. Some were fired from their jobs for "patriotic reasons"; others were put into internment camps. Indeed, rather than keeping them on the relief rolls, government officials began to divert many unemployed aliens to the camps. There were, in fact, very few acts of sabotage or espionage committed.

For other immigrants the war could not have come at a better time. Many had been left destitute by the depression which had settled on Canada in 1912 and refused to lift. Unemployment had skyrocketed and many newly arrived immigrants found themselves without jobs, money, or homes. For large numbers, soup kitchens and Salvation Army hostels provided life-giving solace. But in some areas of western Canada, hungry men raided stores and restaurants for supplies to clothe and feed themselves and their families. When war broke out, thousands of these unemployed men, particularly the Britons, rushed to enlist. For others, the demands of the war soon provided new and better-paying jobs and brought prosperity to Canada. With Europe desperately in need of Canadian food, supplies, and munitions, labour was at a premium. Anyone who wanted to could work, and indeed *had* to work, since the Government late in the war passed an "antiloafing" law compelling "every male person" to be "engaged in some useful occupation." Many interned aliens were released to feed labour-starved industries.

For some government officials, the outbreak of war came none too soon. It provided them with a convenient opportunity to translate their fears of immigrant radicals into ameliorative legislation. Encouraged by a strong business lobby, a series of laws were passed affecting the rights of aliens and such immigrant pacifist groups as the Mennonites and the Hutterites. In 1917 the Wartime Elections Act disenfranchised Canadian citizens born in enemy countries who had not been naturalized before 1902. While some foreign workers were sent to jail for going on strike, employers were actively warning government officials that more would have to be done to remove the threat of a radical uprising. Already frightened by the rapid rise of organized labour during the war, with the Russian Revolution many Canadians saw radicalism as a real threat.

Capitalizing on the propitious wartime conditions, Canadian trade unions began furious organizing campaigns. Thousands of new members, including many immigrants, were brought into the labour movement. A record wave of strikes swept the nation in 1917 and 1918 as the newly potent union movement flexed its muscles. Even though the vast majority of strikes were caused by labour's frantic attempts to keep pace with inflation, some industrialists warned the Borden Government that, for some foreign workers, the major purpose of the strikes was to sabotage the war effort. One mine owner even urged the Prime Minister "to make the foreigners work at the point of a bayonet." In addition, police and military reports were pouring into Ottawa warning of the growing militancy of foreign workers, particularly Finns, Slavs, Russians, and Ukrainians. A government enquiry, conducted by the Montreal lawyer C.H. Cahan, concluded that many immigrant workers were "being thoroughly saturated with the Socialist doctrines . . . [of] the Bolshevik faction in Russia" and that Soviet agents had arrived in North America "to organize and inflame their comrades." Though there seems to have been little real evidence to support Cahan's revelations, little was really needed. The Borden Cabinet had already made up its mind to act against foreign political associations. Immediately following Cahan's report, the Canadian Government started banning socialist organizations, suppressing the foreign-language press, and prohibiting meetings where an "enemy" language was used.

Welcome to Our City!

The war heightened ethnic tensions greatly. This cartoon, from the famous Calgary Eye Opener *of September, 1918, shows one cartoonist's attitude to the influx of Mennonites from the United States.*

To many native Canadians whose contempt and fear of the aliens in their midst had grown exponentially during the war, the Government's response was both tardy and insufficient. Many wanted these immigrants deported; indeed, even the Minister of Militia and Defence, Sam Hughes, had called them a menace and initially urged that "they be encouraged to go to the United States." And passions did not subside with the end of hostilities in Europe. Before the last shot was fired, spokesmen for veterans' groups were already demanding that aliens be rounded up and shipped back home. Newspapers were questioning their worth and their loyalty to the country. Petitions were pouring into Ottawa demanding the deportation of enemy aliens, including Russian immigrants, who were now subject to "Soviet infection." And underscoring the urgency of the situation, confidential police reports were being forwarded to the Government warning of the increasing involvement of immigrants in "Bolshevik subversion."

For Canada's immigrant community, as well as for its labour movement, 1919 was a watershed. Never had the labour movement been so militant and the foreigner so unpopular. There were more organized workers in the country and more strikes than ever before. The key role played by immigrant workers in these strikes, as well as their prominence in the newly created One Big Union, convinced most government officials and businessmen that something had to be done. Many aliens were deported; police agents were instructed to infiltrate radical organizations; companies began firing their foreign workers; mobs of returning veterans attacked immigrants with impunity; and a royal commission was established to investigate the state of industrial relations in the country and particularly the role played by non-Anglo-Saxon workers. But it was too late. The Winnipeg General Strike ensured that the problems of both the worker and the immigrant would be met not with ameliorative legislation but with violence.

Though alien workers had little to do with events either before or during the strike, they were seen by various establishment groups as the ultimate villains. The city's major newspaper urged that the Government "clean the aliens out of this community and ship them back to their happy homes in Europe which vomited them forth." Perhaps worse, not only were immigrant workers constantly being harassed by government officials and security forces, but their own allies in the trade union movement had turned against them. It was unfortunately not uncommon for vigilante groups of returned soldiers, supported by mainstream unions, to battle eastern European immigrants who backed the O.B.U. Eventually the Immigration Act was amended so that "dangerous" aliens could immediately be sent packing. Even without this amendment, tens of thousands of immigrants, realizing their welcome had been worn out, returned home on their own. To them, Canada was no longer the land of freedom or hope. It now differed little from the countries they had fled.

However, for the vast majority of immigrants the events of the war and immediate postwar period were of little note. Very few had the interest or the time to become involved in politics; they were too involved in their work and daily lives. Whether as farmers or manual labourers, as domestics or factory hands, all were consumed by the unrelenting struggle to survive. Most were only dimly aware of the heated debates which were to envelope their adopted homeland in the 1920s about their future as well as the future course of the country's immigration policy. What was no longer in any doubt was that many Canadians had reservations about the strangers within their gates. These doubts were not new, but were now being officially translated into more restrictive policy.

The Call for Assimilation

The great fear was that the Anglo-Saxon character of the country was being undermined, that the country had already been irreparably "Balkanized," according to a reputable British journal. Paradoxically, the overwhelming majority of those arriving in Canada in this period were from the United Kingdom and the United States. Nonetheless, influential politicians, educators, and journalists, supported by farm and labour groups, maintained a strong anti-immigrant lobby during the twenties. They could point to the patchwork of ethnic settlement across western Canada which seemed totally impervious to assimilation. These groups, mostly Doukhobors and Mennonites, stubbornly maintained their own traditions, religion, language, and way of life. They resisted all efforts to bring them into the Canadian mainstream.

The predominant ideology of assimilation in Canada in these years was what historians have called "Anglo-conformity." In effect, it demanded of immigrants that they forget their culture, customs, and language and adopt those of the majority Anglo-Saxon group, that they renounce their past and "behave like little Englishmen." Most influential Canadians viewed the "melting-pot" experiment in the United States as a failure. As R.B. Bennett told the House of Commons in 1928, "Every thoughtful man in the United States, every keen observer... every author... bewails the fact that uncontrolled immigration has been permitted... to such an extent that there is now... a polyglot population without any distinctive civilization, and one about which many of them are in great despair...." Canada was different, he said, because learning from the American mistake, it was going to make sure "to assimilate these people to British institutions." British civilization, he reminded the House, was "the test by which all other civilized nations are measured." Perhaps no one said it better than the Premier of British Columbia in 1923. "We are anxious to keep this a British country. We want [it] British and nothing else."

The attempt to anglicize a large immigrant population was, predictably, not entirely successful. Despite the valiant efforts of countless educators, missionaries, clergymen, and social workers, many foreigners preferred to maintain their own traditions, much to the chagrin of government officials and often to the shame of the immigrants' own children. The conflict between tradition and assimilation was the hallmark of most European families. As the protagonist of John Marlyn's Winnipeg-based novel, *Under the Ribs of Death*, explains to his father:

> The English... Pa, the only people who count are the English. Their fathers got all the best jobs. They're the only ones nobody calls foreigners. Nobody

ever makes fun of their names or calls them bologny-eaters or laughs at the way they dress or talk. Nobody . . . cause when you're English it's the same as bein' Canadian.

Because many felt these newcomers could never become Canadian, much pressure was applied to the Government to adopt a far more restrictive immigration policy. Nativist sentiment had already forced the American Government to tighten its admission policy. It would shortly do the same in Canada. But even more important than the demands of the xenophobes was the economic situation. The country was suffering from a postwar depression; immigrants were not needed. Canadian immigration policy has always been ethnically selective and economically self-serving. And in the few years following the Great War, it made little political sense for the Government to continue its open door policy. The prewar flood of immigrants slowed to a trickle.

One unusual source for restrictionist propaganda was the medical journals of the country. Many of the doctors who conducted the examinations which determined whether newcomers qualified for admission to Canada had distinctly unfavourable attitudes towards immigrant groups. They were constantly warning of the dangerous contagious diseases foreigners might introduce into Canada and were appalled by what they felt were the frightful sanitary conditions of their homes. As the *Canadian Journal of Medicine and Surgery* editorialized in 1919, "Canada has been the dumping ground for thousands of undesirable immigrants. . . . This must stop. Our asylums and jails are over full of degenerates, criminals and mental defectives." Another journal warned, "We cannot melt in our pot certain peoples from Central Europe. They do not fit in. Too many of them have been dumped in already. They already swell our already overcrowded cities and render life in these urban centres most intolerable." The medical profession throughout the 1920s took the lead in agitating for less liberal immigration policies.

Even the most prized newcomers, the British, were not met with open arms. Government officials were even reluctant to accept British immigrants sponsored by the Empire Settlements Act passed by the British Parliament in 1922 to subsidize those residents of the United Kingdom who wished to emigrate to any of the dominions. Perhaps most noteworthy was the number of British deportees from Canada in these years. As a sop to nativists and other pressure groups, the Government ordered the Immigration Branch to be more vigorous in its deportation program. In particular, it had in mind "those foreigners whose presence in Canada was both dangerous and unacceptable." The vast majority of those sent out of the country were, ironically, not continental Europeans but Britons.

Though Ottawa assumed it was satisfying most Canadians with its new restrictive policy, sections of the business and farm communities were annoyed. Mine owners and railway men, in particular, were outspoken in their criticism of the new arrangements. Where, they wondered, were they going to get the workers they so badly needed? Canadians, they argued, even during a depression, had an aversion to the type of work that needed to be done. Some farmers wanted increased access to the large numbers of central Europeans who made up the bulk of the labour force in agricultural communities throughout the West. With the United States now closed to most Europeans, thanks to newly restrictive legislation, increasing numbers of Canadian industrial and farm workers were spilling south across the border to take up jobs usually reserved for European immigrants; and with fewer of these allowed into Canada, industrialists were concerned that there would be, in the words of one, "no one left to do the work." And for the type of work they were offering and the wages they were paying, that was quite understandable. For the railway, factory, and frontier-resource workers in particular, the work was grinding and unremunerative. Railway navvies and loggers were earning up to $5 a day in the 1920s, but after deductions for board, rent, and clothing they were left with very little. At a time when government statisticians were estimating that it required just over $1000 a year to provide a family with the barest essentials, the average earnings of the unskilled worker were less than half that.

In 1925, with the return of prosperity, the "immigration boosters" finally won over the King Government, and Canada's immigration doors were flung open again. Canada's railways, the C.N.R. and C.P.R., were given permission to recruit bonafide agricultural immigrants throughout Europe. The King Cabinet had convinced itself that immigration was a panacea for the country's economic problems. More settlers would mean more revenue and larger markets. As a shoe manufacturer explained, there were "too many shoes in Canada and not enough feet." To the railways, of course, immigrants were an absolute necessity. There was no problem in Canada, said the president of the C.P.R., that "cannot be solved partially or entirely by new people." These could settle in the West, where the railways fortuitously held land and miles of unused track, and provide both goods for export and, of course, business for the railways. Though immigration officials attempted to sabotage the arrangement with the railways — they resented the competition and feared that it was, in the words of the Deputy Minister, a "pernicious attempt to destroy the selective immigration policy" — the railways, nonetheless, brought 200 000 central and eastern Europeans to Canada. Many of these came because they could not get into their land of first choice, the United States.

To offset the large number of continental newcomers, a massive campaign was undertaken to recruit British immigrants as well. Large subsidies and loans were promised to anyone from the United Kingdom who wished to settle in Canada, especially on a farm. In 1928, attempts were even made to ship ten thousand unemployed British miners to western Canada to act as harvesters. Over eight thousand arrived, their way paid by both British and Canadian authorities. Within a short time, six thousand had gone back home. One crestfallen government official opined that it seemed as if "the British race had lost its pioneering instinct." Another, probably more accurately, attributed the failure to the highly advanced British welfare system: "It's the dole that keeps them home," he said. In fact, most of the miners were shipped back home "in locked and guarded trains," according to the historian of this scheme, because officials feared their radicalism and union background might "contaminate the Canadian countryside as they passed through it." The Department of Immigration estimated that while it cost about fifteen cents to recruit a European immigrant, it cost seventeen dollars for each British arrival. And many of these latter, according to some Canadians, were hardly worth the cost. "We do not want mechanics from the Clyde," wrote Clifford Sifton in 1922, "riotous, turbulent and with an insatiable appetite for whiskey." Nor did he want the "trade union artisan who will not work more than eight hours a day and will not work that long if he can help it."

In any event, the immigration procedures of the 1920s satisfied few. Despite the rhetoric of railway spokesmen who convinced the Prime Minister in 1925 that there were 25 million acres of prime prairie land suitable for at least 300 000 immigrants, the supply of good land had indeed run out. Provinces and municipalities were loudly complaining of the large number of unemployed and unassimilable immigrants within their borders. And in Saskatchewan the Ku Klux Klan was successfully recruiting members largely in reaction to what was perceived as the Liberal Government's attempt to populate Canada with Roman Catholic immigrants. Increasing mechanization of both factory and farm meant fewer jobs for the unskilled foreigners. Massive immigration, argued some leading Canadian academics, drove down both wages and living standards and drove out native Canadians. As Professor A.R.M. Lower put it, " 'Cheap men' will always drive out 'dear' men. The men with the higher standard of living cannot compete with the man with the lower." Good English-speaking farmers and workers were thus forced to go to the United States in order to survive. In applying Gresham's famous monetary law — cheap money will drive out dear money — to immigration policy, Lower was not alone; his views were shared by many government officials. Even the British Government was perturbed by Canadian policy. In a confidential memorandum in 1928 the Dominions Office warned the British Prime Minister that Canada was fast losing its Anglo-Saxon character, that it was allowing in too many foreigners and was therefore no longer "an appealing home" for British immigrants. Perhaps the Toronto *Globe* expressed these views best in a 1928 editorial. "The country," it said, "cannot go on if its national life is made up of races which fall short of the national standard."

Most dissatisfied with federal immigration policies were the French Canadians. Many *nationaliste* leaders saw immigration as a nefarious federal plot to reduce French-Canadian influence in Confederation. Since most new immigrants would undoubtedly assimilate into the English-Canadian culture, few French Canadians supported an open door policy; for them, immigration obviously was a threat to the country's finely tuned cultural balance. To appease them, efforts were made to bring over numbers of immigrants from France and to bring home those Québécois who had emigrated to the New England textile mills. Neither attempt met with much success.

The King Government was fully aware of the political repercussions of its policies. The "nonpreferred immigrants" were acceptable so long as they were out of sight, risking life and limb in the mines and smelters of the North and the West, holed up in lumber camps deep in the woods, or farming the more marginal areas of the western wheat frontier. Those who escaped this life for, perhaps, a worse one in Canada's urban centres were less acceptable. As more and more of these drifted towards the cities in the 1920s, the order went out to restrict the immigration of those on the bottom rungs of the ethnic preference ladder. In addition, the federal government agreed to allow provincial premiers to decide how many immigrants their province could accept annually. As well, the freedom of the railways in bringing over colonists was restricted. As the Deputy Minister of Immigration explained, though the economy was still booming, the Government was clamping down on "non-preferred country immigrants [since they] had drifted into non-agricultural work almost immediately upon arrival . . . and [were] filling positions that might have been filled by immigrants from the Mother Country." Yet significantly, an enquiry into the immigration policies of the Government by a House of

Commons committee in 1928 made it quite evident that while most Canadians wanted fewer "foreign" immigrants, they also did not want any more from Great Britain. Immigrants, it was argued, caused unemployment, and in western Canada this was a serious problem, especially in winter, when thousands of migrant workers poured into the cities from the farms, forests, and mines looking for work.

The Depression Stops the Flow

By 1929 unemployment was becoming a serious problem in the rest of Canada as well. In that year, just as in 1913, the flood of immigrants peaked precisely at the time the economy was diving into a depression. Just when it needed them least, Canada had more immigrants than ever before. The Liberal Government was now coming under severe attack from some of its erstwhile allies because of its immigration policies. The people of Saskatchewan who had voted Liberal since the province entered Confederation in 1905 dealt the provincial Liberals a stunning blow in the provincial election of 1929: one of the major issues of the campaign had been the federal government's "lax" policy in opening Canada to so many foreigners. Now there was a growing clamour across the nation to keep them out. In response, as the economy rapidly deteriorated throughout 1929 and 1930, the King Cabinet frantically attempted to close the door. It passed a series of orders-in-council restricting immigration to Canada only to those with enough capital to establish and maintain themselves on farms. In 1931, the new Bennett Government took the ultimate step of barring all immigrants who were not agriculturalists with capital and not of British or American stock. For all intents and purposes, Canada had shut herself off from the rest of the world. Immigration throughout the depression-ridden 1930s was at a standstill.

Predictably, those who suffered worst during the Depression were those who had arrived most recently. Concentrated in the most insecure and vulnerable sectors of the economy, they were the first to lose their jobs, the first to go on welfare, and the first to be herded into the relief camps. Since the country had imported large numbers of unskilled migrant workers for the farms, railways, mines, and lumber camps of the North and the West, the ratio of single, unemployed men was far greater in Canada than in any other western country. Rather than ride out the economic storm in Canada, many of these young men headed back across the Atlantic. Others had no choice; the Government simply deported thousands of those without work. Fully two-thirds of the deportees in this period — over

Anti-foreign and anti-Catholic sentiment led to the establishment of the Ku Klux Klan in Canada. The Klan was strongest in Saskatchewan, but this 1927 photograph was taken in Kingston, Ontario. (PA-87848/Public Archives Canada)

thirty thousand — were forced to leave because they had become public charges. It was certainly much less expensive to send them back home, argued government officials, than to keep them on the relief rolls. What little money was available for welfare would go to native Canadians.

Never very popular with most Canadians, immigrants were least popular during the 1930s.[5] Not only did many blame them for the unemployment crisis ("If we didn't have so many damn foreigners," said one labour leader, "there'd be plenty of work to go around for everyone"), but they were also seen as a threat to the state. Radical groups proliferated during the 1930s, and none was more feared than the Community party. It was an "exotic" movement, wrote one academic in the *Dalhousie Review*, "led principally by European immigrants." The Slavs particularly, he added,

5. On policy in the 1930s, see particularly Irving Abella and H. Troper, *None is Too Many: Canada and the Jews of Europe, 1933–48* (Toronto, 1982), and Gerald Dirks, *Canada's Refugee Policy* (Montreal, 1977).

"contribute to Communist ideas and troubles." Though relatively few recent European immigrants were involved with the party, in the public mind at least, all were; Finns, Jews, Slavs, and Ukrainians were especially suspect. In many places meetings which were conducted in a foreign language were banned; hundreds of foreigners were arrested and many were deported on the flimsiest of evidence. Even some segments of the ethnic press were silenced: how could the Government remain immobile, for example, when one Finnish newspaper was described by the *Canadian Annual Review* as "seditious, immoral, anti-Christian, anti-Canadian and anti-British"? It obviously could not; nor could it fail to notice that the most militant union of the period, the Communist-led Workers' Unity League, had a large immigrant constituency. Though the Bennett Government attempted to destroy the Communist party by declaring it illegal and by arresting and deporting its leadership, it failed. The party survived the Bennett administration and would play an important role in the labour movement for the next decade. Similarly, many of the radical immigrants in the Workers' Unity League would surface again as the backbone of the industrial union movement which swept the country in the late 1930s and early 1940s.

Xenophobia

The Canada of the 1930s, overwhelmed by the social effects of the Depression, was a country permeated with xenophobia. In the provinces of Alberta and British Columbia, it took the form of a hardening anti-Oriental bias. Not only were Asian immigrants legally barred from entering the country, but in British Columbia they were disenfranchised and prevented from joining various professions. As an attorney general of the province once explained, "The *real objection* to the Oriental and the one that is permanent and incurable is the ethnological differences as between the white and Oriental races. . . . In the Divine arrangement of things it was [not] intended that the blood of the Oriental and the blood of the white should mix." In the rest of Canada there were increasing attacks, both physical and verbal, on the "hunky," "bohunk," "uke," and "dago." But perhaps most nefarious was the rapidly spreading anti-Semitism of the period.

This was most apparent in the staunchly Catholic province of Quebec, where the Church led the onslaught against the Jews. Through sermons and articles in Catholic newspapers the faithful were warned against alien doctrines. In many parishes Jews were regularly denounced from the pul-

English Canadians tended to view immigrants as totally without culture, an astonishing attitude considering the level of Anglo-Canadian culture in the interwar years. (C-111019/Public Archives Canada)

pit as Christ-killers and as exploiters who would cheat and rob the inno-cent *habitant*. Many Church and *nationaliste* leaders led a movement to boycott Jewish businesses, to keep Jews out of public life and out of Can-ada altogether. In many popular journals and newspapers, including the prestigious *Le Devoir*, Jews were portrayed as evil, dishonest, dirty, and troublesome.

But anti-Jewish feeling was not restricted to Quebec; it was also strong, though less vocal, in English Canada. Quotas against Jews existed in most universities, professions, businesses, and the civil service. Almost no Jews taught in schools or colleges, worked in anything but the most menial positions in large companies and banks, or played any important role in the legal, medical, or financial communities of this country. Jews were legally forbidden to buy land or homes in many areas, to vacation in cer-tain resorts, or to join various organizations. Anti-Jewish speeches were given regularly by leading Canadian political, religious, business, and labour spokesmen. There was even some violence as Jews confronted anti-Semites on the streets of Winnipeg, Toronto, and Montreal.

The real tragedy of this anti-Jewish sentiment was that it occurred at the same time that Hitler was persecuting and terrorizing the hundreds of thousands of Jews under his control. There was no popular support, and indeed much opposition to the proposal that Canada provide a haven for some of these people, most of whom were later murdered at Auschwitz, Treblinka, or the other Nazi death camps. Of all the countries in the western world, Canada had perhaps the worst record of providing sanctuary to the hapless Jewish refugees. While the United States took in 240 000, Great Britain 85 000, tiny Palestine 100 000, Argentina 50 000, and even penurious Mexico and Colombia 20 000 each, Canada allowed in a total of under 4000.

The Canadian Government was fully aware of the extent of anti-Semitism throughout the land and many of its members shared the prejudice. Thus any program to admit refugees would meet with deep hostility. Mackenzie King was a consummate politician. Had he believed there were votes to be won by allowing Jewish refugees to enter Canada, he undoubtedly would have done so; but he was convinced there were not, so he did not.

Part of the problem lay with the Immigration Branch. Since its heyday under Sifton, it had once again become the backwater of government service. It now found itself attached to the Department of Mines and Resources, reporting to ministers who knew nothing about immigration matters and cared even less. The branch was made up of a handful of civil servants who, according to one critic, thought their job was to keep people out of Canada rather than to let them in. Inspired by their inflexible director, F.C. Blair, who had spent thirty years in the branch, immigration officers all seemed to have a fetish for regulations and were unbending in their application of them. Few could break through the barrier of orders-in-council which now surrounded Canada; few Canadians wanted them to. Except for the ethnic communities themselves, there were no longer any pro-immigrant lobbies in the country. What Canada needed and wanted least during the Depression was more job-hungry immigrants.

Perhaps Canadians felt they had already done their share. In the first thirty years of this century, just under five million immigrants had arrived; in the next ten, barely one hundred forty thousand came, far less than used to land in one good year during the previous three decades. The arrival of so many new settlers of so many different languages, races, religions, and ways of life had obviously been traumatic to a nation which was itself just finding its feet. To integrate, assimilate, and educate these millions was both essential and enormously difficult. Those who for so long had been calling for a halt, for a period of digestion in which the country could finish absorbing those immigrants who were already here, finally got their wish.

Beginning in 1930, and for most of the next two decades of depression and war, almost no one came to Canada. Her doors were shut as firmly as they could possibly be. Only by 1948 was a newly confident Canada, emerging prosperous and powerful from a victorious war, prepared to accept any of the world's homeless, hungry, and dispossessed. The spirit of Sifton had triumphed over that of Blair, the optimists over the pessimists. Once again Canada was ready to play her role in the world community. Immigrants were again welcome, at least until the next depression.[6]

6. Excellent bibliographies on the immigrant experience are Howard Palmer, "Canadian Immigration and Ethnic History in the 1970s and 1980s," *Journal of Canadian Studies* (Spring 1982) and Roberto Perin, "Clio as an Ethnic: The Third Force in Canadian Historiography," *Canadian Historical Review* (December 1983). Finally the most useful, if dated, record of immigration policy is Book IV of the *Report of the Royal Commission on Bilingualism and Biculturalism*.

Chapter VIII

1939–1957:
The Liberal
Ascendancy

When the Cabinet met on November 1, 1944, the ministers were tired and quarrelsome. The endless debates over conscription, the tension between Mackenzie King and Colonel J.L. Ralston, the Minister of National Defence, and the overwhelming weariness engendered in everyone by five years of war had left them all emotionally and physically drained. Conscientious and hard-working, Ralston was sick in body and spirit, his face, with its pugnacious jaw, now looking drawn and gaunt. The Minister knew that his time in the Cabinet was coming to an end, for he was determined to secure the reinforcements that he believed his men overseas needed to fight the war to its inevitably successful conclusion. And, Ralston knew, the Prime Minister was no more willing to consider conscription than he had been at any time since 1939. To Mackenzie King, the great issue was national unity, and to him that meant it was absolutely necessary to keep French and English Canadians united, something that could not be accomplished if conscription was imposed on a reluctant Quebec by the Anglo-Canadian majority, especially if this took place so late in the war, with victory only weeks or months away.

Mackenzie King called the ministers to order and led them through the statistics that were so familiar to them all. To his surprise, Ralston seemed almost accommodating, prepared to consider measures to avert a break. But to King, determined to remove the cancer of conscription now, this was a trick, "a scheme to make the situation still more difficult for me." The time had come to speak out. "I then said I thought we ought to, if possible, reach a conclusion without further delay." Was there anyone who could "save the government and save a terrible division at this time[?] . . . Was there anyone who could do this[?] . . . If there was, I thought it was owing to the country that such a person's services should be secured. I said I believed I had the man who could undertake the task and carry it out." That was General Andrew McNaughton, the general who had taken the first Canadian troops overseas in 1939 and had built them into the great army that was fighting in Italy and Normandy.

"I then said," King went on, later recording his interpretation of events in his diary, "that the people of Canada would say that McNaughton was the right man for the task, and since Ralston had clearly said that he himself did not believe we could get the men without conscription . . . that I thought if Ralston felt in that way he should make it possible for us to bring McNaughton in at once. . . ." The Cabinet members sat stunned as King finished speaking. Ralston rose at his chair, shook King's hand, and left the room, almost without a word.

One of the greatest political gambles in Canadian history had been carried off without a hitch. Mackenzie King had sacked his Defence Minister because of his attitude to conscription, and he had successfully replaced him with a very popular general — and one who was opposed to compulsory military service. It was a coup, all the more dramatic for being carried out within the confines of the Cabinet chamber, and because he had accomplished it so neatly, the Prime Minister had stunned potentially rebellious ministers into inaction. He had bought precious time with his political victory. However, the irony of the triumph was that within three weeks McNaughton would be driven to appeal to the Prime Minister for a measure of conscription, and this time Mackenzie King would have no choice except to yield to the political and military powers that demanded it.

The Coming of the War, 1939

Few Canadians felt any excitement as the Second World War began in September, 1939. There were no cheering crowds in Montreal singing "La Marseillaise" and "Rule Britannia," as had been the case twenty-five years before, no enthusiasm, no shouts that the boys would be in Berlin by Christmas. Ten years of depression, unemployment, and hard times had sapped the national will, and there were too many families all across the land who remembered the dead and the maimed from the Great War and who did not underestimate the cost of another struggle with German militarism.

In the circumstances, Mackenzie King's cautious policies fit the national mood. Before the outbreak of war, the Prime Minister had made very clear that no government led by him would support a policy of conscription for overseas service, a promise that had obvious appeal to a French Canada that dreaded the prospect of another confrontation with Ottawa on such an emotive subject. More to the point, perhaps, aside from fire-eating imperialists, in 1939 almost no one in English Canada seemed to believe that conscription was wise — or likely to be necessary. The new Conservative leader, Dr. R.J. Manion, who had replaced Bennett in 1938, made it clear that his party took the same stance, although that was not a position that sat easily with some of his supporters. The Prime Minister also stated that Canada's policy was to be one of "limited liability" in this war. We were not a great power, we were far from the scene of the action, we had had little part in the events leading up to the struggle against Hitler. In these circumstances, Canada would simply contribute what it could and use the war to rebuild the depression-ravaged Canadian economy. That was not a glamourous position, to say the least; but it was one that seemed to fit the Canadian mood and reflected that of the "phony war" which saw Britain and France glowering at Germany over the Maginot line in a state of armed hostility that produced little actual combat.

Mackenzie King's policy was a natural one for that most curious of Canadians to follow. King had seen Canada tear itself apart over conscription in 1917; he had watched as the great Laurier was deserted by most of his English-speaking colleagues, and he had sworn that that would not recur. His Government would remain intact, his Liberal party would stay together as the only major national organization that united French and English Canadians, and his Government would produce a war effort that was decent and honourable. "Everything in moderation" might have been King's slogan. The Prime Minister was almost sixty-five years old as the war began, a crafty, experienced politician who had led the Liberals for twenty years and been Prime Minister for a dozen. His successes had not been spectacular ones to that point — his greatest triumph had been to win election after election and to swallow in the great maw of Liberalism the dissident Progressives. He had led the country through the 1920s and into the Depression, and he had returned to power in 1935 on the slogan of "King or Chaos." But he had been unable to end the Depression (who could?) and had he died on September 1, 1939, he would likely have been remembered by Canadians only as another in a long succession of sometimes lacklustre leaders. The war was to alter that.

Mackenzie King's first challenges were political. In Quebec, Premier

Maurice Duplessis announced to a surprised province that he was going to the people for a renewed mandate in October. The reason? Ottawa was using the war as an excuse to centralize power, to crush the provinces. Cynical observers thought Duplessis' reason for seeking an early election was a combination of the difficulties he was having in borrowing money to keep his Union nationale Government going and the expectation that the war had so alarmed French Canadians about conscription that they would back a government that was strong on provincial rights. The conscription issue was soon squelched when Mackenzie King's Quebec ministers announced that if Duplessis won they would resign from the federal Cabinet, thus leaving Quebec naked and defenceless before the power of the Anglo majority and probably making conscription inevitable. The choice was put clearly to Quebeckers — vote Duplessis and get conscription; vote Liberal and we will protect you. The province responded to this appeal (and probably to Duplessis' very bad record) by tossing the rascals out and electing Adelard Godbout's *rouges* with a strong majority in the legislature.

One of Ottawa's battles had been won. The second challenge came from Ontario in January, 1940, where the dissident (and often erratic) Liberal Premier, Mitch Hepburn, had convinced himself that King was running a lackadaisical war effort and letting Britain down. Hepburn put a motion to that effect before the legislature where it was whooped through with the enthusiastic backing of George Drew and the Conservative Opposition. For King, this resolution provided the opportunity he needed. Telling himself that no federal leader could countenance such dissension in Ontario, he advised a surprised House of Commons that he was calling a snap election. The Tories were caught unprepared, Manion and his men having banked on a session of some months to allow them the time to expose the Government's weaknesses in fighting the war. The C.C.F. too were in disarray. J.S. Woodsworth, the party leader, had felt obliged to call for neutralism and pacifism in the special war session of Parliament in September, 1939, and while that was gallant and honourable, it did his party little good. The Liberals were home free, particularly as the Conservatives converted themselves into the "National Government" party and called for a coalition of "the best brains" in the country. Most of "the best brains" declined to serve under Manion in the unlikely event that he would win, and many French Canadians apparently believed that the recycled Tories were again putting Union Government forward as their platform — and could conscription be far behind? The result, on March 26, was a sweeping Liberal victory. The Government was in power for the duration with 181 seats, while the Tories had lost their leader and won only forty seats, twenty-five of them in Ontario. The C.C.F. was reduced to eight seats, Social Credit won ten, all from Alberta, and independents and others captured six. Any assaults on King's policies could now come only from the press — or from within his own party.[1]

There was little sign of that initially. The Cabinet had some strong men, and most of their time was devoted to gearing the nation up for war. At the onset of the struggle, Colonel J.L. Ralston had become Minister of Finance. A courageous man who had been a battalion commander in the Great War, Ralston was a somewhat dour Nova Scotian with enormous force of will. In June, 1940, he would become Minister of National Defence, a post in which he would be aided by Air Minister Chubby Power, a gregarious, bibulous Irish Canadian from Quebec City who was one of the ablest men in the ministry, and by Angus Macdonald, the Liberal Premier of Nova Scotia, brought to Ottawa by King to be Navy Minister. That was a first-rate trio. To mobilize the economy, King was fortunate in being able to draw on the organizational talents of C.D. Howe, the grain-elevator builder from the Lakehead. Howe took over responsibility for the new Department of Munitions and Supply in early 1940 and made it the driving force of Canada's industrial contribution to the war. J.L. Ilsley was another of King's ministers who blossomed during the war, and when he succeeded Ralston in the Finance portfolio, he became, with his flinty honesty and administrative skill, that most unlikely of creatures, a popular Minister of Finance. There was also the Minister of Justice, Ernest Lapointe, a French Canadian whose special task it was to make sure that Quebec's considerations received their due. It was as strong a Cabinet as any that Canada had ever had, and the changes that the war forced on it only strengthened it further.

To formulate and direct war policy, the Prime Minister created a Cabinet War Committee, a grouping of the key ministers. The War Committee's members controlled the major departments, employed the ablest officials in the bureaucracy, and effectively created and directed Canada's war. But even before the Committee was created in December, 1939,

1. Books on the politics of the war include J.W. Pickersgill, *The Mackenzie King Record*, vols. I-II (Toronto, 1960, 1968); J.L. Granatstein's *The Politics of Survival: The Conservative Party of Canada 1939-45* (Toronto, 1967); John Kendle's *John Bracken: A Political Biography* (Toronto, 1979); Granatstein's *Canada's War: The Politics of the Mackenzie King Government, 1939-45* (Toronto, 1975); Neil McKenty's *Mitch Hepburn* (Toronto, 1967); Walter Young, *The Anatomy of a Party: The National CCF 1932-61)* (Toronto, 1969); H.F. Quinn, *The Union Nationale* (rev. ed., Toronto, 1979); and Reginald Whitaker, *The Government Party: Organizing and Financing the Liberal Party of Canada 1930-58* (Toronto, 1977).

Ernest Lapointe, King's Quebec lieutenant and closest colleague from the early 1920s until his death in November, 1941. (C-9796/Public Archives Canada)

the basic outlines of the war effort had been laid down. In September, King announced that Canada would raise a division of infantry for service in Europe, and the First Canadian Infantry Division, under the command of Major General Andrew G. L. McNaughton, had arrived in England by mid-December. The small Royal Canadian Navy was put to work shepherding convoys, a vital if unglamourous task. And the Royal Canadian Air Force was given the job of running the British Commonwealth Air Training Plan, a magnificent and costly enterprise that took advantage of Canada's open spaces and relative safety from the enemy to make this country "the aerodrome of democracy." Air crew trainees from all across the Commonwealth came to Canada to be turned into pilots, navigators, wireless operators, and bombardiers. It was a splendid plan, and the 132 000 aircrew produced by the B.C.A.T.P. were, arguably, Canada's major contribution to the Allied victory.

Canada's modest war effort might have been sufficient had the course of the war followed the plans laid down by Allied staff officers in London and Paris. The war of 1939 was in some respects a continuation of the Great War — with a twenty-year armistice separating the two parts. But there were differences. Italy had switched sides and, although neutral until the summer of 1940, was on the Axis team. So too was Japan, although its entry into the war did not occur until Pearl Harbor signalled the conversion of a European War into a world war on December 7, 1941. The Soviet Union was also neutral in 1939, another shift from the course followed by Russia in 1914, and Stalin's nation was a wary partner of Hitler's Germany in the partition of Poland in September, 1939. The last great neutral was the United States. President Franklin Roosevelt's country wanted to be free of European entanglements, a traditional attitude but one that had been reinforced by disillusionment after the First World War. However, the President feared Hitler's power and wanted to help the Allies as much as he could, but he was usually constrained by Congress and public opinion.

Britain's Ranking Ally

That American help — and a greater Canadian effort — would be needed became clear in the spring and summer of 1940. The Nazi *blitzkrieg* swept over Denmark and Norway in April and then turned on Belgium, the Netherlands, Luxembourg, and France the next month. The European balance of power changed dramatically in a single month: France was beaten, and England, having rescued its armies at Dunkirk in a brilliantly improvised evacuation, found itself defended only by the Royal Navy, the small but effective Royal Air Force, and a few well-equipped army formations of which the First Canadian Division was the best. Hitler was the master of western Europe, and Canada, from being a cautious dominion fighting a war of limited liability, had suddenly become Britain's ranking ally; it remained so until Hitler invaded Russia in June, 1941, and the United States came into the war in December, 1941.

Increased efforts were undertaken from Ottawa, and limited liability was tossed out the window. Recruiting was stepped up, war production increased (as the British for the first time in the war began to place orders in quantity), and units of infantry, armour, artillery, and R.C.A.F. squadrons were hurried across the ocean. Mackenzie King also gathered his courage and put in place, through the National Resources Mobilization Act, a policy of conscription — but for home defence only. Young men were to be called up for thirty days training, an attempt, as some army officers saw it, to begin the process of whittling away at twenty years of pacifism. Surprisingly there was little opposition in Quebec, although Camilien Houde, the mayor of Montreal, was interned for urging his compatriots not to register for the draft. French Canadians, just as they had always claimed, were willing to serve to defend Canada, and after June, 1940, there seemed to be a threat to Canada. Eventually the home defence draft was extended to four months and then, in April, 1941, for the duration of the war, but for domestic political reasons the Government refused to send the conscripts abroad. The result was the creation of two armies — one of volunteers for service anywhere, and one of draftees (called Zombies after the living dead of Hollywood horror films) who could serve only in Canada and later in Alaska and the West Indies. Two great national crises over conscription, in 1942 and 1944, followed the creation of these armies, and each upheaval almost destroyed the King Government. But that was still in the future.

More immediately, the crisis of the summer of 1940 forced Canada to look to its own security. What if Britain fell? What of Canada's defences? What of Canada's trade? Those hard questions were also being posed in Washington by President Roosevelt and his brain trust, and the answers in both countries seemed to demand closer cooperation between them. There had been some movement in this direction even before the war, for Roosevelt and King were friendly, their Governments had worked together to negotiate two trade agreements in 1935 and 1938, and there had even been some tentative military staff talks in 1938. Now something more was needed, and in August Roosevelt called the Prime Minister on the telephone to suggest that the two leaders meet at Ogdensburg, New York. There they agreed to establish a Permanent Joint Board on Defence to plan for the defence of the continent and to coordinate the deployment of their forces. It was a historic decision (made, interestingly, without any consultation whatever with Parliament or Congress) and one, in retrospect, that marked Canada's shift from the British to the American sphere of interest. It was also essential, for if Canada had failed to look to its own security, the Government would have been foolish indeed. Evidence that the public realized this can be seen in the popular approbation the Ogdensburg Agreement received — and in the harsh words with which Winston Churchill greeted its conclusion. Ogdensburg let Canada go all out to help Britain, but the British Prime Minister, with his long view of events, recognized the significance of the agreement and its *permanent* defence board.

This blotter was distributed by the manufacturers of a Canadian patent medicine. Such things annoyed Mackenzie King, who worried that Canadians might forget that he was their leader.

Canada was also going all out to help Britain economically. But, given the limited capacity of Canadian industry, this meant that components, raw materials, and machine tools had to be imported from the United States — at a cost of some $400 million a year, payable in American dollars — and this quickly began to pose difficulties. Before the war Canada could use its surplus earned in trade with Britain to pay for the perennial deficit in trade with the south, but the British barred the exchange of sterling for dollars, and Canada was soon in a bind. The more it tried to help England, the more it had to import and the greater its dollar deficit. Efforts were made to control nonessential imports and holiday travel, notably through the War Exchange Conservation Act of December, 1940, but the U.S. dollar shortage increased rapidly, threatening the Canadian economy.

The solution came in April, 1941, when Mackenzie King again travelled to see Roosevelt, this time at the President's family home in Hyde

Park, New York. If the Americans could buy more raw materials and manufactured goods in Canada, then our difficulties would be eased, King told the President. And if the components that Canada had to import for incorporation into munitions for Britain could be supplied under Lend-Lease and charged to the British account, then the difficulties would disappear altogether. Lend-Lease was the ingenious attempt of a still-neutral America to help Britain secure the supplies for which a nearly bankrupt England could no longer pay. The President, a man who had as long a view as Churchill, readily agreed, and he inscribed the Hyde Park Declaration to say that it had been done by Mackenzie and Franklin on a "grand Sunday in April." It was a grand Sunday for the Prime Minister indeed, for Canada's economic problems virtually dissolved at a stroke, and the Canadian war economy went from strength to strength. So powerful did industry and agriculture become, in fact, that Canada was soon in a position to give away billions of dollars in munitions and foodstuffs. A great loan of $700 million to Britain was followed by a billion dollar gift and then by massive Mutual Aid contributions of $2 billion to Britain and other Allies. In total, Canada gave Britain $3.5 billion in aid.[2]

The Condition of the People

The war's transformation of Canada was miraculous. The blighted prairie farms regenerated and began again to produce first quality wheat in abundance — and for a good price. The war effort needed every foot of lumber that the British Columbia forests could yield, every fish that the Maritimes could produce, every ounce of ore that the mines of the Laurentian Shield could process. Unemployment disappeared, soon to be replaced by a labour shortage and government controls that required a man or woman to seek permission from National Selective Service before changing jobs. Peace on the labour front was essential if production was to be maintained, and Ottawa passed regulations which recognized labour's rights to bargain collectively and to organize, to fair wages and a fair deal. That was a marked change from past attitudes, and union strength during the war doubled from 359 000 in 1939 to 711 000 in 1945. Business-

2. On Canadian-American relations during the war, see S.W. Dziuban, *Military Relations between the United States and Canada 1939–45* (Washington, 1959); C.P. Stacey, *Arms, Men and Governments: the War Policies of Canada, 1939–45* (Ottawa, 1970); Stacey's *Canada and the Age of Conflict*, vol. II (Toronto, 1981); J.L. Granatstein, *A Man of Influence: Norman A. Robertson and Canadian Statecraft, 1929–68* (Ottawa, 1981); and R.D. Cuff and J.L. Granatstein, *Ties that Bind: Canadian-American Relations in Wartime* (Toronto, 1977).

men may not have been altogether happy with that development, but the war was a good time for them as well. After the hard years of the 1930s, there was all the work that every factory — if it made goods needed for the war effort — could handle, often on cost-plus contracts that eliminated risks. There was government aid for construction of plant, there were easy write-offs of costs and for depreciation, and although taxes were high, there was still a good profit. But there were other prices to pay. Unnecessary industries were squeezed out of the marketplace and ordered to convert to war production. Factories that had produced refrigerators in 1939, by 1941 were making Bren guns or tank tracks. The state began to intervene in every sphere of life, allocating resources, controlling production, determining wages. Prices and wages were frozen in November, 1941, when inflation seemed on the verge of a spiralling increase, and the Wartime Prices and Trade Board, headed by the tough-talking Donald Gordon, a previously little-known officer of the Bank of Canada, became a giant agency that controlled the lives of businessmen and ordinary citizens alike. Ration cards for scarce foods and for gasoline became the norm; tokens were necessary to purchase meats; car tires became scarce as hen's teeth; and every housewife was urged to grow vegetables in her backyard, to report waste, and to save money, edible fats, and even milkweed for life preservers. Canada was mobilized for the war in a fashion that made the effort of 1914–18 look amateurish.

Astonishingly, despite the great war effort there was enough left over to improve living standards all across the country. Families that had had no breadwinner during the Depression years now found that even if the husband was overseas, the wife and eldest daughter had all the work and overtime they wanted. At their peak of wartime employment in the fall of 1944, more than one million women were working full time, a figure that excluded part-time workers and the eight hundred thousand women on the farms who were doing their share — as they always had — to produce the food that Canada and her allies needed. Approximately 439 000 women worked in the service sector, 373 000 in manufacturing, 180 000 in trade and finance, 31 000 in transportation (including those who drove streetcars and buses in the large cities), and even 4000 in construction. In October 1943, for example, there were 261 000 women employed in war industries where they made artillery pieces, tanks, ammunition, ships, and aircraft. "Rosie the Riveter" was a popular American wartime caricature of the female munitions worker — but it was no sham in Canada. Women did much the same work as the men in the factories, and they earned substantially higher wages than were possible

VALUE OF WAR PRODUCTION ($ MILLIONS)

	1939–40	1941	1942	1943	1944
Merchant ships	—	$29	$183	$232	$170
Naval vessels	$27	73	73	164	204
Aircraft	45	110	232	361	403
Motor transport	119	198	368	435	462
Armoured vehicles	—	21	155	203	146
Guns, small arms	1	20	162	213	156
Ammunition	16	111	257	277	233
Defence construction	94	138	219	194	100
Govt.-financed plant expansion	103	221	185	200	57

Source: *Canada at War*, No. 45 (1945)

PERSONAL INCOME TAXATION

Earnings	Tax in 1939	1940	1941	1943	
$1500	—	$14	$35	$24 plus $24	compulsory savings
$3000	$10	97	215	334 plus 334	compulsory savings
$5000	134	427	735	1062 plus 600	compulsory savings
$10,000	738	1921	2710	3346 plus 1200	compulsory savings

(rates for a married man with two children)

Source: *Canada at War*, No. 45 (1945)

in the "traditional" factory jobs they had held before the war. There were also (as the chart on page 283 shows) a substantial number of women in the army and in the other services. In all, nearly fifty thousand women enlisted in the Canadian Women's Army Corps, the R.C.A.F.'s Women's Division, and the Women's Royal Canadian Naval Service, and almost forty-five hundred more served as nursing sisters in the forces. The war did not emancipate women and give them equality with men — attitudes shaped over centuries could not change so quickly — but it did increase their opportunities.[3]

3. The best work on women in wartime is by Ruth Roach Pierson. Her "Canadian Women and the Second World War" (Canadian Historical Association Historical Booklet No. 37, 1983) is a handy summary of women's role, and the bibliography lists most of the available literature, including Pierson's many articles.

Certainly the war increased family savings and the country's wealth. The gross national product rose from $5.6 billion in 1939 to $11.8 billion in 1945, an incredible increase, and average wages, personal savings, and government expenditures rose with it. All the while the cost of living remained virtually static, particularly after the imposition of the freeze of November, 1941. There was, in spite of high taxes, more money in Canada during the war than there had been for years, but because of war production there was little to buy — except Victory Bonds — and Canadians gave their earnings and savings back to the government by the billions. It was a people's war in Canada, fought by the people with equipment produced by the people and paid for by the people, and for once the people seemed to get some of the benefits.[4]

Overseas, the Canadian army sat in Britain, protecting the little island against an invasion that never came. The army, swollen by late 1941 to more than 250 000 volunteers, was fit, well equipped, well trained — and bored. There was no action for the boys as the Government and the overseas commander, General McNaughton, insisted that the troops be employed *en bloc*. However, the R.C.A.F. squadrons in Britain and elsewhere were in the thick of the air war, as were thousands of Canadians who had been integrated into the R.A.F. Some flew in fighter squadrons or in army cooperation squadrons that provided tactical air support to the infantry and armour. But the greatest effort was put into the Royal Air Force's Bomber Command, into the great air armadas that carried the war into the heart of Germany each night. The bombers dropped their payloads into the vitals of Hamburg, Berlin, and Frankfurt, into the steel plants of the Ruhr, and the German interceptors took a terrible toll in retribution for the huge civilian casualties and the destruction the bombers wrought. In a single night, more airmen could be lost than in the entire Battle of Britain, and bomber crews statistically had only one chance in four of surviving a thirty-operation tour of duty. Many did more than a single tour. At sea, the risks statistically were not as high, but the officers and seamen of the Royal Canadian Navy, taking on an ever-increasing part in the battle for the Atlantic, were in deadly peril too. The German U-boats preferred to sink the fat, slow tankers and merchant ships on their way to Britain, but the destroyers and corvettes who accompanied

4. On the war economy and war finance, see particularly Robert Bothwell and W. Kilbourn. *C.D. Howe* (Toronto, 1979); A.F.W. Plumptre, *Three Decades of Decision: Canada and the World Monetary System, 1944–75* (Toronto, 1977); and J.L. Granatstein, *The Ottawa Men: The Civil Service Mandarins, 1935–57* (Toronto, 1982).

STRENGTH OF THE CANADIAN ARMY

Year end		Male	Female
1939		63 327	149
1940		117 302	508
1941	Volunteers	256 208	1 958
	N.R.M.A.	16 647	
1942	Volunteers	360 016	4 536
	N.R.M.A.	55 840	
1943	Volunteers	396 867	13 488
	N.R.M.A.	69 299	
1944	Volunteers	411 574	16 581
	N.R.M.A.	63 769	
1945	Volunteers	250 291	10 974
	N.R.M.A.	40 843	
1946	Volunteers	29 684	304
	N.R.M.A.	1 054	

Source: C.P. Stacey, *Six Years of War* (Ottawa: Queen's Printer, 1955), Appendix "A."

them were targets as well. In winter, the North Atlantic claimed virtually every man unlucky enough to have his ship shot out from under him, and there were the hazards of burning oil, of attack from U-boat machine guns or aircraft, of exhaustion. But the convoy service was essential if Britain was to survive, and the little escorts went out again and again, manned by businessmen and stockbrokers turned officers, by weekend sailors, farmers, and shipping clerks, as crew. Astonishingly, they had learned their trade by 1943 and prevailed, eventually chasing the submarines from the sea and winning the Battle of the Atlantic.[5]

But the victories initially seemed small to the Canadian public. There were few heroes for those who remembered the glorious efforts of the Canadian Corps in the Great War and who nostalgically pined for similar efforts in this war. In vain the Government pointed to the vast air force and navy; in vain it argued that defending Britain was a vital chore. In vain. Conscription talk — initially disguised as a demand for "total war"

5. Some of the best books on the fighting in Europe in which Canadians participated include Murray Peden, *A Thousand Shall Fall* (Stittsville, 1981); Jeffrey Brock, *The Dark Broad Seas*, vol. I (Toronto, 1981); C.P. Stacey, *Six Years of War* (Ottawa, 1955) and *The Victory Campaign* (Ottawa, 1960); and G.W.L. Nicholson, *The Canadians in Italy* (Ottawa, 1957), the latter three titles being official histories. The best book on the R.C.N. is Marc Milner, *North Atlantic Run* (Toronto, 1985).

— began in earnest in Canada in the summer and fall of 1941, and newspaper editors and politicians alike began to grumble that Quebec was not doing its share in the war. In one sense that was so. Quebec enlistments, while much higher proportionately than in the Great War, *were* less than in the rest of the country, but the N.R.M.A. home defence conscripts, despite popular English-Canadian perceptions, were not all French Canadian by any means. The mood was becoming ugly as the war dragged on in late 1941 and as Allied defeat followed Allied defeat. Hitler had invaded the Soviet Union in June and his panzer armies were at the gates of Moscow, Leningrad, and Stalingrad; in Africa, General Erwin Rommel toyed with ill-led imperial forces; and on December 7, 1941, the Japanese lashed out at the United States, Britain, and the Dutch East Indies. The attack on Pearl Harbor in Hawaii brought the war close to North America — and created near panic in British Columbia and along the California coast.

The first victims of the growing fear on the coast were the Japanese Canadians. Some twenty-three thousand Japanese, not all Canadian-born but almost all citizens, lived in British Columbia, making their living for the most part by fishing or market gardening. Racism in the province had long been endemic, but the Japanese assault on Hawaii raised it to a fever pitch, and there were demands from provincial and municipal politicians, the newspapers, and alarmed citizens' groups that Ottawa do something. The federal government was repeatedly told by its officials, by the R.C.M.P., and by the military that the Japanese Canadian posed no threat, but the political pressure was so intense, and not least from British Columbia's representative in the Cabinet, Ian Mackenzie, that the government felt obliged to act. The Japanese were rounded up, deprived of their livelihoods, and shunted off to the interior or dispersed across the country. Later their property was sold at sacrificial prices, and after the war the Government attempted to deport as many of the Japanese as possible back to their ancestral islands. It was the most shocking violation of civil liberties in Canada during the war, a manifestation of panic and racism that besmirched the ideals for which Canadians were supposedly fighting. However, it was almost completely understandable in the panicky atmosphere of 1942.[6]

6. Among many titles on the treatment of the Japanese, see T.U. Nakano, *Within the Barbed Wire Fence* (Toronto, 1980); Ken Adachi, *The Enemy that Never Was* (Toronto, 1976); Ann Sunahara, *The Politics of Racism* (Toronto, 1981); and F.E. La Violette, *The Japanese Canadians and World War II* (Toronto, 1948). One novel is Joy Kogawa, *Obasan* (Toronto, 1981).

Conscription Talk

Canadians were frightened then, unhappy and complaining. The Conservative party, in ruins since the elections of 1935 and 1940, began to press stridently for a greater war effort, and a party meeting in November, 1941, turned unexpectedly into a leadership meeting that put Senator Arthur Meighen at the party's helm once again. Meighen had been the draftsman of the Military Service Act of 1917, he had been the "ready, aye, ready" statesman of the 1920s, and his name was anathema in Quebec — and to Mackenzie King. With his great intelligence and acid tongue in debate, Meighen clearly frightened the Prime Minister, and his return to the scene altered events.

One immediate change was the Government's decision to seek release from its promises against overseas conscription through a plebiscite. The electorate of all Canada was to be asked to release King from his pledge to Quebec that this war was to be different. French Canadians were outraged. Nationalistic groups denounced the Government and declared that Ernest Lapointe, dead of cancer in November, 1941, would never have permitted such a thing. Lapointe's sucessor in the riding of Quebec East and as Minister of Justice, Louis St. Laurent, a distinguished Quebec City lawyer, spoke against the mounting hysteria in his province, but he was as yet unknown, his prestige not nearly as great as Lapointe's, and his and his Cabinet colleagues' efforts against the forces campaigning for a *non* vote on the plebiscite were ineffectual. There were no such problems in English Canada, where the Meighen-led Tories and the C.C.F. found themselves in the uncomfortable position of being obliged to support King's plebiscite. The result was a great national split, as virtually all French Canadians, wherever in the country they were, voted on April 27, 1942, not to release the Government from its pledge, while the great majority of English Canadians voted yes to the referendum. In Quebec, 72.9 per cent voted no; in Ontario, by contrast, only 17.7 per cent did so. The exceptions to the general trend in English Canada were constituencies that were heavily French Canadian, German Canadian, or Ukrainian Canadian — which amounted to a few ridings in New Brunswick, Ontario, Alberta, and Saskatchewan.[7]

---

7. On conscription, see Pickersgill, *Mackenzie King Record;* Stacey, *Arms, Men* and *Governments;* J.L. Granatstein and J.M. Hitsman, *Broken Promises: A History of Conscription in Canada* (Toronto, 1985); André Laurendeau, *La Crise de la conscription, 1942* (Montréal, 1962); and W. Denis Whitaker and Shelagh Whitaker, *Tug of War* (Toronto, 1984).

Mackenzie King now faced a dilemma (one that had been eased somewhat by the surprising and decisive defeat of Meighen by Joe Noseworthy, an unknown high school teacher and the C.C.F. candidate, in a Toronto by-election on February 9). If he did not act to enforce conscription, now that the national majority had declared for it, he would be in difficulty with the electorate, the media, and strong elements within his Cabinet, most notably Colonel Ralston and Navy Minister Macdonald; if he did impose conscription for overseas service, he could split the country and perhaps destroy his party's base in Quebec irrevocably. His solution was characteristically clever — too clever, his critics argued. Legislative action, in the form of bill 80, that deleted the restrictive geographic clause of the National Resources Mobilization Act would be taken to make overseas conscription possible, but conscription would never be enforced unless and until it was necessary to do so. Not necessarily conscription, the Prime Minister told a bewildered and bemused House of Commons and nation, but conscription if necessary. One senior Quebec minister, P.J.A. Cardin, resigned, and Ralston, too, almost left in disgust, but the Government survived and the crisis of 1942 passed uneasily into history.

The Boys Overseas

Perhaps the increasing casualties overseas had snapped some Canadians back to reality. The Japanese attacks of December had included an assault on the British Crown Colony of Hong Kong, an indefensible island to which, inexplicably and foolishly, the Government, at Britain's request, had despatched a very much understrength Canadian brigade late in 1941. The troops, with their British comrades, fought well but had been overwhelmed, killed, or captured. On Christmas Day, 1941, Hong Kong was lost and 1975 Canadians with it. That was bad enough, but in August, 1942, a large portion of the Second Canadian Infantry Division went to a similar fate at Dieppe. Again, inexplicably and foolishly, a landing was mounted against a heavily defended port, one whose shale beaches were

The Canadian Army in Italy ▶

"We're the D-Day dodgers," Canadian and British troops on the forgotten front bitterly sang. Italy was largely forgotten once the invasion of Normandy took place, but it was a long struggle for the Canadians who faced crack German troops all the way from Sicily to Florence. The hardest fighting was at Ortona around Christmas, 1943, when the Loyal Edmonton Regiment, the Seaforth Highlanders, and the Princess Patricia's Canadian Light Infantry slogged it out with Germany's First Parachute Division. (Adapted from Canada's Soldiers, *by George F.G. Stanley, published by Macmillan of Canada, p. 371.)*

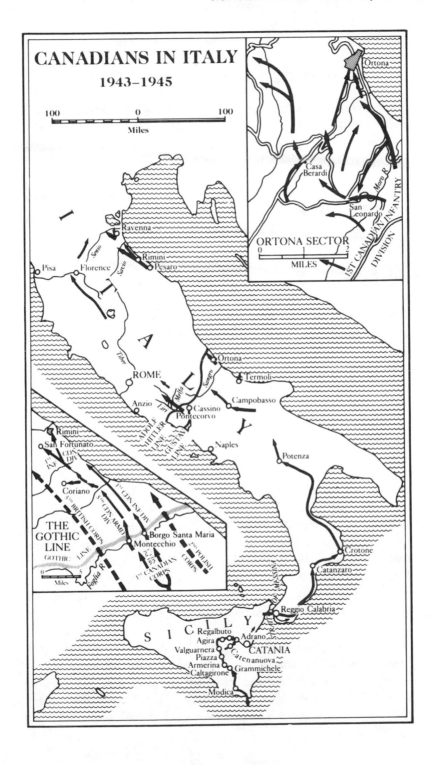

CANADIANS IN ITALY
1943–1945

100   0   100
Miles

ORTONA SECTOR

Ortona

Casa Berardi

San Leonardo

1ST CANADIAN INFANTRY DIVISION

Moro R.

0   1   2
MILES

Ravenna
Pisa
Florence
Rimini
Pesaro
Serchio
Serio
Tiber

I T A L Y

ROME
Anzio
Tanaro
Melfa
Cassino
Pontecorvo
ADOLF HITLER LINE
GUSTAV LINE
Naples
Ortona
Sangro
Termoli
Campobasso
Potenza

Rimini
San Fortunato
1ST CDN INF DIV
Coriano
5TH BRITISH CORPS
5TH CDN ARMD DIV
1ST CDN INF DIV
THE GOTHIC LINE
GOTHIC LINE
0   5
Miles
Foglia R.
Borgo Santa Maria
Montecchio
2ND POLISH CORPS
1ST CANADIAN CORPS

Crotone
Catanzaro

STRAIT OF MESSINA

Reggio Calabria

S I C I L Y

Regalbuto
Agira
Valguarnera
Piazza
Armerina
Caltagirone
Adrano
Catenanuova
CATANIA
Grammichele

Modica

unsuitable for landing tanks and one whose defences commanded the likely landing areas from high ground with every kind of fire. The result was a slaughter that recalled the ghastly battles of 1916, and whole battalions were lost in the Canadian toll of 907 dead and 2000 captured. Lessons about amphibious operations presumably had been learned, and the assault was claimed to have persuaded Marshal Stalin of the Soviet Union that the western Allies were serious about the war, something he was said to have doubted. It was a heavy price to pay for those alleged benefits.

Nonetheless the war was beginning to go better. American entry put a huge industrial machine fully at the Allies' service, and vast armies were soon in the field under the American flag. The Russians, to universal astonishment and awe, held against the *Wehrmacht*, while in North Africa General Montgomery's victory at El Alamein marked the turning of the tide, as did the almost simultaneous Allied landings in Algeria and Morocco. It was the end of the beginning.

Sicily was the next stage, and over McNaughton's protests a Canadian division was assigned to that invasion. The Italian island fell fairly quickly, and there followed an invasion of the mainland and, inevitably, an increased commitment of Canadian troops to the campaign. Casualties began to mount, and the hometown newspapers had their lists of the dead, wounded, and decorated each week. The war at last began to hit home to Canadians. For those at the front, slogging their painful way up the Italian boot, the fighting was extraordinarily difficult. The terrain favoured the defenders, and every river crossing, every mountain was contested. The *Wehrmacht* must have known that the tide had turned, but that seemingly only made the German soldiers fight more fiercely, and the Canadian, American, and British armies paid dearly for every inch of ground.

Rome was captured in June, 1944, just at the time that the Allies launched their long-awaited invasion of France. The Third Canadian Infantry Division was in the initial landing force, and R.C.A.F. squadrons and R.C.N. ships also participated as the Canadians quickly seized most of their D-Day objectives. A new slogging match began as the bridgehead was slowly expanded and Allied forces reinforced. The culmination came in the great Canadian struggle for Caen and in the near-successful effort to close the Falaise Gap and trap a large part of the Nazi armies. Had that effort succeeded, the Germans in France might have succumbed immediately, but since it did not, the Canadians and their allies had to battle through France. The First Canadian Army, a massive formation under the command of General H.D.G. Crerar, a professional soldier who had

Canadian bodies and equipment litter the beach at Dieppe. In 1942, this German photograph made splendid propaganda about the strength of Fortress Europe. (C-14160/Public Archives Canada)

graduated from the R.M.C., served in the trenches in the Great War, and worked his way up the promotion ladder in the tiny prewar Permanent Force, was in reality an international army with Polish, British, and a few other national contingents serving under Canadian command. The army had the left flank of the Allied advance, a position that involved the clearing of the Channel ports (including a joyful liberation of Dieppe by the reconstituted Second Division), the freeing of Holland, and the clearing of the great Scheldt estuary. Again, casualties were heavy, and soon it became apparent that there was a growing shortage of infantry.

In one sense this was inexplicable. The Canadian army had enlisted 650 000 men in the course of the war and had sent overseas five divisions and ancillary troops. But because Canada insisted — and properly — on controlling its own forces in this war, a long supply line and reinforcement chain was necessary. That absorbed manpower, as did the need, both political and military, to keep forces in Canada, most notably in

British Columbia. The result was that the army's "teeth-to-tail" ratio — or its balance of fighting to supporting troops — was low, probably the lowest of any of the Allied forces. It was also true that misjudgements had been made by British planners, who had overestimated the effectiveness of the *Luftwaffe* and had prescribed a heavy quota of reinforcements for rear area troops and such supporting arms as the artillery. Happily, the German air force was controlled, but the infantry took heavier casualties than expected, and reinforcement shortages arose. Soon, recently wounded Canadians were being returned to the front, and claims that untrained men were being posted to infantry battalions also began to be heard by the late summer of 1944. The final crisis over conscription had arrived.

The Politics of Conscription

Mackenzie King was not ready for it. The Prime Minister had watched events in Europe with some satisfaction since D-Day. Canada's forces had served with distinction and valour, and no one doubted that Hitler was doomed, squeezed between the Russians moving westwards and the Allies coming from the south and east. And, King believed, he had brought Canada through this titanic struggle without a divisive internecine struggle over compulsory military service. Who could call for conscription now, with the war all but won?

Colonel Ralston, the Minister of National Defence, had gone to the front in September, 1944, to see for himself if the complaints of infantry shortages were true. To his horror, he found that they were, and the Minister returned to Ottawa in October, tired, ill at heart, but determined to press for the necessary reinforcements for the fighting men overseas. After all, had Mackenzie King not promised in 1942 that there would be conscription if necessary? Of course he had, a startled King admitted, but he had meant necessary to win the war, and the war clearly was already won. The battle lines were drawn for one of the greatest Cabinet struggles in Canadian history.

Ralston had a steely determination to get his way, and he was prepared to resign and to take as many of his colleagues as possible along with him if he could not. Mackenzie King had a similar determination, masked though it was by his soft, puffy appearance and reputation for indecision. He was committed to preventing the destruction of his country, Cabinet, and party. King was to prevail when, as we have seen, in a stunning move he sacked Colonel Ralston at the Cabinet meeting on November 1, 1944, and put in his place General McNaughton, the former army commander in

England who had been returned to Canada because of ill-health and British dissatisfaction with his command capabilities. Andy McNaughton, nonetheless, was a man with a very powerful personality, extremely popular in the country and with the forces, and King believed that the general could persuade enough of the sixty-eight thousand N.R.M.A. home defence conscripts to volunteer for service overseas. For that was the Government's chosen — and seemingly only — course.

McNaughton failed, despite his best efforts. The N.R.M.A. men were as determined to resist volunteering as men could be, telling their pleading chaplains and commanding officers that they were willing to fight if the Government had the courage to send them but they would be damned if they would let King off the hook by going voluntarily. For McNaughton, this was personally shattering, and, finally advised by the military staff that volunteers could not be secured, he told Mackenzie King so. King's

*The most popular military cartoonist of the Canadian army here illustrates scrounging, a favourite activity of Canadian soldiers in Europe. (*Toronto Telegram *Collection, York University Archives)*

problem now was to justify a change of policy to himself, first, and then to his Cabinet, party, and country. Characteristically, he managed to do so, persuading himself that the military advice to McNaughton amounted to a challenge to civil authority, one that could only be countered by imposing conscription for overseas service on the N.R.M.A. That did the trick with King and with his ministers, many of whom were on the very verge of resignation, and the political crisis was resolved by the decision to send sixteen thousand N.R.M.A. men overseas. The military crisis was resolved when casualties at the front, fortuitously, were less than anticipated, and only 2463 of the N.R.M.A. soldiers reached the front lines. Those that did, by all reports, fought and died as well as any other soldiers. Sixty-nine N.R.M.A. soldiers were killed, a tiny proportion of the army's 22 917 dead, the navy's 2204, and the R.C.A.F.'s 17 101.

The crisis had been caused by planning failures far more than anything else but it was a crisis nonetheless. King had survived with his Cabinet more or less intact, and above all he had prevented French Canada from deserting the Liberal party and, King was convinced, abandoning faith in the promises of their federal leaders. Still, the reaction in Quebec was sharply critical, many apparently believing that the betrayal of 1942 (for so the plebiscite was seen) had produced its inevitable result. Nonetheless, bad as he was, Mackenzie King still seemed the best of a bad lot of Anglo politicians to French Canadians. Could they support the Conservatives, that party that was ferociously in favour of compulsion and pressed for it to be used in the war with Japan as well? Could they support the C.C.F., a socialist party that, while no longer condemned by the Church, still seemed too radical for a traditionalist society? Could they support the Bloc Populaire Canadien, a protest party that had sprung into existence as a result of the plebiscite campaign of 1942? The B.P.C. had some able leaders in men such as André Laurendeau, but its policies mixed reformism with nationalism in a way that seemed forced to many. Provincially, French Canadians had taken out their frustrations by returning Maurice Duplessis and the Union nationale to power in August, 1944, but there was no apparent desire to isolate Quebec from the rest of the country.

If Quebec made Mackenzie King nervous for the fate of his Government, so too did English Canada. Feelings were high on the conscription issue, and many in Ontario and the West were convinced that they had been gulled by King in 1942 and betrayed by him in 1944. The Conservatives fed on this resentment, but the party was in some difficulties of its own. In 1942, after Meighen's defeat in Toronto, the party was left leaderless, convinced that its fate was sealed unless it could find a new base of support. That turned Conservatives to the West and to social reform simultaneously, and in December, 1942, the assembled party faithful picked John Bracken as leader and changed the party's name to the Progressive Conservative party. Bracken had been a very successful Liberal-Progressive premier of Manitoba, a skillful and shrewd operator who had come to power at the beginning of the 1920s directly from the faculty of the Manitoba Agricultural College. But Bracken, who was really more conservative than progressive, foolishly decided not to seek a seat in Parliament, and, thus deprived of a national forum, he devoted himself to delivering dry speeches across the land. Conservatives quickly became disillusioned and many looked wistfully to George Drew, the Ontario leader who had led his party to a minority victory in 1943. The ideologically divided and weakly led Tories seemed stronger than they were.

The Move to the Left

As did the Cooperative Commonwealth Federation. J.S. Woodsworth, the saintly socialist, was dead and gone, and the C.C.F. was led now by M.J. Coldwell, a decent and able man, and the party organization was directed largely by the forceful, brilliant David Lewis. The defeat of Meighen had put the socialist party into the news, and the next year the C.C.F. had risen from zero to thirty-four seats in the Ontario provincial election and to a narrow lead over the old parties in the national opinion polls. Something was happening to Canada as the war went on. The C.C.F. began to win federal by-elections and astonishingly, under Tommy Douglas's leadership, it captured control of Saskatchewan in 1944, the first elected socialist Government in North America. The challenge from the left was a real one.

Mackenzie King was fully aware of this, although the demands of the war forced his and his Government's attention away from political and domestic affairs. Tired ministers wrestling with intractable problems of state had little time for politicking. But by 1943 the Liberals had to reorganize and rethink their role if the party was to survive the war. The direction that people wanted to go seemed clear — virtually every opinion poll taken openly by the Canadian Institute of Public Opinion and secretly by the Government's Wartime Information Board demonstrated that Canadians were afraid that depression conditions would return with the peace. People wanted jobs, security, a good standard of living, and if the C.C.F. promised those things, then people would vote C.C.F. King himself had always claimed to want similar things — after all, he had written *Industry and Humanity* in 1918 as a virtual manifesto of social welfare — but the times had never before been right. Now the war had demonstrated that Canada could produce goods in profusion and that billions of dollars worth could be given away to our allies. Could the country not do as much for its own citizens?

More to the point, perhaps, the federal bureaucracy had become converted to Keynesian economics, convinced that a prosperous Canada could be erected only if the federal government played a major role in directing the economy. When times were tough, officials in the Department of Finance now believed, the state should prime the pump with money. And as everyone believed that the reconstruction period was certain to be difficult, that it would strain the country to reintegrate the servicemen and to convert industry from producing tanks to once again building automobiles, preparation had to be made now. One step had been taken in 1940 with the establishment of a contributory scheme of unemployment insurance. Another came in 1944 with the creation of a great plan for family allowances. The "baby bonus," as some sneeringly described it, was deliberately designed to give mothers (and not fathers) a monthly payment for each child. This money would buy milk, shoes, and clothing; it would help raise the standard of living for everyone; it would lead to healthier children; and it would put money in the hands of those who would spend it and thus stimulate the economy. It would also convince millions of Canadians that the Liberal party was their salvation, that Liberals — and not C.C.F.ers or Tories — were the party that delivered the goods. It would and did. So too did a whole series of additional government measures to move towards the welfare state, to re-establish industry and stimulate exports, to encourage housing construction, to resettle veterans in the cities or on the land, and to give demobilized servicemen a chance for an education or all the medical care they needed. The country had changed with the war, and the ideas of state intervention that in the 1930s had been denounced as unjustified interference with the laissez faire tradition were now hailed as essential.[8]

The Liberals were the beneficiaries of all this, in part because they happened to be in office when the shift in attitude occurred and could react to it, in part because they had the good sense to listen to the advice

---

8. On reconstruction, see Bothwell and Kilbourn, *C.D. Howe*; Granatstein, *Canada's War*; R. Bothwell, I. Drummond, and J. English, *Canada Since 1945* (Toronto, 1980); and Leonard Marsh, *Report on Social Security for Canada 1943* (Toronto, 1975).

*Tommy Douglas campaigned for the C.C.F. in the Saskatchewan election of 1944.
Douglas's victory frightened the old parties and helped push the federal government
along the road to social welfare programs. (Saskatchewan Archives, R-A7917[1])*

of an extraordinarily able bureaucracy. Whatever the reason, the Liberals
stole the social welfare planks away from the Opposition, and in the election of June, 1945, they were returned to power. The Tories won only
sixty-seven seats, a reflection of the party's lack of wisdom in harping on
conscription for the Japanese war while Canadians, fresh from victory in
Europe in May, were looking only to the peace. The C.C.F. — badly
battered by a sometimes vicious anti-socialist campaign that denounced
them as both Nazi and Communist, authoritarian and academic — won
only twenty-eight. It was the socialists' best showing yet, but it was a far
cry from the party's expectations. And King and the Liberals received
127 seats, a bare majority in a House of 245 members. Quebec, restive
and unhappy, had nonetheless opted for King, giving him 50.8 per cent
of the vote and fifty-three seats. Considering that such a leader as Winston Churchill was deposed by an ungrateful British electorate as soon as
possible after the war, King's triumph might fairly be seen as one of the
most remarkable in our history. He had been saved by Quebec, to be

sure, but he had deserved to be. He had guided the country through a long and terrible war, he had produced an astonishing military and industrial war effort, and he had remade Canadian society in the process. In 1939 Mackenzie King seemed an eminently forgettable Prime Minister; by 1945 he had to rank with Macdonald and Laurier, although both his contemporaries and historians have been grudging with this judgement.

A Nation on the World Stage

The coming of peace was a tremendous relief and release to Canadians. At last the killing was over, at last the boys and girls would come home. But the atomic bombings of Hiroshima and Nagasaki, however necessary they had seemed to the President of the United States and his political and military planners, and however they had been hailed as casualty-saving weapons in Allied countries, heralded a new and dangerous world. So too did the defection of a Soviet cipher clerk, Igor Gouzenko, from the Russian embassy in Ottawa. Carrying with him documents that irrefutably demonstrated that the Soviet Union had been operating major spy rings in Canada throughout the war, Gouzenko's flight might be said to have launched the Cold War.

Almost as surprising as the revelation that the U.S.S.R. had been spying in Canada was the realization that there might be something worth spying on here. That surely would not have been the case in 1925 or 1935, but by 1945 Canada had suddenly blossomed forth as a Middle Power, an important ally of Britain and the United States, and as the nation that had put together the third largest navy and fourth largest air force and a large, powerful, and well-equipped army in the course of the Second World War. By itself, that made Canada important, but so did its close relationship with its Anglo-American allies on atomic research, its cooperation with them in other scientific research and in intelligence matters, and the general friendliness with which Canada, the United States, and the United Kingdom worked and cooperated as partners. That too was a change from the prewar years or even from the opening years of the war.

In 1939, for example, Canada had gone to war for much the same reasons and in much the same way as it had in 1914. There was little Canadian involvement in the events preceding the British and French declaration of war, notwithstanding the long process of Canada's movement towards autonomy and the Statute of Westminster of 1931. Canada went to war not because Hitler was a monster who had invaded Poland, not to fight for democracy, not to save the Jews of Europe but simply because Britain had gone to war. If the Chamberlain Government had managed to welsh on its commitments to Poland (promises made without any consultation with Canada), then Canada would have stayed out of war too. But Chamberlain's Cabinet insisted on honouring its pledges, and after a week of semi-neutrality that let Mackenzie King honour *his* promise that "Parliament will decide," Canada was at war. It was almost as if the long struggle for autonomy, from 1914 to 1939, had never occurred.

Nor did matters alter much with the first years of war. Canada was occasionally feisty and jealous of its rights, but Ottawa never claimed or sought any share in Anglo-French strategic or economic planning, contenting itself with the right to a say only in how Canadian troops could be employed. London took Canada for granted, and while Mackenzie King grumbled about this, he did little to rectify it, although on economic questions he and his ministers sometimes struggled forcefully with Whitehall.

Relations with the United States prior to Pearl Harbor were, as we have seen, friendly and close on both economic and defence fronts, but

The victory in Europe produced a great celebration all across the country. This Toronto mother's display, showing photographs of her sons in Europe and an effigy of a German soldier, must have been among the most impressive. (Toronto Telegram *Collection, York University Archives)*

that was as much a function of the American desire to make the hemisphere inviolate as it was a genuine concern for Canadians. And as war in the Pacific threatened in mid-1941, and as the British and American military staffs began secret consultations about actions in the event that America entered the war against the Axis, Canada began to find itself forgotten in Washington too. After Pearl Harbor matters grew worse, for the Anglo-American leadership created a whole series of combined agencies, boards, and military planning staffs, blithely forgetting Canada and all the other junior partners in the struggle against Hitler.[9]

For the first time in the war the Canadian Government — or its civil servants — began to be upset at the treatment the country was receiving. In the Great War, Sir Robert Borden had complained that London could not expect Canada to put a half million men into the field and then treat it like a colony; the same thing might have been said in 1942. But in the Second World War, Canada already had won its formal autonomy from Britain, and its efforts this time were directed at achieving genuine influence in the councils of the Great Powers.

The chosen tactic was the functional principle. The idea was not uniquely Canadian, but the way Ottawa used it was. It was developed by Hume Wrong, the very intelligent professional diplomat who was then at the Canadian legation in Washington, and refined by Norman Robertson and Lester Pearson, two senior officers of External Affairs in Ottawa, both men with great ability and a desire to see Canada play its proper role. The functional principle took shrewd advantage of Canada's strengths in certain key areas. For example, Britain and the United States had created a Combined Food Board to allocate scarce foodstuffs. But with the United States, Canada was the greatest food exporter on the Allied side; in those circumstances, surely justice and common sense required that Canada have a part to play in the decision-making. The same type of situation applied in a number of other areas and the Canadians mounted a skillful attack on Britain and the United States, and occasionally on France, the U.S.S.R., and China as well, with the aim of obtaining a larger voice for itself. In the end, and after very tough bargaining that saw Ottawa threaten to cut off financial assistance to Britain, the Canadian point was made. Alone among the smaller countries Canada received a place on some of the combined boards; alone among the lesser powers Canada received a

9. On wartime foreign policy, see the volumes in the *Canada in World Affairs* series (Toronto); John Holmes, *The Shaping of Peace: Canada and the Search for World Order, 1943-57*, vols. I, II (Toronto, 1979, 1982); Stacey, *Canada and the Age of Conflict*, vol. II; Granatstein, *Canada's War;* Cuff and Granatstein, *Ties that Bind;* Granatstein, *A Man of Influence.*

crucial role in the United Nations Relief and Rehabilitation Administration. And in a very real sense, those achievements amounted to a declaration of responsibility. For the first time Canada was seeking a share in carrying out tasks, not simply autonomy for its own sake, not status alone.

This could be seen in the discussions and negotiations that led to the creation of the United Nations. The Canadian argument, advanced as well by such other countries as Australia, New Zealand, the Netherlands, and Belgium, was that there were a number of Middle Powers with special capabilities, nations that had shown during the war that they could carry their own weight and more. Surely such countries were entitled to a place in the new world organization that distinguished them from small countries that had not contributed much to the Allied victory. The Big Four — the United States, the United Kingdom, the Soviet Union, and China — were not particularly receptive to this, being more interested in securing a veto for themselves, and Canada had little success. A Canadian delegation was slightly more successful at the United Nations Conference on International Organization in San Francisco in the spring of 1945 when it sought to secure guarantees that the U.N. Security Council would not be able to commit Canadian forces to collective security operations without Canadian participation in the decision-making. The long history of Canadian resistance to Whitehall's imperious demands required such a guarantee, and although Ottawa won its point, it turned out to be a hollow victory, as the relevant clause has never been employed.

The San Francisco conference was also an eye opener to many Canadians in what it told them about the Soviet Union. The Russian delegation was large and able, but the Soviet stonewalling tactics sometimes seemed disruptive and reprehensible. The good feelings of the war, the great admiration in the West for the U.S.S.R.'s doughty resistance to Hitler (even if it had involved forgetting the excesses of Stalin's Russia in the 1930s), were rapidly beginning to dissipate, a casualty of mutual Soviet and Western suspicions and of the powers' postwar jockeying for control in eastern and central Europe, the Balkans, and Asia. This posed serious problems for Canada, situated as it was on the direct bomber route between Moscow and Washington, and Canadian planners — for the first time ever there *were* planners in Ottawa and this fact deserves to be noted — had already carried out staff studies on Canada's role in the cold peace. There was no doubt that Canadian interests were seen to require cooperation with Washington, for the United States, in its own defence interests, would require this of us in any case. The Gouzenko revelations made the point more clearly still.

L.B. Pearson speaking to members of one of the committees at the United Nations Conference on International Organization at San Francisco in 1945. (C-18532/ Public Archives Canada)

The result was that Canada quietly began to ready itself to play a part in the defence of the Western world. This was a slow process of accommodation to the new realities, and the Canadian forces, rapidly demobilized after 1945, were in no condition to undertake operations against any enemy, however weak. But to Ottawa's officials, the need, by 1947, was becoming clear: the West had to organize itself to resist Soviet Communism and, above all, the United States had to be dragged out of its self-satisfied isolationism and made aware of its responsibilities to the rest of the world. In other words, Ottawa was not dragged into the Cold War, kicking and screaming by Washington; the reverse was more nearly the case, and officials in External Affairs, National Defence, and the Department of Finance were present at the creation of the postwar world as participants. The North Atlantic Treaty of 1949, the result of an idea first advanced by Escott Reid of External Affairs in August, 1947, and advocated again and again by others such as Louis St. Laurent, the Secretary of State for External Affairs, and his deputy minister, Lester Pearson, was in many senses a Canadian creation. To Ottawa and to most Canadians, the treaty seemed the definitive burial of the old prewar years of evasion of responsibility. The war had altered Canada and Canadians dramatically.

Dollars and Trade

This was also demonstrable in postwar Canadian trade policy. Officials and politicians alike had realized by 1944 that while postwar trade was certain to be disrupted, there were opportunities to be seized. Europe and Asia were in ruins, their industrial plant and agricultural production virtually destroyed. What should Canada do in these circumstances? One plan was to press for a great measure of free trade to end the prewar system of tariff barriers that had done so much to breed suspicion and enmity, and that plan culminated in 1947 in the General Agreement on Tariffs and Trade that brought together all the great trading states. Canada also realized that most of its traditional trading partners had no money to buy Canadian goods, their scanty resources being necessary to rebuild homes, factories, and lives. In such circumstances, the answer was clear: Canada had to give credits to Britain, France, and the Low Countries. However, this was not charity, although it involved the realization that our allies had suffered greater hardships in the war than we; instead, this policy was pragmatically based on the hard-headed understanding that unless Canada could trade, the nation would face massive unemployment and unrest at home. In the circumstances, and in keeping with the war-time policy of mutual aid that had seen us give away goods when Britain could no longer pay for them, and also in keeping with the conclusion, arrived at during the war, that the most important task of a nation was to give its people work and security, the Canadian Government in 1946 offered $2 billion in credits to Britain and Western Europe. It was purposeful generosity, it was good business, and it demonstrated more than anything else could that Canada had grown up.

Trade with the United States was also crucial, for most of Canada's exports and imports travelled in a north-south direction. With the peace, and after ten years of depression and six years of war, the Canadian people wanted luxuries again. They wanted trips to Florida, radios, cars, refrigerators, and clothes dryers. But all those things cost American dollars, and although Canada had emerged from the war with its reserves of American currency in good shape, it did not take long before there was a major exchange crisis facing Douglas Abbott, the Minister of Finance in 1947, and Clifford Clark, his deputy minister and one of the ablest civil servants in Canadian history. The situation was strikingly similar to that of 1941. Then Canada had been caught in a situation where every effort we made to support Britain with munitions forced us to import more from the south and to slide deeper into debt, largely because we were unable to convert the sterling surplus that our large trade balance with Britain had earned into U.S. dollars. In 1947, the Canadian Government was paying almost the entire cost of its exports to Britain and Europe, getting almost nothing back in return, and imports from the United States were skyrocketing. The crisis must have seemed inevitable.

How to resolve it was unclear. One response was to restrict the flow of imports as a dollar conservation measure, but that produced little more than nickels and dimes. Another was to initiate discussions with Washington for a full-scale free trade arrangement. Those discussions, in 1947 and 1948, had been agreed to by Mackenzie King and conducted in great secrecy, but when the Canadian negotiators came back to Ottawa with the draft agreement, the Prime Minister became nervous. The old man was almost seventy-four now, worn down by the war and the unceasing strain of office. He was at the end of his career, he knew, and he did not want to go into history as the Prime Minister who had tied Canada irrevocably to the United States — or as the leader who repeated the Liberal disaster of 1911. For King, the decision to veto the free trade deal was finally reached when he pulled a book down from his shelves and opened it by chance to a page discoursing on the spiritual meaning of

PERCENTAGE OF TOTAL NONRESIDENT INVESTMENT

	U.S.	U.K.	Other
1914	23%	72%	5%
1920	44	53	3
1939	60	36	4
1945	70	25	5
1947	72	23	5
1949	74	22	4
1952	77	18	5

INVESTMENT BY NONRESIDENTS IN DOLLARS (MILLIONS)

	U.S.	U.K.
1914	$ 881	$2778
1920	2128	2577
1939	4151	2476
1945	4990	1750
1947	5201	1647
1949	5906	1717
1952	7997	1886

Source: F.H. Leacy, ed., *Historical Statistics of Canada* (Ottawa: Statistics Canada, 1983).

the Empire. That was fate, and King closed off the talks, perhaps saving the country, as he believed, or losing the opportunity of the century, as many in the bureaucracy argued.

What then could rescue Canada from its dollar shortage? The answer again reproduced the events of the war. Then the Hyde Park Agreement had allowed Canada to import components from the United States and to have these charged to the British Lend-Lease account. This time, skillful Canadian negotiators in Washington persuaded the Americans to allow European countries, and mainly Britain, to use funds allocated by Congress under the European Recovery Program — better known as the Marshall Plan — to cover purchases in Canada. That was clever, and in the inflationary postwar years, when genuine shortages existed, the Truman administration was willing to agree. The result was that almost a billion dollars flowed north in 1948 and 1949 to pay for wheat shipments to Britain and food and manufactured goods for countries as diverse as France,

Norway, and Italy. That was sufficient to restore equilibrium in the Canadian economy, although one effect was that virtually all of Canada's trade went either to the United States or was subsidized by it, a dangerous state of affairs. Another was that in its desperate efforts to build up its holdings of American dollars, the Government encouraged American investment at every opportunity. Money poured north to develop iron mines, mineral production, and oil fields and to buy up Canadian industries, creating problems for the future at the same time as it resolved the difficulties of the present.

Korea and Suez

The economy also received an extraordinary fillip as a result of war in an unlikely place, the small Asian peninsula of Korea. Korea had been under Japanese control until 1945; then, by a wartime agreement, it was divided into a northern zone, to be under the control of the Soviet Union, and a southern zone under the United States. While it had been anticipated that the two zones would be merged into a single, independent country, the Cold War had frozen matters, and when the two great powers departed in 1948 they left two mutually antagonistic states behind. On June 25, 1950, the armies of North Korea invaded the south, sweeping the disorganized armies of Syngman Rhee's Republic of Korea before them. The United States intervened, bringing the United Nations in its train, and many in the West perceived the struggle as the first shot in a world war against Communism. The North Koreans could not have attacked, people in the West — and in Canada — believed, without the go-ahead from Moscow and/or from Peking, where the Communists now ruled also. If Moscow was prepared to go to war in Korea, could Western Europe not expect a similar fate? The answer was massive rearmament and the enlistment of new armies.

For Canada, this meant the raising of a brigade group to fight in Korea, a decision squeezed out of a Government somewhat reluctant to fight in Asia only by substantial American pressure. Had Mackenzie King been the prime minister, Canadian participation would have been unlikely; King was always too worried about conscription and national unity to consider such a foreign adventure. But King was gone, retired in the fall of 1948 and, by a striking coincidence, dead and buried in Toronto at the very height of the Korean crisis. Indeed, it was on the way back from King's funeral that most of the Cabinet, gathered in a private rail car, decided that Canada had to participate in the Korean conflict. The new

Prime Minister, Louis St. Laurent, although a Quebecker, had none of his countrymen's worries over conscription and much more confidence in the strength of Canada's unity than Mackenzie King. To him Communism was an evil, the anti-Christ, and if it had to be stopped in Korea, so be it. But even St. Laurent must have become alarmed at the impact of the Cold War on Canada. Korea sparked fears that the U.S.S.R. might strike in Europe, and these fears prompted the decision to raise an additional brigade for service in Germany with the North Atlantic Treaty Organization's forces, the first permanent peacetime commitment of troops abroad in Canadian history. The brigade was to be joined by an air division of the R.C.A.F., flying twelve squadrons of Canadian-made F-86 Sabre jets in an interceptor role. The R.C.N. was strengthened as well, its destroyers plying the waters of the Atlantic and Pacific. The armed forces' strength rose rapidly — the army increased from 20 369 in July 1950 to 42 622 a year later, and the other services' manpower increased similarly — and costs increased more rapidly still. In 1949, Canadian defence spending had been $361 million, or 2.2 per cent of G.N.P.; in 1951 it was $1157 million, or 5.5 per cent; and in 1953 it was $1907 million, or 7.6 per cent of G.N.P., the highest level in peacetime Canada to that point.

Many of the volunteers for Korea or N.A.T.O. were old "sweats" from the Second World War, and very quickly they were whipped into shape. The Korean brigade did not fight as a unit until well into 1951, although one battalion of the Princess Patricia's Canadian Light Infantry, arriving in Korea before the main body, saw action early in that year. The Canadian brigade served as part of a Commonwealth division and fought well, especially the Princess Patricia's at Kap'yong in April, 1951, and the Royal Canadian Regiment on the Sami-ch'on River in May, 1953. In all, 22 000 Canadians served with the brigade in Korea under the United Nations flag; 309 were killed, 1202 were wounded, and 32 became prisoners of war. "By way of comparison," the official army history of Korea notes a bit drily, "in 1950, 2289 persons in Canada were killed in traffic accidents."

That U.N. service in Korea was something of a foretaste of future efforts to keep the peace. Korea had been described by President Truman as a police action; but the United Nations was also playing different military roles in other parts of the world. A war, after independence, between Pakistan and India had resulted in a truce, and a U.N. observer group, on which Canadian personnel served, was involved. There was a similar situation along the borders of the new state of Israel after 1948. And in 1956, after President Nasser of Egypt nationalized the Suez Canal, an act

Canadian troops moved through this Korean village in 1951.
(PA-110828/Public Archives Canada)

symbolic of an irresistible upsurge of Third World nationalism against
the old imperialist and colonial powers, U.N. peacekeeping reached its
pinnacle in the attempts to resolve matters when Britain, France, and
Israel combined to attack Egypt.

The Suez crisis caused a dramatic series of events. For the first time
ever, the Canadian Government found itself deeply opposed to actions
undertaken by its two mother countries, for to Ottawa the Anglo-French
attack — and the collusion between Paris and Tel Aviv — seemed like
nothing so much as a foolish attempt to reverse history, one that was
certain to redound to the discredit of the West's position in the Middle
East and throughout the Third World. Ottawa's policy, largely directed
by Lester Pearson, the Secretary of State for External Affairs since 1948,
was to salvage as much face as possible for the British and French, to

preserve what remained of the N.A.T.O. alliance, and to keep Washington, itself bitterly opposed to the invasion that occurred in the final few days of a presidential election campaign, talking with London and Paris. A subsidiary, but no less important goal, was to preserve the Commonwealth, for nations such as India were on the verge of breaking all ties with London. Difficult as those tasks may have been, Pearson's splendid and supple diplomacy largely accomplished them.

The locus of action was the United Nations in New York. Heading the Canadian delegation, Mike Pearson worked tirelessly to improvise a U.N. peacekeeping force that could be interposed between the combatants and preserve a truce. Indeed, Pearson got Cabinet support to offer a Canadian battalion for the U.N. force, an effort that was well intentioned but more than a little maladroit. Egypt had been invaded by the Queen of England's soldiers, English-speaking and wearing uniforms and flying flags not at all dissimilar to those carried by Canadians. No one should have been surprised when Nasser refused to have the Canadian battalion, but the shock to Canadian pride was terrible. It was only with the greatest of difficulty that Nasser was persuaded to permit Canadian logistics troops to be part of the United Nations Emergency Force. The Canadian triumph in creating the U.N.E.F. and easing the tense situation was recognized by Pearson's being awarded the Nobel Peace Prize; the humiliation of Nasser's rejection of the Canadian infantry and English-Canadian resentment that Canada was not "ready, aye, ready" to support Britain, were likely reflected in the general election results of 1957.

But in a sense, the anger in Canada over the Government's treatment of Britain was a last gasp of the old Anglocentrism. Too many of Canada's business, trade, and defence ties were with the United States now, and the arrival of television was bringing American culture directly and intensely into all parts of the country. The population mix was altering as well under the impact of postwar immigration, and although Canadians of British ancestry still occupied the key places in the business, media, and political elites, demographic power was shifting. The old Canada was going, and the Suez crisis and the responses it provoked demonstrated that fact.[10]

---

10. On foreign policy to 1956, see Holmes, *The Shaping of Peace*, vols. I. II; Stacey, *Canada and the Age of Conflict*, vol. II; L.B. Pearson, *Mike: The Memoirs of the Rt. Hon. Lester B. Pearson*, vols. I, II (Toronto, 1972, 1973); Pickersgill, *The Mackenzie King Record*, vols. III, IV (Toronto, 1970); Granatstein, *A Man of Influence;* R.D. Cuff and J.L. Granatstein, *American Dollars/Canadian Prosperity: Canadian-American Economic Relations 1945-50* (Toronto, 1978); James Eayrs, *In Defence of Canada*, vols. III, IV (Toronto, 1972, 1980); Denis Stairs, *The Diplomacy of Constraint: Canada, the Korean War, and the United States* (Toronto, 1974); and the biennial volumes of the *Canada in World Affairs* series.

Postwar Immigration

Immigration had been one of the central facts of the Canadian experience before the Great War, and it had been a moral question in the 1930s. But after the Second World War, immigration became less contentious and more accepted. The newcomers brought skills and wealth, different religions and cultures, and they immeasurably altered the Canada they found. The first waves after the war were refugees from Hitler or Stalin — Jewish survivors of the death camps or anti-Communist Poles, Ukrainians, and others who had not wanted to return home after the war. By the time of the Cold War, security considerations were beginning to become important, and applicants for admission to Canada could be denied entry for political reasons — a policy that was little known but one that probably would have been enthusiastically accepted by Canadians. Who wanted former Nazis in Canada? Who wanted Reds? However, members of both of those groups sometimes slipped through the cursory checks.

The checks had to be cursory because the numbers coming were enormous — even though many Canadians were unenthusiastic about accepting more foreigners. From 22 722 in 1945 (a number that included thousands of war brides, married to soldiers overseas), immigration to Canada increased to 64 127 in 1947, 125 414 in 1948, and 194 391 in 1951. Thereafter, for every year of the 1950s, immigration was above a hundred thousand, and in 1957, a year that saw Hungarians who had fled their homeland after the abortive revolution of 1956 admitted along with thousands of Britons, disillusioned by the Suez fiasco and declining economic opportunity in England, immigration reached the amazing total of 282 164. In all, between 1945 and 1957, 1.7 million people left their homes in Europe and came to the New World, firmly expecting to find the streets paved with gold.

Most of the newcomers went to Ontario, almost half heading for the factories of Toronto, the mines of the north, or the booming construction industry of the cities. The next largest group chose Quebec, but as many were British in origin or opted to send their children to English-language schools, the demographic implications were serious for French Canadians, ever conscious of their language and culture and sensitive to their declining relative numbers within Confederation. There was little support in Quebec for mass immigration if the children of Italian workmen after one generation became part of the Anglophone community. The rest of the country, less threatened, was more tolerant. British Columbia received more than a hundred thousand immigrants between 1945 and 1957, and many, such as the entire forestry faculty and student body of Sopron University in Hungary, brought crucially needed skills.

J.W. Pickersgill, the Minister of Citizenship and Immigration in the St. Laurent Government, had arrived in Vienna to administer Ottawa's crash program of assistance to Hungarian refugees, heard about the Sopron foresters, and sprang into action. "I telephoned Jimmy Sinclair [a Cabinet colleague] who was in Vancouver, and he succeeded in a few hours in making arrangements to have the Forestry Faculty of Sopron affiliated with the University of British Columbia. Through Harold Foley of Powell River Paper Company, Sinclair was able to arrange to have a lumber camp at Powell River provided as a reception centre for the faculty and students from their arrival in British Columbia until the university term opened in September 1957." The foresters came and greatly benefited the country.

Not everyone was happy at the influx of Hungarians, of course. In Toronto, Pickersgill noted, Gordon Sinclair, a popular broadcaster, was bemoaning the costs to the taxpayers, and the provincial government, too, was worried about the costs of integrating into Canadian society people who arrived with little but the clothes on their backs. "These people are arriving with absolutely nothing," one Ontario minister complained, "not even an extra suit of underwear. Who is going to pay for the underwear?" Pickersgill paused for breath and then said, "We will." Ottawa did. In all, thirty-five thousand Hungarians came to Canada as a result of the revolution's failure.

If the Hungarians brought skills, so too did many others. Over 50 per cent of British immigrants between 1946 and 1963 were professionals. However, the percentage of professionals was infinitesimal among Italian immigrants, most of whom were destined for the labour force. The Italians amounted to the second largest national group to come to Canada, 139 000 entering the country between the war and 1957, and most settling in Toronto, Montreal, and Vancouver. But if the Italians were not managers or doctors or lawyers when they arrived, their children would be. Hardworking and industrious, the Italian immigrants quickly began to play a role in the cities they were helping to build. The Toronto subway, opened in 1954, was largely built by Italian labourers, as were most of the skyscrapers that began to sprout in the downtown.[11]

11. On immigration policy, see Freda Hawkins, *Canada and Immigration* (Montreal, 1972); Alan G. Green, *Immigration and the Postwar Canadian Economy* (Toronto, 1976); Gerald E. Dirks, *Canada's Refugee Policy* (Montreal, 1977). There is a substantial literature on various ethnic groups, most notably in the *Generations* series, published by McClelland and Stewart in association with the Multiculturalism program of the Department of the Secretary of State, and in the publications of the Multicultural History Society of Ontario. The best periodical in the field is *Canadian Ethnic Studies*, published at the University of Calgary.

Federal-Provincial Wrangling

Immigration, particularly when it involved a crash program such as the one organized for the Hungarians in 1956-57, demanded close federal-provincial cooperation. That cooperation increasingly was required across a wide range of activities, and cooperation between Ottawa and the provinces had never been easy to secure. The report of the Royal Commission on Dominion-Provincial Relations (usually called the Rowell-Sirois Commission after its first and second chairmen) was received in Ottawa only in 1940, at a time when the war was absorbing everyone's attention. A federal-provincial conference in 1941 to consider the subject of the report collapsed in disagreement, and Ottawa, desperate for money to finance the enormous costs of the war, soon announced its intention to take the areas of personal and corporate taxation from the provinces and to offer the provinces an annual payment in return. This had been one of the major recommendations in the Rowell-Sirois report, and the provinces grumbled but went along. At war's end they would not be so accommodating.

The wartime tax rental agreements expired in 1947, and while no one wanted to return to the prewar system where the two levels of government levied taxes without reference to each other, the provinces insisted on receiving a high price for their abandonment of certain rights of taxation. The federal proposals, usually called the Green Book proposals, aimed at securing a continuation and broadening of Ottawa's control of corporate and income taxation so that it could implement a series of national programs with the revenues gained. The Green Book laid out a complex and interrelated program of public works and social welfare. T.C. Douglas, the C.C.F. Premier of Saskatchewan since 1944, later called the federal plan "one of the most comprehensive pieces of work that has ever been done in Canadian history — in laying out a blueprint for establishing the beginning of a planned economy in Canada. . . . The general idea was that in times of prosperity we should be pulling money out of circulation, and in times of depression we should be pumping money into circulation. . . . Both the provincial and federal governments should have a whole series of public works projects on the shelf — already drafted with all the specific details — which could be taken off the shelf at any time that unemployment began to reach menacing proportions." In addition Ottawa proposed a series of social welfare plans — universal old age pensions financed by Ottawa alone for those over seventy years, and a program shared with the provinces to finance pensions for those from sixty-five to sixty-nine years who qualified after a means test; assistance for the able-bodied unemployed to be administered by Ottawa through the existing unemployment insurance system; and plans for the beginnings of a system of health insurance with Ottawa picking up 60 per cent of the costs. Ottawa also offered unconditional subsidies to the provinces in return for their giving up the levy of corporation and income taxes (and now succession duties as well) for a trial period of three years. The subsidies were to be determined by comparing the gross national product per capita in each of the three years with that of 1941. Most of the have-not provinces — the Maritimes and the Prairies — stood to gain from renting their tax fields to Ottawa, but Ontario and Quebec did not. Both believed their taxpayers would be subsidizing the rest of the country, and neither Premier Duplessis nor Premier Drew (joined by Angus L. Macdonald of Nova Scotia, who

Louis St. Laurent addressing an outdoor meeting, probably in the 1957 election campaign. (Matheson Papers, Queen's University)

hated King) were willing; Duplessis, in addition, saw in Ottawa's proposals yet another attempt to centralize power and to destroy the autonomy of Quebec. The failure to reach agreement led to the shelving of the federal proposals for social security. In the end, Ottawa drafted tax rental agreements with seven provinces, Ontario and Quebec refusing to the end. A great opportunity had been lost.

One opportunity was seized, however. On April 1, 1949, Newfoundland joined Canada, at last making the country's motto "A Mari Usque Ad Mare" a reality. The great island had been a Dominion until the Depression of the 1930s forced it into virtual bankruptcy and back to the status of a Crown Colony of Britain. The war had brought tens of thousands of Canadian sailors and troops to Newfoundland and the close links they forged had helped to erode centuries of suspicion. But the war had also brought visiting British delegations and free-spending American soldiers, and in a real sense the postwar fate of Newfoundland was a problem of the old North Atlantic triangle. The Americans probably had some desire to get the island, but in Washington's eyes Newfoundland was not worth a bitter fight with Ottawa so long as they could keep bases there; the war-ravaged British wanted out as cheaply as possibly — austerity demanded that; making no bones about it, the Canadians wanted Newfoundland to be the tenth province. And the people of the island? They were torn. Many wanted Dominion status back again, others sought a link to the United States, while still others, led by the redoubtable broadcaster and labour leader, Joey Smallwood, wanted Confederation. After two plebiscites and after a narrow victory for Confederation on the second one, hard negotiations produced a bargain. Smallwood became the leader of the new province's Liberal party and the first premier, and for a time, as baby bonus cheques and unemployment insurance poured in to help redress the island's seasonal unemployment, Newfoundlanders thought they had struck the mother lode at last. Those feelings would alter over time, as new defence costs strained the federal treasury.

The provinces and the federal government met again in December, 1950, in the shadow of the Korean War. Prime Minister St. Laurent made it clear that this Government hoped to renew the tax rental agreements, and Ontario, this time led by Premier Leslie Frost, went along with the plan, thus preserving the possibility of double taxation only for taxpayers in Quebec. In addition, St. Laurent won the support of all the premiers for the implementation of a program of old age security, universal for everyone over seventy. Ottawa would in addition share the costs of pensions for needy citizens between sixty-five and sixty-nine with any province willing to join in such a scheme. All the provinces agreed to this, and a constitutional amendment that provided for concurrent jurisdiction over old age pensions was duly passed. The old age pension was fixed at $40 a month, with the supplemental scheme with the province also providing the same sum.

There was one final and major federal initiative in the area of social welfare — hospital insurance. The idea of freeing Canadians from the crippling costs of hospitalization had first been legislated in Saskatchewan in 1946, and Tommy Douglas's Government had long been pressing Ottawa for assistance with the costs, which rose each year. In the end, and thanks to the efforts of Paul Martin, the Minister of National Health and Welfare, Ottawa had committed itself to supporting such a scheme whenever a majority of the provinces, representing a majority of the population, were ready to put into effect programs to provide hospital insurance. The Hospital Insurance and Diagnostic Services Act of 1957 came into effect on July 1, 1958, and committed the federal government to paying 50 per cent of the cost of provincial hospital insurance plans covering a basic range of in-patient services. Eventually every province was compelled by public opinion to offer hospital insurance to its people; the province of Saskatchewan and its C.C.F. Government had led the way.

St. Laurent and Duplessis finally resolved the differences over taxation between their two Governments in 1954. Duplessis had announced his intention to impose personal income taxes — as he had not yielded that right to Ottawa, he could certainly do so — but the result would be that a taxpayer in Montreal, for example, would pay 15 per cent more than one in Ontario and have two forms to fill in. That was not Duplessis' position, however; the premier argued that as the constitution gave taxation powers to the provinces, Quebec had priority and taxpayers there could deduct their provincial taxes from their end-of-April payments to Ottawa. A war of speeches between Ottawa and Quebec City went on for some months, until the two leaders met in Montreal on October 5, 1954. The resulting agreement saw Duplessis withdraw his claim of provincial priority. In response, St. Laurent offered Duplessis — and all the other premiers — the right to reduce their federal taxes by 10 per cent; since a federal tax abatement of 5 per cent was already in place, this meant that Quebeckers escaped double taxation. Duplessis had probably won the day, yielding a spurious constitutional premise to St. Laurent in return for substantial cash benefits.

In 1956 St. Laurent suggested a new system of revenue sharing with the provinces. In effect, he proposed to offer a choice to the provinces —

tax rentals as before, or a system of provincial taxation of up to 10 per cent of federal personal or corporate income taxes and 50 per cent of federal succession duties. In any case, most of the provinces would receive a new equalization grant which represented the difference between what any province could collect at the standard rates and the average that could be collected by the two wealthiest provinces, Ontario and British Columbia. One advantage of the scheme was that Quebec could continue to impose its own taxes and still be eligible for equalization grants, something that St. Laurent believed essential to the unity of the country. The very word "equalization" also suggested that all citizens, wherever they happened to live, had a right to equivalent services and standards of living. That too would assist unity. In the end the new system was accepted by Parliament, and eight of the provinces made tax rental agreements for all their taxes; Ontario made an agreement covering personal income taxes alone; and Quebec, though it made no agreement, accepted the equalization grant.[12]

The Postwar Boom

One reason that Ottawa could afford to be generous was that the country was riding the crest of a great, almost unprecedented boom. The difficulties that had plagued the economy after the war had largely disappeared, thanks initially to a billion dollars in American Marshall Plan money, but thanks, too, to vast quantities of American investment capital that poured into Canada. By 1950, the United States was beginning to worry about its own resources and sources of supply in the uncertain world of the mid-twentieth century. If China expanded in the East, if Russia expanded its frontiers, where could America turn for crucial minerals and metals? One answer was Canada, and, pressed by strategic necessity — as well as by geographical proximity, common attitudes and ideals, and the unwavering eagerness of the Canadian Government — American corporations poured billions of dollars into Canada. Oil gushed from the ground in Alberta and most of the money for exploration, drilling, and development was American. Iron ore from Quebec was developed by American corporations, loaded on American ships, and transported to the blast fur-

12. Studies of federalism and federal-provincial relations for the period from 1939 to 1957 include *The Rowell/Sirois Report/Boook 1* (Toronto, 1963); R.M. Burns, *The Acceptable Mean; The Tax Rental Agreements, 1941-62* (Toronto, 1980); Wilfrid Eggleston, *The Road to Nationhood* (Toronto, 1946); F.R. Scott, *Essays on the Constitution* (Toronto, 1977); and A.R.M. Lower, *et al.*, *Evolving Canadian Federalism* (Durham, 1958).

naces of Pittsburgh, Cleveland, or Gary. New industries leapt the tariff wall (a leap that was no longer as high as it had been under the National Policy or under the tariff revisions of the late 1930s, thanks to the General Agreement on Trade and Tariffs) and set up shop in Montreal, Toronto, Hamilton, and a hundred other communities, providing employment and good wages. The country was booming, and every index reflected this. The gross national product increased from $11.8 billion in 1945 to $18 billion in 1950 and to $31.9 billion in 1957. The average wage of a male factory worker increased over the same period from $30.47 per week to $44.03 and then $64.96.

The good times encouraged organized labour to try to heal the wounds in its ranks. The Canadian Congress of Labour and the much more conservative Trades and Labour Congress of Canada had been feuding for years, and in 1954 the two organizations, representing some 960 000 of the 1.25 million unionized workers in the country (a record 33.8 per cent of the work force), began negotiations to put labour's house in order. By 1956, as the C.C.L. and the T.L.C. emulated the peace between the American Federation of Labor and the Congress of Industrial Organizations in the United States, the Canadian Labour Congress had come into being. Approximately three-quarters of the C.L.C.'s membership were affiliated with American unions. The bulk of the country's unaffiliated workers were in Quebec, members of the Canadian and Catholic Federation of Labour (which in 1960 changed its name to the Confederation of National Trade Unions) which chose not to join the C.L.C. There was great optimism for the future.

Women workers did not fare so well. The gains women had made during the war when a range of hitherto closed jobs had suddenly been opened to them evaporated. Women, always lower paid than male workers, had been the first to be laid off to make room for demobilized veterans, and the percentage of women in the labour force dropped rapidly, as many seized the chance to return to being full-time homemakers and to raising children after the interruption of the war years (the birth rate after 1945 remained high for almost twenty years). By 1948 only 23.5 per cent or 835 000 women were in the non-farm work force — and there were only tiny numbers in managerial jobs and in professional positions (other than nurses and teachers). By 1957, after years of boom, the situation was not much better. Labour force participation was up only to 25.8 per cent, or 1 263 000 women workers, and the small numbers in managerial and professional posts, while higher all across the board, demonstrated that Canadians still remained overwhelmingly a patriarchal society, resistant to change in the relations between the sexes.

The Americanization of Canada

But in view of the general prosperity, few questioned the direction of the country or its economic policies. In a sense, this was understandable. Everyone could remember the Great Depression and its catastrophic impact on the living standards of the population. In a time of unrelieved boom, when everyone's life was improving each year, surely the Government's policy was proving itself. But some were looking askance at the unchecked influx of American capital that seemed necessary to fuel the boom. One such was Walter Gordon, a wealthy Toronto businessman and chartered accountant who had worked in Ottawa in the senior bureaucracy during the war and who had the best of connections with the Liberal party and the Government. From the mid-1950s Gordon had become fretful about the dangers to Canadian economic independence from unchecked foreign investment, and he had begun to believe that economic control could lead to American political control as well. Some of those concerns were advanced in an article he drafted for an academic journal, one calling for a royal commission to investigate the state and direction of the economy. The article was not to be published, for the Government, to which Gordon had sent a draft, took over the idea and appointed Gordon as chairman of the Royal Commission on Canada's Economic Prospects in the spring of 1955. His investigation, carefully based on the best academic research then available, demonstrated the extent of American penetration of every sector of the economy. An interim report was issued before the election of 1957, and it probably fed the growing feeling that Canada had somehow become too close to the United States and, for some, strayed too far from her British roots — an idea intensified by the Suez crisis.

The extent of American cultural penetration also worried many. A Royal Commission on National Development in the Arts, Letters and Sciences had been created in 1949 and put under the chairmanship of Vincent Massey, the former minister to the United States and high commissioner to Britain from 1935 to 1946. Massey's report, released in June, 1951, bemoaned Canadian culture's struggle to survive on the fringes of society, and called for the creation of a Canada Council, an arm's-length federal agency that could use tax dollars to foster the arts in Canada. Massey also called for strengthening such agencies as the Canadian Broadcasting Corporation, formed by the Bennett Government in the 1930s, and the National Film Board, created by Mackenzie King just before the Second World War, to make them carriers of Canadianism in the face of massive American intrusions in cultural areas. There was some real need for concern. American magazines held an increasing share of the market and absorbed high percentages of the advertising revenues in Canada. *Time* and *Reader's Digest* led the way. American radio stations near the border captured much of the Canadian audience, and the advent of television, seductive in its appeal and particularly mindless in its content, worsened matters. From the end of the 1940s Canadians in cities near the border purchased expensive television sets and erected high antennae to bring in the C.B.S., N.B.C., or A.B.C. stations from nearby American cities. The advent of Canadian broadcasting in 1952 — the C.B.C. first appeared on Toronto screens with its logo upside down — partially redressed the balance, but increasingly the public corporation found itself compelled to buy American programs to hold a satisfactory share of the viewing audience. Massey's prescriptions were to be hard to achieve. One of his recommendations was finally implemented in 1957 when the Canada Council was set up, its revenues being provided by succession duties from the huge estates of two recently deceased millionaires, Isaac Walton Killam and Sir James Dunn. The Council, over the years, would alter the lot of Canadian artists and scholars; it would also, by helping such nascent organizations as the Stratford Festival (started in 1953), the National Ballet (1951), Le Théâtre du Nouveau Monde (1951), and Toronto's Crest Theatre (1951), foster and encourage the development of a Canadian culture that was often vigorous and experimental. American cultural penetration, nonetheless, continued.

Liberal Arrogance

The parties that worried most about the American presence in Canada were the C.C.F. and the Progressive Conservatives. The socialist party was still led by M.J. Coldwell of Saskatchewan, one who fought the good fight every day in the House of Commons. The C.C.F. had made little headway nationally — although in Saskatchewan Tommy Douglas continued to lead his Government to election victory after victory — but the party could be counted upon to speak out for democratic socialist alternatives. The C.C.F. supported Canada's adherence to N.A.T.O., and it went along with participation in the Korean War, but it fretted about American policies and strategy and called for distinctively Canadian positions.

So too did the Progressive Conservatives, although often that party's idea of a distinctive position was for Canada to follow Britain's course. The Tories had chosen John Bracken as their leader in 1942, but when Bracken only marginally improved the party's position in the general election of 1945, unrest in the ranks increased. The answer in 1948, after Bracken's resignation, was the election of George Drew, the Premier of Ontario since 1943. Tall, good-looking, a man with a good record from the Great War, Drew had easily defeated a little-known Saskatchewan M.P. named John Diefenbaker on the first convention ballot. The difficulty was that Drew, too, failed to improve the party fortunes. In June, 1949, running against Louis St. Laurent, the new Prime Minister, he suffered a grievous defeat as St. Laurent swept to the largest majority in Canadian history to that point. Only 41 Conservatives and 13 C.C.F. M.P.s were returned to the House of Commons, against 193 Liberals. Drew, with his central Canadian attitudes, his seeming inability to understand French Canada or the West, and his stiff, rather shy exterior (one that was said to mask a warm personality), simply was no match for "Uncle Louis," a smooth Liberal machine, and prosperity. The same thing proved to be true in August, 1953, when St. Laurent again enjoyed a comfortable majority with 171 seats, the Conservatives taking 51 and the C.C.F. 23. The Liberals seemed able to go on forever.

C. D. Howe

But cracks were developing. The debate in 1955 on the renewal of the Defence Production Act of 1951, a measure that gave C.D. Howe, St. Laurent's "Minister of Everything," quite extraordinary potential powers over the economy, revealed some of them. There seemed less need for sweeping powers than there had been at the peak of the Korean War two or three years before, and that stirred the Opposition and public concern. So too did Howe's stubborn and almost arrogant defence of *his* need for the act's renewal. Drew and his front-benchers, Donald Fleming, a Toronto M.P., Davie Fulton from British Columbia, and Diefenbaker, harried and harassed the Government, delaying other business with a filibuster. In the end St. Laurent caved in, agreeing to a compromise with Drew that renewed Howe's powers only for a limited four-year term. The unbeatable Government had suffered a tactical defeat.

The next year there was to be another and more serious blow. Howe had become convinced that a pipeline had to be built to carry Alberta's natural gas to central Canadian markets, a good idea but one that was to be carried out by a largely American-controlled corporation. That was bad enough for the increasing number of Canadians concerned with American investment in Canada, but the company, Trans-Canada Pipelines, was in financial trouble and needed government assistance if its project was to be completed on schedule. One plan was to create a Crown corporation to build a pipeline through the difficult (and financially unrewarding) terrain of northern Ontario. Another was to loan the company enough money to build its western section of pipeline. Most Canadians probably understood few of the details of the contract or even of the supposed necessity of the pipeline. But what all understood, what the combined Conservative and C.C.F. Opposition made them understand, was that the Liberal Government was using improper methods to ram its pipeline bill through the House. Using Parliament's rules to advantage, the Opposition resisted at every turn, consistently outmaneuvering the Government. With irrevocable deadlines approaching, Howe, in desperation, resorted to closure, a legitimate but unpopular measure, to cut off debate and force a vote. The ensuing struggle, characterized by the apparent abandonment of impartiality by the Speaker, by the expulsion of Conservative Donald Fleming from the House and the draping of his seat with a Union Jack, and by a long, unruly series of sittings, resulted in the bill's passage and the Government's disintegration. The Liberals had won, but their highhandedness had shocked the country. C.D. Howe had served Canada well during the war and after, but by 1956 Canadians were beginning to wonder if he had overstayed his welcome in the seats of power.

Still, no one truly expected the Government to be defeated in the election of 1957. St. Laurent remained as Prime Minister and leader of the Liberal party, and although he was seventy-five years old and clearly tired, he still projected personal decency and integrity. Coldwell also remained in his place at the head of the C.C.F., his party bolstered by its sterling performance in the pipeline debate. But the Tories had changed leaders, Drew resigning after the pipeline affair because of ill-health. At a convention in Ottawa at the end of 1956, the assembled Progressive Conservatives chose John Diefenbaker as their leader. In Parliament since 1940, Diefenbaker had a reputation as a fierce partisan, a civil libertarian, and a fine orator. Many in his party also thought of him as a prima donna, but because the new chief was sixty-one years old, those who worried over the Prince Albert lawyer's stewardship doubtless thought he would not stay long. Certainly, few thought him likely to amount to much, and *Maclean's* magazine, caught by a deadline that forced it to produce an election editorial before the votes were cast on June 10, took what it believed to be a safe gamble and noted that Canadians had once again returned the most powerful government in the Western world. For once, events did not proceed the way the editors — or the Liberals — had planned.[13]

13. Works on Canadian politics from 1948 to 1957 are not numerous. The first volume of Diefenbaker's memoirs, *One Canada* (Toronto, 1975), and Dale Thomson's *Louis St. Laurent: Canadian* (Toronto, 1967), are useful guides; so too is J.W. Pickersgill's *My Years with Louis St. Laurent* (Toronto, 1975). Academic studies include Whitaker's *The Government Party*, John Meisel's *The Canadian General Election of 1957* (Toronto, 1962), Bothwell, *et al.*, *Canada Since 1945*, and Donald Fleming's memoir, *So Very Near*, vol. I (Toronto, 1985).

Chapter IX

The Pinnacle of Bureaucratic Power

"I spoke of what it meant to have Norman Robertson and Arnold Heeney associated with myself," Mackenzie King wrote in his diary on February 18, 1946, describing the small dinner party he had staged at his home for his Under Secretary of State for External Affairs and his Clerk of the Privy Council, their wives and aged parents. The Prime Minister had fussed over the arrangements, worrying over the details of the menu and seating plan as if the dinner was for a head of state, and when he told the elder Heeneys and Robertsons that he was grateful for the "gift" they had given the country in the form of their sons, he meant every word.

So he should have. Arnold Heeney had organized the work of the Cabinet and its key committee, the Cabinet War Committee, so effectively that the Prime Minister for the first time in Canadian history had a measure of control over the topmost operations of government. Norman Robertson had taken charge of External Affairs, the department of which King himself was minister, after the irreplaceable O.D. Skelton's death in January, 1941, and Robertson had filled the small department with the ablest collection of officials in the capital, men who could carry abroad Canada's new power and influence; during the Second World War and after, for the first time, other nations took notice. The bureaucrats had played a critical role for Mackenzie King, changing the country greatly. In the years to come, the period of continuous boom that lasted through the war, the Cold War, and the forging of a new relationship with the United States, their influence would be greater still.

Building a Civil Service

The Canadian civil service that was created after Confederation was not one known for its competence and ability to offer advice to ministers on thorny policy questions. In fact, its one notable characteristic was its patronage basis. The principle of appointment and promotion by merit was often paid lip service, but almost never accepted in practice, no matter the political colour of the Government or its promises while in Opposition. The victorious party, swept into power by the votes of its friends, naturally enough felt obliged to reward those same friends with positions in the public service and on the public payroll. Postmasterships were changed in small towns and large cities; the lock-keepers and workmen on the canals turned over; and the senior and junior administrators in Ottawa flowed in and out of office with the tide of political success. There were some exceptions, fortunately, some continuity, or else the government could scarcely have carried on. Some men — almost no women could rise to any position of influence in the civil service before the Second World War began to alter attitudes and produced a manpower shortage — managed to keep their positions despite political shifts and became indispensable adjuncts to their political masters. Sir Joseph Pope, for example, had been the son of one of Macdonald's ministers and an aide to the Old Man himself, but he nonetheless survived through the Laurier, Borden, and early King years, retiring only in 1925. Pope was a clever man, a skilled negotiator in international bargaining, a shrewd player of the Ottawa game. However, what he was not was an advisor to ministers, one who could propose courses of action and weigh advantages and disadvantages. That was not the role Pope or his colleagues envisaged for themselves — and it was probably not the role the politicians wanted them to play.

But who was to proffer policy advice if not the public servants? Could one assume that a lawyer from a small town in Prince Edward Island or Ontario or Alberta, elected by an usually indifferent populace and selected for the Cabinet by a prime minister who had to balance regional, racial, and religious considerations, was an expert in the arcane workings of the Departments of the Interior, Public Works, or Finance? Should anyone expect that minister to be able to shape a new direction for the country? To raise the question is to answer it. Most textbooks suggest that the task of a minister of the Crown in our system is to bring a fresh eye to the problems of state and to select from the options presented to him by his staff those that best serve the interests of country and party. But if no options are produced, then what? This argument overstates the absence of advice moving from the bottom up, but the general outlines are correct enough. How could the matter be altered?

The situation could not be improved very much until the public service was freed from the demands of pork-barrel patronage. A royal commission before the Great War had recommended this, and Sir Robert
Borden's Union Government had made major alterations in the structure
of the civil service in 1918. Teams of management experts (from the
United States) were brought to Ottawa to study the organization charts
and to produce a rational system of bureaucratic organization. The result
was more a farce than an improvement, for some senior bureaucrats suddenly found themselves outranked by and paid less than their subordi-
nates, while others saw the organizations they had created swept away.
Protest produced a return to the status quo *ante* in many cases, but the
very idea that efficiency could be considered important and that rational-
ity had a place in the public service made its effect felt. Patronage did not
die, but never again would its use be quite so common in Ottawa.[1]

It was not at all coincidental that Oscar Douglas Skelton came to Ottawa
in the aftermath of the postwar reorganizations. Skelton was a political
economist, the biographer of Laurier and Galt, and one of the country's
leading academic writers on the economy and affairs of state. He was a
nationalist and a Liberal and a man close to Mackenzie King, the Liberal
Prime Minister, but he was no patronage appointee. Instead, the Prime
Minister had brought him to Ottawa in 1924 from Queen's University in
Kingston to help create a Canadian foreign policy and a department to
run it. Skelton came because he believed those to be important and worthy goals, and also because he had become convinced, through his obser-
vations of Ottawa, that Canada needed a civil service corps of able men.
The postwar reorganization had created a structure of gradations in each
type of task: one began as a lighthouse keeper, grade one, and progressed
through the ranks to the pinnacle of lighthouse keeping. But what if that
keeper proved to be a brilliant formulator of policy or an administrator
supreme? No provision had been made for thinkers, and Skelton, who
was one, believed that to be foolish. His task, once he became the Under
Secretary of State for External Affairs in 1925, was to alter that situation,
at least in his own department.

1. On the old civil service, see J.E. Hodgetts, *Pioneer Public Service* (Toronto, 1955); R.M.
Dawson, *The Civil Service of Canada* (London, 1929); J.E. Hodgetts, *The Canadian Public
Service* (Toronto, 1973); W.L. Grant, "The Civil Service of Canada," *University of Toronto
Quarterly*, III (July, 1934); Sonja Sinclair, *'Cordial But Not Cosy': A History of the Office of the
Auditor-General* (Toronto, 1979); Maurice Pope, ed., *Public Servant: The Memoirs of Sir Joseph
Pope* (Toronto, 1960); O.M. Hill, *Canada's Salesmen to the World* (Montreal, 1977); J.
Swettenham and D. Kealy, *Serving the State* (Ottawa, 1970); and Sandra Gwyn, *The Private
Capital* (Toronto, 1984).

He was in a good position to do it: he knew the universities intimately, then a repository of intelligent generalists and good ideas, and he could draw on his contacts to recruit. He was, as Under Secretary, the Prime Minister's deputy in the department. But King was cautious, fearing that if the Department of External Affairs expanded too quickly his critics in the House of Commons would cry that he was expanding his personal empire and squandering the public's funds to do it, and so Skelton had to move carefully. His recruiting was slow but of high quality.

Skelton persuaded the Civil Service Commission, the watchdog body for appointments and staffing, that he should run a competition for a first secretary and a third secretary for his department. Those competitions in 1928 attracted a host of applicants and resulted in the eventual appointments of Lester Pearson, Norman Robertson, and Hugh Keenleyside, three uncommonly able men who were as far removed from the kinds of civil servants who had preceded them in Ottawa as one could imagine. All were young and well educated, with graduate degrees in history or economics from the best institutions in the United States or Britain. All were generalists, men with the capacity to apply their broad intelligence to differing problems and to improvise solutions. All were willing and — thanks to Skelton's guidance — unafraid to propose policy to their political masters. Their advice was often declined, but that it was offered was the key. In a few years Skelton had turned the Department of External Affairs from a post office that filed British dispatches and sent back form replies into a policy agency, one that had the capacity to offer advice to the Prime Minister and Cabinet, who were desperately in need of it. Skelton had made himself and his men indispensable, something that R.B. Bennett, taking power in 1930, was quick to discover. He had probably intended to sack Skelton, a Grit, but, perhaps to his surprise, Bennett found that he received prompt and effective advice from the Under Secretary, and as a result he kept him on. An important milestone on the road to the ideal of an impartial public service had been reached.

If the public service was now becoming impartial, it was also remaining completely masculine and English-speaking at the top. No women filled senior posts in the bureaucracy and none would for another thirty years or more. Women were the secretaries and clerks, the indispensable cogs in the wheels of bureaucracy, but no one seemed to believe that they might ever help make policy. In a sense, that omission is understandable for the era; less so is the complete absence of French Canadians from the corridors of power. There were French-speaking civil servants in Ottawa, but as with women, most were junior functionaries without power. Quebec ministers surrounded themselves with aides and offered patronage posts on boards and commissions to their friends, but only a rare Québécois could crack the policy-making upper levels of the public service; if one managed the trick, he was certain to be fluently bilingual — all the government's work was carried out in English. That lack of consideration was to have serious consequences for Canada before too many years passed.

With the onset of the Depression, Skelton knew well that his tiny crew in External could not cope with all the problems of the country. The Department of Finance, for example, was a mess, a swamp of bureaucratic incompetence and maladministration where the nation's funds had literally been stolen by a senior official. There was no effective agency to control or shape monetary policy and few officials able to understand the complexities of it. And the Cabinet had no organizational back-up, no agenda, no minutes, no staff papers to assist it in its work. The Prime Minister's Office similarly spent more time clipping the newspapers and answering letters than it did in helping the Prime Minister run the country. Matters had to be altered, and over the decade of the 1930s Skelton immeasurably changed Ottawa and the public service as a whole, much as he had already changed his own department.

His first move was to persuade Prime Minister Bennett to appoint W. Clifford Clark as Deputy Minister of Finance in 1932. Clark was a Queen's economics professor, a friend and former student of Skelton's, one who had worked in business in the United States. He was a bouncy little man with a kewpie-doll face, and although his economics were orthodox in the early 1930s, he was as convinced as Skelton of the necessity of bringing able men to the capital to work in government. Indeed, he was also a firm believer in the need for Canada to establish a central bank to make monetary policy and to control the currency, and he and Skelton soon had their eye on a young banker, Graham Towers of the Royal Bank. Still in his thirties, Towers was a cool customer, a very shrewd technician who understood how the money supply and credit could be manipulated and how monetary policy could be employed as a tool to serve the interests of the state. In 1934, after a royal commission (carefully structured by Clark so that the right answers would be produced) had recommended the creation of the Bank of Canada, Towers became its first Governor at the then-extraordinary salary of $30 000, and the next year the bank opened its doors. At last Ottawa had in place the necessary organizations for effective fiscal control, and in Towers and Clark it had two very able men. Both also recruited wisely and well.[2]

Organizing the Prime Minister

The job of organizing the Prime Minister and Cabinet was next. The key man here was Arnold Heeney, a Montreal lawyer whose father, an Anglican clergyman, was a friend of Mackenzie King's. Heeney was brought to Ottawa in 1938 as Principal Secretary to the Prime Minister, and he very quickly saw the problem. The system as it existed was geared to service a parish council, not the operations of a nation, and Heeney began to press a sometimes reluctant King towards a rational organization. The coming of the war in September, 1939, made Heeney's importunings more urgent, and the stress of events won his case.

The Cabinet War Committee was established by the end of 1939, bringing the most powerful ministers together. For the first time, a civil servant — Heeney — sat in on the meetings as a matter of course, taking minutes of the discussions, circulating papers, and providing the necessary follow-up to ensure that decisions were carried out. That sounded simple, but it amounted to a revolution in Canadian practice. Gradually an agenda was introduced, a change that King feared might destroy his ability to control discussions, and slowly the Cabinet began to require more administrative back-up as committees proliferated. The Privy Council Office began to become a powerful central agency of government, and as Clerk of the Privy Council and Secretary to the Cabinet from 1940, Heeney became a key bureaucratic player.

Similarly, the Prime Minister's Office altered too, handling more political questions. The nominal head of the office after 1940 was Walter Turnbull, an official on loan from the Post Office, but the effective operative direction was provided by J.W. Pickersgill, a young Manitoban who had joined External Affairs in 1937, after teaching history at United College in Winnipeg, and promptly been put on the Prime Minister's staff. Pickersgill loved his work as he loved politics, and his fertile mind was fully at King's

---

2. On Skelton, Clark, and Towers, see J.L. Granatstein, *The Ottawa Men: The Civil Service Mandarins, 1935-57* (Toronto, 1982); G.N. Hillmer, "The Anglo-Canadian Neurosis: The Case of O.D. Skelton," in P. Lyon, ed., *Britain and Canada* (London, 1976); W.A. Mackintosh, "O.D. Skelton," *Canadian Journal of Economics and Political Science*, VII (May, 1941); W.A. Mackintosh, "William Clifford Clark," *Queen's Quarterly*, LX (Spring, 1953); R.B. Bryce, "William Clifford Clark," *CJEPS*, XIX (1953); R.T.L., "Mr. Towers," *Maclean's* (15 Oct., 1934).

service. The Prime Minister's Office became, much as the Privy Council Office, a reservoir of talent and the key point of contact between bureaucratic and political decision-makers.

Thus by 1940, the key agencies in Ottawa were in place and functioning. The Privy Council Office and Prime Minister's Office provided the key politicians with administrative back-up and policy advice. The Bank of Canada and the Department of Finance were fully occupied with the mammoth task of raising the huge sums necessary for a vast war effort, but both had the skilled staff they needed to do it. And the Department of External Affairs, the Prime Minister's own department, had King's ear and a crew of exceptionally able men. The change in administrative terms was very important, but the number of key bureaucrats was still very small, no more than fifteen or twenty. The creator of the system, and there can be no doubt of this, had been Skelton. He had found Clark, and he and the Deputy Minister of Finance had discovered Towers. All had backed Heeney in his efforts to impose system on the top ranks of government. And Skelton, Clark, Towers, and Heeney were recruiting able men as fast as they could. The old civil service was not gone, but it had been by-passed by the new.[3]

Making a Foreign Policy

Skelton's Department of External Affairs was surprisingly tiny. When Skelton came to Ottawa in 1924 (for one year, he said), there was only Sir Joseph Pope, the Under Secretary, and an assistant, and both men were little more than clerks. Once Skelton took over as Under Secretary in 1925, he very quickly made himself into King's senior advisor on foreign policy — and on domestic questions too. But the staff at his command remained small. A few appointments were made and one or two missions abroad opened up before the onset of the Depression. A legation in Washington was opened in 1927 with the millionaire dilettante Vincent Massey as Minister and Hume Wrong, Laurent Beaudry, and Tommy Stone as officers, all men that Massey had personally selected. A legation in Paris was in the care of Philippe Roy, a long-time Canadian government employee in France. In Tokyo, the millionaire Sir Herbert Marler was in

3. On Heeney and the organization of the P.C.O. and P.M.O., see Arnold Heeney, *The Things That Are Caesar's* (Toronto, 1970); J.W. Pickersgill, *My Years with St. Laurent* (Toronto, 1975); Granatstein, *The Ottawa Men*; Heeney, "Cabinet Government in Canada...," *CJEPS*, XII (1946); Heeney, "Mackenzie King and the Cabinet Secretariat," *Canadian Public Administration*, X (September, 1967).

charge. And in London the Canadian High Commissioner was Peter Larkin, yet another millionaire who had assisted King and his party. The one additional post abroad was at the League of Nations in Geneva, where W.A. Riddell, an academic, was the advisory officer. That was Skelton's empire abroad; at home, by 1929, there was a counsellor, a legal advisor, and a first, second, and third secretary to watch over the entire world, to prepare and negotiate treaties, and to provide advice to the Prime Minister and his Government, as well as to supply a "fire-fighting" crew that moved from job to job and crisis to crisis. Lester Pearson, for example, was the First Secretary in Ottawa, and he handled disarmament questions, filled in at the Washington legation, served as secretary to two royal commissions, and took on a host of additional responsibilities before he was posted abroad in 1935. Others did much the same variety of work out of necessity.

And yet Skelton's department and his officers built up a splendid reputation in Ottawa. They were all professionals, educated, intelligent, sophisticated, and genuinely idealistic in a town that lacked such qualities. More to the point, they were all competent men in a civil service that desperately needed competence, and both Mackenzie King and R.B. Bennett after him came to rely on External. Skelton worked himself to the point of exhaustion trying to create a foreign service and a foreign policy while simultaneously advising the Prime Minister on the myriad questions of domestic policy. Perhaps Skelton's exhaustion was responsible for the administrative chaos that seemed to surround External Affairs and that led the caustic Hume Wrong, frustrated at what he saw as the do-nothing policies of his Minister, Massey, and his Prime Minister, Mackenzie King, to characterize Canada's foreign service as farcical.

Was it? On one level it was. Mackenzie King (and to some extent R.B. Bennett, too) was a cautious man in foreign policy, anxious not to get too far ahead of public opinion. The Canadian people — or at least those few who were interested in foreign policy — were still generally concerned with keeping in step with British policy, and, while King wanted to move in the direction of autonomy, he could not proceed too quickly or openly. That succession of events — Chanak in 1922, the Halibut Treaty of 1923, the Imperial Conferences of 1923 and 1926, and finally the Statute of Westminster in 1931 — that marked the road to autonomy had been care-

◀ *Dr. O.D. Skelton, the Under Secretary of State for External Affairs and the creator of the modern civil service, with one of his prize recruits, L.B. Pearson, in the mid-1930s. (PA-117595/Public Archives Canada)*

fully handled to suggest evolution and not revolution, and many Canadians failed to realize what had occurred. The prime ministers did, but both Bennett and King were sentimental imperialists and devoted to Britain, however much they might quarrel with London on economic questions or quibble with English policy in the world.

But for someone like Hume Wrong, probably the most brilliant man in the foreign service, the fuzzy atmosphere in which policy existed in Ottawa was an affront. What would happen if Britain went to war once more? he asked in letters to Ottawa in the late 1930s. Skelton, who shared Wrong's concerns and felt even more deeply about them, was realistic enough to recognize that this was the ultimate political question. Mackenzie King had the task of bringing a reluctant French Canada into a war, of restraining an eager public opinion in English Canada, and of reconciling the two. Squaring a circle was easier. But King managed the job adroitly, issuing bellicose statements one day and cautionary ones the next, warning the British High Commissioner not to count on Canada in an eastern European war, while telling Adolf Hitler that Canadians would swim the Atlantic to participate in a war that pitted Germany against Britain. Mackenzie King knew what he was doing, but his grand design was hidden from almost everyone else. The difficulty was, as Stephen Leacock put it in an article in the *Atlantic Monthly*, that if you asked any Canadian if he had to go to war if Britain did, the answer was certainly no. But if you asked him if he *would* go to war if Britain did, the answer was certain to be yes. If you then asked why, the answer, reflectively, would be, "Because we'd have to." In essence that was precisely true; Canada did not have to go to war, thanks to the Statute of Westminster, but it would go to war because English Canada, whose elites still controlled the media, business, and public opinion, would insist on going. King knew this, shared the same attitudes, and directed the process.

Wartime Nationalism

The Second World War altered all this and gave the officers of External Affairs their heads. Mackenzie King quickly became too busy to watch over every aspect of foreign policy or to concern himself with the location of telephone extensions and expense allowances. The Prime Minister's every waking hour was devoted to the manifold tasks of directing a fractious Cabinet and a huge war effort, and he was soon reduced to meeting with the Under Secretary once or twice a year to discuss departmental administrative matters. And after 1941, when Skelton was gone — he died on a January day at the wheel of his car while on his way home for lunch — and Norman Robertson was in charge, the department had a different cast to it. Robertson was only thirty-six when he took over as the top professional in the department, wide in his knowledge, realistic, and unafraid to try to have his country play a role in the world. Assisting him were Hume Wrong and Lester Pearson, both young and vigorous, extremely skillful diplomats, and men who similarly wanted Canada to have its proper place in the Allied councils. There can be no doubt that these three men, backed up by their colleagues in the department, effectively altered Canadian policy during the war and postwar years.

Their first task was to ensure that Britain and (once the Americans had come into the war after Pearl Harbor) the United States did not take Canada for granted. There was every sign that the great allies would do so when, for example, they created the Combined Chiefs of Staff to plan

Hume Wrong, one of Canada's ablest professional diplomats.
(C-45196/Public Archives Canada)

the war's fighting and a series of combined boards to plan the economic effort at the beginning of 1942. What was Canada's place to be in this scheme? No one in London or Washington had concerned themselves with this, simply expecting the Canadians to do as they were told, whatever that might be. But Hume Wrong, stationed in Washington at the time, was not about to let this pass. "The principle," he wrote to Ottawa, on which Canada and the Great Powers should operate was that "each member . . . should have a voice in the conduct of the war proportionate to its contribution to the general war effort. A subsidiary principle is that the influence of the various countries should be greatest in connection with those matters with which they are most directly concerned."

That was very shrewd. There was no way that Canada could claim a position as a coequal with the United States, Britain, the Soviet Union, or China, the acknowledged Great Powers. Their contribution to the war was simply too great for a country like Canada, with only 10 million people, to expect to match. Nonetheless, Canada had raised very substantial military forces and was straining every nerve to produce vast quantities of food, munitions, and raw materials for the common war effort. In the case of food, for example, the British and Americans had created the Combined Food Board to control the allocation of food; but Canada, as the greatest food producer in the Allied ranks next to the United States, had no place on that Board. Wrong's principle, soon to be described as the functional principle, suggested that in such an area Canada had the right to be consulted and to participate in decisions. The same thing could be said of Canada's role in munitions production or even of its development of civil aviation. In certain areas, in other words, Canada had the attributes of a Great Power and should be treated as such.

But to claim this was different from securing it. British and American officials, harassed beyond measure by the demands of global war, craved peaceful cooperation more than anything else, and importuning Canadians quickly became pests. But the Canadians pressed their case. Ottawa was giving Britain vast sums in aid by 1942, a billion dollars in that year alone, and Canadian officials, most notably the nationalistic Clifford Clark in the Finance Department, began to tell visiting officials from London that the tap would be turned off unless Britain recognized Canada's new status. That had some impact, naturally enough, but in the crucial negotiations in Ottawa in the late summer of 1942, Mackenzie King caved in and accepted British support for Canadian membership on the Combined Production and Resources Board, already the one combined board of little consequence, instead of a place on the Food Board. Mike Pearson complained that all too often Canadian policy seemed to be the strong glove over the velvet hand.

But the next year the Canadians were back at the charge once more. There were too many difficulties in allocating food because Canada, a great producer, had no place on the Food Board, or so Ottawa officials claimed. The Board dealt with commodities Canada produced in large quantities, and Canada's special place had already been recognized by putting Canadians on most of the Board's subcommittees. Moreover, Canadian public opinion was demanding that Canada's contributions be recognized, and under this repeated, interminable hammering both London and Washington gave way. Canada won its place on the Combined Food Board in October, 1943, adding this to its place on the Production and Resources Board.

In a very real way, the achievement of membership on the boards was important only as a symbol. No other country had achieved such recognition, not the Netherlands, France, Australia, or New Zealand. Clearly that appealed to Canadian nationalism. But what was more important than securing a place on the boards was that Canada had set out to fight for its rights. In the 1920s and 1930s, Canadian politicians had fought for and won autonomy — but then had to go to war in 1939 much as they had in 1914. Arguably, the nation had entered the war in as colonial a fashion the second time as it had the first. But now Canadian diplomats were beginning to take their autonomy seriously and were pressing the Great Powers for a greater Canadian share in decision-making. In other words, it was no longer only *status* that was being sought (although that still remained important) but *responsibility* too. Give us a share and let us show what we can do, the Canadians argued, waving the banner of the functional principle aloft. And the Great Powers to some extent recognized the justice of the Canadian case. That was a marked advance.

The same arguments were advanced by Robertson, Pearson, Wrong, and their political masters at the United Nations Conference on International Organization at San Francisco in 1945. The San Francisco conference created the new world organization, and Canadians were concerned that the United Nations should not simply be a vehicle for the Great Powers. There had to be a role for the smaller states, and there should be some way of differentiating among those states, some method of enshrining the functional principle and establishing a category that Canadians were beginning to think of as Middle Powers. Canada had more international clout than Guatemala, for example, and it had proved its good faith by its contribution in the war; why not then give Canada and other countries of similar status more weight than nations whose major export was postage stamps?

It was a good argument, but not one that made much headway. The Great Powers were already beginning to create the Cold War and were more concerned with establishing their right to veto U.N. actions than with protecting the rights of lesser states. Canada won only a few token recognitions of its new power in the U.N. Charter, but again it was the effort that was important, not the results. The war had changed the country immeasurably, given it confidence and clout. No longer were Canadians afraid to speak up and speak out.[4]

Getting On with Washington

The war had changed Canada, but its effects on the United States were still more striking. Before the Second World War, the United States, like Canada, had been sunk in depression, often unwilling to play its part in world affairs, and certainly unwilling to assume the leadership of the western democracies. The events of 1940 and 1941 had altered that condition permanently, plunging Franklin Roosevelt and his administration pell-mell into the conflicts in the Atlantic and the Pacific theatres and obliging America to assume the role of the great arsenal of democracy. That shift served the interests of Britain, the Soviet Union, and Canada during the war, but there could be no doubt that it posed problems for all of them, not least for Canada.

Before the war and for the first eighteen months or so of America's neutrality, Canadians rested secure in the assumption that they were held in high regard in Washington as the best friends of the United States. Naturally, there had been difficulties on such matters as trade and tariffs, but the relations between the two countries had been conducted with a level of cordiality that was possibly unmatched in other international negotiations and that could lead Norman Robertson to write to Mackenzie King that Canadians "have tended to take it for granted" that the U.S. administration would "always regard Canadian interests as a close second to their

4. On the development of External Affairs and its policy, see H.B. Neatby, *William Lyon Mackenzie King*, vols. II-III (Toronto, 1963, 1976); C.P. Stacey, *Canada and the Age of Conflict*, vol II (Toronto, 1981); J.W. Holmes, *The Shaping of Peace: Canada and the Search for World Order*, vols. I-II (Toronto, 1979, 1982); J.L. Granatstein, *The Ottawa Men*, and *A Man of Influence: Norman A. Robertson and Canadian Statecraft, 1929-68* (Ottawa, 1981); also by Granatstein, *Canada's War: The Politics of the Mackenzie King Government, 1939-45* (Toronto, 1975).

own and appreciably ahead of those of any third country." The Ogdensburg Agreement and the Hyde Park Declaration of 1940 and 1941, both of which had resolved pressing Canadian defence and economic problems, had only confirmed that view, or so it seemed in Ottawa.

But Canadians had been startled by the way the United States had forgotten about Canadian concerns when the combined boards were set up and had even suggested on occasion that Ottawa should resolve its concerns in London so the Americans would not have to deal separately with Ottawa. All of this worried Ottawa, particularly the "rather abrupt and not too tactfully handled" shift in attitude, or so Robertson characterized it. The Americans had become convinced anew of their "enormous strategic importance and strength," imbued with "a new sense of... 'manifest destiny' " and a corresponding willingness to make decisions and accept responsibility. "The change of attitude," Robertson noted at the end of 1941, a few weeks after the Japanese attack at Pearl Harbor at last had brought the U.S. into the war, "is very encouraging from the standpoint of the world in general, but it does imply quite an important modification of the special relationship in which Canada has hitherto stood with regard to the United States." So it did, and Canadian relations with the United States ever after would be at the top of Ottawa's agenda. Power had shifted in the world, and Britain clearly was never again to be a giant. The new empires were directed from Washington and Moscow; by the end of the war there was hostility between them; and Canada had to create a new relationship with its neighbour to the south. This was essential, first, because the war's demands had put substantial numbers of American troops into the Canadian north and because the coming Cold War had increased interest in the Pentagon in the defence of North America against threats across the Pole. It was also vital because of the way the war had established a web of interconnections between the two North American economies, tying them more tightly than ever before.

The Canadians were conscious of the problems, and on the economic front they tried to meet them with a generosity and creativity that deserve note. Most of the world, other than Canada and the United States, was in ruins in 1945, and Canada's trading partners in Western Europe had little money to pay for the food, raw materials, and manufactured goods they needed to re-establish their economies. If Canada was to find markets for its products other than in the United States, and if it was to locate sources of the goods it needed elsewhere, then Canada had to treat trade in a very different fashion than it had before the war. In other words, if Canada wanted to avoid total dependency on Washington for its exports and imports, it had to give Britain and the Europeans credits with which to buy Canadian goods. Foreign aid was not yet in vogue, but spurred on by the economic analyses of Graham Towers in the Bank of Canada and a startling degree of consensus among the key officials in Finance, External Affairs, and the Privy Council Office, the Mackenzie King Government offered substantial sums to its friends. The British were given $1.25 billion, a vast sum and fully one-third of that the United States proffered, although the American economy was at least ten times larger than the Canadian. An additional $750 million was offered to the Western Europeans so they could buy wheat, timber, and manufactured goods. It was generosity of an unparalleled sort, but it was absolutely essential, or so the Ottawa planners believed. It was equally essential for the sake of the Canadian economy — all those returning servicemen and munitions workers had to have jobs to go to or else the Depression would return with a vengeance.

If only the plan had worked. The devastation in Britain and Europe was worse than anyone had calculated, and the Canadian credits did not go very far to rectify matters. Britain, the major importer of our wheat and foodstuffs, was very quickly into a state of financial emergency, desperate for dollars, virtually forced to cut back on the imports it needed for want of them. Worse, the British wartime ban on the conversion of sterling into dollars remained in place, thus preventing Canada from using any of the pounds it earned in London to pay the costs of the goods it imported from the United States. This was becoming a critical matter, for Canadians, after fifteen years of depression and war, wanted the luxuries they had been denied for so long. They wanted fresh fruit from Florida and winter vacations; they wanted new cars, refrigerators, jukeboxes, and radios, and they wanted them now.

The problem became apparent by the middle of 1947. The U.S. dollar reserves Canada had built up after the Hyde Park Declaration began to melt away to pay for the goods Canadians imported. During the prewar period those imports had been paid for by converting pounds earned in London into American dollars, but now that was impossible. Worse still, Canada was putting up $2 billion of its own money to assist its friends. Very quickly, because of generosity and a desire on the part of Canadians for a good life, the country was in the midst of a great foreign exchange crisis.

How could this be resolved? To Clifford Clark and Robert Bryce in the Department of Finance and to Graham Towers and Louis Rasminsky in the Bank of Canada, four of the officials most directly involved, the choices were few. Canada could opt for self-sufficiency, cutting its links with the world and living off its own resources. That approach pleased no one and was quickly dismissed. Or Canada could tie itself to the sterling bloc, to Britain and its dependencies. That choice too had little to recommend it — given the parlous state of the British economy, it was akin to tying oneself to a corpse. The remaining option was to take the American road, to recognize that the United States, in 1947 and for the immediately foreseeable future, was the strongest economy in the world.

But what did the choice mean? To most of the officers in the Department of Finance, and particularly to those who had been making regular trips to Washington to discuss Canada's difficulties with their counterparts in the Treasury Department, it meant striking a deal with the United States that saw the Americans give a loan to Canada and agree to purchase far more goods in Canada than hitherto. John Deutsch was the key Finance representative in these talks. The son of a German immigrant farmer in Saskatchewan, he had risen from dire poverty, working his way through Campion College in Regina and then through Queen's University in Kingston. Tough and solid, a man with the thick fingers of a farmer, Deutsch had one of the quickest minds in Ottawa, and he saw in Canada's difficulties a chance to strike a bargain with the United States that would ease long-standing domestic problems. What issue had wracked western Canada for years? Deutsch might have asked. The answer was clear: high tariffs and a desire for reciprocity with the United States that would mean less expensive manufactured goods for prairie farmers. With the rest of the world gripped by economic dislocation and possibly prey to communism, surely now was the time for the United States and Canada to join economic forces in the interests of both.

Deutsch and his colleagues secretly put this proposition to Mackenzie King and received the go-ahead just days after the Canadian Government had been obliged to put restrictions on American imports and on tourist travel to the United States in an attempt to stem the hemorrhage of U.S. dollars. Through January and February, 1948, the Canadian and American teams met to discuss the free trade scheme, their secrecy precautions being severe. One American official privy to the talks believed that the Canadians were anxious for the arrangement because King was soon to retire and was the person best able to get public support for the package. (The import restrictions were unpopular and would, with time, build up vested interests which would make their removal very difficult.) That was probably true enough, and the Americans themselves had the international situation much in mind. Psychological factors, the official wrote, "favor immediate action. The widespread popular concern over Russian policy will undoubtedly lead to an acceptance of the international political and strategic implications which will override the supposed economic difficulties in the minds of many people."

The draft agreement negotiated by the officials by March, 1948, was comprehensive. It envisaged the immediate removal of all duties by both countries, the prohibition of restrictions on imports after five years (though with important exceptions for both countries), and joint consultation on agricultural export marketing. Under the plan, Canadian manufacturers would have five years to adapt to U.S. competition, but almost all Canadian goods secured immediate access to the American market. Sir John A. Macdonald had said seventy years earlier that his National Policy was designed only to protect infant industries. Deutsch and his negotiating colleagues were saying that those industries had had time to grow, and if after five years of adaptation they could not survive, then they did not deserve to live.

However, by this point, Mackenzie King was beginning to have second and third thoughts. He was on the verge of retiring after more than two decades as Prime Minister. Would he go down in history as the man who had carried out Laurier's great dream — or would he be the traitor who had sold Canada to the United States? To King, ultimately, the latter concern was the more pressing, the feeling that the free trade arrangement would "absolutely destroy the significance" of the whole of his career. That was bad enough, but King soon persuaded himself as well that the proposal could lead toward the achievement of "the long objective of the Americans . . . to control this Continent." And shortly after, his officials having tried once more to press the free trade deal on him, King complained bitterly in his diary that he got "alarmed beyond measure at the casual way in which a few officials take it into their hands to try and settle the great national policies; force the hands of the Government, etc., without the least knowledge of the political side of matters of the kind or the least kind of political judgment." That judgment was grossly unfair; nonetheless, the free trade idea was dead, killed by Mackenzie King in his final months in office.

But Canada's dollar shortage still remained, and it had to be resolved. Thanks to skillful negotiation by the same officials with whom he was so furious, Mackenzie King and his country were rescued by the Americans. The great European Recovery Program — or the Marshall Plan, as it was usually called — was working its way through Congress in the winter of 1948, and the Canadians persuaded their friends in Washington to agree that funds from the plan could be used to pay for "off-shore purchases," that is, goods bought in countries other than the United States. The arrangement was sufficiently flexible, for example, that even Canada's contract to sell wheat to Britain could be covered. In other words, instead of using its own hard-earned dollars, or instead of paying with the $1.25 billion credit from Canada, Britain could get wheat from Alberta and the American taxpayer would pick up the tab. This generous arrangement rescued Canada, pouring a billion dollars in U.S. funds into the foreign exchange reserves by the end of 1949. The dollar crisis was over.

However, its legacy would not disappear so quickly. In the first place, the immediate result for Canada of the Marshall Plan's support was that virtually all of Canada's exports were either to the United States itself or subsidized by the United States, a dangerous and vulnerable position for Canada. Secondly, in order to boost foreign exchange holdings, Canadian negotiators had been forced to urge the Americans to buy more and invest more in Canada, a situation that increased our dependency on the U.S. market and one that significantly increased American foreign investment — and economic control — in Canada. Perhaps Mackenzie King had been correct to resist free trade with the States. That was an emotive issue that could only have sharply divided Canadians. But the remedies selected by his Government, the only remedies that could have been selected, had much the same effect as free trade might have had. By the end of the 1940s, Canada had become a virtual economic colony of the United States.[5]

The Coming of Social Welfare

If the war altered Canada's relations with the United States, so too did it dramatically change the way individual Canadians were treated by their government. During the hard years of the 1930s, the federal government played relatively little part in attempts to ameliorate the lives of those who were suffering because of unemployment or deprivation. There was no unemployment insurance, no health insurance or hospital insurance, and no family allowance. All there was, in fact, was a patchwork of inade-

5. On Canadian-American relations in this period, see Stacey; Holmes; J.W. Pickersgill and D.F. Forster, eds., *The Mackenzie King Record*, vols. III-IV (Toronto, 1970); R.D. Cuff and J.L. Granatstein, *Ties That Bind: Canadian-American Relations from Great War to Cold War* (Toronto, 1977); R.D. Cuff and J.L. Granatstein, *American Dollars/Canadian Prosperity: Canadian-American Economic Relations 1945-50* (Toronto, 1978).

quate relief programs run by provinces and municipalities with some (and sometimes substantial) financial support from Ottawa.

The ethos of the day accepted that such a limited role for the federal government was proper. The constitution, for one thing, sharply circumscribed Ottawa's powers in such areas. The gospel of laissez faire remained powerful, and the general attitude was that if a man was out of work, it was probably his own fault; if a farmer suffered from the hard times, then he was at fault for not being more prudent when times were good. Many in the country had begun to recognize the poverty of such beliefs, and after 1932 the Cooperative Commonwealth Federation was becoming a vocal force for a more humane society under social democracy. In England, John Maynard Keynes was arguing brilliantly for a new economic philosophy, one that would use public works and government spending to prime the pump when times were tough, and in the United States Franklin Roosevelt's New Deal was attempting to implement policies that had strong Keynesian overtones.

But not in Canada. Bennett's New Deal of 1935 might have been a slight gesture in this direction, but both Bennett and his proposals were massively rejected by an electorate that had lost faith in the Tories. King's Liberals were liberals, not economic experimenters, and there were few initiatives of any sort from Ottawa until the National Employment Commission in the late 1930s began to argue for greater government expenditures and to suggest that a balanced budget was not necessarily the highest virtue in the state.

However, within a few years the orthodoxy that had dominated the Depression years was virtually gone, swept away by vast wartime budgets, by changing attitudes to the role of the state and to social welfare, and by a virtual bureaucratic revolution in Ottawa. The Keynesian message had been brought to the Department of Finance in 1938 by Robert Bryce, a University of Toronto graduate who had attended Keynes' seminar at Cambridge, picking up the new gospel from the master himself. Brilliant as a student, concerned by the impact of the Depression on the lives of ordinary people, Bryce had become one of the leading preachers to the orthodox economists and doubters of Keynes in England, and when he went to Harvard University in the mid-1930s, he played a substantial part in persuading economists there of Keynes' prescriptions. His influence in Ottawa would be much the same when Clifford Clark brought him into the department in the midst of the Czech crisis of 1938.

The budget of 1939 had some Keynes in it, thanks to Bryce, but the war soon altered everything. Money that could not be found in peacetime for the people's needs suddenly was available to produce arms and munitions and to mobilize those same people in vast armies. The state began to intervene in every aspect of life, exercising the power to fix prices and wages, to deny people the right to change jobs, and to control the amount of meat or butter a family could purchase. And, contrary to the fears of laissez faire economists, the system worked — and worked efficiently. People were earning more and saving more than they had ever done before, and the standard of living rose markedly, despite rationing and shortages.

But what of the situation when peace returned? Did that happy event have to bring a renewed depression in its train? And if it did, could the society survive? Promises had been made to soldiers and workers that this was a people's war, a war for freedom *and* a better life. If those promises were not fulfilled, then the anger would be enormous, possibly so strong as to make the Winnipeg General Strike of 1919 look like a tea party. The state had to cushion the economic blows that a capitalistic system seemed so prone to inflicting, or else that system would be toppled.

One of the first measures put in place by the federal government was unemployment insurance, implemented in 1940 when the provinces at last agreed to an amendment to the British North America Act to permit such legislation. The scheme was literally *insurance*, requiring that contributions from workers and employers go to build up a fund from which payments could be made in periods of unemployment. As such, the act could only be put in place in good times if the fund was to be established on a firm basis, and there was a cruel irony about that, for the war had largely resolved the problem of unemployment. Unemployment insurance nonetheless was a giant step.

So too was the baby bonus, a scheme that was intended to put a monthly payment for each child in the hands of its mother. Incredibly, the family allowance plan was expected to cost $250 million a year, a sum that was almost 50 per cent of the total prewar budget. That was the most striking indicator of the way attitudes had altered.

The baby bonus was an idea that had been around since the 1920s, but it had never made much headway against the balanced-budget governments of the interwar period. But during the war a number of factors worked in its favour. One was that the C.C.F., challenging the Liberals from the left, had family allowances as part of its social welfare program. Another was that the National War Labour Board, chaired by a Conservative judge, C.P. McTague, had endorsed the idea in 1943 as a way to put more money in the hands of workers whose wages were tightly controlled by the wage freeze in force since late 1941. That idea won the support of the Economic Advisory Committee, the key committee of bureaucrats that brought together all the leading mandarins in the civil service. But there were problems here, as all recognized. The public might see the family allowance plan as simply an election bribe; many in English Canada might feel it was a reward to French Canada — whose support for the war effort was darkly viewed — for its continuing return of Grits to Ottawa. And then there was Prime Minister Mackenzie King, who had his own doubts. On October 1, 1943, King told his Cabinet that "to tell the country that everyone was to get a family allowance was sheer folly; it would occasion resentment everywhere. Great care had to be taken in any monies given out from the Treasury. . . ."

The Prime Minister remained as tightfisted about public funds as he had ever been, and he seemed either blind to the political gains to be made or simply ready to overlook them. He maintained that position until he was bearded by J.W. Pickersgill, an officer from the Department of External Affairs who had been seconded to the Prime Minister's Office shortly after he came to Ottawa in 1937. Clever, absorbed in politics, and with a good liberal cast of mind, Pickersgill had risen from rural poverty in Manitoba to get a good education and build a successful career. This had taken place, he told King, only because his mother had received a pension as a result of his father's death from war wounds after the Great War. What was the difference between a war pension and the family allowance scheme, if the latter would let other bright but poor children get an education and a chance? As Pickersgill describes it, King realized the point instantly and altered his position.

He had the full support of the senior bureaucracy. Clifford Clark, for example, cared very little for the social welfare aspects of the scheme. He was "completely sold on family allowances," one reporter learned confidentially, as "the only effective way to deal with slum clearance. You have to give the boys the money to buy the houses you intend to build for them." That was almost exactly it. If Canada was to avoid the troubles that had wracked the country after 1918, then it had to have planning in place for reconversion from war to peace. That meant efforts to stimulate the economy so that soldiers could find jobs. And one way to encourage spending was to put money in people's hands. Clark had been slow to accept Keynesian economics, but under the tutelage of Robert Bryce and under the pressure of events, he had swung round completely.

Of course, once the key reasons had been laid out and accepted, the other and more political reasons were obvious. Family allowances would steal the C.C.F.'s thunder. The proposal would have great public appeal in Quebec. It would frustrate the Conservatives. There was a fight in Cabinet over the scheme, but Mackenzie King weighed in to argue that "I thought the Creator intended that all persons born should have equal opportunities. Equal opportunity started in days of infancy and the first thing, at least, was to see that the children got the essentials of life. . . ." Clifford Clark was brought into the Cabinet chamber to speak about the country's ability to pay and to give the economic rationale. And in the end the measure won approval. In Parliament too the plan won wide support, although, happily for the Government, several Conservative members complained bitterly, one virulent Toronto M.P. even being expelled from the House for saying that the baby bonus was a bribe to Quebec. What could have been more calculated to enrage Quebec against the Tories? Family allowances, scheduled to begin on July 1, 1945, just a few weeks after the election of that year, turned out to be splendid campaign material.

Just as important, the plan was a social revolution. Based on $5 a month for a child five years old and under, $6 for those from six to nine, $7 for those from ten to twelve, and $8 for those thirteen to fifteen, the plan put substantial sums of money into the economy, $28 million a year in the Maritimes and $54 million a year in the Prairies, for example. And thanks to the fact that the cheques went directly to the mother — the government of Quebec objected to this most strenuously, implicitly arguing that paternal control over the family would be weakened by the suggestion that fathers could not provide for their families — the plan also gave many women the first money under their own control that they had ever had. That was a form of practical emancipation, a major step out of the kitchen for women. But not all women approved the plan. The country's leading social worker (and a Conservative party supporter), Charlotte Whitton, denounced the scheme on the grounds that it would encourage the weakest in society to breed more — the pseudoscience of eugenics remained popular — and that it was "a disgrace" to spend millions on children "at a time when such expenditure was never needed less. . . . Canada," she complained, "is leaving adequate and humane care of the aged without attention." That last was true enough, but governments seem able to attend to only one social need at a time, and in 1944–45 the women and children were at the top of the list. One reason, as some later observers have suggested, was a government planner's hope to encourage women to return to the home and leave the work force to open up space for demobilized veterans. There was also much worry about the way the baby bonus would be spent. The Government could not control what happened to the money once it was disbursed; undoubtedly some of it was taken by husbands and squandered on drink or foolishness. But most of the money seems to have been used as intended, to purchase food and milk and shoes. Relatively well-off parents opened bank accounts for their children, building up funds for their education. And although $5 a month per child today sounds like very little, it was not so in 1945 when the average wage was still about $25 a week.

The family allowance scheme had emerged during the war for a variety of reasons. It helped the Government against its political opponents. It raised wages without seeming to violate wage controls. It liberated women and helped their children. But most important to Ottawa, it served the fiscal needs that had been identified by the Department of Finance and the key bureaucratic players in Ottawa. If Jack Pickersgill had not been in the Prime Minister's Office to make the case for the baby bonus, it might not have passed; if Clifford Clark and his officials had opposed the scheme, it could never have got political support. Social welfare came to Canada during the war primarily because it was seen as one essential way to keep the economy going in the peace. Only one thing need be added. The plan worked.[6]

Creating N.A.T.O.

Another plan that worked had two purposes. One was to see the United States play an appropriate part in world events, a direct reaction to the interwar period when, in the eyes of Canadians and others, the United States had largely withdrawn and thus contributed to the coming of the Second World War. The second purpose of the plan was to see Canada take up its fair share of the load in an alliance of democratic states in the North Atlantic area.

The North Atlantic Treaty and its military product, N.A.T.O., were to a substantial extent Canadian creations. It was not that the Canadian officials in the Department of External Affairs were particularly prescient or that they assessed Soviet intentions with a perspicacity that others

6. On the development of social welfare during the war, see *The Mackenzie King Record*, vols. I-II; Granatstein, *Canada's War* and *The Politics of Survival: The Conservative Party of Canada, 1939-45* (Toronto, 1967); Walter Young, *The Anatomy of a Party: The National CCF* (Toronto, 1969); Dennis Guest, *The Emergence of Social Security in Canada* (Vancouver, 1980); and Leonard Marsh, *Report on Social Security for Canada 1943* (reprinted; Toronto, 1975).

lacked; it was simply that an organization such as N.A.T.O. appeared to serve so many Canadian needs. The free trade initiative, launched from within the bureaucracy and scuppered by the aging Mackenzie King, had failed and new efforts were needed to balance the Canadian export economy. What better way than to create an alliance that encompassed all of Canada's historic trading partners? The presence of the United States as a giant power immediately to the south invited the creation of some multilateral organization through which American direct influence on Canada might be moderated. What better way than in a North Atlantic alliance that reunited the democratic partners of the Second World War? And the threat exerted by the Soviet Union, and almost as important, by the Communist parties that operated — and seemed to thrive — in France, Italy, and elsewhere had to be checked. How better to do this than to revitalize the spirit of democracy in Western Europe? The North Atlantic Treaty might have been designed to fill Canadian needs.

The key bureaucratic players in the Canadian service were Escott Reid and L.B. Pearson in Ottawa, Hume Wrong, the Ambassador to the United States, and Norman Robertson, the High Commissioner to Great Britain. These four men had all served in External Affairs during the war, and they had seen the United States and Britain arrogate all power to themselves in planning Allied strategy and economic policy. They had determined then that this could not be permitted, and they had invented the functional principle to serve their ends. They had worried about the United States as it became messianic, and as they saw it, full again of a spirit of manifest destiny. But with the peace, paradoxically, the old-style isolationism seemed to be finding its feet again in Congress, and there was alarm in Ottawa at the abruptness with which Lend-Lease had been cancelled as soon as Japan surrendered and at the American reluctance to take up the burdens that Britain and France were so clearly unable to carry. President Truman seemed willing to press ahead, but Congress was the difficulty, and Wrong and other Western ambassadors in Washington spent much time talking to senators and representatives, trying to persuade them of the urgency of providing money and energy to a Europe desperately in need of both.

The Marshall Plan, passed by Congress in the spring of 1948, was a sign that Washington was beginning to recognize the needs of Western Europe. However, that great and generous plan had in it a desire to dispose of American surpluses and to bolster an economy that was beginning to sag, almost as much as it had a desire to prop up Europe. And the bill, seemingly stalled in Congress, had been sped through only because of the Soviet takeover in Czechoslovakia and the fear that event created and enhanced. That plan too had served Canadian needs, as we have seen, and the Canadians had pushed very hard for it, probably harder than a foreign mission in a national capital should ever do.

But what could be done to ensure that a fickle Congress could not change its mind tomorrow and go off half-cocked in a fit of either rabid anticommunism or Fortress America-style isolationism? An alliance that bound the United States to take its place in the defence of Western Europe seemed the solution, a guarantee of commitment.

The idea of a treaty had been gaining ground every since Escott Reid, the Assistant Under Secretary of State for External Affairs, had raised it in a speech at the Canadian Institute of Public Affairs' annual conference at Couchiching, Ontario in the summer of 1947. Still in his early forties, Reid was one of the brightest of the senior officials in Ottawa, a determined man with a crusader's zeal. He had been on the left in the 1930s, a strong neutralist and an advocate of Canadian isolationism from the follies of Europe. But the war had driven that out of him, and his role in the creation of the United Nations had convinced him that the new world organization was the salvation of mankind. However, Reid had become increasingly alarmed over Soviet actions in Eastern Europe and at the United Nations, and he had gradually become convinced that the U.S.S.R. was destroying the world body. Those concerns were probably in his mind when he told his Couchiching audience of academics and others that if "the peoples of the Western world want an international security organization with teeth . . . they do not need to amend the United Nations Charter in order to create such an organization. . . . They can create a regional security organization to which any state willing to accept the obligations of membership could belong. In such an organization," he said, referring to the way in which the Soviet Union had largely paralyzed the operations of the U.N. Security Council, "there need be no veto right possessed by any great power. In such an organization each member state could accept a binding obligation to pool the whole of its economic and military resources with those of the other members if *any* power should be found to have committed aggression against any one of the members." That was likely the first public call for an alliance of democratic states.

At the same time, Reid set out other aspects of his thinking in a secret memo to Pearson, the Under Secretary, that he called "The United States and the Soviet Union." In it, Reid argued that Canada's major goal had to be to influence the United States to accept membership in a North Atlantic alliance. "In the event of war we shall have no freedom of action in any matter which the United States considers essential," he argued. "We shall be out-and-out belligerents from the day the war starts." That posed problems reminiscent of the Second World War, but Reid also noted that "if we play our cards well we can exert an influence at Washington out of all proportion to the relative importance of our strength in war compared to that of the United States. The game is difficult; the issues will be delicate; but with skill we can play it successfully."

Norman A. Robertson, Under Secretary of State for External Affairs from 1941 to 1946 and High Commissioner to England during the critical years of the Cold War.

The important point here is that Reid's assessment, ultimately accepted by Pearson and soon by the whole Canadian Government, was based on an appraisal of the United States *and* the Soviet Union. The two superpowers, in their separate ways, were the Canadian problem. Equally important was that Canadians believed that the situation held some opportunities which could be exploited. Norman Robertson, the deepest thinker in External Affairs, noted this from his post in London when he wrote in

April, 1948, that Canada's problem had always been "the antinomies created by our position as a North American country and as a member of the Commonwealth, by our special relationship with the United Kingdom and at the same time, though in a lesser degree, with other countries in western Europe as well." Now, with the possibility of a North Atlantic treaty, there was a chance. "A situation in which our special relationship with the United Kingdom can be identified with our special relationships with other countries in western Europe and in which the United States will be providing a firm basis, both economically and probably militarily, for the link across the North Atlantic," he noted, "seems to me such a providential solution for so many of our problems that I feel we should go to great lengths and even incur considerable risks in order to consolidate our good fortune and ensure our proper place in this new partnership."

In other words, Robertson was saying, Canada could solve its long-standing economic problems through creative use of a new alliance. A North Atlantic arrangement might be used to secure Canada permanent access to markets that were fragile, it could solidify links with Western Europe, and it could even help to ease the problems involved in sharing a continent with the United States. The alliance, while necessary to deal with the Soviet Union and to put heart into Western Europe, also could be an instrument of Canadian economic policy abroad.

Indeed, all through the long negotiations that eventually produced the North Atlantic Treaty in April, 1949, that concern was at the forefront of the Canadian negotiating position. The Americans thought of the treaty as a simple military alliance and were impatient of the Canadian concerns that could cause them problems in the Senate; most of the other participants in the discussions were lukewarm; and even Hume Wrong, charged with the task of presenting the Canadian case in the day-to-day talks, believed that Ottawa's emphasis was misplaced. But Wrong, a superb bargainer, hid his concerns from the representatives of the other allies, and after a titanic struggle won acceptance for what came to be called Article II or "the Canadian article." That article bound the signatories of the North Atlantic Treaty to "seek to eliminate conflict in their international economic policies and . . . encourage economic collaboration between any or all of them."

Article II was an effort to eliminate trade wars among the democracies as much as it was an attempt to achieve peculiarly Canadian aims. But its importance proved less than Robertson and Reid had hoped, for, particularly after the outbreak of the Korean War on June 25, 1950, N.A.T.O. was convinced that the U.S.S.R. was beginning openly to use force to achieve its ends and so became much more of a military alliance than some had expected or hoped. Indeed, it was not long after the onset of hostilities in Korea that Canada began to raise a brigade of troops for service with N.A.T.O. in Germany and to build a large fighter aircraft division for service there. N.A.T.O. had created a situation in which, for the first time, Canada stationed troops abroad as part of an alliance in peacetime. The era of isolationism, the days of "Parliament will decide" as the only policy Canadians had were over for good — even if N.A.T.O. as the centrepiece of Canadian policy lasted no more than two decades. Now Canada was playing its part in the world, bargaining actively and with skill in negotiations with its friends, and using its resources and such clout as it could muster to make its case. Some, in fact, see the years from 1947 onwards as a golden era in Canadian foreign policy, and they are likely correct.[7]

Suez: Pearson's Triumph

If there was a golden era in foreign policy, its very pinnacle came during the Suez crisis of 1956. Led by Lester Pearson, by this time the Secretary of State for External Affairs, the Canadian foreign service produced its most important intervention in world events, a difficult feat of mediation between Britain and the United States, a demonstration of enormous skill in politicking at the United Nations but also a rather risky venture in terms of Canadian public opinion.

The key figure unquestionably was Pearson. In 1956, Pearson was fifty-nine years old, but his unwrinkled face still had a boyishness to it, and his legendary charm was as powerful as ever. Pearson had served in the Great War, he had attended university at Toronto and Oxford, he had taught history, and he had spent twenty years in the senior ranks of the Department of External Affairs before he abandoned the security of his civil service position for the vagaries of politics in 1948. Of course, Pearson had started at the top, entering the Cabinet as Secretary of State for External Affairs. That had troubled some in the Opposition who were beginning to worry that the senior bureaucracy was too close to the Liberal Government, but that storm had passed (although five years later,

7. On Canadian policy with regard to the formation of N.A.T.O., see Pickersgill and Forster, *The Mackenzie King Record*, vols. III-IV; Holmes; Stacey; James Eayrs, *In Defence of Canada*, vol. IV: *Growing Up Allied* (Toronto, 1980); Escott Reid, *Time of Fear and Hope: The Making of the North Atlantic Treaty 1947-49* (Toronto, 1977); and Cuff and Granatstein, *American Dollars/Canadian Prosperity*.

when J.W. Pickersgill resigned as Clerk of the Privy Council to enter St. Laurent's Cabinet, the concern, redoubled, would emerge again). As Minister, Pearson had demonstrated the same skills he had shown as a diplomat and ambassador. He was the master of the compromise phrase, the helpful fixer who could cajole two or three sides into reaching a mutual accommodation that might leave no one happy but all more or less satisified. He had shown his skills at the United Nations in negotiations that had led to a cease-fire in Korea, an action that angered some in the United States but that built lines of trust to India and even China. He was at the peak of his powers in 1956, a still tireless man who understood how men thought and how nations worked.

He had to have that kind of broad understanding, for the Suez crisis stood the world — or at least the comfortable Canadian world — on its ear. Who could have envisaged a situation in which Britain and France would stage an invasion of Egypt in collusion with Israel? Who would have expected the United States, with President Eisenhower in the midst of his campaign for re-election, to have been misled by its senior European allies? Who could have expected that the breach in the ranks of N.A.T.O. could have occurred at precisely the moment that the Soviet Union was sending in its tanks to crush a democratic revolution in Hungary?

The world was in an uproar those days at the end of October and the beginning of November in 1956. London and Paris had virtually ceased to communicate with Washington, except through the medium of Ottawa. And the telegrams between Prime Minister St. Laurent and Anthony Eden, the British leader, had developed a tone of asperity that was unequalled in the long history of Anglo-Canadian relations. From London, Eden wired disingenuously that Britain and France had intervened in the Israeli-Egyptian war only to separate the combatants and to protect the Suez Canal, nationalized a few months earlier by Egypt's President Nasser. It had been a difficult, even agonizing decision, but Britain was certain it was right, Eden said. St. Laurent was not so sure. "I think we have a sympathetic understanding of you and France's position but we still regret you found it necessary to follow the course you are taking. Of course the motives and the known character of the actors do make a difference, but it is unfortunate that the events in the Middle East have cloaked with a smoke screen the renewed brutal crimes of the Soviets." The cries of outrage from President Eisenhower and Secretary of State John Foster Dulles, and from India's Jawaharlal Nehru were even more pointed.

In the circumstances, the task of Canadian diplomacy seemed clear. Canada had to work to rescue the British and French from the consequences of their folly; it had to restore communication between Washington and London and Paris; it had to try to save the Commonwealth, sorely tested in Asia and Africa by the reappearance of old-style gunboat colonialism; and, if possible, it had to work to make the Suez crisis a stepping-stone to a permanent resolution of the hostilities between Arab and Zionist in the Middle East. That was an agenda and a half; the astonishing thing is that Pearson and his colleagues largely carried off all but the last point.

Pearson was the heart and soul of the operation, but he was assisted by an extraordinary crew. In London, Norman Robertson was serving his second term as High Commissioner, and there was no one with better entrée to high places or more wisdom among the array of foreign representatives there. In Washington, Arnold Heeney was Ambassador, forthright, skillful at arguing cases, and a supremely organized man. At the United Nations, John Holmes served as Pearson's strong right arm, cajoling wary Third World delegates and arguing the Canadian case. And in Ottawa, the Under Secretary of State for External Affairs was Jules Léger, the senior Francophone in the public service and a man whose intelligence and character were recognized by all.

But Pearson was the key. His initial idea on hearing of the Israeli attack against Egypt and the subsequent Anglo-French ultimata was to go to New York and to suggest at the United Nations that the Anglo-French invaders be transformed into a U.N. force, "not to give United Nations respectability to the ... intervention but to change its character and make it serve different ends." That idea was a nonstarter, Pearson discovered on arrival, the tone of the U.N. membership tending far more to branding the invaders as aggressors. In the early hours of November 2, an American resolution calling upon the "parties now involved in hostilities in the area" to accept a cease-fire was easily carried. Canada had abstained, and Pearson explained his vote:

> I regret the use of military force ... but I regret also that there was not more time, before a vote had to be taken, for consideration of the best way to bring about that kind of cease-fire which would have had enduring and beneficial results ... We need action, then, not only to end the fighting but to make the peace ... I therefore would have liked to see a provision in this resolution ... authorizing the Secretary-General to begin to make arrangements with Member Governments for a United Nations force large enough to keep these borders at peace while a political settlement is being

worked out . . . My own Government would be glad to recommend Canadian participation in such a United Nations force, a truly international peace and police force.

That idea ultimately would get Pearson his Nobel Peace Prize, but his greatest achievement came as he worked out the details with U.N. Secretary General Dag Hammarskjöld over the next harrowing days.

Shuttling from delegation to delegation at the United Nations, flying back to Ottawa for consultations with the Prime Minister, the Cabinet, and the officers of the Department of National Defence, Pearson seemed to be everywhere at once. Early in the morning on November 4, the U.N. General Assembly accepted Pearson's resolution that directed "as a matter of priority, the Secretary General to submit . . . within forty-eight hours a plan for the setting up, with the consent of the nations concerned, of an emergency international United Nations force to secure and supervise the cessation of hostilities. . . ." Because of Canadian lobbying, that resolution carried fifty-seven to zero, with nineteen abstentions. It seemed only logical, given the origins of the United Nations Emergency Force, or U.N.E.F. as it soon was called, that a Canadian officer, General E.L.M. Burns, who was in the area on U.N. duties, should be named commander of the force.

While the fighting around the Suez Canal intensified, the work at New York continued. Working with Hammarskjöld and an advisory group of U.N. members, Pearson prepared a major document for the General Assembly. Presented on November 6, the report made very clear that the British and French could have no place in the U.N.E.F.; neither could the United States nor the Soviet Union. Political control of the U.N. force was to be in the Secretary General's hands, assisted only by the advisory group, and U.N.E.F. was to be more than a corps of observers but "in no way a military force temporarily controlling the territory in which it is stationed." Within days troops were on the way to staging areas in Europe, wearing hastily painted U.N.-blue helmets.

It had been a triumph for Pearson and Canada thus far, a genuinely major achievement. The Suez fighting was halted, and if the face of the British and French had not been saved, at least they had not been irretrievably labelled aggressors. And Washington, its rage mollified by Eisenhower's sweeping election victory, was at last beginning to speak, if still sternly, to its friends overseas. But now for Canada the triumph began to turn into a farce.

The Department of National Defence had selected one of Canada's premier infantry regiments for service with U.N.E.F. The Queen's Own

L.B. Pearson and his wife Maryon just after he received the Nobel Peace Prize in 1957. (C-94168/Public Archives Canada)

Rifles of Canada, with their British-cut battle dress and their British-pattern weapons, would proudly enter Egypt behind the U.N. flag and the Red Ensign, with the Union Jack occupying the upper corner. Curiously, no one had stopped to think that Nasser, under assault by the British, might object. After all, had Canada not worked so hard to save Egypt? But Nasser did object, and his Foreign Minister told General Burns that "the trouble was that Canadian soldiers were dressed just like British soldiers, they were subjects of the same Queen — the ordinary Egyptian would not understand the difference, and there might be unfortunate incidents." That was by no means a foolish response, but it could not easily be accepted by Canada.

The public response in the country to Pearson's role at the United Nations had not been completely favourable. Anglophile sentiment was still fierce in Canada in 1956, and the Conservative party was sharp in its criticism, denouncing Canada for letting down its friends and declaring Nasser to be another Hitler. Arthur Meighen, the former Tory prime minister who had said in 1922 that Canada should have been "Ready, aye, ready" at Chanak, had not allowed thirty-four years to alter his views and he regretted that Canada had not followed Australia in backing Britain. And the Toronto *Globe and Mail* charged that Canada had "added nothing to its prestige... by its conduct" at the United Nations. In the circumstances, if Egypt rejected Canadian soldiers in U.N.E.F., the political costs would be incalculable.

Pressure was put on Cairo from every direction. The Canadian Ambassador, Herbert Norman, was trusted by Nasser, and Norman argued the Canadian case. In New Delhi, Escott Reid, the Canadian High Commissioner, spoke fervently to Nehru, who had been impressed by Canadian efforts at the U.N. — and by Reid's arguments that the Commonwealth deserved to survive, notwithstanding the British action — and Nehru, the senior statesman of the nonaligned world, added his support to the Canadian case. So too did Hammarskjöld, although the Secretary General had to be more interested in seeing U.N.E.F. created than he was in rescuing a Liberal Government in trouble with its English-speaking voters. The result was a compromise, accepted and papered over by General Burns, who told Pearson in writing that "the most valuable and urgently required contribution that Canada could make to the Force at the present time would be to supply an augmented transport squadron of the R.C.A.F. to lift the troops assembling at Naples to Egypt. It would also be of great assistance if the administrative elements of the army contingent could go forward at an early date in order to help in organizing the administration at the base of the force in Egypt." In other words, instead of the Queen's Own, Canada would be represented on the ground in Egypt by administration, supply, and signal troops. Temporarily, Canada's face had been saved.

But if U.N.E.F. was a great achievement for Pearson and his officials, its results were probably damaging to the St. Laurent Government in the election of June, 1957. Although the Conservatives, now led by John

Diefenbaker, did not assail the creation of the U.N. force as such (Diefenbaker, in fact, claimed to be the originator of the idea), they took every advantage of what they saw as an anti-British cast of mind on the part of the Liberals. In the House of Commons, St. Laurent had remarked in anger that the British and French were among "those supermen of Europe whose days are about over," giving the Opposition a large target. There were cries that the Liberals had made Canada into the chore-boy of the United States, and Howard Green, a British Columbia M.P., said it was "high time Canada had a government which will not knife Canada's best friends in the back." To what extent this affected the election results is uncertain. There were innumerable other issues and particularly the perceived arrogance of the entrenched Government. But it seems probable that the U.N.E.F. episode had not helped the Liberals.[8]

Still, it was a great achievement; even if it failed to produce permanent peace, it was the absolute culmination of Canadian influence and power. In the postwar world Canada *had* influence and power, it had idealism and skilled diplomats, it had money and the willingness to spend it in the furtherance of its aims. Suez had brought all this together, and if the Egyptians had not trusted the Queen's Own, they seemed to be almost the only nation that didn't. But the world was already altering, and the events of 1956 probably marked the end of Canada's golden age. The ruined countries of Europe and Asia were largely rebuilt, and Germany and Japan already were playing important roles. The Europeans were moving toward the creation of the Common Market to pool their strength. The Third World countries were becoming both more numerous and more concerned to play off East against West, and the United Nations, as a result, was altering too. Never again could a country such as Canada have quite so much influence.

And if the golden age was over in foreign policy, so too was it at its end for the civil service mandarins who had given Canada arguably the best public service in the world for a decade and a half. Death had removed some of the major figures like Clifford Clark and Hume Wrong; others, such as Graham Towers at the Bank of Canada, had retired. But that was only part of the story. Pearson and Pickersgill had enlisted with the Lib-

8. On Suez and U.N.E.F., see Holmes; Granatstein, *A Man of Influence*; Alastair Taylor, *et al.*, *Peacekeeping: International Challenge and Canadian Response* (Toronto, 1968); L.B. Pearson, *Mike: The Memoirs of the Right Honourable Lester B. Pearson*, vol. II (Toronto, 1973); Terence Robertson, *Crisis: The Inside Story of the Suez Conspiracy* (Toronto, 1964); James Eayrs, *The Commonwealth and Suez* (London, 1964); and Eayrs, *Canada in World Affairs 1955-1957* (Toronto, 1959).

erals, provoking suspicion of the senior bureaucracy on the part of Conservatives such as John Diefenbaker, and later many of Diefenbaker's ministers took the same attitude. After a time, many of the deputy ministers began to feel mistrusted and to reciprocate the suspicion. And as important, the great consensus that had shaped Canadian policy at home and abroad since the war had begun to break up. That consensus had been devoted to nationalism and internationalism, to centralization in Ottawa and to social security, but the problems had altered. The different world scene, with its fragmenting loyalties, was one sign of this, and the stirrings in the provincial capitals were but another. The golden age of the bureaucracy was at an end.

Chapter X

1957–1985:
Responding
to
Social
Change

The huge crowd gathered in the city's Chinatown was festive. There were placards with the names of the local candidates, a few Canadian flags, and a host of posters with the leader's face and name boldly displayed. Advance men circulated through the throng handing out buttons to the children and teen-agers, of whom there were far more present — as well as many more very pretty young women — than one usually found at political meetings. When one of the organizers went to the microphone on the decorated stage and tested it — "Testing, one, two, three . . . ," he drew a cheer, a sign that the throng was becoming impatient.

At last the official party appeared, suddenly emerging from the rear of the platform. There were the ritual speeches of welcome, the introductions of party notables, the exhortations to vote in the coming general election. But none of this was what the people had come to see or hear. They wanted the Prime Minister, and soon the crowd's shouts were almost drowning out the droning speakers.

Finally, the moment arrived. "Ladies and gentlemen, the Prime Minister of Canada." As the leader appeared from behind the official party, the crowd literally went wild, pressing even closer to the stage, shouting out the Prime Minister's name, throwing him kisses. Girls jumped and squealed, reaching out to try to touch him. Not even the Prime Minister's calming words could quiet everyone down, not even his speech, when he finally got a chance to deliver it. There was very little content in the leader's remarks; there didn't have to be much. The party strategy was simply to show the man to the country, to allow his style and grace — so very different from the politicians who had preceded him in power — to come across. It was the new Canadian politics of 1968 that was being tested, and it was working.

At the end of the Prime Minister's remarks, he hopped lightly down off the platform and moved into the crowd, much to the despair of his security men. But no harm would come to Pierre Trudeau unless a man could be hurt by kisses, by people reaching out to touch him. It was Trudeaumania, 1968, and the Canadian people had gone slightly mad with giddy excitement. Politics, the wise journalists covering the love-in sagely agreed, would never be the same in Canada.

Canada in 1957

The decade from 1957 to 1967 was the most turbulent decade in Canada's political history, with five federal elections, two changes of government, and four minority governments.[1] It is tempting to explain this in terms of the rivalry between John Diefenbaker and Lester B. Pearson, the respective leaders of the Progressive Conservative and Liberal parties, who differed sharply in personality as well as policies. However, this rivalry was made possible by profound changes in the attitudes and the aspirations of Canadians in these years. Political leaders did not initiate these changes. They could only respond to them and attempt to give a new sense of common purpose to a society which seemed open to change without knowing where it was going.

Technology helped to create the impression that a new world was emerging. Canadian children of the late 1950s and early 1960s were the first to grow up with television, to see satellites and space ships and a man on the moon. It was the age of supersonic jets and supertankers, of Xerox and the computer. Closer to home, it was the age of instant foods, automatic dishwashers, and polyester suits, of transistors and tapedecks and stereophonic sound. Medical science held out the promise of revolution-

1. R. Bothwell, Ian Drummond, J. English, *Canada Since 1945: Power, Politics and Provincialism* (Toronto, 1981), is a good study of the postwar years, especially for economic issues. The best reference for events is the *Canadian Annual Review*, founded and directed by J.T. Saywell from 1960 and edited by R.B. Byers since 1978. Statistical data can be found in the *Canada Year Book*, in various publications of Statistics Canada, and in F.H. Leacy, ed., *Historical Statistics of Canada* (Ottawa, 1983).

izing human behaviour, beginning with tranquilizers and birth-control pills. There seemed no limit to the ability to control the environment and to shape human existence.

The rising expectations based on this technological revolution were also encouraged by the apparent capacity of governments to direct the national economy. The postwar administrations had concentrated on maintaining full employment and averting another depression; success had shifted the emphasis to economic growth. There were some disturbing economic indicators, however. In 1958 and again in 1960 unemployment reached 7 per cent, the highest rate since the Depression, and the cost-of-living index, which rose at an average rate of less than 2 per cent through the 1950s and early 1960s rose to an average of over 4 per cent for the last half of the decade. But unemployment could be attributed to a rapidly expanding labour force and a government which had been slow to apply Keynesian remedies, while inflation could be blamed on profligate politicians spending too much money. It was still assumed that competent governments applying wise fiscal and monetary policies could ensure sustained economic progress.

Associated with this faith in material progress was a demographic revolution with far-reaching consequences. The baby boom of the postwar period and the immigration of the 1950s had produced a population with an unusually large proportion of young people; by the mid-1960s almost half of Canadians were under twenty-five years of age. Even more significant was the decision of young parents to have small families. The birth rate, which had remained just above twenty-seven births per thousand since the war, dropped abruptly in the 1960s until it was just below eighteen per thousand by the end of the decade. The contraceptive pill made family planning easier, but the decisive factor appeared to have been the desire of many Canadians to enjoy higher living standards.

The most obvious impact of these demographic changes could be seen in the labour force, which grew from 6.5 million to 8.6 million over the decade. The number actually declined in farming, lumbering, fishing, and mining, where machines replaced unskilled labour while increasing production. Manufacturing and construction absorbed only a small proportion of the additional workers with the major increase coming in the service industries. Changing family patterns also affected the labour force. Women had more time to work outside the home and could contribute directly to family income, and the number of women in the labour force rose from 1.8 to 2.9 million. By the end of the decade 40 per cent of all Canadian women and one-third of married women were working. Two-income families were no longer unusual and day-care centres were beginning to be seen as a necessity. However, in one area there was little change. Women were still concentrated in the clerical and service jobs where wages were relatively low and within those occupations they earned about half as much as male workers.[2]

These changes in society were deeply disruptive, and Canadians responded differently to the consequences of economic growth. The upwardly mobile and ambitious looked forward to an ever higher standard of living, whereas the more conservative saw only a threat to traditional community and family values. With increasing national wealth, distribution became a contentious issue. The 1960s also saw the emergence of a "counterculture" in reaction against an economic system which seemed to produce material wealth and profits by exploiting the poor and by destroying the environment. Some tried to change the system; others threatened to opt out by openly flouting middle-class manners and morals. It was a decade of intense political involvement and of mass protests against nuclear weapons and pollution. It was also a decade when a growing number of young Canadians of both sexes adopted long hair and jeans, experimented with marijuana, and hitchhiked across the country in the summer.

Although Canadians had rising expectations, there was no consensus on what they wanted. In a country which had gained confidence in its political leadership during the war and postwar era, Canadians now looked to politicians to provide leadership in this age of change. And the politicians shared in the rising expectations, in the faith that sound administration could ensure sustained economic growth. Naturally enough, they promised more than they could deliver. More damaging to their fortunes in the long run was the fact that even modest growth meant disruptive social changes. Technology was altering the Canadian way of life and not all Canadians were convinced this was desirable.

The greatest impact was in Quebec. There the technological advances coincided with radical changes in French Canada. A society which had survived by resisting change suddenly decided to join the modern world and share in its benefits. The result was revolutionary for French Canada and for the federal union.

2. The best study on the impact of economic changes on Canadian women is Pat and Hugh Armstrong, *The Double Ghetto* (Toronto, 1978).

Dief the Chief

The Conservative victory of 1957 was a stunning upset. It was also difficult to assess. John G. Diefenbaker had campaigned against an arrogant
and insensitive Liberal Government and his apocalyptic intensity had
tremendous impact. A million more Canadians went to the polls than in
the previous election. The freshness, vigour, and charisma of the new
leader seemed to account for the public's interest in politics and for the
increased support for the Conservative party, but the victory was far from
decisive. The Conservatives won only 112 of 265 seats; they faced an
Opposition of 105 Liberal, 25 C.C.F., 19 Social Credit, and 4 independent seats. And although it was clear that Diefenbaker was against the
Liberals, it was less clear what he was for — other than a change. It was
difficult to predict what the new Government would do, or indeed, whether
it would be able to survive.

Diefenbaker soon showed himself to be a masterful tactician.[3] He
attracted favourable publicity at a Commonwealth prime ministers' meeting
in the summer of 1957 with a promise to divert Canadian trade from the
United States to Great Britain. He humiliated Lester B. Pearson, the
newly chosen Liberal successor to Louis St. Laurent, when his Government lowered taxes and increased housing loans and old age pensions.
He then promptly dissolved Parliament and went back to the hustings in
search of a majority.

The election of 1958 was a rout. Diefenbaker promised to end unemployment and regional disparities and waxed eloquent about developing
northern resources. It did not matter that his "vision of the north" lacked
substance and that his "roads to resources" were (foolishly) ridiculed by
Pearson as running from "igloo to igloo"; Canadians responded to his old-
style, evangelical rhetoric because they wanted to believe. The total number of voters rose by another half million, and this time the Conservative
support was overwhelming. The party swept Prince Edward Island, Nova
Scotia, and the four western provinces and won decisive majorities in
every other province except Newfoundland. The most startling results
were in Quebec, where Maurice Duplessis' Union nationale organizers
openly supported the Conservatives; the fifty Conservative seats in Quebec were the most since the days of John A. Macdonald. In all, the Con-

3. Peter Newman, *Renegade in Power* (Toronto, 1963), is a journalist's account of the
Diefenbaker years. Diefenbaker's own memoirs, *One Canada*, vols. I-III (Toronto, 1975-77),
are quite unreliable; Donald Fleming's *So Very Near*, vol. II (Toronto, 1985), is remarkably
revealing. See also J.L. Granatstein, *Canada 1957-67* (Toronto, 1986).

servatives won 208 seats, with the Liberals reduced to 49 and the C.C.F. to 8. John Diefenbaker had won the most decisive election victory in the history of Canada.

Diefenbaker had stressed regional economic grievances in his election campaigns, a testimony to his sound political instinct — regional grievances had intensified during the St. Laurent administration. The federal government had relied on broad fiscal and monetary policies to maintain a high level of employment. These measures stimulated manufacturing and the exploitation of natural resources, but the economic benefits had been unequally distributed. Some sectors of the economy, such as farming and fishing, had suffered from declining prices for their products. They could only share in the national prosperity by becoming more efficient, which meant enlarging their scale of operations, investing heavily in machinery, and reducing labour costs. The point was bluntly made by the Royal Commission on Canada's Economic Prospects under Walter Gordon, a Liberal accountant from Toronto. The Gordon report, released in 1958, paid special attention to the Maritimes, where incomes had been consistently below the national average; its long-range solution was for more capital investment in the rural and fishing communities in the Maritimes, with the displaced workers migrating to central and western Canada where there were jobs and higher wages. This economic argument may have been right, but it ignored the social consequences. It was proposing the death of the old-fashioned family enterprise and the end of the stable life style of traditional rural and fishing communities. The Conservative Government rejected this social revolution, and the party swept the Maritimes.

In Nova Scotia, Robert L. Stanfield, the slow-speaking but able Conservative premier who had taken office in 1956, was already undertaking a different approach to economic recovery. He was concerned with rural communities where small farms and marginal lands kept incomes low, with fishing villages where the inshore fisheries were less and less productive, and also with the mining towns of Cape Breton where antiquated equipment and less accessible coal seams were increasing the costs of production. His response was to lend government funds to entrepreneurs who would establish local industries in these communities and so provide employment for the surplus labour force. Over the next decade the Nova Scotia Government helped to establish small textile, hardboard, and fish-packing plants across the province with mixed success. The Diefenbaker Government provided support for such projects through a $25 million annual adjustment grant to the Maritime provinces.

*The Diefenbaker Govern-
ment released this advertisement in the first months of
the new adminstration.*

Macpherson /Reprinted with permission—The Toronto Star Syndicate

Such projects did provide jobs and income for local communities, but they were not a long-range solution to the economic problems of the family farm. Alvin Hamilton, the innovative Minister of Northern Affairs and later of Agriculture, introduced a more direct approach with the Agricultural and Rural Development Act (A.R.D.A.), which initiated a wide range of shared-cost programs to increase rural incomes. Much was done to improve farming procedures and to make farm lands more productive. However, the problem of rural poverty was not so easily resolved. In the Maritimes and in many rural areas in other parts of Canada, the unpalatable fact was that profitable farming now depended on large farms. Farm improvements and efforts to stimulate tourism could increase rural incomes, but a long-range solution had to involve more fundamental changes in the rural economy.

In Newfoundland the problem was the modernization of the logging industry. The major pulp and paper mills relied on the part-time work of farmers and fishermen to supply many of their logs. The International Woodworkers of America successfully organized the full-time loggers in 1959 and called a strike to win the wages and working conditions of loggers elsewhere in North America. These demands had far-reaching social implications. The higher labour costs would inevitably lead to mechanization and reliance on a small corps of highly paid professional woodsmen. The part-time jobs, the supplementary income on which many farmers and fishermen depended, would disappear.

The strike was broken by the intervention of Joey Smallwood, the volatile and partisan provincial Premier. Smallwood, once a socialist, may have sympathised with the strikers, but he could not face the disruption in the farming and fishing communities. After the strike had gone on for a bitter six weeks, Smallwood decertified the I.W.A. and certified a rival union which promptly signed a less favourable contract with the mills.

The federal government became involved when violence broke out during the strike. The R.C.M.P. acted as both the provincial and federal police force in Newfoundland, as they did in all provinces except Ontario and Quebec. Smallwood asked for R.C.M.P. reinforcements to maintain order. After some hesitation, Diefenbaker refused the request, despite a clear legal obligation, because he did not wish to appear to support strike-breakers.

The political consequences of the strike attracted the most attention. In Ottawa, Diefenbaker's refusal to send reinforcements led the Commissioner of the R.C.M.P. to resign. In Newfoundland, Smallwood's reputation as the champion of the underprivileged was tarnished, and this was a factor in his eventual defeat years later. But in the logging industry the political intervention had little effect in the long run. Within a few years mechanization had arrived, and logging had become the monopoly of a few specialized, full-time workers, in spite of the reluctance of politicians and businessmen and the unwelcome consequences for farmers and fishermen.[4]

The federal policy of transfer payments to the Atlantic provinces was not a resounding success. Average per capita income rose in the four eastern provinces, as it did in all Canadian provinces, but in relative terms it improved only slightly and remained well below the national average. The sense of regional grievance may have grown even stronger in these years. Television programs and advertising, as well as political campaigns, helped make the less privileged regions aware of their relative poverty, and the rising standard of living only whetted their appetites for more. There was also some backlash because prosperity tied the Maritimes to an industrial economy which rewarded adaptability but also brought insecurity and eroded the traditional values of family and community.

In contrast to the Maritimes, some regions in Canada were prospering greatly. In British Columbia, the growing demand for minerals and forest products in the United States stimulated economic development. Confident that a depression was no longer a threat, businessmen and politicians on the West Coast advocated rapid expansion; capital investment in resource industries would create jobs and exports. British Columbians were critical of federal transfer payments which taxed the wealthier provinces to subsidize the less fortunate ones. From their point of view, federal funds would contribute more to the national income if they were invested in growth industries. Not surprisingly, this would mean federal support for industries in British Columbia.

W.A.C. Bennett, the Social Credit Premier of the province from 1952 to 1972, was the most vocal exponent of this regional approach. Bennett was flamboyant and brash, but his free-enterprise rhetoric came from an authoritarian politician, and the perennial smile concealed a tough-minded negotiator. His commitment to vast water-power projects on the Columbia and Peace Rivers brought him into direct conflict with an unsuspecting federal government.

The growing demand for industrial power in the American northwest

4. Geoffrey Stevens, *Stanfield* (Toronto, 1973), and Richard Gwyn, *Smallwood: The Unlikely Revolutionary* (Toronto, 1968), are well-written biographies by journalists without access to private papers. Another study of a provincial premier is Allan McDougall's *John P. Robarts* (Toronto, 1985).

had already led to major hydro-electric installations on the Columbia River south of the border. Dams on the Canadian side could store the spring runoff and increase the power developed at these downstream installations, as well as contribute to flood control. An American proposal for a storage dam which would flood Canadian territory led to international negotiations for joint development of the entire Columbia watershed. The discussions were conducted on the Canadian side by the federal government, but provincial jurisdiction meant that any final agreement would require British Columbia's consent. A major breakthrough in the negotiations came when the Americans agreed to pay for a portion of the downstream benefits from storage dams in Canada.

The treaty was delayed because the federal and provincial governments disagreed over how this payment should be made. The federal government favoured low-cost electricity which could be delivered from the state of Washington to the Vancouver area, where there was a growing demand for power. The provincial government preferred to sell the downstream benefits for cash which could then be used for yet another huge development on the Peace River to supply the needs of the lower mainland. Ottawa, convinced that its solution would mean cheaper power and that it would have the support of most British Columbians, nonetheless signed a treaty with the United States which provided for the construction of three large storage dams in Canada in return for low-cost power.

Bennett rejected the agreement. He strengthened his bargaining position by suddenly expropriating B.C. Electric, the private utility serving Vancouver, which then agreed to buy power from the proposed Peace River installation. The Premier ultimately had his way because the majority of British Columbians supported his ambitious projects. The treaty was finally ratified in 1964 when the newly elected Liberal Government in Ottawa recognized that, if there was to be a treaty, it would have to be on Bennett's terms.[5]

Going Wrong

Federal relations with Quebec also deteriorated. The Conservative hopes of 1958, when they won fifty seats in Quebec, were never fulfilled. In large measure, this was the result of developments within Quebec. Maurice

---

5. Neil A. Swainson, *Conflict over the Columbia* (Montreal, 1979), is a detailed study of the negotiation of the Columbia River Treaty. Additional material is available in the Diefenbaker and Fleming memoirs.

Duplessis, whose support probably accounted for most of the Tory gains, died in 1959 and the Union nationale Government was defeated by the Liberals under Jean Lesage in the following year. This was more than a transfer of power from one party to another. Duplessis had defended the traditions of rural Quebec, whereas the Liberal Opposition increasingly drew its support from French Canadians who believed that this policy was misguided. The Liberal victory in 1960 marked the beginning of the Quiet Revolution, when French Canadians rapidly began adapting their institutions to meet the needs of an urban and industrial society. There were differences in the new government and in the progressive sectors of the society about what changes were necessary and about the speed of change, but there was general agreement on the final objective. The aim was still the survival of French Canada as a cultural entity but now the goal was survival by becoming a modern society rather than survival by rejecting the modern world. Among the changes was a shift from the Roman Catholic Church to the state as the major instrument of *la survivance*. In this case, the state meant the provincial government, and inevitably this implied conflict with Ottawa over respective spheres of authority. Any federal government, Conservative or Liberal, was bound to clash with the Government of Quebec under these circumstances.

John Diefenbaker, nonetheless, aggravated the situation because he never understood French-Canadian aspirations. He knew that political support from Quebec was important, and so he made some gestures towards the province. He spoke some French on public occasions even though he was far from fluent in the language, and he introduced long-needed simultaneous translation into the House of Commons. However, his French-Canadian ministers held only minor portfolios and none exercised much influence. It was easy, therefore, for French Canadians to believe that the Government in Ottawa represented English Canada and that only the Government in Quebec represented them. Diefenbaker's failure to understand French Canada was also illustrated by his Canadian Bill of Rights, which he considered the greatest achievement of his political career. In his Saskatchewan experience, ethnic minorities wanted to eliminate invidious distinctions and merge with the English-speaking majority. His bill reflected this experience by protecting all citizens against the exercise of arbitrary power by the federal government, regardless of their race or ethnic origin. It was limited in scope because it gave no protection against the actions of provincial governments and because it could not bind future federal Parliaments, but the objectives were certainly commendable in an era of expanding government activities. But to French

Canadians, Diefenbaker's emphasis on individual rights ignored their rights as a cultural group, and his ideal of "unhyphenated Canadianism" seemed to them to be a policy of assimilation.

In an earlier era the consequences of this insensitivity to French-Canadian aspirations would have been less serious. However, in these turbulent years, with French-Canadian nationalism rising, the political results were disastrous. The fifty Conservative seats of 1958 plummeted to fourteen in 1962 and to eight in 1963. The Progressive Conservative party was once more confined largely to English Canada.

Diefenbaker was more in sympathy with those Canadians who felt a sentimental attachment to Great Britain. Sentiment is not always a clear guide to what should be done, and Diefenbaker's rhetoric about the Commonwealth was not always consistent with his actions. He was also apprehensive about Canada's close economic and military associations with the United States. He was not anti-American — on the contrary, he had great respect for the United States' political and economic achievements — but he was concerned that its dominance as Canada's trading partner and the integration of continental defence under American control were threats to Canadian autonomy. His concern was well founded, but his policies were vacillating and inconsistent. The problems may have been insoluble, but they could have been more fully understood.

Diefenbaker had a romantic view of the British Empire — he took a world tour in 1958 which included an elephant ride in Ceylon, a tiger hunt in Bengal, and a side trip to the Khyber Pass — but he also saw Great Britain as a counterweight to the United States. Shortly after taking office in 1957, he proposed shifting 15 per cent of Canada's imports from the United States to Great Britain. It was a well meaning but irresponsible proposal because there were no available incentives to create the necessary market in Canada for British goods. His response to the British application for entry into the European Economic Community in 1961 was no more constructive. Membership in the Common Market would certainly weaken Britain's economic links to the Commonwealth and hurt Canadian trade, but to the British the alternative seemed to be a continuing economic decline. The Liberal Opposition in Canada accepted the British decision and tried to make the best of it by arguing that the E.E.C. could become a major trading bloc and a counterbalance to the United States. But the Conservative Government publicly insisted that Britain had an obligation to the Commonwealth which was inconsistent with E.E.C. membership. Charles de Gaulle ended the debate in 1963 by vetoing the admission of the United Kingdom, delaying its entry for almost a decade, but Diefenbaker's position seemingly showed only a nostalgic longing for a Commonwealth which no longer had much meaning.

The British economic difficulties only aggravated the concern for Canadian economic independence. American firms continued to invest in the development of Canada's natural resources, and Canadians continued to debate the implications of American ownership in newspapers and academic journals. There were even isolated cases of American branch plants in Canada conforming to restrictive American trade legislation directed against countries such as China or Cuba. More significant for Canada's long-term economic development was the argument that American firms would conduct all their research and development in the United States, leaving Canada far behind in the competition for technical innovation. There was not much consolation in the counterargument that Canadian-owned firms did even less research than American subsidiaries in Canada. On the other hand, the rate of economic growth was levelling off,

John Kennedy's first presidential visit was to Ottawa in May of 1961. The result was a developing antipathy between him and Prime Minister Diefenbaker. (John F. Kennedy Library, ST-120-21)

and higher than usual rates of unemployment in 1958 and again in 1960 meant that the Conservative Government, sensitive to any suggestion of economic mismanagement, saw advantages in any investment, foreign or domestic.

In the summer of 1961 the debate over American ownership focussed on the activities and policy prescriptions of James Coyne, Governor of the Bank of Canada. Coyne was convinced that foreign investment should be discouraged, but his reasons apparently had more to do with his personal philosophy than with economic theory. Canadians, he argued, should live within their means by tightening their belts and investing their own savings instead of borrowing from the United States. He advocated "tight money" — restraining credit by raising interest rates. Most Canadian professional economists disagreed with Coyne: they favoured economic growth, and the national origin of the investment dollar seemed irrelevant to them. A more telling argument was that even if the Government accepted Coyne's objective, his proposal would be self-defeating because higher interest rates would actually attract foreign capital. His monetary policies would probably have had to be accompanied by rigid import regulations and a level of government intervention which almost no one favoured.

However, the debate quickly shifted from monetary policy to the role of the Governor of the Bank of Canada. The Government had no clear policy of its own and Coyne's public statements were an embarrassment. Diefenbaker and his Finance Minister, Donald Fleming, seized on the fact that the Governor of the Bank of Canada should not be discussing monetary policies in public. His duty, they argued, was to advise the Government and then to administer and defend Government policy. A bill for his dismissal was introduced in the House of Commons, but it proved to be a major political blunder when the Liberal majority in the Senate gave Coyne an opportunity to defend himself before a Senate committee. The Coyne affair had no apparent effect on Canadian monetary policy, but it did have political consequences. It created an image of a vacillating Conservative Government, looking for scapegoats to blame for its own shortcomings and indecision.

The Government did agree with the objective of reducing imports and encouraging domestic production. But instead of tight money it eventually opted for a tentative policy of inflation. The difficulty was to control the value of the floating Canadian dollar so that it would drop, but not drop too far. Confidence in the Government had been weakened by the prolonged debate over monetary policy and by the Government's growing reputation for indecision in a number of spheres. Investors began to hedge by exchanging Canadian dollars for foreign currencies. In May, 1962, in the middle of the federal election campaign, there was a sudden run on the Canadian dollar, and the Government was forced to peg it at 92.5 American cents. It was a difficult and embarrassing political decision at the time, but in retrospect it showed sound judgement. The dollar stayed at that level until 1970, when once more it was allowed to float and to find its own level against the U.S. dollar.

The Diefenbaker Government found defence policy even more controversial than monetary policy. The logic of a continental defence policy seemed self-evident when technological advances in atomic weapons and missiles made cooperation all the more necessary. However, the need for rapid response to any attack would make it more difficult for Canadians to be consulted before the button was pushed. The North American Air Defence Agreement of 1957 was one answer to technological changes; it integrated the air defence forces of the two countries under an American commander and a Canadian second-in-command. The N.O.R.A.D. agreement provoked little controversy at the time — it was negotiated by the St. Laurent Government and quickly ratified by the Diefenbaker Government as soon as it took office. But it was not safe to assume that Canadians would always agree with American decisions. In 1962 the Americans uncovered Russian missile sites in Cuba and demanded their immediate withdrawal. The American defence forces were alerted during the crisis; the Canadian Government, slow to admit that there was a crisis, hesitated. This could be seen as an affirmation of Canadian autonomy, but it left the American Government — and many Canadians — wondering about the reliability of its defence partner.[6]

National defence was also intimately linked to economic strength. Defence research and development could lead to technological innovations and the development of skills which could spawn profitable high-technology industries. In the 1950s the Liberal Government had invested heavily in the CF-105 Arrow, a supersonic fighter, in an attempt to foster the aeronautics industry in Canada. The Arrow was an ambitious project, but its success depended upon sales to other countries, and production

---

6. There is no standard survey of Canadian foreign policy since 1957. Two volumes of essays by John Holmes in the *Carleton Library Series*, *The Better Part of Valour: Essays on Canadian Diplomacy* (1970), and *Canada: A Middle-Aged Power* (1976), touch on the major issues. The same series has published two volumes of documents, edited by Arthur Blanchette, *Canadian Foreign Policy 1955-1965*, and *Canadian Foreign Policy 1966-1976*, Stephen Clarkson, ed., *An Independent Foreign Policy for Canada?* (Toronto, 1968), gives the tenor of the debate in the 1960s.

The devaluation of the dollar during the 1962 election led the Liberals to issue "Diefendollars."

The balloteers

◀ *Prime Minister Diefenbaker, Governor General Vincent Massey, and Howard Green, the new Secretary of State for External Affairs, after his swearing-in in 1959. (PA-114895/Public Archives Canada)*

delays and spiralling costs eventually made foreign sales less and less likely. In 1959 the Diefenbaker Government cancelled the project, provoking an outcry from those who believed that Canada needed an aircraft industry in order to have access to the high technology it involved. The cancellation of the Arrow was, in fact, a tacit admission that the stakes were too high for Canada to compete with the superpowers in this high-risk game. The alternative was an agreement which allowed Canadians to share in American defence projects. There would be Canadian jobs but defence poduction would be organized on a continental basis, with the major decisions on military equipment being made in the United States.

Under the impact of the Arrow, the Coyne affair, and a shaky economy, the Diefenbaker charisma of 1958 had faded by 1962. In the federal election of that year the Conservatives elected only 116 members, a stunning loss of ninety-two seats. The results also showed intensified regional divisions. The Atlantic provinces continued to support the Government, and the Prairie provinces remained overwhelmingly Conservative, a reward in part for wheat sales to China which had compensated for declining markets in Europe. Local issues played a part in these results, but it was no coincidence that these two Conservative strongholds were less urban and less industrialized than the rest of the country. The same pattern emerged in Ontario, where most of the thirty-five seats which Diefenbaker retained were in rural ridings. The thirty Ontario seats lost to the Liberals, on the other hand, were mainly in urban communities. There was a growing cleavage between smaller, more traditional communities and larger industrial centres. The pattern showed clearly with the New Democratic Party, the reorganized and revampd C.C.F., which appealed directly for labour support and whose nineteen seats came mainly from industrial ridings in Ontario and British Columbia. The Liberal party still retained some support in smaller communities, but its strength now clearly lay in the industrial areas of central Canada. The same divisions emerged in Quebec, although there the Conservatives were not the beneficiaries in the rural areas. The Social Credit party under Réal Caouette, a fiery orator and an intense campaigner, came from nowhere to take twenty-six seats in northern and eastern Quebec. The Créditiste slogan — *Il n'y a rien à perdre* — was an appeal to voters disoriented by the changes of the Quiet Revolution to reject both major parties in favour of one which offered a simple monetary panacea to restore the good old days. The Conservatives retained only fourteen seats in Quebec. A divided House of Commons and a minority Government mirrored an uncertain country divided by regional and social differences. The bloom was off the roses of 1958.

Prime Minister Diefenbaker continued in office, but even within his party there were growing doubts about his ability to regain some of the support he had lost. A controversy over defence policy provoked an open challenge to his leadership. The continental defence plans against Soviet

This is a Prime Minister.
He is at breakfast.
Should he have orange juice or a grapefruit?
It is a hard decision. He dreads decisions.
Perhaps he will never have breakfast.
Colour him hungry.

In the 1963 election the Liberals concentrated on attacking Diefenbaker's indecision. This cartoon from The Election Colouring Book *had an impact — on the Liberals, who were denounced for lowering the tone of the campaign.*

An enthusiastic crowd cheered at an N.D.P. rally in Toronto's Maple Leaf Gardens during the 1965 election. (Toronto Telegram *Collection, York University Archives)*

bombers included the construction of a number of Bomarc missile sites, two of them in Canada. Canada had agreed in 1959 to install the Bomarcs; by 1962 construction was almost completed and all that remained to make them operational was to install the nuclear warheads. However, by this time the antinuclear movement had gained adherents, Diefenbaker's relations with President John F. Kennedy had deteriorated, and the Prime Minister found excuses not to arm the Bomarcs. The American State Department took the unusual step of a press release to refute some of his statements. Then in February, 1963, his Minister of National Defence, Douglas Harkness, resigned in protest and the three Opposition parties combined to defeat the Government. After the parliamentary defeat other ministers resigned as well.

The Conservatives were defeated in the following election, although the results could hardly be called decisive. Diefenbaker ignored a divided Cabinet and a sharply hostile press and conducted an emotional and effective campaign against "them" — an omnibus group that included the Liberals, the Americans, and big business. To the surprise of the pundits, the Conservatives again swept the Prairies, held most of their seats in the Maritimes, and survived in rural Ontario. The Liberals won 128 seats, just short of a majority, while the number of N.D.P. and Social Credit seats was almost unchanged.

John Diefenbaker was not a man to accept defeat gracefully. Though he was now almost sixty-eight years old, the Chief rallied his followers in the House and attacked the Pearson Government with a force and viciousness that were surprising. The Liberal Government's errors provided the target, and Diefenbaker, always good in Opposition, was at his destructive best. As a result, in the election of 1965 the fragmented Conservative party came together once more, many of the rebels of 1963 returning to work for the defeat of Pearson. But when the results demonstrated that Conservative support was more than ever confined to rural Canada, and when Diefenbaker still showed no sign of being willing to step down as party chieftain, the grumbling increased. Led by Dalton Camp, the party president, a movement began for a change in leadership: it became a struggle that tore the old party apart. Finally, after many vicissitudes and a long fight, the challenge to Diefenbaker succeeded. At the Progressive Conservative party's leadership convention in Toronto in September, 1967, the Chief belatedly decided to attempt to succeed himself, but his decision came so late and his organization was so weak that he ran a humiliating fifth on the first ballot. Robert Stanfield, the Premier of Nova Scotia and Camp's choice for the succession, won out on the fifth ballot, but the party remained sorely divided. John Diefenbaker himself remained a Member of Parliament, his very presence a rebuke to the new leader.

Pearson at the Helm

The Liberal party in 1963 was a sharp contrast to the dispirited Conservatives. The Liberals had attributed their earlier defeats to their own inadequate public relations and to Diefenbaker's demagogy. They were convinced that the Diefenbaker administration had been indecisive and incompetent and that any regional dissatisfaction could soon be resolved by restoring economic growth; grievances would disappear with rising incomes. In the election campaign of 1963 they had boldly promised "60 days of decision" as an alternative to Conservative ineptitude.

The social policies of the Pearson Government over the next five years were a far-reaching effort to adapt both to the demands and to the insecurities of an industrial economy. The need for a skilled labour force was obvious, and although education is a provincial responsibility in the Canadian federal system, federal governments had been convinced that manpower training was too important to be left to the provinces. In 1960 the Conservative Government had offered generous financial incentives for technical and vocational training. But sociologists were talking of a "postindustrial" society in which the benefits of high technology would go to countries with highly trained researchers and skilled technicians. The Economic Council of Canada, appointed in 1963 to advise the Government on economic policy, explained in its first annual report that "the potential Canadian economy we visualize for 1970 is a high-standard-of-living and a high-employment economy, and it must therefore be a high-education economy, a high-resource-mobility economy, a high-research economy, a high-investment economy, and a highly competitive economy." The emphasis under the Liberal administration shifted to university education.

There were dramatic changes in Canadian universities in the 1960s. Full-time undergraduate enrolment rose from 100 000 in 1960 to 300 000 by 1970. There were more young people reaching university age and an ever higher proportion sought university education, encouraged by parents, by governments, and by an economy which offered financial rewards for higher educational qualifications. The demand for advanced training had an even greater impact at the graduate level, where enrolment rose from six thousand to thirty thousand over the decade. Old universities expanded and new universities — Simon Fraser, York, the Université de Québec and others — were built. The costs of this expansion were more than provincial governments were willing or able to meet. The federal government had introduced per capita grants to the provinces for university education in 1951; the grants had risen to $1 per capita by 1957, had been doubled by the Conservatives in 1962, and increased again to $5 in 1965. In 1967 the federal government changed its policy to encourage further expansion and undertook to reimburse the provinces for half the costs of all postsecondary education. The cost to the federal government in the first year of the program almost doubled to more than a billion dollars.

The Government tried even more to provide economic security in an industrial society. The Canada Assistance Plan of 1965 was a major re-structuring of federal grants-in-aid for "the further development and ex-tension of assistance and welfare service programs." Under this plan, the federal government agreed to share the costs of a wide range of income support programs, including child care, mothers' allowances, health care for the needy, and the costs of welfare administration. Special programs included rehabilitation and work projects to prepare individuals for employ-ment. The plan removed a substantial financial burden from provincial and municipal governments and also reduced the demands on private charity.

This major extension of social assistance was supplemented by other social security programs. Hospital insurance had done nothing to protect individuals against other medical costs. In 1962 the N.D.P. Government of Saskatchewan once more took the initiative when it introduced a com-prehensive medical insurance scheme. The plan provoked a bitter doc-tors' strike in the province, but a compromise was negotiated which made some minor concessions to the medical profession while preserving the major outlines of the scheme. Three years later the Pearson Government adopted the broad outlines of the Saskatchewan plan and offered to share the costs of any provincial medical insurance scheme which provided universal coverage for "all medically necessary services." Some provinces would have preferred to encourage the expansion of voluntary insurance plans, but the demands of their people, the lure of federal funds, and the federal insistence on universal coverage meant that all provinces were virtually forced to participate in the program by the end of the decade.

Government programs paid special attention to young people because throughout the Western world restless youth seemed a threat to social stability in the 1960s. Affluence allowed the children of middle-class fami-lies to postpone their careers, and idealism led some of them to challenge the discrimination and inequalities in their society. Canadians found no cause in Canada comparable to the civil rights movement in the United States, but Canadian youth did agitate in support of the Indians and the poor and showed an interest in the emerging nations of Africa. Ironically,

The introduction of Medicare into Saskatchewan caused enormous controversy. This photograph shows a rally at the legislative buildings in Regina sponsored by the Keep Our Doctors Committee, an anti-Medicare group. (Saskatchewan Archives, R-B3980[1]).

young English Canadians were less interested in French Canada. University students were at the centre of most of the agitation, and the federal government made special efforts to placate them. Ottwa established the Canada Student Loan Fund in 1963. A much more imaginative response was the Company of Young Canadians, designed to channel youthful enthusiasm into projects for the underprivileged. The experience of the C.Y.C. showed that idealism has its problems: local officials protested when young people encouraged the Métis or slum tenants to organize, and federal bureaucrats complained when the C.Y.C. workers ignored proper accounting procedures. Funds for the company were cut, and within a few years it was disbanded.

The aged also presented a special problem in Canada in these years because improved health care had increased life expectancy. The federal government had taken over the full responsibility for old age pensions in

1951, but in 1963 it proposed a radical shift to a universal and contributory pension plan. Individuals and employers would contribute to a fund which would then provide a retirement pension after the age of sixty-five or benefits for the contributor's widow or dependents. The Canada Pension Plan was accompanied by a federal Guaranteed Income Supplement for the benefit of the elderly with low incomes who retired before establishing full benefits under the plan. The plan itself was generous, and it avoided the humiliating means test, with its taint of charity.

There was almost no opposition in Canada to these extensions of social security; the costs did not seem excessive in a period of economic growth, and aid to the less fortunate had general approval in an egalitarian decade. However, the federal initiatives did provoke strong criticism for constitutional reasons, since they encroached on the legislative powers allocated to the provincial governments. Prime Minister Pearson stressed the efficiency and equity of uniform social security measures across Canada, and his constitutional justification was that his Government was not imposing any programs on provincial administrations; it was merely offering assistance to provinces which agreed to introduce the programs. The provincial governments were not impressed with this argument. The Ontario Government of John Robarts, for example, had made it clear that it was strongly opposed to the federal Medicare Plan. But once the offer was made and accepted by other provinces, it was difficult to resist federal generosity and deprive the people of a popular program. Federal initiatives, in fact, were imposing federal priorities on provincial administrations.

Not surprisingly, the strongest opposition came from Quebec, where provincial autonomy was linked to cultural survival. When the federal government first proposed its pension plan to the provinces, the Liberal Government in Quebec responded with its own plan. The eventual compromise was a Canada Pension Plan which accepted some features of the Quebec proposal and a separate Quebec plan which was parallel to Ottawa's and permitted workers to carry pension rights from one plan to the other. In lieu of the federal grant paid to the other provinces, the Quebec Government received an equivalent sum through an increase in the provincial income tax balanced by an equal reduction in the federal income tax for Quebec residents. This opting-out procedure was adopted for a number of other federal measures. It had the advantage of maintaining broadly uniform programs across the country while conceding formal administrative control to Quebec. Critics did argue that opting out would weaken the links of Quebec residents with Ottawa and dilute their sense of belonging to a national community, but in these years of militant nationalism in Quebec, some special recognition of provincial autonomy seemed inevitable.[7]

This debate was part of the larger problem of the future of French-Canadian society within Canada. The problem had become more acute with the sense of alienation from the Diefenbaker administration in Ottawa and with the social changes produced by the Quiet Revolution in Quebec. Pearson had committed the Liberal party to fuller recognition of the French fact in Canada, and in 1963 the Government appointed a Royal Commission on Bilingualism and Biculturalism "to recommend what steps should be taken to develop the Canadian Confederation on the basis of an equal partnership between the two founding races."

The Commission adopted as basic the principle that Canadian citizens should have the right to be served by the federal administration in either English or French. This principle seemed obvious and straightforward, but it required major changes within the federal public service before it could be put into effect. English had always been the language of work. Documents now would have to be translated, and communication with citizens would have to be available in the two languages. Within the civil service this meant that supervisors would often have to be bilingual. Furthermore, if French Canadians were to be attracted to the public service and were to have equal chances of promotion, their language had to have a status equivalent to that of English. This meant a massive second-language training program for both Anglophones and Francophones (two new words that appeared in the 1960s).

The federal government accepted the principle of federal services in both languages and began the slow process of altering language patterns within the public service. There was strong resistance from unilingual Anglophones who saw their careers threatened, and progress was slow. But there was progress, and in 1969 the Government passed the Official Languages Act, which established the legal right of citizens to federal services in either English or French.

The principle of "equal partnership between the two founding races" also had constitutional implications, but here the Commission was less helpful. The survival of French-Canadian society depended on more than linguistic rights: its distinctive cultural identity would have to be assured. The Quebec Government under Premier Jean Lesage claimed to represent the interests of French Canada as the only government in which

7. Richard Simeon, *Federal-Provincial Diplomacy: the making of recent policy in Canada* (Toronto, 1972), is a detailed study of constitutional discussions from 1963 to 1971.

French Canadians were a majority, and Lesage demanded expanded legislative and administrative powers in recognition of this special status without clearly defining what those powers should be. However, in 1966 the provincial Liberal Government was defeated by the Union nationale under Daniel Johnson. The Quiet Revolution had lost some of its impetus and a rural backlash against sweeping educational reforms contributed to the election results. The new Government was more cautious about social change, but it was equally determined to extend Quebec's constitutional powers. The choice, according to Johnson, was equality or independence.[8]

Some English Canadians feared that equality would mean independence. Pearson advocated "cooperative federalism" and was willing to make substantial concessions to meet Quebec's demands. But each concession seemed to be followed by further demands. Would it be possible to satisfy Quebec and at the same time preserve the federal system? Opposition grew to any further concessions to this creeping separatism.

French-Canadian representation in the federal Parliament was also a matter of concern because, whatever the powers allocated to Quebec, the federal government would still exercise substantial jurisdiction over French-speaking citizens. Pearson did not make any formal changes in the structure of the federal legislature, but through his choice of Cabinet ministers he did give French Canada an influence in Ottawa it had never had before. This influence was further strengthened when, in 1965, he persuaded Jean Marchand, Gérard Pelletier, and Pierre Trudeau, three French Canadians who had played prominent roles in the Quiet Revolution in Quebec, to join the federal Liberal party. Their arrival in Ottawa after the election of that year and their obvious influence meant that the federal government could no longer be dismissed as an English-Canadian government, and the Quebec Government could no longer claim to be the sole interpreter of the interests of French Canadians.

In addition to extending social security and trying to improve French-English relations, the Pearson Government was committed to establishing Canadian independence on a firmer basis. Pearson saw the Commonwealth as one of Canada's windows on the world but no longer as a major factor in Canadian foreign policy. As a symbol of Canada's new status, he proposed a flag that did not include the Union Jack. In the heated debate that followed, the critics, led by Diefenbaker, represented a nostalgic

8. For a discussion of French Canada and the Quiet Revolution, see Kenneth McRoberts and Dale Posgate, *Quebec: Social Change and Political Crisis* (revised ed., Toronto, 1980). For additional readings see the footnotes in Chapter XI.

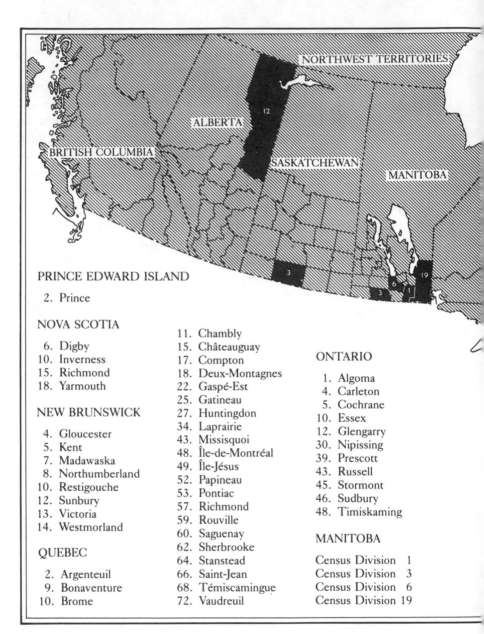

PRINCE EDWARD ISLAND

2. Prince

NOVA SCOTIA

6. Digby
10. Inverness
15. Richmond
18. Yarmouth

NEW BRUNSWICK

4. Gloucester
5. Kent
7. Madawaska
8. Northumberland
10. Restigouche
12. Sunbury
13. Victoria
14. Westmorland

QUEBEC

2. Argenteuil
9. Bonaventure
10. Brome
11. Chambly
15. Châteauguay
17. Compton
18. Deux-Montagnes
22. Gaspé-Est
25. Gatineau
27. Huntingdon
34. Laprairie
43. Missisquoi
48. Île-de-Montréal
49. Île-Jésus
52. Papineau
53. Pontiac
57. Richmond
59. Rouville
60. Saguenay
62. Sherbrooke
64. Stanstead
66. Saint-Jean
68. Témiscamingue
72. Vaudreuil

ONTARIO

1. Algoma
4. Carleton
5. Cochrane
10. Essex
12. Glengarry
30. Nipissing
39. Prescott
43. Russell
45. Stormont
46. Sudbury
48. Timiskaming

MANITOBA

Census Division 1
Census Division 3
Census Division 6
Census Division 19

Official Language Distribution

The Royal Commission on Bilingualism and Biculturalism recommended the creation of official language districts wherever 10 per cent or more of the population spoke the minority language. The map, taken from the Commission Report, shows the designated areas. The problem was that in some parts of the country, the

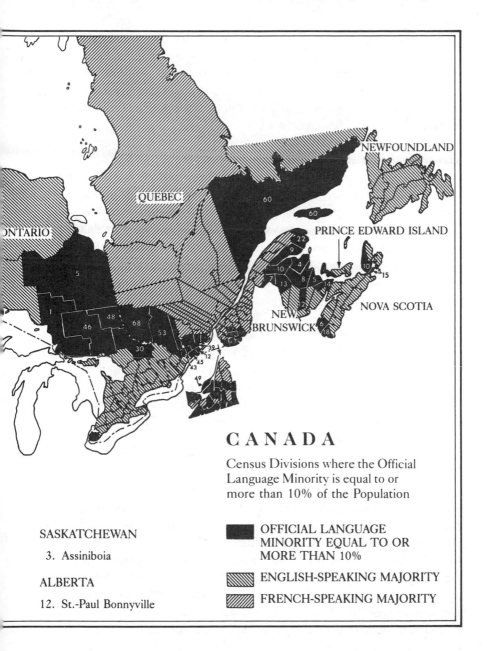

CANADA

Census Divisions where the Official
Language Minority is equal to or
more than 10% of the Population

SASKATCHEWAN

3. Assiniboia

ALBERTA

12. St.-Paul Bonnyville

■ OFFICIAL LANGUAGE
MINORITY EQUAL TO OR
MORE THAN 10%

▨ ENGLISH-SPEAKING MAJORITY

▨ FRENCH-SPEAKING MAJORITY

Prairies particularly, more spoke Ukrainian or German, say, than French, a cause of much hard feeling.

Source: *Report of the Royal Commission on Bilingualism and Biculturalism*, Bk. I, page 108
(Ottawa, 1967). Reproduced by permission of the Minister of Supply and Services Canada.

view of the importance of the British tradition; however, the popular approval of the new flag after its adoption was a reflection of an emerging pride in Canada as a separate nation. But national identity would not be resolved by a flag. Relations with the United States now were infinitely more decisive than the British connection. On this issue the Pearson Government had an ambivalent record.

Walter Gordon, the Minister of Finance when the Liberals returned to office in 1963, was a spokesman within the Government for Canadian nationalists who wanted to limit American investment in Canada. His first budget, part of the promised "60 days of decision," included discriminatory taxes on Canadian company shares sold to nonresidents and on Canadian dividends paid to nonresidents. Aside from businessmen and their press, there was general approval in Canada for these takeover and withholding taxes, but they became a major embarrassment to the Government when they proved to be uncollectable and had to be withdrawn. Gordon was further embarrassed when a proposed American tax on foreign loans threatened to weaken the Canadian dollar, and he had to beg the American Government to exempt Canada from the tax. In 1965 Gordon's budget attempted to limit the distribution of American journals in Canada by disallowing income tax deductions for advertising in non-Canadian publications But as a result of pressure from the United States, the two leading American magazines, *Time* and *Reader's Digest*, were exempted. Gordon's economic nationalism was frustrated by the interdependence of the Canadian and American economies — and by Pearson's unwillingness to risk a confrontation with the United States or with those in the Cabinet who favoured close links with the United States.

The Auto Pact of 1965 actually fostered an even greater integration of the two economies. Canadians had long objected to a branch-plant automotive industry in which most parts were manufactured in the United States and only assembled in Canada. The United States in turn objected when the Canadian Government subsidized Canadian car exports at the expense of American exporters. A distinctively Canadian automotive industry was out of the question; existing Canadian plants built American cars and, equally important, Canadian buyers wanted the choice of models which international corporations could offer. The Government's solution was an even more closely integrated automotive industry. The Auto Pact established continental free trade in automobiles and parts, limited only by guarantees that Canadian production would be equivalent to Canadian sales. The agreement made economic sense — and in 1965 provided substantial benefits to Canada — but it bound the Canadian economy more closely than before to that of the United States.

Shortly after coming to power in the 1963 election, Prime Minister Pearson flew to Hyannisport, Massachusetts for a meeting with President Kennedy to restore good relations with the American administration. (John F. Kennedy Library, ST-250-4-63)

Misgivings about Canadian autonomy were not restricted to matters of trade. At the diplomatic level the two governments had long discussed problems freely while avoiding public confrontations. This "quiet diplomacy" assumed a community of interests and a basic accord on major issues, an assumption that was to be sorely tested by the American involvement in Vietnam. Canadians feared that major Communist powers might be drawn into the conflict there and that Canada would be forced into a wider war as a reluctant participant. Massive American bombing of North Vietnam in 1965 increased this concern. In a speech in Philadelphia Pearson had the temerity to suggest a halt in the bombing as an invitation to negotiations for a peaceful settlement of the war. President Lyndon B. Johnson was furious at this criticism, and he made no bones about telling Pearson so. If there was a lesson to be learned from this affair, it was that Canada's influence on American foreign policy was limited. Since any public confrontation ran the risk of American economic retaliation, Canadian government representatives became more guarded in their public comments on the American conduct of the war. This, in turn, led Canadian critics of the war to denounce their own government's spinelessness.

In five years the Pearson Government had some major accomplishments to its credit, but the high hopes of 1963 were never fulfilled. It had introduced major social security programs, had adopted the principle of linguistic equality within the federal administration, and had altered the division of powers within the federal system. And yet the government, which came into office as a minority government, never significantly broadened its popular support. Pearson called a snap election in 1965, assured by his advisors that he would win a clear majority. The odds were in his favour; with the Conservatives under Diefenbaker deeply split, pollsters and journalists disagreed only on the margin of victory. But the voters had minds of their own, and the results were almost a repeat of the previous election. Only a small number of constituencies changed hands, and the Liberals, with 131 seats, were still in a minority position. It was a political setback from which the Pearson Government never recovered.

Part of the explanation lay in the intensely partisan politics of those years. The Liberal claims of administrative competence were thinly veiled attacks on what they considered to be Diefenbaker's incompetence and indecision. Their scorn for him partially blinded them to the new complexity of the nation's problems and, beginning with the first Gordon budget, they projected an image of both arrogant overconfidence and vacillation. The Conservatives, faced with internal divisions which could not be resolved, seized every opportunity to embarrass the Government, and in the charged atmosphere of those years their attacks often went beyond discussions of policy to concentrate on allegations of corruption and personal dishonesty. Had Department of Justice officials tried to win bail for Lucien Rivard, a criminal with Mafia connections? Had Yvon Dupuis, a Minister without Portfolio, accepted a bribe? Were political favours exchanged when two other ministers acquired furniture with no down payment? Evasive answers by Pearson hinted at an awareness or tolerance of corruption which even a royal commission investigation and the resignation of some ministers could not dispel. The partisan bitterness was sharpened when the Liberals retaliated by drawing attention to an alleged breach of security by one of Diefenbaker's ministers who had consorted with a German prostitue and potential spy. It was all very sordid and had little to do with national policies.[9]

---

9. For an account of the partisan debates, see Richard Gwyn, *The Shape of Scandal* (Toronto, 1965), and Granatstein, *Canada 1957-67* (Toronto, 1986).

However, the inability of the Liberals to gain wider support also had its roots in the deep divisions within Canadian society. The erratic pattern of the Government's relations with the United States frustrated both nationalists and continentalists. The sweeping social security measures provoked debates on the distribution of powers between the federal and provincial governments. But the most striking division was over the place of French Canada within the union. The Government's efforts to respond to Quebec's demands had convinced some French Canadians that the federal system, with its inevitable compromises, could never be satisfactory. The survival of French Canada, they concluded, required a separate, independent Quebec. The emergence of separatist parties in the province was an ominous sign. At the same time, the concessions to Quebec had provoked a backlash among those English Canadians who resisted the idea of linguistic or cultural duality in Canada. The election of three minority Governments within three years was the response of a society that could not agree on its future.

The divisions might well have been more serious. Mike Pearson was a diplomat, even as Prime Minister, and his instinct was to search for consensus rather than to impose a solution. Many Canadians interpreted his willingness to compromise as weakness, and there were many occasions when policy reversals strengthened the image of bumbling indecision. However, in the 1960s Canadians were faced with major changes. Decisive policies might well have led to confrontations; compromises at least provided time for discussion and debate and a wider awareness of the issues involved. Pearson had no dramatic solutions, but he was sensitive to the social changes, and he did begin the painful process of adjustment.

The culminating event of the Pearson years, the celebration of Canada's centennial in 1967, gave a different perspective. Despite their political controversies, Canadians had enjoyed a decade of rising living standards, and this affluence had provided the impetus for an impressive development in the arts. The endowment income of the Canada Council was handsomely supplemented by large annual grants from the federal government. Canadian theatre groups, orchestras, and ballet companies established loyal audiences at home and the best of them toured the United States and Europe where they usually received good reviews. Canadian playwrights, composers, and choreographers received less acclaim than Canadian performers, but there was beginning to be a conscious effort to produce Canadian works. Both English and French Canada showed a heightened interest in the works of Canadian poets and novelists. However, the widest international recognition went to two literary scholars: Marshall McLuhan, who articulated the sense of a revolutionary elec-

Canada's centennial was celebrated at Nepean Point, Ottawa. Among those in attendance were the Queen, Prime Minister Pearson, and former prime minister John Diefenbaker. (Toronto Telegram *Collection, York University Archives*)

tronic age, and Northrop Frye, who provided an analytical framework for the whole of literature. The developments on so many fronts seemed to mark the passing of a colonial and derivative culture and to portend the emergence of a culture that would be uniquely and distinctively Canadian.

Expo 67, for a brief and heady moment, was seen as a showcase for Canada's cultural maturity. It not only opened on schedule, despite the well-publicized problems of the project, but it was an exhilarating success from the beginning. The architecture and environmental design reflected a modern and sophisticated society, but there was also a human and personal scale and even a playful whimsy which seemed distinctively Canadian. The pageant of the opening ceremonies was impressive without being solemn, and the artistic performances and films over the summer seemed to show an essential vitality beneath the characteristic

Expo 67 was a great success as a fair and as a stimulus to nationalism.
(C-30085/Public Archives Canada)

Canadian restraint. Expo 67 was clean and efficient — no mean accomplishment — but it also had the friendly atmosphere of a national birthday party.

But even Expo 67 could not be isolated from unresolved problems. General Charles de Gaulle, President of France, was one of the many heads of state to visit Canada, but his triumphal journey from Quebec City to Montreal, carefully staged by the Quebec Government, ended in a deliberate provocation of the federal government when de Gaulle publicly proclaimed *"Vive le Québec libre,"* the rallying cry of the Quebec separatists. The enthusiasm of many Quebeckers and the outrage of many federalists showed the depths of the cultural division. Expo 67 would also be remembered for its cost. This was partly the resentment of some English Canadians at being taxed for the construction of roads and pavilions in Montreal, but it was also a dawning recognition that there were limits to what governments could afford. The next decade brought this home to everybody.

Modern Canada

The high hopes of the 1960s became the hopes deferred of the 1970s. Technology showed no signs of losing its momentum — satellite communications and the silicon chip were extending the revolutionary potential of science — but there was a growing scepticism about the benefits of technology. Innovations were now associated with costly consequences: atomic power meant radioactive wastes, industrial growth meant acid rain. The zeal for warring against poverty at home and abroad was tempered by the apparent failure of research or financial aid to have much impact on economic inequalities. The world seemed more complex and more resistant to change, and the crusading zeal was gone.

There was no return to an earlier age, and the lost deference to traditional institutions was not restored. There was even a tendency late in the 1960s and early in the next decade for the radicals to become even more militant, to question the possibility of gradual reforms and to provoke confrontation to bring on the revolution. The more common pattern was a shift from broad social concerns to narrow self-interest. Physical fitness became almost an obsession: books on jogging were best sellers; smoking in public buildings was banned or confined to restricted areas; families took up bicycling and cross-country skiing. Religion, too, reflected this new self-absorption. Evangelical preachers attracted large crowds and television audiences; even conservative and middle-class congregations had charismatic groups which stressed individual religious experience. It was a decade of credit cards and lotteries. University students, once the cutting edge of social criticism, showed less interest in broader social problems and more interest in the high marks and professional degrees which might bring them material rewards in a tight job market.

The egalitarian idealism of the 1960s did not disappear entirely, but there was a shift of emphasis from economic equality to equality of status. Economic disparities were not ignored, but more attention was paid to legal inequalities and individual rights. Homosexuals received more public support in their fight against discrimination. Wife-beating and child abuse were recognized as serious social problems. Innocent victims of crimes were compensated by the state for losses or injuries. The disabled were provided with easier access to public buildings. Individual consciences were pricked and civil rights were extended, but shoulders were often shrugged at the wider issues of war and poverty.

Demographic changes contributed to the mood of the 1970s. There were 24 million Canadians by the end of the decade, but the continuing low birth rate meant an aging population. The population bulge was still swelling university enrolment, but graduates found themselves competing for a limited number of jobs. Young people were less inclined to take time off to meditate or to agitate when admission to a professional school or a job depended on good marks. Reforming the world was postponed until personal security was assured.

Economic developments contributed to this more individualistic orientation. The average family income rose during the decade, even after inflation was taken into account, but there was less confidence that these gains would continue. The consumer price index doubled during the 1970s, in spite of efforts to control inflation. The rise in interest rates was even more disturbing. Interest rates were the highest in Canadian history by the end of the decade, and the cost of money made it difficult for young people to own a business or a home. At the same time unemployment rose to the highest levels since the war, averaging over 7.5 per cent for the last half of the decade. By the end of the decade Canada was sharing in a recession affecting most industrial countries, and Canadians, many of them for the first time in their lives, were worried about the possibility of a depression and its impact on their way of life.[10]

Organized labour was directly affected by the social and economic changes. The labour force grew over the decade, but trade union membership grew even faster. More significant was the fact that the new members were largely teachers, public servants, and white-collar workers who in the past had considered themselves closer to professionals than workers. However, in the 1970s they found themselves squeezed by inflation and government retrenchment; they swallowed their pride and joined trade unions in an effort to maintain their standard of living. The new unions were also remarkable for their militancy. Teachers and hospital workers, once so proud of their devotion to their charges, staged strikes to win better contracts. Even doctors united to protect their economic

10. The Ministry of Supplies and Services has recently begun publishing a series, *Perspectives Canada*, which provides a useful range of economic and social statistics.

status. It was beneath their dignity to join a union, but their professional associations did negotiate with governments for higher Medicare fees and were prepared to withdraw medical services to support their demands. The family doctor of an earlier age would not have approved.

The new public service unions created problems which were not easily solved. In the private sector the strike could be an effective negotiating tool because it reduced the employer's profits, but governments do not have profits. Strikes in the public sector inconvenienced the employer only indirectly. The people directly affected were the citizens who had to rely on the services provided by postal workers or air traffic controllers and whose protests encouraged the government to reach a settlement. Federal and provincial governments were also unlike private employers because they could declare a strike illegal and pass back-to-work legislation, a tactic which became increasingly common in the 1970s. Such laws were temporarily successful, but they embittered labour relations for the future. While it was obvious to everyone that the strike was an unsatisfactory negotiating tool in the public service, it was not easy to find a satisfactory alternative. With almost one-third of the workers employed directly or indirectly by governments by the end of the decade, labour relations were a major concern.

The changing mood of the 1970s also had its impact on the status of women. There was significant improvement in the legal protection for married women. The Divorce Act of 1968, which accepted mental cruelty and a three-year separation as causes for divorce, gave women a protection they sorely needed. Even more important were provincial laws which, by the end of the decade, gave divorced wives across Canada a claim to half the property acquired during the marriage. Less progress was made in the workplace. The labour codes of most provinces did guarantee equal pay for equal work, but the codes were not easily enforced. In any case, the problem was more deep-rooted. By 1980 half the women over the age of fifteen were employed, but they were still concentrated in low-income occupations. It was encouraging that more women were graduating from university with professional degrees, but in the higher income levels they were still trying to break into a man's world. Few of them occupied positions of power.

In politics the decade saw the fuller exploitation of techniques which had been developed in the 1960s. Political organizers had come to depend on opinion polls to assess voters' interests and attitudes, and they planned political campaigns on the basis of their surveys. The other major development was the use of television. Politicians still campaigned, but their primary concern was now the television audience. They hopped from one region to another overnight, and rushed from one organized rally to the next during the day, with brief statements and much handwaving, all in the hope of being considered noteworthy enough to be shown on the evening news broadcast. Press releases and interviews became carefully orchestrated to project the image and the message which opinion polls indicated would be most effective. The voters had the advantage of seeing political leaders in their own living rooms; they also had the problem of judging the party and its policies by watching a carefully planned performance. Would the package conceal the contents?

The Coming of Trudeau

In 1968 the Liberals chose Pierre Trudeau as Pearson's successor. In many ways he was a surprising choice. Trudeau had been an activist in the Quiet Revolution and a harsh critic of many federal policies before entering federal politics in 1965. However, being a newcomer was an advantage in the 1960s. Many Canadians were looking for an alternative to the indecision and the compromises of recent years and were attracted to this unorthodox bachelor who expounded philosophy or talked slang in both French and English, whose life style included sandals, beautiful women, and sports cars, and who seemed attuned to the modern world. He had attracted attention by easing abortion and divorce laws ("The state," he said, "has no place in the bedrooms of the nation") and by a televised debate with Premier Daniel Johnson of Quebec in which he had argued for a strong central government. At the Liberal leadership convention he was the overwhelming favourite of the media, and, although Liberal delegates had some reservations, he was elected on the fourth ballot.[11]

Trudeau dominated the election of June, 1968. Journalists coined the word "Trudeaumania" to describe the response of the large and enthusiastic crowds who seemed more fascinated by his personality than his policies. But political issues were also a factor. Trudeau was an outspoken critic of separatism and even of special status for Quebec, and English Canadians unsympathetic to the demands of the minority saw a leader who would end the concessions to that province. But the election results

11. The most useful of the many biographies of Trudeau is George Radwanski, *Trudeau* (Toronto, 1978). See also Richard Gwyn, *The Northern Magus* (Toronto, 1980); Christina McCall-Newman, *Grits* (Toronto, 1982); and Trudeau's *Federalism and the French Canadians* (Toronto, 1968).

L.B. Pearson photographed with his Minister of Justice, Pierre Trudeau, at the constitutional conference. Trudeau's performance there shortly before the 1968 leadership convention gave his as yet unannounced drive for the brass ring a huge boost. (C-25001/Public Archives Canada)

showed that Trudeau's popularity had not effaced the regional and social differences. The Liberals won 155 seats, most of the gains coming in Ontario and the West, to form the first majority government since 1958. But it was by no means a landslide victory: less than half the voters had supported Liberal candidates.

Pierre Trudeau did bring a new style to Ottawa. For all his uninhibited manner, he was an intellectual who believed that government policies should be based on a definition of social objectives and a logical analysis of how to achieve them. He appeared to welcome debate and confrontation as part of the process of participatory democracy, and he was seemingly prepared to consider untried measures to achieve social goals. It was not a style to which Canadians were accustomed.

The Government's Indian policy was an early example of this approach. The three hundred thousand Indians in Canada had attracted attention in the 1960s as victims of poverty and racial discrimination. A white paper in 1969 argued that the goal should be equality for Indians and that this meant that Indians should receive the same services as other Canadians. The white paper, therefore, proposed that the special status which isolated the Indians should be gradually eliminated until they merged with other Canadians as equal citizens. However, equality of status was no guarantee that individual Indians would achieve social and economic equality. The Indians, who had not been consulted, were shocked by this threat to their privileges and protection under the Indian Act, and they protested so vehemently that the white paper was shelved. The unintentional result was to make the Indians more conscious of their collective identity and more insistent on their special status. The federal government later gave a tacit recognition to aboriginal rights, including compensation for the infringement of fishing and hunting rights by the James Bay hydro development project, but the attempt at a more comprehensive solution of the Indian problem was dropped.

A more sustained effort was made to reappraise Canadian foreign policy. Trudeau was sceptical of Pearson's emphasis on Canada's role as a peacekeeper and "helpful fixer" in international affairs. He was specifically critical of Canada's participation in N.A.T.O., being less impressed than the Department of External Affairs with the dangers of Soviet aggression. He favoured a less ambitious foreign policy tailored to fit Canada's national interests. But how could these national interests be defined, and how could they be balanced against the interests of other nations?

In *Foreign Policy for Canadians*, a study prepared in the Department of External Affairs and completed in 1970, the emphasis was placed on economic interests. The new approach to foreign policy was illustrated by the recognition of mainland China in that year, an indication of China's growing importance as a market for Canadian wheat. But economic intersts were not easily isolated from other concerns. The talk of withdrawal of Canada's N.A.T.O. forces from Europe brought strong protests from N.A.T.O. allies. The Government eventually reduced the N.A.T.O. forces, but left some Canadian troops in Europe. Economic interests were used to justify increased aid to less developed countries, with much of the aid linked to their purchase of Canadian goods, but there was also a sense of obligation to the less privileged. "Canada's foreign policy," Trudeau declared in 1974, "would be nothing if it were not caring." In the long run, the hard-headed talk of economic considerations proved to be less radical and less innovative than it sounded.[12]

The issue of French-English relations at home did have a direct impact on Canada's foreign relations. In 1968 the former French colony of Gabon, at the instigation of President de Gaulle, had invited Quebec to send a delegation to a conference of French-speaking nations on education. The federal government was willing to accept provincial nominations for a federally appointed delegation but insisted on its constitutional authority over foreign relations and maintained that the invitation should have been issued through Ottawa. When the invitation to Quebec was not withdrawn, Canada cut off diplomatic relations with Gabon as a warning to France that the federal government would not tolerate any further meddling. But there were also positive effects of the French-English tension at home. Membership in the British Commonwealth had created links with some African countries, and, in the 1960s, most of Canada's foreign aid to Africa went to former British colonies. Under Trudeau the emphasis on cultural duality led to increased contacts with French Africa, and by the end of the decade, Canadian aid was divided almost equally between former French and British colonies.

Canada's relationship with the United States was one example of a constant in foreign policy. The importance of this relationship — and Canada's vulnerability — was underlined in 1971 when the United States, facing a serious balance of payments crisis, levied a special tax on imports. This time, when Canada asked for an exemption, it was bluntly refused. The Canadian Government advocated strengthening trade relations with other countries in order to reduce dependence on the United States, but this was more easily said than done. Two-thirds of Canada's foreign trade continued to be with its North American neighbour. American investment in Canada also continued to attract attention. In 1973 the Government established a Foreign Investment Review Agency which could intervene to block the takeover of any Canadian company or any foreign investment which was not considered to be of any "significant benefit" to Canada. F.I.R.A. was much resented by Americans and by expansionists in

12. On this reappraisal of Canadian foreign policy in the early Trudeau years, see especially Bruce Thordarson, *Trudeau and Foreign Policy* (Toronto, 1972).

Canada, but it had little impact. Americans owned just over 25 per cent of the shares of all Canadian corporations, excluding financial institutions, and this proportion remained almost unchanged over the decade.

The foreign policy developments in Africa reflected the high priority given to domestic issues and particularly to the French-Canadian question. Trudeau had been one of the leading advocates of modernization in Quebec; as a liberal he had consistently argued that French Canadians must be prepared to compete on equal terms with their compatriots. He had no sympathy for a narrow French-Canadian nationalism which he saw as restricting individual rights and isolating Quebec, and he had entered federal politics in reaction to Quebec's demands for a special status. He saw the need for a strong central government to regulate the national economy, and he understood French-English relations largely in terms of civil liberties. French Canadians would become loyal Canadians, he believed, when they were no longer treated as second-class citizens outside the province of Quebec. The solution, according to Trudeau, was not a transfer of powers to the provinces or special status for Quebec, but the provision of education and other services in French in all parts of Canada where French Canadians lived. Trudeau's accession to power set the stage for a confrontation with the Quebec Government, which was demanding broader economic powers. The election of a Liberal Government in Quebec in 1970, under Robert Bourassa, eased tensions only slightly because the separatist Parti Québécois, under the former Liberal René Lévesque, was now the official Opposition and the champion of *nationaliste* sentiment in Quebec.

Attention was distracted from the constitutional issue by the October Crisis of that year. For some time a handful of Quebec's extremists had advocated the use of violence in the fight for the "liberation" of their province. Terrorists had dynamited some federal buildings and blown up a few mailboxes in Westmount. The tension grew in October, 1970, when they kidnapped James Cross, a British trade commissioner, and demanded the freeing of some "political prisoners" from jail as a condition for his release. Five days later, Pierre Laporte, a provincial cabinet minister, was abducted. The most disturbing aspect of all this was the apparent support for the kidnappers among Quebec's *nationalistes*. The fear of widespread civil disorder even led some provincial leaders to suggest negotiating with the terrorists.

Other leaders, including Trudeau, rejected any compromise. When police forces failed to find the kidnappers, Ottawa declared "a state of apprehended insurrection" in Quebec and invoked the War Measures Act, which permitted the arbitrary arrest and detention of suspected sympathizers. This suspension of civil liberties was widely supported in English and French Canada, and it effectively ended the demonstrations of support for the terrorists. It was less effective in apprehending the kidnappers. Over four hundred persons were arrested, of whom sixty were brought to trial and only twenty convicted, but no useful information was obtained. Laporte was murdered and his body found two days after the War Measures Act was proclaimed. Eventually Cross was located and his release was arranged in exchange for a safe passage to Cuba for his abductors. The murderers of Laporte were later caught and convicted. Public opinion, in retrospect, concluded that the fears of insurrection were exaggerated and that the federal government had overreacted.

When constitutional discussions reopened at Victoria in 1971 a tentative accord was reached. The federal government obtained the extension of French language rights, although the western provinces were not included, and in exchange it conceded greater provincial authority in social legislation. An amendment procedure would give a veto to Quebec and Ontario and to a majority of the Atlantic or western provinces. However, popular opinion in Quebec interpreted the agreement as an obstacle to further extensions of provincial authority, and Premier Bourassa eventually refused to ratify the agreement. A decade would pass before the next constitutional agreement.

Economic problems could not be shelved so easily, especially with an election in 1972. The unemployment rate, which had fallen below 4 per cent in the mid-1960s, rose to over 6 per cent in the early 1970s. This could be attributed to an expanding labour force or even, as some argued, to the generous social security measures which encouraged "welfare bums." Far more disturbing was the rate of inflation, as measured by the consumer price index, which rose to an average of 4 per cent per year despite the high unemployment. In the election campaign, the Liberals shrugged off the economic difficulties as temporary and offered only a banal slogan—"The Land Is Strong." David Lewis of the N.D.P. tried to shift attention from the poor to the "corporate welfare bums" — wealthy corporations thriving on tax exemptions. The Conservatives, under Robert Stanfield, concentrated on the Liberal Government's economic mismanagement. The election results were the closest in Canadian history. The Liberals lost some urban support in Ontario and British Columbia and dropped to 109 seats compared to 107 for the Conservatives, 31 for the N.D.P., and 14 for the Créditistes in Quebec. The Liberal losses were widely interpreted as a protest against the insensitivity of the party and its leader to the economic problems of individual Canadians.

Over the next two years, the Liberal minority government tried to regain political support by showing its concern. The emphasis was once more on social security. Unemployment insurance benefits were extended, and, in response to inflation, family allowance and pensions were increased and linked to the consumer price index. Even income tax exemptions were to rise with the cost of living. However, in economic terms the situation grew worse. Unemployment came down only slightly and inflation shot up to over 10 per cent by 1974, partly because an international cartel, the Organization of Petroleum Exporting Countries, dominated by Arab countries in the Middle East, doubled the price of oil. In political terms the N.D.P. supported the Liberal measures and kept the minority government in office until opinion polls encouraged Trudeau to call another election.

The election of 1974 seemed to offer voters a clear choice. Robert Stanfield, the Conservative leader, had reluctantly come to the conclusion that the economy was out of control, that traditional fiscal and monetary policies were ineffective, and that wage and price controls were needed to meet the crisis. Many Conservatives were dubious, but the party was officially committed. The Liberals, on the other hand, believed the crisis was a temporary result of the jump in oil prices. Canada was almost self-sufficient in oil, with imports to eastern Canada balanced by exports to the United States from western Canada, and so Canada could cushion the shock by keeping domestic oil prices well below the world price. It seemed probable that within a few years Canada would be relatively better off than other industrialized countries. Trudeau himself treated Conservative arguments rather flippantly (what was Stanfield going to say to Americans and to Arab sheiks: "Zap, you're frozen"?) but differences between the two parties seemed clear. It was less clear whether Canadians voted for policies or personalities, but the results, at least, were beyond dispute. The Liberals won a clear majority with 141 seats, most of the gains coming in Ontario at the expense of both the Conservatives and the N.D.P.

A year later, in a stunning flip-flop, Trudeau announced the imposition of wage and price controls. With double-digit inflation continuing and with unemployment rising sharply to 7 per cent, even the Government had lost confidence in the orthodox response of fiscal and monetary restraint. The problem seemed to be psychological. The expectation of high rates of inflation led businessmen to raise prices and trade unions to negotiate higher wage settlements, and this in turn fuelled further inflation. When voluntary appeals for restraint had no effect, the Government appointed the Anti-Inflation Board to limit wage and price increases in accordance with certain guidelines. It was seen as an emergency measure, an attempt to stop the wage and price spiral and to end the expectations of continuing inflation. The anti-inflation program did have some effect. Wages were held in check and the rate of inflation dropped below 10 per cent, although it was difficult to determine how much of this could be attributed to the program and how much to other economic factors. However, political events in Quebec, culminating in the provincial election of 1976, diverted attention from economic problems.

In 1972 the Bourassa Government had been re-elected on a platform of job creation and continuing economic growth. But the stress on economic issues did not silence the fears of Quebec's *nationalistes*, who were convinced that the combination of the low French-Canadian birth rate and the tendency of newly arrived immigrants to become part of the English-language community was a direct threat to French-Canadian survival. Bourassa attempted to placate his critics by proposing some tentative restrictions on admission to English-language schools, but his response only angered English Canadians without satisfying the *nationalistes*. His Government became even more unpopular when its economic initiatives failed to prevent higher rates of unemployment.

The language issue in Quebec was greatly exacerbated by a strike of English-speaking air traffic controllers in 1976. The controllers argued that air safety was endangered by the increased use of French at Quebec's airports, although concern for their own careers was clearly a factor also. The strike became a major political issue when English Canadians across Canada supported the strikers; the support was so strong that the federal government reluctantly yielded and appointed a commission to study the problem. French Canadians, who believed that air safety could only be improved by giving instructions in French to French-speaking pilots, were shocked at this evidence of English-Canadian prejudice against their language. By 1979 reason prevailed and the commission report, which unequivocally supported bilingual air traffic control in Quebec, was accepted without any protests. But the incident had some substantial bearing on the election in Quebec in November, 1976.

In this election the Parti Québécois focussed on the shortcomings of the Bourassa Government. René Lévesque promised an honest and competent administration and reassured the uneasy by promising a referendum on the question of independence before any other steps were taken. The verdict, a large majority for the P.Q., was a stunning defeat for the Liberals and a vote of confidence in Lévesque, who was an enormously engaging personality. Whether it was a vote for an independent Quebec was less certain.

The first step of the P.Q. Government was to deal with the language question. Bill 101 established French as the official language in Quebec and made it compulsory for all children to attend French-language schools; only the children of parents who themselves had attended English-language schools in Quebec were exempted. The legislation was criticized outside of the province as an infringement of individual rights, but it was generally popular among French Canadians in Quebec, who saw it as a guarantee of their survival as a people. However, there was less support in Quebec for independence, and so the P.Q. Government postponed the referendum. The fate of Canada remained undecided.

In Ottawa, the shock of the election could not divert attention for long from the pressing economic problems. The rate of inflation was still unacceptably high — in 1977 it was at 8 per cent — and with lower wage settlements it was necessary to look elsewhere for the cause. For some, the answer was to be found in the federal deficits. By 1975 the combination of tax concessions, federal projects to fight unemployment, and the spiralling federal contributions to the provincially administered social security and education programs had begun a series of federal deficits which

Macpherson / Reprinted with permission — The Toronto Star Syndicate

"A little self-restraint, s'il vous plaît."

by 1978 had risen to 10 billion dollars. The Auditor General had already warned that "Parliament — and indeed the Government — has lost or is close to losing effective control of the public purse." The deficits were surely inflationary, but in a time of high unemployment it seemed inappropriate to reduce expenditures or to raise taxes. The Canadian dollar, which had been floating since 1970 and had stayed close to par with the American dollar, began to drop sharply in 1977 and by 1979 was worth about 85 American cents. Foreign investors had lost confidence in the financial administration of the Canadian Government.

By 1979 one of the federal government's major expenditures was on oil. Low domestic oil prices, insulated against the increases of O.P.E.C., the oil cartel, had led to increased oil consumption, and Canada quickly became a net importer of oil. In 1979, when O.P.E.C. raised its price abruptly towards \$35 per barrel, the federal subsidy to maintain the domestic price of \$15 per barrel rose to over \$2 billion. In 1975 the federal government had established Petro-Canada, a national petroleum company, to negotiate oil imports and to stimulate domestic production by exploring for oil and developing the Alberta tar sands, but this could not help the Government in 1979. It was obvious that the domestic price would have to be raised, but by how much? Alberta demanded something close to the world price, but Ontario, on the other hand, feared that any increase would raise manufacturing costs and cause greater unemployment. After a prolonged confrontation with Premier Lougheed of Alberta, the Trudeau Government eventually negotiated annual increases of \$2 per barrel, with 10 per cent of the additional revenue coming to the federal government and the rest being divided between the provincial government and the oil companies involved.

It was not clear that this was an issue in the federal election of 1979. The Conservatives promised to sell Petro-Canada to private interests, but this had more to do with ideology than oil policy. The Conservatives had chosen Joe Clark as Stanfield's successor in 1976, but he was young and inexperienced, a compromise choice of a party which had no clear sense of direction. The Liberals were convinced that an emphasis on leadership during the campaign would be to their advantage, and they focussed on Trudeau's forceful personality and the need for strong national leadership. In an election where all parties agreed on the objectives of cultural harmony, regional equality, and prosperity, but no parties knew with confidence how these could be achieved, it was probably inevitable that leadership should become an important election issue.

The results seemed decisive. The Liberals, with 114 seats, were defeated after sixteen years in office. Their popular support in Quebec increased, but the decline in their support in Ontario and the western provinces was interpreted as a rejection of the party, and, more particularly, of its leader. Trudeau resigned as Prime Minister and six months later he announced his resignation as party leader. The Conservatives, with 141 seats, were in a minority government position, but they seemed securely in office with time to consolidate their gains.[13]

Appearances were misleading. The voters who had lost confidence in Trudeau were not committed to Clark, and over the next few months he failed to win their support. It was not his fault that the inflationary pressures, which had led to a bank rate of 11 per cent by early 1979, pushed the rate to a then-historic high of 14 per cent by October. However, on the crucial issue of energy policy Clark's Government seemed inconsistent. Clark did not dismember Petro-Canada, in spite of his campaign promises to do so, but he did concede the off-shore petroleum rights to the Maritime provinces as a concession to provincial demands. The prolonged and indecisive negotiations with Alberta over domestic oil prices and the distribution of the profits also suggest a readiness to defer to provincial governments. But in the November budget, the Government gave evidence of forceful leadership by imposing an unpopular 18 cents-a-gallon tax on gasoline in spite of provincial protests. The tax would help reduce the federal deficit and at the same time would bring Canadians closer to the reality of high energy costs. The ambiguity of the Government's position may explain why Canadians failed to respond to this appeal to accept the burden of higher fuel costs. The Opposition parties, after reading the public opinion polls, combined to defeat the budget and force an unexpected election.

The election of 1980 did not offer a clear choice to the voters. The Conservatives defended a record which had not yet clearly taken shape. The Liberals persuaded Trudeau to return to lead the campaign but left policies and future leadership to be decided later. The election results confirmed the political pattern which had emerged over the previous twenty years. The Conservative party was almost eliminated from Quebec; the Liberal party barely survived west of Ontario. There was a slight shift in popular support in the Atlantic provinces and Ontario, this time towards the Liberals. This shift was nonetheless enough to increase the Liberal representation to 146 seats and to elect a majority Liberal Government.

13. The best account of the political events of this period is Jeffrey Simpson, *Discipline of Power: The Conservative Interlude and the Liberal Restoration* (Toronto, 1980).

New Nationalism?

The political consequences were more dramatic than anybody had expected. The Trudeau administration, apparently affected by the criticism that it had accomplished so little in its previous term of office, tried to resolve some long-standing national problems by decisive action. Its controversial approach to energy and to the constitution dominated national politics for the next two years.

The National Energy Policy, announced in 1980, was an aggressive attempt to achieve Canadian ownership in the petroleum industry, and to gain a larger share of the profits for the federal government. It provoked bitter opposition from the oil-producing provinces, led by Peter Lougheed of Alberta; but because it held out the prospect of lower energy costs for the manufacturers and people of central Canada, it had the restrained support of William Davis of Ontario. The federal initiative might have succeeded if oil prices had risen as expected. Instead, increased world oil production and a world recession that decreased oil consumption led to lower prices, and the federal government was forced to make financial concessions to the producing provinces and to the oil companies. By mid-decade the N.E.P. had lost its momentum. Canadian self-sufficiency in oil was still a remote goal, although the policy had succeeded in expanding Canadian ownership of petroleum resources and the federal share of revenues from the petroleum industry had increased.[14]

The attempt to revise the Constitution was even more controversial. The impetus for constitutional change had been lost with the rejection of the Victoria charter, but for Trudeau the election of the Parti Québécois in 1976 had given the issue new life. Some revision of the existing federal constitution seemed necessary to win a majority of the French Canadians to the federal cause. Trudeau had convened a series of federal-provincial conferences, but the results had been disappointing. The provinces differed among themselves over the desirability of a charter of rights, over the distribution of powers between federal and provincial levels of government, and over an amendment procedure for a new constitution. Nor was there a sense of urgency; as one western premier candidly explained, out of one hundred items of concern to his province, constitutional amendment was the hundred and first. By 1979 constitutional revision once more seemed a dead issue. The Conservative Government took no new initiatives, and the constitution was scarcely referred to in the election campaign of 1980.

14. G. Bruce Doern and Glen Toner, *The Politics of Energy*, (Toronto, 1985), provides an informed and judicious assessment of the National Energy Policy.

Quebec's referendum in May of 1980 revived the issue. The referendum itself was far from decisive. The provincial government was careful not to pose the question of independence directly; the question it put to the voters was whether the Quebec Government should begin negotiations with Canada for "sovereignty-association." The federalists in the referendum campaign, who included some politicians from English-language provinces and Ottawa, were also cautious. They appealed for support while reassuring Quebeckers that the existing constitution would be revised. The result, with 60 per cent voting against negotiations, could be interpreted as a rejection of independence, but it could not so easily be interpreted as a vote for the existing federal union.

Trudeau interpreted the federalist campaign as a commitment to constitutional revision. Since previous negotiations with the provincial governments had accomplished nothing, he now decided to act unilaterally. In October of 1980 he introduced a resolution in the House of Commons to patriate the constitution, while at the same time adding a charter of rights and a formal amendment procedure. This arbitrary action was bitterly denounced by the Opposition and by most of the provincial premiers, although Ontario and New Brunswick supported the federal measure. A reference to the Supreme Court delayed any decision but did not end the controversy; the Court ruled that unilateral action by the federal government was legal but also affirmed that the agreement of most of the provinces was a constitutional convention. Eventually the federal government and nine provincial premiers reached an eleventh-hour compromise. René Lévesque was the isolated opponent.

Public protests forced the premiers to make some minor modifications. At the insistence of the New Democratic Party, a guarantee of the aboriginal rights of native peoples had been added to the federal government's original proposal. Some western premiers were fearful of the land claims that these rights might entail, and this clause had disappeared in the last minute negotiations. Public sympathy for the native peoples' claims forced the premiers to agree to the insertion of a clause guaranteeing the "existing" aboriginal rights. Women's organizations were also concerned about the guarantee against legal discrimination on the basis of sex. Earlier in the year they had forced the federal government to insert a special section to strengthen this guarantee. One of the compromises of the last minute revision, however, had been a clause that would permit provincial governments to override some sections of the charter. Did this include the clause on women's rights? Nobody was sure until a public campaign by women forced the premiers to affirm that this clause could not be overridden. By December, 1981 the modified resolution was passed by the House of Commons and the Senate, and in the spring of 1982 for the last time the British Parliament passed the necessary legislation. Canada possessed its own constitution and the power to alter it.

The debates over the National Energy Policy and the constitution seemed to have exhausted the Government. Canada felt the impact of the world recession acutely because its manufacturers suffered from foreign competition and because its exports were affected by the trend towards protectionism. The record levels of inflation subsided but unemployment rose beyond 10 per cent and showed no sign of declining. It was widely believed that structural changes were needed to reduce unemployment to an acceptable level but there was no agreement on how these changes could be introduced. In the meantime, decreased revenues and increasing social security costs produced record government deficits and limited the initiatives that governments could take.

Politicians were blamed for the economic frustrations. In part it was their own fault; they made promises that they could not keep, and they seemed more concerned with public opinion polls than with economic strategy. On the other hand, regional and class divisions made it difficult for any party or any leader to defend economic initiatives or even to receive a hearing in all parts of the country. In western Canada, for example, a combination of resentment against French-Canadian influence in Ottawa and economic exploitation by central Canada crystallized into a virulent personal hostility to Pierre Trudeau and made any policy introduced by his government suspect from the beginning. Trudeau's confrontational approach only confirmed the suspicions.

Mulroney's Canada

The Liberal Party responded in 1984 by replacing Pierre Trudeau with John Turner, a Liberal politician who had left federal politics a decade before for a business career. Turner was not identified with Trudeau and so might regain the confidence of westerners and of businessmen, or so Liberal convention delegates hoped. The Conservative Party had also changed its leader. Joe Clark was blamed for his government's defeat in Parliament and for failing to win support in Quebec. Brian Mulroney, a bilingual Quebecer, challenged Clark and in 1983 won the party leadership in a bitterly contested convention. In 1984 when the newly installed John Turner called a snap election, the stage was set for a choice between new leaders.

The election marked the end of an era. Television debates between the party leaders underlined the changes in Canadian society over the last generation. The debates showed the political influence of women — one debate was initiated by the National Action Committee on the Status of Women and focussed on women's issues, especially the issue of equal pay for work of equal value. They also illustrated the linguistic changes in Canada; there were debates in English and French. But it was not clear what options for the future were being offered. Each party promised more jobs and reduced federal deficits but was reluctant to be specific. The voters nonetheless expressed a clear preference. The Conservatives under Mulroney won even more seats than Diefenbaker in 1958.

Any comparison with the Diefenbaker era, however, would show more differences than similarities. Canadians had eagerly adopted technological innovations and had become accustomed to material comforts unimagined by earlier generations. They had also begun the painful process of adjusting to the social consequences of this affluence. The isolation of rural communities was gone, but wider opportunities brought stresses and insecurity. The economic disadvantages of French Canadians, of women, and of westerners had been challenged with some success. Affluence had also made it possible to expand and improve educational and health services. More economic assistance was now provided for the aged, the infirm, and the unemployed.

By the mid-1980s, however, the debate over the distribution of the national income was being overshadowed by challenges to the national economy. The years of plenty had given way to years of restraint. Technological change was continuing and even accelerating, requiring ever-increasing human and capital investments. Canadian export markets were threatened by the protectionist tendencies of major trading blocs, while Canadian manufacturers were facing strong competition from foreign producers. The national priorities were changing. At the same time, the politicians who had dominated politics for a generation were also leaving the stage. Trudeau's retirement had been followed by the resignations of Premiers William Davis of Ontario, René Lévesque of Quebec, and Peter Lougheed of Alberta. New leaders and new governments would now be drawing up the national agenda. They would be leading a sober and uncertain nation.

NON
merci

Chapter XI

From
Canadiens
to
Québécois

In the Paul Sauvé arena a delirious crowd sang "*Gens du Pays*" and waited
for their leader. When a diminutive, balding man finally approached the
microphone, the cheering audience drowned out the amplifiers. René
Lévesque tried in vain to silence them, shrugged his shoulders, and waited
with a look of benevolent resignation. It was now official. That day, November 15, 1976, the voters of Quebec had elected the Parti Québécois, a
party committed to making Quebec a sovereign and independent country. When his followers finally quieted down, Lévesque attributed the
victory to the pride of Quebeckers, to their determination to complete
the work of the Quiet Revolution and to become truly "*maîtres chez nous.*"
It was the birth of a new country. A stunned Pierre Trudeau, watching
events from Ottawa, offered a different explanation. The people of Quebec, he argued, had only elected a new provincial government. "I am
confident," he said grimly, "that Quebeckers will continue to reject separatism because they still believe their destiny is linked with an indivisible
Canada."

By 1976 nobody would have expected Lévesque and Trudeau to agree
on the destiny of Quebec. They had been associates in the early years of
the 1960s, sharing an intense dislike of the reactionary regime of Duplessis
and the desire to bring French Canada into the twentieth century, but
they had never agreed on how this was to be done. Lévesque was a democrat and a *nationaliste*, convinced that only French Canadians could decide

how French Canada should adapt to survive in the modern world. As a consequence, Quebec must have as much autonomy as it needed to make the necessary decisions. Truedeau, on the other hand, was a liberal with a deep respect for individual rights, one who mistrusted the arbitrary and discriminatory power of nationalism and saw federalism as a safer way to become a modern society. In the 1960s they had gone their separate ways, and by 1976 they had become bitter political opponents. And yet, each in his way was a spokesman for Quebec.

The election of 1976 was not decisive for Quebec. It was clearly a victory for Lévesque, but the war was far from over. For almost twenty years French Canadians had been debating their past and their future, and in those years there had been dramatic changes in the way French Canadians saw themselves. There had been a revolution — the Quiet Revolution — in which men and institutions had been altered. But what did Quebec want? Neither Lévesque nor Trudeau nor anyone else could be sure. The only thing on which everyone could agree was that French Canadians in 1976 no longer wanted what they had wanted twenty years before.

Quebec Nationalism

French Canadians had long thought of themselves as a distinctive society.[1] In the nineteenth century they reached the consensus that they were essentially and fundamentally a Roman Catholic society. It was this that distinguished them and set them apart from the rest of the continent, which they saw as Protestant and increasingly secular. Survival in this context meant reinforcing and strengthening their Catholic identity. Even the fact that they spoke French in a predominantly English-speaking country was of secondary importance. The language was useful because it was a barrier to heretical ideas — *la langue, gardienne de la foi* — and pro-

---

1. For an analysis of the Quiet Revolution in English see Kenneth McRoberts and Dale Posgate, *Quebec: Social Change and Political Crisis* (revised edition, Toronto, 1980); William D. Coleman, *The Independence Movement in Quebec 1945-1980* (Toronto, 1984); and Michael Behiels, *Prelude to Quebec's Quiet Revolution* (Montreal, 1985). John Saywell, ed., *The Canadian Annual Review* (Toronto, 1961 ff.) is an invaluable reference for the political events; the sections dealing with Quebec are published separately in John Saywell, *The Rise of the Parti Québécois 1967-76* (Toronto, 1977). Douglas Fullerton, *The Dangerous Delusion: Quebec's Independence Obsession* (Toronto, 1978) is an opinionated account of events by a minor participant. Most of the sources on the Quiet Revolution are in French. Those which have been translated can be found in Philip Stratford, ed., *Bibliography of Canadian Books in Translation* (2nd edition, Ottawa, 1977).

tected them from alien influences. In the 1860s, Bishop Laflèche had talked about the destiny of French Canada and of its sacred mission "to expand the Kingdom of God by developing a predominantly Catholic nationality." In the twentieth century the Abbé Groulx had rewritten the history of French Canada as a stirring epic of martyrs and patriots carrying out the will of God. Religion gave this minority a sense of purpose and a justification for survival.

But it was not enough merely to want to survive as a Catholic society. There also had to be agreement on how this was to be achieved. French Canadians, nor surprisingly, looked to the clergy for leadership; its authority was based on training in the faith and dedication to Catholicism. But survival was also associated with the rejection of the values and patterns of the rest of North America. In Quebec, according to Maria Chapdelaine, nothing would change and nothing should change. On a continent which was becoming urban and industrial, French Canadians held to the folkways of a rural society. The ideal for the leaders of French Canada became the rural parish, where citizens could live simple Christian lives under the paternal guidance of the parish priest, far from the temptations of the godless, alien cities.

This ideal required the adaptation of social institutions. Education provides the most striking example. Nineteenth century English-speaking North America had developed a system of nondenominational, tax-supported public schools which reflected the values of a liberal and secular society. With different values, French Canada developed a much different system. Instead of one publicly supported system it created two systems divided along religious lines, thus separating Roman Catholic from Protestant students. The Catholic schools were tax-supported, but they were not run by a department of education under a cabinet minister; instead a Catholic committee controlled by the Catholic bishops in the province set curriculum and standards. The Church was even more dominant at the secondary level. There were no French Catholic high schools, only classical colleges which were religious institutions, often residential, offering eight years of liberal arts instruction based on Latin and Greek language and literature. Only a small minority attended these colleges. The graduates became an elite who dominated the liberal professions and became the leaders, clerical and lay, of French-Canadian society.

The system was well suited to the needs of rural, Catholic French Canada and its leaders. The curriculum was imbued with traditional values. The classical colleges reinforced the hierarchical social pattern by limiting the number of students beyond the elementary level; they did not offer the technical and vocational options appropriate to an industrial society which had found a place in the curricula of secondary schools elsewhere in North America.

None of this meant that Quebec had truly remained a rural province. There were major developments in pulp and paper and in mining, and Montreal became a major manufacturing centre. By 1921 half the population of the province lived in urban communities. However, it did mean that this industrial development was unique in one way. In Quebec the entrepreneurs and the managers were almost all English-speaking; the unskilled workers were mainly French Canadians drawn from the surplus rural population. The division between management and labour, a feature of all industrial societies, was more marked in Quebec because it was based on language as well as status.

Not all French-Canadian leaders were hostile to industrial growth. Most clerical leaders extolled the rural life and saw urban society as immoral and corrupt, but French-Canadian politicians regularly cooperated with English-Canadian entrepreneurs, offering privileges and concessions to attract capital investment and providing a number of technical and vocational institutes to train the labour force, a task which the traditional school system ignored. Maurice Duplessis, for example, was a French-Canadian *nationaliste* who cooperated with the Church and the rural elite, and his Union nationale drew its political strength from the rural ridings. But Duplessis saw no contradiction between this and the encouragement of industrial development in Quebec. Revenues from the industrial sector would reduce taxes or improve government services in the rural areas. In northern Quebec the exploitation of natural resources could even provide part-time jobs and encourage agricultural settlement. Industry, it was assumed, could exist in Quebec without endangering the values of rural French Canada.

However, this political system left the industrial workers with little protection. The traditional French-Canadian elites, committed to the survival of a rural society, showed little interest in the health or welfare of the urban proletariat. The provincial government under Duplessis was no better. Eager to attract new industries, Duplessis was unsympathetic to any labour demands which would increase costs. His Padlock Law of 1937 was used against labour "agitators" who tried to organize industrial workers, and postwar legislation restricted the right to strike and outlawed any unions with Communist officials. It was a striking anomaly of the system that in labour disputes a *nationaliste* Government consistently sided with English-speaking industrialists against French-Canadian workers.

The Church authorities similarly showed little sympathy for these workers. The clergy continued to extol the virtues of rural life long after most French Canadians lived in urban communities, and it encouraged opening up new farming communities long after most of the arable land in the province was occupied. Some priests did organize Catholic trade unions as a desirable alternative to international unions, but the objectives were more cultural than industrial. They were benevolent associations, guided by a chaplain, but were often little better than company unions when it came to negotiating contracts.

The focus on a Catholic society isolated from the rest of North America also shaped Quebec's place within the federal system. Provincial governments in Quebec advocated a federalism of watertight compartments in which the federal and provincial governments were autonomous.

There were crises in French-English relations when other provinces tried to assimilate their French-speaking minorities; Quebec protested any attempts to limit the religious or linguistic privileges of these minorities. There were also crises in both world wars over conscription, which French Canadians interpreted as an attempt by the English-Canadian majority to force them to fight in British wars. But for most of the time French Canadians within the province of Quebec lived within the federal system with very little friction. The federal government did not interfere with Quebec's distinctive institutions and respected its cultural identity — by entrusting federal patronage in Quebec to French Canadians, for example. Quebec, in turn, ordinarily allowed the federal government a free hand in its economic policies. Provincial autonomy was a policy of isolation.

The federal context changed after the Second World War. Wartime experience and the economic theories of John Maynard Keynes encouraged the federal government to play a more active role in planning the national economy. This expanded role included a federal monopoly of income taxes in exchange for larger federal subsidies to the provinces, massive federal projects such as the St. Lawrence Seaway, and a wide range of measures to improve industrial skills and to provide more social security. Almost all of the English-Canadian provinces broadly agreed with the federal objectives and even encouraged an expanded federal role. Maurice Duplessis, Premier of Quebec from 1944 to 1959, had a different reaction. He saw the federal policies as a threat to the traditional way of life in Quebec and consistently opposed federal initiatives. The financial costs were not insignificant — Duplessis spurned lucrative tax agreements with Ottawa and prevented Quebec's universities from accepting federal grants — but he accepted the costs as part of the price of French-Canadian survival.

Prelude to the Quiet Revolution

In 1949 there was a strike in the asbestos mines in Quebec. It was not the first and it would not be the last. Technically it was an illegal strike because when negotiations broke down the workers set up picket lines instead of following provincial procedures and waiting for arbitration. The companies involved appealed to the provincial government, and Duplessis responded by denouncing the strike and sending in his provincial police to break up the picket lines and arrest the strike leaders. The workers, nonetheless, held firm and stayed out for four months until a new contract was signed.

In the history of Quebec's industrial relations, the Asbestos Strike was no more violent and no more significant than many other strikes, but it has since been given a huge symbolic importance and has come to be seen as a turning point in the history of the province. It was noteworthy that one of the unions involved was a Catholic union and that this union was among the most militant in its defiance of its employer and of the provincial government. Even more unusual was the fact that leading clergymen, including Archbishop Charbonneau of Montreal, openly supported the strikers. *Le Devoir,* another pillar of French-Canadian nationalism, also gave its approval. French-Canadian university students joined the workers on the picket lines. Still, French Canada was far from unanimous. Duplessis and the provincial government had the support of many clerical and *nationaliste* leaders, who saw the strike as a challenge to all the established authorities. But to have *any* support for a strike seemed significant. It was interpreted as evidence that, slowly but surely, the social perspective of French Canadians was changing.

It was also noteworthy that English Canadians in Quebec were not divided. Their leaders and press strongly supported Duplessis and his repressive measures. In Quebec the English minority was clearly on the side of the industrialists.

The shifting attitudes within French Canada must be linked to important changes in the province during the postwar years. Quebec had become an urban, industrial province even before the war, but during and after World War II the shift from rural to urban accelerated. In two decades, from 1941 to 1961, the rural farm population dropped from one million to half a million. In the same period the urban population doubled; Montreal alone had a population of two million by 1960. But the changes were more than numerical, for in these years people not only migrated to the cities, but the cities, by way of radio and television, moved out to the smaller communities and eroded the traditional values held there. The leaders of French-Canadian society might deplore the changes, but they could not turn back the clock. French Canada had become an urban, industrial society. The Quiet Revolution of the 1960s was a consequence of the tardy recognition of this fact.

By the 1950s a growing number of social critics were responding to these social changes. They realised that rural French Canada, even if it could be preserved, would have no vitality; it would be no more than a quaint survival of a bygone age. The future lay with the world which French Canada had rejected for so long. A group of historians at the University of Montreal reflected this new perspective by their reinterpretation of the past.[2] French Canada, they argued, had no providential mission. New France had been a colony like other European colonies in North America, with a commercial base and a developing middle class. Under normal circumstances it would have developed much like the British colonies in North America, with a partnership of local politicians and businessmen promoting local commerce and industry. But circumstances had not been normal. The colony had been conquered and British entrepreneurs had replaced the French-speaking middle class. French Canadians were left in control of only the rural communities and the Roman Catholic Church. According to the Montreal historians, this accounted for the myth that French Canadians were an agricultural people with a religious mission and for their rejection of the modern world. "It must never be forgotten," wrote Michel Brunet, one of these historians, "that the fundamental weakness of French-Canadian thought stems from the inability or the refusal to understand the real meaning of the Conquest of 1760."

Brunet's was a pessimistic view of the past. He and his colleagues offered an explanation for French Canada's economic inferiority but held out no hope for the future. The Conquest could not be undone, and French Canada seemed fated to remain a backward society. However, some younger critics found this pessimism unacceptable. They share the historian's view that a modern society required a strong industrial base and that the ideal of a rural Catholic society was absurd. But they refused to believe that French Canada's future had been determined forever on the Plains of Abraham. They believed that, given the opportunity, French

2. The viewpoint of the Montreal school is most readily accessible in two Canadian Historical Association pamphlets: Guy Frégault, *Canadian Society in the French Regime*, and Michel Brunet, *French Canada and the Early Days of British Rule 1760-1791*. Ramsay Cook, "La Survivance French Canadian Style," in *The Maple Leaf Forever* (Toronto, 1971), is a brief essay on French-Canadian historiography. The articles in this collection and in Cook's earlier *French Canada and the Canadian Question* (Toronto, 1966), provide an essential historical context for French Canada and French-English relations in the 1960s.

Canadians could compete successfully in the modern world and could provide the economic basis for social and cultural development.

One group of critics was associated with Pierre Trudeau, a wealthy young law professor and intellectual with a talent for debate, self-contained, reputed to be something of a dilettante, but deeply committed to individual freedom.[3] Trudeau and Gérard Pelletier, a journalist who had been active in the Catholic youth movement, founded a journal, *Cité Libre*, in 1950. *Cité Libre* expressed a liberal point of view, with an emphasis on individual rights and democratic procedures. It assumed that political power and cultural development depended on economic power and that this in turn depended on exploiting technology in a world increasingly subject to automation, computers, and nuclear energy. *Cité Libre* was harshly critical of the traditional French-Canadian elites who had turned their backs on the modern world. Its most scathing criticisms were directed against the paternalistic and authoritarian attitudes of these elites and their insistence on conformity. The Asbestos Strike was seen as proof that French-Canadian workers could act responsibly and effectively, and social reforms would follow if these workers gained more political power. A liberal and democratic regime, responsive to the urban voters, would encourage and train French Canadians to compete within the industrial system and eventually to share in the direction of the industrial economy. The workers were seen as the key to the modernization of French Canada.

Cité Libre saw no need for constitutional reform. Trudeau argued that the federal system was the best guarantee of a liberal regime because it diffused political power. But it was also the essence of Canadian federalism that each province should be responsible for its own social policies. *Cité Libre* insisted that a more centralized federal system was not a short cut to reform. Thus, Trudeau approved of more money for universities but he opposed federal grants to universities; education was a provincial responsibility and it was up to the voters of Quebec to persuade the provincial government to provide the funds. At the same time he opposed separatism for Quebec; the provincial government already had all the powers it needed to introduce social reform and nationalist passions seemed to him more likely to bring despotism than liberty. However, in the 1950s the main target for *Cité Libre* was the Duplessis regime, which was both

3. The best biographies of Trudeau are George Radwanski, *Trudeau* (Toronto, 1978), and Richard Gwyn, *The Northern Magus* (Toronto, 1980). Trudeau's own view of the traditional ideology can be found in his long introduction to P.E. Trudeau, ed., *The Asbestos Strike* (Toronto, 1974). Some of his comments on French Canada in the 1950s and 1960s are available in P.E. Trudeau, *Federalism and the French Canadians* (Toronto, 1968).

reactionary and corrupt. The first step towards social reform in Quebec was a democratic government, and this meant defeating Duplessis.

Others were equally critical of the traditional view of French Canada and equally committed to French-Canadian participation in the modern industrial world, but they were less willing to trust a federal system in which French Canadians were a minority. They feared that competing within a Canadian economy would mean adopting English-Canadian patterns and that success could mean assimilation. It was not enough to exercise economic power in a modern, industrial society; that society must be distinctively French Canadian. For these critics the provincial government was of crucial importance because it could be the agent of economic planning and because it was the only government which French Canadians controlled. Few of these *nationaliste* critics were separatists in the 1950s but, like André Laurendeau, editor of *Le Devoir*, they defended provincial autonomy.

These neo-nationalists were ambivalent about Duplessis. They shared his concern for provincial rights and his suspicions of any extension of federal authority. At the same time they deplored his cooperation with English-speaking businessmen at the expense of French-Canadian workers. For them the Asbestos Strike was significant not merely because the workers had united against their employers, but also because the workers were French and the employers were English. By the mid-1950s *Le Devoir* had ended its ambivalence and decided that provincial autonomy was no longer enough. Laurendeau compared Duplessis to the "negro-king," the figurehead allowed by the British to govern a colony despotically so long as he protected British property and British economic interests. *Le Devoir* became a leading advocate of an interventionist provincial government, one that would use its autonomy to enhance the economic power of French Canadians.[4]

The municipal government of Montreal became yet another focus of opposition to Duplessis in the 1950s. Camilien Houde had been mayor in the early postwar years, kept in office by his popularity in the working-class districts of the city and by his willingness to cooperate with business interests and the provincial government in keeping down the costs of municipal administration. A combination of civic reformers who wanted improved services, especially in transportation, and moral reformers who

4. Philip Stratford, ed., *André Laurendeau: Witness for Quebec* (Toronto, 1973), is a collection of Laurendeau's writings, including some editorials from *Le Devoir*. See also Ramsay Cook and M. Behiels, eds., *The Essential Laurendeau* (Toronto, 1976).

wanted to eliminate prostitution and gambling, elected Jean Drapeau in 1954. Drapeau's demands for greater autonomy for Montreal were frustrated by Duplessis, and soon Drapeau was numbered among the critics of the provincial regime.

The French-Canadian clergy did not play a decisive role in this criticism of the old regime. For almost the first time, some priests, disturbed by the poverty and alienation of the urban proletariat, wanted the Church to identify itself with the cause of the workers and to fight for their economic as well as their spiritual needs. Archbishop Charbonneau forcefully expressed these sentiments. "The working class is the victim of a conspiracy . . . ," he declared, "and it is the duty of the Church to intervene." Other bishops were more conservative. They deplored the insidious materialism of the modern world and preached the need to return to the Christian virtues of humility and submission. Rome, for reasons which are still a matter of controversy, removed Charbonneau from office, but his successor, Cardinal Léger, eventually became identified with the reform wing within the Church. Individual priests also contributed to the attacks on the regime — two of them denounced political corruption in the province, and a teaching brother, in a best seller called *The Impertinences of Brother Anonymous*, described with bitter wit the fearfulness of a people who hid behind authority rather than thinking for themselves — but these priests spoke as individuals. The Church as an institution was divided and uncertain. This in itself was significant. The Church was not in the vanguard of reform but neither did it lead a rearguard action against change.

The evolution that occurred in the Catholic trade unions illustrates the declining role of the Church. These unions had been organized and supervised by priests who were reacting to the secular materialism of international unions, but by the 1950s laymen had taken over union leadership and their objectives had become more worldly. The emergence of lay leadership coincided with an increasing militancy in both industrial and political disputes. In the years after the Asbestos Strike the Catholic unions played a prominent part in the organized opposition to the provincial labour policies and became a significant element in the anti-Duplessis coalition.

By the end of the decade the Liberal party had united most of the dissident elements within the province. Jean Lesage, who left a successful career in federal politics to become provincial leader in 1958, managed to retain the support of the moderates while winning the confidence of those committed to change. This might not have been enough to unseat the entrenched Union nationale Government, but in 1959 Maurice

Duplessis died, and six months later his successor died. Even under these circumstances the reformed Liberal party did not win an overwhelming majority in the provincial election of 1960. Only a bare majority of Quebeckers had voted for what would become known as the Quiet Revolution, and Lesage held only fifty of the ninety-five seats in the legislature.

La Revolution Tranquille

The election of Lesage was much more than a change of governments. In politics it meant a shift from a defensive nationalism to an active government committed to change. However, the revolution in government was only part of the story. Almost every part of Quebec's society was affected. A pattern was quickly established of criticizing existing institutions and customs, of rejecting the past and identifying change with progress. For many French Canadians it was an intoxicating experience. There was a sense of liberation, of being freed from suffocating traditions and of suddenly living in a society where there were no limits, where innovation was welcomed and talent would be rewarded. In an era of rising expectations, French Canadians were doubly optimistic. For a few exhilarating years it was possible for them to believe that they could shape their own destiny.

The rejection of the past included a sharp turning away from religious faith and from clerical leadership. Church attendance dropped precipitously. Young people showed little interest in taking religious vows, and an increasing number of priests and nuns left their orders. At the same time, responsibility for education, welfare, and health shifted from the Church to the state. French Canada, which had once seen itself as essentially Catholic, was becoming a secular society.

The reforms in education were the most striking as well as the most controversial examples of this transformation. It had long been obvious that the system of elementary schools and classical colleges was inadequate for an industrial society. A bewildering number of separate technical and vocational institutions had appeared to supplement the public schools, and new colleges had been founded and the curricula adapted in response to social pressures. But in the changed mood of the 1960s it was no longer enough to adapt the established system. Instead, the old institutions were discarded and a new system was erected in their place.

The Lesage Government began by appointing a royal commission to study the problem. For the next five years the Parent Commission was never far from the headlines. The public debate began with the Commission's hearings, continued with the release of its report in five volumes between 1963 and 1966, and then focussed on the legislation which followed. Emotions ran high and sometimes obscured the issues, but the public concern was justified. French Canadians were debating what kind of education was most appropriate for the modern world.

The first volume of the report dealt with the thorny question of the roles of church and state. The Commission advocated an integrated educational system, planned and coordinated to meet the diverse needs of a complex society, and it concluded that only the provincial government could administer such a system. The Commission accepted the existing pattern of separate Catholic and Protestant school systems, but it recommended that ultimate control of both be given to a ministry of education. To devout Catholics the Commission promised that this did not mean secular schools. So long as French Canadians remained Catholic, their government would reflect their religious beliefs. The Government promptly introduced a bill based on these recommendations.

The measure was bitterly debated. The spokesmen for the traditional point of view — and there were still many — denounced government control as the first step towards eliminating religion entirely. They were not satisfied with the Church's control over the teaching of religion as a subject; if the schools were to be Catholic, there must be some assurance that the other subjects and the teachers who taught them would reflect their religious character. This opposition forced the Government to withdraw the bill and to negotiate a compromise with the Roman Catholic bishops. The revised bill muted the criticisms by establishing an advisory committee on religious matters, but the Government nonetheless remained the final authority. Control of education in Quebec had shifted from church to state.

The subsequent recommendations of the Commission led to a radically restructured educational system. It argued that "modern man no longer lives in the same universe as his ancestors," and concluded that Quebec needed a system that would train young people for a world transformed by science and technology. Education was to be democratic, in the sense that all children should acquire some essential skills and should then have the opportunity to develop their individual talents. The major change was at the secondary level, where the classical colleges were replaced by five-year secondary school and two-year colleges offering technical and vocational as well as academic programs.

Naturally enough, such sweeping changes threw the educational system into chaos. By the end of the decade enrolment at the secondary level had increased by almost half a million students, and there were almost forty thousand students attending the two-year colleges. The young found themselves in new institutions without established traditions, still in the process of defining goals and procedures. They faced teachers who were either novices or who had been trained for traditional institutions. It did not help that in Quebec, as elsewhere, the 1960s was also a decade when students and faculty were resentful of any authority. The immediate results were predictable. Classes were held in schools still under construction, programs were constantly being revised, and students and faculty were frequently on strike. Social change can be disruptive, but more important in the long run was the fact that the aims and structures of education were reformed.

Another area of controversy was hydro-electricity. René Lévesque, Lesage's Minister of Natural Resources, was the key figure in this debate. Lévesque, an intense chain-smoker with an extraordinary talent for simplifying complex ideas, had come to politics after a brilliant career as a television journalist with his own program on current events.[5] He was a *nationaliste*, convinced that the provincial government was the instrument through which French Canadians could direct and control their economic future. Electricity in Quebec had initially been generated and distributed by private power companies, and although the provincial government had taken over the Montreal Light, Heat and Power Company during the war, most of the power was still generated by foreign-owned private companies. Lévesque, who wanted the Government to plan and direct industrial growth, saw the need for more electricity to power industrial growth. His solution was to expropriate the private power companies and to give Hydro-Québec a monopoly and allow it to develop new water power sites. He persuaded a reluctant Lesage to agree to the take overs and to fight a provincial election on the issue with the *nationaliste* slogan of "*maîtres chez nous.*" The Liberals won the provincial election of 1962 with an increased majority.

Hydro-Québec quickly became one of the success stories of the Quiet Revolution. This provincial power company, after taking over the private power companies in the province, undertook power installations to produce some five million kilowatts on the Manicouagan River. The significance of Manicouagan was, in part, that it was a French-language enterprise.

---

5. Peter Desbarats, *René: A Canadian in Search of a Country* (Toronto, 1976), is an informative popular biography. Lévesque's *Option Quebec* (Toronto, 1969), is a useful statement of his views at the time of the founding of the Parti Québécois. Graham Fraser, *P.Q.: René Lévesque and the Parti Québécois in Power* (Toronto, 1984) is an excellent study of the events and personalities associated with Lévesque's career.

The private power corporations had operated in English, and it was widely assumed that English was the only possible language for major engineering projects in North America. However, with Hydro-Québec, the language of work became French, and the construction on the Manicouagan was planned and carried out in French by French-Canadian engineers and managers. The experience contributed greatly to French-Canadian self-confidence.

Not all of the Government's projects were as successful. The Société Générale de Financement (S.G.F.) was a provincial agency to encourage French-Canadian entrepreneurs by providing capital for industrial and commercial enterprises. An even more ambitious project was the establishment of a steel mill. Sidérurgie Québec (Sidbec) produced steel from the iron ore of Labrador; it was also a status symbol because heavy industry was considered the hallmark of an industrial nation. Both S.G.F. and Sidbec were high-risk enterprises undertaken by a government eager to foster French-Canadian industry; both projects lost money.

Reaction in Quebec to the provincial government's initiatives was varied. There was a new-found assurance, especially among the middle-class youth, better educated than their parents, with confidence in technology and the social sciences, and eager to apply the new skills of computing and management. They were the privileged beneficiaries of the Quiet Revolution. As technocrats, they replaced clerical administrators in education, welfare, and health services. Even more encouraging, if French Canada was to win its proportionate share of economic power, they were the French Canadians who would succeed to the management posts in Hydro-Québec, in the bureaucracy, and in industry, which until now had been a virtual monopoly of English Canadians. For ambitious young French Canadians, the Quiet Revolution was the road to power.

Others were ambivalent. Most French Canadians probably shared the satisfaction of belonging to a society that no longer thought of itself as an insecure minority and that was affirming its place in the modern world. But for some the Quiet Revolution was disruptive in a negative sense. The questioning of tradition and the challenge to authority was unsettling, especially to those for whom religious and social institutions brought order and meaning to life. In the areas outside of Montreal there was a growing resistance to change.

Some French-Canadian workers had a different reaction. The Liberals in Opposition had championed the rights of labour and, once in office, had encouraged the growth of trade unions. Much of the growth came in the public sector, with unions for public servants, hospital employees, and teachers. A reluctant Lesage was even persuaded to concede the right to strike to public servants. However, by the mid-1960s, the trade union leaders were losing confidence in the Quiet Revolution. The technocrats might be prospering, but workers were finding that it was almost as difficult to bargain with the Quebec Government as it had been with English-language corporations in the private sector.[6] A number of strikes in the public sector were ended by back-to-work legislation, and it became clear that the Quiet Revolution apparently did not mean power to the workers.

But much of the publicity relating to the Quiet Revolution focussed on the clashes between Quebec and Ottawa. Disputes between the two levels of government were inevitable. Duplessis had resisted the encroachments of the federal government, but under Lesage it was no longer a matter of resisting federal intervention. It was no longer enough to defend provincial autonomy — the provincial government was now required to take the initiative in economic and social matters. Quebec City needed increased revenues to achieve its aims, and Lesage peremptorily demanded a larger share of income taxes and succession duties to finance his projects. To this point Lesage could count on the support of other provinces which also wanted more money from Ottawa.

But Lesage could not stop there. His Government represented Quebec, but it also considered itself the spokesman for some four million French Canadians, and the survival of French Canada was still the ultimate objective. The rules and regulations of the industrial milieu would have to be consistent with and should even reinforce French Canada's distinctive cultural identity. With its English-speaking majority, Ottawa could not be expected to discriminate in favour of the French-speaking minority or even to understand its needs. Quebec, therefore, was not a province like the others. Its provincial government had a special obligation to preserve the cultural identity of its French-Canadian citizens. It must have jurisdiction over all matters which touched on their cultural identity.

Lesage favoured opting out as a solution. Quebec would not participate in national programs which had cultural implications but would receive equivalent funds in the form of federal grants and so be able to finance similar programs of its own design. However, federalist critics argued that in the long run opting out would weaken the federal union. Fewer and fewer

---

6. Pierre Fournier, *The Québec Establishment* (Montreal, 1976), is a class interpretation of the links between business and government in Quebec.

federal programs would operate in Quebec, and the provincial government would have a virtual monopoly of the legislation for the province.

Proposed pension legislation led to a major confrontation in 1964. The Liberal Government under L.B. Pearson had proposed a contributory pension plan. Quebec had objected to this federal initiative in a provincial field and had devised a pension plan of its own, one that had the advantage of quickly accumulating a large reserve fund upon which the provincial government could draw for other purposes. Given Lesage's constant need for revenue, this was a most attractive aspect of provincial control. On the other hand, Ottawa was committed to a national scheme that allowed workers to move from one province to another without losing their pension rights. Both Pearson and Lesage wanted to avoid an open breach, and at the last minute Ottawa proposed a funded pension plan that gave all provincial governments the right to draw on the funds. Quebec insisted on administering its own pension fund, but agreed to introduce a plan which would be compatible with the federal plan and so permit labour mobility.

The participants on both sides believed that the compromise had saved the federal union, and there certainly had been significant concessions on both sides. However, the pension plans did not provide a blueprint for future disagreements. The federal government might not want to adapt another program to suit Quebec, and the Quebec government might not always be willing to restrict its autonomy by conforming to a national plan. It was still by no means clear how a dynamic Quebec could be accommodated within a federal constitution.[7]

The War Between Ottawa and Quebec

The Quiet Revolution had lost its impetus by the mid-1960s. The exhilaration of a new beginning was tempered by experience. Reformers who had made common cause against Duplessis now found it less easy to agree on positive measures. French Canada, which for so long had been a cohesive minority, obedient to its leaders, was now a pluralist society, divided into groups and factions, each with its own aims and ambitions. For the next ten years the changes of the early 1960s were consolidated, but there was no consensus on further reforms. There were still debates

7. The best account of federal-provincial relations from 1963 to 1971 is Richard Simeon, *Federal-Provincial Diplomacy* (Toronto, 1972). Claude Morin, *Quebec versus Ottawa: The Struggle for Self-Government 1960-72* (Toronto, 1976), is the personal interpretation of an active participant.

and confrontations, but now the focus shifted. Differences over the nature of French-Canadian society were muted by a growing emphasis on the status of that society within the federal union. Decisions over what kind of society it should be were put aside until the relations between French and English Canada were more clearly defined.

English Canadians outside of Quebec had already been drawn into the debate. English-Canadian commentators and academics had expressed sympathy for the critics of Duplessis and for the shift from a clerical to a more secular society. But the Diefenbaker Government showed little awareness of French Canada, although the Liberal Government of L.B. Pearson was more sensitive. In 1963 Pearson appointed a Royal Commission on Bilingualism and Biculturalism — the Laurendeau-Dunton Commission, after the co-chairmen — to advise on how the federal system could accommodate "an equal partnership between two founding races."

The Commission offered only a partial answer. It made recommendations on behalf of the French-Canadian minorities outside of Quebec, and its main thrust was for a federal public service which would reflect the cultual duality implicit in an equal partnership. These were complex and controversial problems, but increased services for French Canadians did not involve a direct reduction of services for the majority. A thornier problem was the redistribution of legislative powers between Ottawa and Quebec to reflect the more active role of the provincial government. Giving to Quebec meant taking away from Ottawa. In the end, the Commission never did present its views on constitutional reform.

The Commission ended abruptly because Pierre Trudeau succeeded Pearson as Prime Minister in 1968, and Trudeau already had firm opinions on the constitution. Along with Gérard Pelletier and Jean Marchand, a prominent trade union leader, Trudeau had joined the federal Liberal party in 1965 in reaction to the growing nationalism in Quebec. He was convinced that this nationalism would create an isolated Quebec which would be as conformist and as intolerant as it was under Duplessis. His alternative was a federalism which provided equal opportunity regardless of individual differences of language and culture. Trudeau, therefore, favoured a constitution which guaranteed linguistic and educational rights for French and English Canadians in all parts of Canada. His emphasis was on individual rights and not on minority rights, and as a consequence he was opposed to any special constitutional status for the province of Quebec. This was a popular view in English Canada, where the continuing demands of Quebec for greater autonomy were widely seen as a threat to national unity. The extraordinary Trudeaumania in the federal election of 1968 was largely a response to his personal style, but it was far from irrelevant to English Canadians that Trudeau seemed prepared to end the concessions to Quebec, or, as some saw it, to put Quebec in its place.

Meanwhile, the political situation in the province was becoming more confused. Lesage had always been a cautious reformer, ready to do what was necessary to keep his party united but not entirely sure where the Quiet Revolution was taking him. The initiatives had come from *nationalistes* within his Government — René Lévesque, for example, was convinced that the "powers of the nation-state that is Quebec must become as broad and autonomous as the federal system can stand." When provincial ministers could not persuade their more conservative colleagues in Cabinet, they regularly discussed the issues in public and appealed for public support. Lesage's Government soon gave the impression of being divided and irresolute.

The Union nationale was also ambivalent. Daniel Johnson, party leader after 1961, had been associated with the Duplessis regime, but as Leader of the Opposition he sought support where he could find it. He showed concern for those who found the Quiet Revolution disruptive, but at the same time he spoke for the *nationalistes* by criticizing Lesage for not being more forceful in his negotiations with Ottawa. He put more emphasis on provincial status than on social change, and his slogan — "Equality or independence; a new constitution or separation" — deliberately failed to define the kind of society he envisaged.

The shift towards nationalism was also illustrated by the founding of two separatist parties before the provincial election of 1966. The Ralliement national looked to a state in Quebec which would return the province to its traditional values; the Rassemblement pour l'indépendance nationale, at the other extreme, advocated a socialist state.

The election was an unexpected victory for the Union nationale. The Liberals received a larger popular vote than Johnson's party, but much of their support came from Montreal, which was under-represented in the legislature. Only 9 per cent of the popular vote went to separatist candidates, but the results suggested that Quebec voters were as undecided about their future as their political leaders.

Johnson and his successor, Jean-Jacques Bertrand, tried to ride the whirlwind. The costs of the educational reforms and the economic initiatives of the Liberal Government meant heavy deficits despite increased taxes. Demands for more generous terms from the federal government fell on deaf ears; the federal government had deficits of its own to worry about, and, after 1968, with Trudeau in power, it was hostile to any suggestion of special status for Quebec. The Johnson and Bertrand Governments did not initiate any new major programs and blamed the federal government for their own inactivity. The excitement and the optimism of the Quiet Revolution were gone.

One sign of the change was the emergence of the new term *les Québécois*. Until the 1960s French Canadians in Quebec had called themselves *les Canadiens*, implicitly including French-speaking minorities outside Quebec in the same category. But the attitude towards these minorities changed with the Quiet Revolution. The French Canadians in Quebec increasingly thought of themselves as citizens of the province, with the provincial government as their government. The distinction was even more marked because French Canadians outside Quebec looked to the federal government for support and showed no interest in championing provincial rights. The new provincial perspective required a new vocabulary, and within a remarkably short time *les Québécois* was in general use, and *les Canadiens* had almost disappeared.

For *les Québécois* the problem of survival once again became a pressing concern. The danger was two-fold. French Canadians had long had the highest birth rate in Canada. This birth rate had dropped slowly after the Second World War, but suddenly, in the 1960s, it plummeted until, by the end of the decade, it was the lowest in Canada. The postwar period had also been one of massive immigration to Canada, with many of the immigrants settling in Montreal. The majority of these immigrants, with an eye for economic opportunity, sent their children to English-language schools. The combined effect of the low birth rate and high immigration threatened to produce an English-speaking majority in Montreal by the end of the century.[8] It did not matter that the danger was greatly exaggerated. For a group which now associated its survival with a greater role in industry and commerce, even the possibility of becoming a minority in Montreal was frightening. There was little inclination to return to large families, so the only solution was to make the newcomers join the French-speaking community.

The issue flared up in St. Léonard, a district in Montreal with a high proportion of Italian immigrants. The Catholic school board, at the request of the Italian parents, had provided bilingual schools with both English and French as the languages of instruction. Militant Québécois *nationalistes*

8. Richard Joy, *Languages in Conflict* (Toronto, 1972), is a clear account of demographic developments, although it does not go beyond the 1961 census data. See also the many volumes published by the Royal Commission on Bilingualism and Biculturalism.

objected to this compromise and demanded unilingual French-language schools. Disturbed by the increasing nationalism, Montreal's English-Canadians denounced this as an infringement on the right of parents to choose between English- or French-language schools. The provincial government attempted to defuse the issue in 1969 by reaffirming freedom of choice but, at the same time, undertaking to improve the teaching of French as a second-language in the English-language schools. The *nationalistes* rejected the compromise. They could not feel secure until the law gave French a privileged status.

A few young French Canadians were not prepared to wait. To them the language issue was part of the broader issue of economic imperialism. They saw Quebec as a colony, still controlled by English-speaking capitalists, and they believed that cultural inferiority was the inevitable consequence of this economic servitude. In many parts of the world, the end of the decade was marked by student demonstrations and violence; in Quebec some young radicals saw violence as a necessary part of the crusade for Quebec's liberation. They organized demonstrations, supported strikers, and exploded bombs in federal armouries and Westmount mailboxes. The authorities, especially in Montreal, were deeply disturbed. They exaggerated the number of terrorists, but there was some justification for their concern because of the number of young people who vociferously expressed approval of the resort to violence.

Quebec's nationalism found wider expression in the arts. The decade of the 1960s was remarkable for the outpouring of songs, poems, plays, and films, and even more remarkable for the popularity of the artists. This cultural explosion was an aspect of the Quiet Revolution, linked in some way with the release from conformity and the sense of shaping a new society. The songs of Gilles Vigneault and the plays of Michel Tremblay gave common experiences and popular language a cultural significance and became a celebration of the distinctive identity of *les Québécois*. From there it was but a short step to politics, and most of these artists were open advocates of independence for Quebec.[9]

The October Crisis and After

The political situation changed significantly with the provincial election of 1970. The Union nationale, with its balancing act in constitutional and

---

9. Malcolm Reid, *The Shouting Signpainters* (Toronto, 1972), is an essay on the links between French-Canadian literature and nationalism in the 1960s. Also helpful is F. Dumont, *et al.*, *Idéologies au Canada Français 1940–1976* (Quebec, 1981), in three volumes.

domestic affairs, was crushingly defeated. The Liberal party, under Robert Bourassa, a young economist, offered a different choice. It attempted to divert attention from controversies over language and culture by stressing economic goals, and Bourassa promised to make federalism profitable. The alternative to the Liberal party was now the Parti Québécois, a party which united a number of separatist groups under the leadership of René Lévesque. The new party included a wide range of conservative and radical *nationalistes*, but Lévesque, who had been frustrated by the constraints of the federal system, gave the new party an instant credibility. The Liberals won the election, but the Parti Québécois received almost a quarter of the popular vote. Quebec's electorate was becoming polarized.

The newly elected Government was quite unprepared for the October Crisis of 1970. In that month terrorists kidnapped James Cross, a British trade commissioner, and then Pierre Laporte, the Minister of Labour in the Bourassa Government. Bourassa had no sympathy for the kidnappers, for his "profitable federalism" depended on foreign investment which, in turn, depended on social stability. But Bourassa did not want to defy the moderate *nationalistes*, who seemed prepared to negotiate with the terrorists. His hesitation was interpreted as weakness, and there was talk of a coalition to resolve the crisis. Bourassa's reputation as a leader was further eroded when federal authorities under Trudeau invoked the War Measures Act and took charge. Subsequently, when many French Canadians concluded that the federal government had over-reacted, Bourassa was criticized for his collaboration with Ottawa. It was a difficult initiation for a Government which had hoped to distract attention from divisive constitutional questions by concentrating on economic issues.[10]

The Québécois response to a constitutional accord in 1971 confirmed the wisdom of avoiding constitutional controversies. Trudeau and the provincial premiers, meeting in Victoria, British Columbia, proposed a constitution that would extend French language rights in the eastern provinces and concede a wider provincial authority in social legislation. The amendment procedure would give a veto to Quebec, as well as to Ontario and to a majority of the Atlantic and western provinces. After initially accepting the Victoria Charter, Bourassa soon discovered that many in his province objected vehemently to an agreement which might inhibit

---

10. Gérard Pelletier, *The October Crisis* (Toronto, 1971), presents the federal position; Denis Smith, *Bleeding Hearts . . . Bleeding Country* (Edmonton, 1971), is a criticism of federal policy. Other titles include Ron Haggart and A. Golden, *Rumours of War* (Toronto, 1971); Pierre Vallières, *The Assassination of Pierre Laporte* (Toronto, 1977); and M. Bellavance et Marcel Gilbert, *L'opinion publique et la crise d'octobre* (Montréal, 1971).

further extension of Quebec's autonomy in the future, and he soon refused to ratify the proposal. As a result, constitutional change was stalled for more than a decade.

Bourassa's major undertaking was the development of hydro-electric power in the James Bay region. It was a massive project, with three rivers to be diverted, installations to a total of 10 000 MW, and 1000 km of high-voltage transmission lines to bring this power to southern Quebec. Critics objected to the estimated cost of $15 billion, although ten years later, when the first turbines turned, the high cost of oil helped mightily to justify the project. In the meantime, the enterprise did mean investment and construction jobs.

The emphasis on economics did not prevent a confrontation with trade union leaders. By the 1970s prominent trade union leaders had lost confidence in governments, whatever their political colouration, and had concluded that the capitalist system was to blame for their problems. In 1972 the Confederation of National Trade Unions, an association of the former Catholic unions, together with the Quebec Federation of Labour, representing the international unions, and the Quebec Teachers Corporation formed a common front in their negotiations on behalf of government employees. A massive strike, including hospital workers and teachers as well as public servants, provoked yet another law ordering the strikers back to work. This time both sides were intransigent. The presidents of the three labour federations, using references to the class struggle and to colonialism, advised the workers to ignore the law. They were arrested, convicted, and jailed. The Government won that battle, but it lost some friends.

To take advantage of the popular reaction against labour disruptions and radicalism Bourassa called a snap election in 1973. The Liberals painted a frightening picture of the dire economic consequences of a separatist victory, graphically symbolized by the departure of a fleet of armoured cars on the eve of the election, supposedly carrying the contents of safety-deposit boxes to the security of Ontario. The polarization of the electorate was more marked than before. The Liberals won a majority of the votes and a vast majority of the seats, but the Parti Québécois vote rose to 30 per cent.

The emphasis of the Bourassa Government on economic growth could not suppress the language controversy for long. In 1974 Bourassa tried to resolve the issue by legislation to encourage the use of French as the language of work and to restrict admission to English schools to those children able to pass tests of proficiency in English. Bill 22 was intended to reassure the *nationalistes* without worrying the federalists, but it was a failure on both counts. As the consequence of a decade of agitation, both French and English Canadians were suspicious of a law whose impact depended upon how it was administered. The controversy over Bill 22 continued until the next provincial election.

The economic policies of the Government were also criticized after 1973. Rapidly rising oil prices contributed to a higher cost of living and to unemployment. The James Bay development continued, but there was disturbing evidence of corruption and excessive costs. In an effort to avoid disruptive strikes, the Government had given a monopoly to some construction unions which had then taken advantage of their position. Rivalries between unions and factions within unions had led to sabotage and violence, and public hearings on these events discredited both the Government and the unions.

A dispute over air traffic control in the summer of 1976 raised the language issue in a new form and to new heights. Communications between

Aislin—The Montreal Gazette

pilots and their controllers had been in English, but there were now more French-speaking pilots, and they found it easier to communicate in French, especially at some of the smaller airports in Quebec. English-speaking traffic controllers protested that the use of French was a safety hazard, but Quebeckers were outraged by opposition to French-speaking pilots communicating with French-speaking controllers in their own language in their own province. They were more incensed still when the federal government yielded to massive English-Canadian pressure and appointed a commission to study the question. Three years later the commission would approve the use of French, and the Government would establish bilingual air traffic control, but for the moment the entire province of Quebec only saw that the use of French was being restricted.

The Parti Québécois did not fail to take full advantage of the situation. It tried to broaden its appeal by promising honest and efficient administration, a clear contrast to the corruption and favouritism of the Liberals. It tried to defuse the constitutional issue by denying that a vote for the party was necessarily a vote for independence, and Lévesque promised, if elected, to hold a referendum on the issue. He would negotiate sovereignty-association (a common-market arrangement with Canada) only after a majority of Quebeckers had voted for it. It was a concession which the militants within the party accepted only because of Lévesque's prestige — and the possibility of gaining office. On November 15, 1976, the Parti Québécois did win the election. Its share of the popular vote rose to 41 per cent, while the Liberal vote dropped to 34 per cent. Federalists could argue that it was not a vote for independence. Lévesque, on the other hand, could promise that "we will have the Quebec of which our ancestors dreamed." Whatever else the election results were, they were not a vote for the existing union.

P.Q. in Power

By this time the French language had unquestionably replaced the Catholic religion as the essence of French-Canadian identity, and survival had become directly linked to the preservation of French. The two previous administrations had tried to reassure les Québécois, but their legislation had not allayed their fears. The first measure introduced by the new Government attempted to resolve the language issue once and for all. Bill 101 declared French to be the official language of Quebec; it was to be the language of the courts, of government, and of business in the province, and English-language firms were given a limited time to give priority to

French. The educational changes were also drastic. All children would attend French-language schools except the children of English-speaking parents who had themselves been educated in Quebec. The Liberal Opposition wanted the exemption extended to children of English-speaking parents educated elsewhere in Canada but, significantly, no party in Quebec argued on behalf of the children of immigrants to Canada. For those children, French schools would be obligatory: the survival of French Canada seemed to depend on forcing foreign newcomers to become French-speaking. Even Lévesque expressed regret for this illiberal policy. "There is an unhealthy aspect to it," he conceded with the frankness that was his most attractive characteristic, "but what the hell can we do — just go down the drain?"

The threat to survival may have been exaggerated. The Québécois birth rate, which had dropped so dramatically, levelled off at a rate close to that of Ontario, and immigration, which had threatened to flood Montreal, declined sharply from the peak of the 1950s as the economy slowed. Bill 101 also coincided with a shift of corporate head offices from Montreal to Toronto and even to Calgary, a westward migration which was a North American phenomenon. The legislation accelerated or even precipitated the shift in some cases since the working language of most head offices was English. Whatever the reason, there was a net decline of English Canadians in the province over the decade. Quebec was becoming more French, and, economically, Montreal was becoming more and more a provincial city with the entire province as its hinterland. However, psychologically, Bill 101 did give the assurance that French was to be the dominant language. In that sense the legislation was effective.

The long-term effects of Bill 101 may be more complex. French-language schools in the past had been culturally homogeneous and had played a major role in strengthening the sense of cultural identity. These schools now include children of diverse ethnic origins, with a wide range of customs and traditions. The school language is French, but the cultural milieu is more cosmopolitan.[11]

In other areas the years after 1976 were anticlimactic. Even with a separatist government the sky did not fall, for the new administration was cautious. The successive budgets were austerity budgets, limiting expenditures in an effort to control the size of the deficits. The Government did introduce some reforms — "no fault" automobile insurance, a

11. Dominique Clift and Sheila McLeod Arnopolous, *The English Fact in Quebec* (Montreal, 1980), deals with the impact of the Quiet Revolution on the Anglo-Quebeckers.

higher minimum wage, and supplements to family income — but these were not *nationaliste* and not very controversial. Nor did Lévesque accede to trade union demands. In its negotiations with the Common Front in 1979, his Government obliged the union negotiators to submit its proposals to the workers, and when Hydro-Québec went on strike it passed back-to-work legislation. Lévesque had promised sound and honest government, and public opinion polls showed that Quebeckers believed he had kept his word. But for the new Government this was not enough. Québécois

For the referendum campaign the Lévesque Government established stringent rules that obliged proponents of federalism, whatever their political inclinations, to organize one committee and to channel all financing through that body. The illustration shows the cover of a pamphlet explaining the set-up.

— and Canadians in the rest of Canada — were holding their breath until the constitutional status of the province was settled.

The promised referendum was seen as crucial. All policies and public statements from Quebec and from Ottawa were coloured by and directed towards the promised referendum. The in-fighting was not always edifying. When the provincial government declared June 24, St-Jean Baptiste Day, as Quebec's national holiday and funded the celebrations, the federal government reacted by making even more generous contributions to the celebrations on the first of July. When the federal budget offered compensation for reductions in the provincial sales tax, Quebec responded to this federal intervention by a selective reduction and a demand for reimbursement; when Ottawa instead sent income tax rebates directly to Quebec's residents, the provincial government altered the provincial income tax exemption so that it ended up with the money. There would be no cooperative federalism until the fate of the federal union was resolved.

The referendum was long delayed. Lévesque was doubtless discouraged by opinion polls which showed that, although most Québécois favoured changes in the federal system, only a minority wanted separation. In the meantime, the federal government talked of revising the terms of union, but a federal task force and a federal proposal to the provincial premiers failed to produce a consensus. The situation was further confused when the provincial Liberal Opposition, now led by Claude Ryan, a distinguished journalist, produced its own blueprint for a new federation along lines known to be unacceptable to Trudeau. When the provincial government finally set the date of the referendum in 1980, the wording of the question showed its uncertainty. Instead of asking Quebeckers to vote for or against independence, the question merely asked whether voters would authorize the provincial government to begin negotiations with the federal government for sovereignty-association.

The question may have been ambiguous, but the results were not. Almost 60 per cent voted *non*. Even among the French-speaking Quebeckers a bare majority had voted against negotiations for even a mitigated sovereignty. The results could not be interpreted as a vote for the status quo, but they did imply a commitment to some form of federal association. It was a major setback for a Government committed to separation, a major blow to Lévesque and his Péquistes.

The provincial election in April of 1981 nonetheless returned the Parti Québécois with an even larger majority than before. Voters who only a year before had voted against negotiations for sovereignty-association now re-elected a government committed to this objective. As usual, it seemed

UN CANADA DE PLUS EN PLUS ANGLAIS

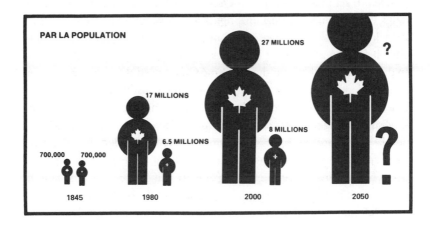

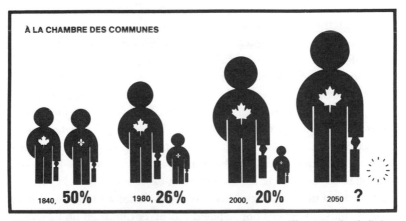

This chart from the Parti Québécois referendum literature illustrates the declining influence of French Canadians in Canada in terms of population.

easier to say what Quebec did not want. It did not want separation; but neither did it want a loss of provincial autonomy. *Les Québécois* hoped to survive and flourish as a cultural group within the federal union. They still saw the need to defend their identity, and they still had more confidence in Lévesque than in the provincial Liberal alternative.

The election also can be seen as an incident in the continuing constitutional debate. Pierre Trudeau believed that in the referendum campaign the federalists had committed themselves to a reformed federalism, and after the referendum he was determined to honour this commitment. When the provincial premiers failed to agree on a revised constitution, he decided to act unilaterally and in October of 1980 proposed a charter of rights which included educational rights for provincial minorities, whether French or English. Lévesque's unequivocal opposition to this federal initiative helped to account for his victory in the Quebec election of 1981. In the summer of that year the Supreme Court ruled that unilateral action by the federal government, while legal, violated constitutional convention. In a last-minute attempt to reach some agreement, Trudeau and the nine English-speaking premiers accepted a modified version of the federal proposal. The education rights for minorities were included, but the new amendment procedures required the consent of the legislatures of two-thirds of the provinces, representing at least half of Canada's population. It was a humiliation for Lévesque. Not only had the other provincial premiers left him isolated but the new procedure meant that Quebec would have no automatic veto over future changes in the federal constitution.

The constitutional revision split the Parti Québécois. Committed separatists interpreted it as a deliberate affront, and at a party convention they succeeded in passing a resolution opting for independence without the qualification of association with the rest of Canada. Lévesque rejected this option and threatened to resign. A mail vote — derisively known as the Renérendum — reversed the decision but did not unite the party. Rising unemployment and a climbing provincial deficit added to the internal differences. Contracts with the public service unions, negotiated before the referendum, had provided for generous annual increases. The government now arbitrarily imposed new contracts with salary roll-backs and reacted to the subsequent strikes with back-to-work legislation. Lévesque had alienated the left wing of his party. This followed the debate over strategy for the next election. Should the party campaign on its record with some chance of winning, or should it affirm its commitment to separatism and go down to honourable defeat? When Lévesque opted for the former, hard-core separatists resigned from the government and even from the party. In 1985 a beleaguered Lévesque himself resigned and left it to the party to choose a new leader before the next provincial election.

Lévesque's resignation was the end of an era. The Quiet Revolution had not resolved Quebec's problems and, after a quarter of a century, the future of French Canada was still unclear. But there had been irreversible changes. *La survivance* had been given a new meaning. The provincial government had replaced the Church as the institution to which French Canadians looked for strength and guidance. The Catholic religion was no longer the touchstone of cultural identity; in its place now was the French language. A society that had revered the traditions of a simple rural existence now had a frame of reference that was urban, industrial, and secular. It was still searching for a balance between protective isolation and the risks of a more open society. French Canada had, for a time at least, rejected independence as an option, but only because the changes over a quarter of a century had secured a place within Canada that seemed to make cultural survival possible.

Chapter XII

Conclusion

General histories often end with a clarion call. The 1957 edition of Donald Creighton's *Dominion of the North*, for example, concluded by observing that Canadians "had survived the perils of the nineteenth century. The ordeals of the first half of the twentieth had toughened them. And they now expectantly faced the most exciting, rewarding, and dangerous period in their collective existence." Creighton later finished his distinguished scholarly career by arguing bitterly that Canadians had flunked the challenge of history by taking the wrong fork in the road; the ringing note nonetheless had sounded clearly. In W.L. Morton's 1969 edition of *The Kingdom of Canada*, a book whose very title dated it in a Canada that was at last creating distinctive national symbols of its own, the great Manitoba historian concluded: "New men were in authority, new methods were under trial. The years of frustration were perhaps behind; the years of decision at last at hand. This the future and Prime Minister Trudeau would reveal."

For many Canadians, the future that Pierre Trudeau revealed ultimately seemed to embody frustrations and disappointments very similar to those that Professor Morton had found in the years prior to 1968.

There had been continual federal-provincial battles, most notably confrontations with Alberta's Premier Peter Lougheed over energy policy and with Quebec about the very future of the Canadian nation; the implementation of bilingualism had seriously divided the country; the economy had been sluggish at best and in outright decline at worst; and relations with the United States were testier than at any time since their nadir during the Diefenbaker years. But hope springs eternal. The election in September, 1984 of the fluently bilingual "boy from Baie Comeau," Brian

Mulroney, and his Progressive Conservative party's overwhelming majority in the House of Commons briefly stirred optimism in some Canadians about their future. Once again, new men were in authority, new methods were under trial.

Most notably, Mulroney's Conservatives had broken the age-old barrier of Quebec hostility and elected a large and seemingly vigorous contingent of French-speaking *bleus*. The Liberals, dominant for so long in Quebec, were left in tatters in that province, their once mighty party reduced to a status that approximated their pitiful state in the federal house and in the legislatures of the Maritimes and the Prairies. The Conservative resurgence in Quebec was a healthy development in Canadian politics, a sign that there was at last one truly political party with representation in every region, something Canadians had not had for years. The federal election results also gave Mulroney a historic opportunity to re-build the great French- and English-speaking coalition that the Conservative Party had been unable to establish since John A.'s day. The same election left the federal Liberals, their shrunken forty-member caucus now led by Trudeau's successor John Turner, briefly in danger of losing second place to the New Democratic Party or even, some observers suggested, of disappearing altogether.

More important still for the future of federalism, the Parti Québécois Government was in grave difficulties with its electorate. René Lévesque had hung on for some time (despite disastrous opinion polls) by sacrificing the political, social, and economic principles that had brought the P.Q. to power in 1976. But even this effort to keep alive some glimmer of electoral success failed, and Lévesque announced his retirement from the premiership in late June, 1985. The P.Q.'s founder had already abandoned the idea of independence as a concession to the economic realities of the mid-1980s, and the fear in the rest of the country that Quebec would opt for separate nationhood greatly diminished, while the promise of a future francophone nation dwindled in Quebec, along with the P.Q.'s caucus and membership.

And with separatism's troubles and Mulroney's success the bitter struggles between Ottawa and the provinces that had characterized the Trudeau era were — temporarily at least — a thing of the past. In part, this was a result of political compatibility. By the middle of 1985 all the provincial governments except those in Quebec, Ontario (where the Liberals had scored a stunning upset victory in the election of May), Manitoba, and British Columbia were led by Tories, and B.C.'s Premier Bill Bennett, while he headed a Social Credit regime, managed to cooperate easily with the Conservative forces in his province. One cheerful sign of the new ways was that Ottawa and Newfoundland in 1985 concluded an energy agreement to develop the huge potential of the offshore oil fields, something that had seemed an impossibility a year earlier. Another optimistic sign was the agreement in the same year between Ottawa and the western oil and gas producing provinces to move the Canadian price for oil to world levels. The Liberals' National Energy Policy was quickly being dismantled (along with the Foreign Investment Review Agency), and while that upset Canadian nationalists, there was no doubt that an easier mood, one small benefit in itself, was prevailing in federal-provincial relations.

The new Prime Minister had also taken another symbolic step of great importance. By putting more women into the Cabinet than ever before and by giving them important portfolios, including, for example, Manpower and Immigration and Environment, Brian Mulroney had shown some sensitivity to the new political realities in Canada. The 1984 election campaign discussed women's issues seriously for the first time in a national race and, in part at least because Mulroney had been burned by the issue, the Prime Minister had to show that he had learned from his mistakes. As a result, the political process could never again be as closed to women as it had been in the chauvinist old days.

Equally important, in March, 1985 the Conservative Government put forward a cautious package of measures to improve women's job prospects in Crown corporations and in companies doing business with Ottawa. The publicly owned corporations were instructed to implement plans to end discrimination against women, minorities, and the disabled, and to report to Parliament on their progress. Federally regulated businesses, including the banks, had to do the same and report publicly on progress within three years, while private companies dealing with the federal government would be denied contracts unless they adopted and fulfilled employment-equality plans. This was not quite as firm a position as women's groups had hoped for, and the details of implementation announced in the summer of 1985 were weaker still, but it was more than any previous government had offered. The coming into force in April, 1985 of the equality provisions of the Charter of Rights also improved women's rights to equality — although court battles faced every group and individual seeking change.

But the signs were by no means all propitious for the new Conservative Government. The economy remained in difficulty with the resource industries, still the engine of Canadian prosperity, struggling in a sluggish world market and reeling in the face of competition from the Third World —

despite a very weak Canadian currency when measured against the American dollar, something that should have enhanced the attractiveness and competitiveness of Canadian exports. That hurt domestic programs too. For example, in British Columbia the provincial Government's public revenue from natural resources declined from $1.3 billion in 1979–80 to $473 million in 1983–84, and corporation and personal income tax receipts also dropped. In the circumstances, the Government cut back wherever it could. Fed by the slump in the resources sector and by weakness in manufacturing, unemployment all across the country was very high, staying stubbornly at levels unmatched since the Great Depression of the 1930s, and with the burden falling heaviest on the youngest, least educated, and least skilled. Automation and the quickening introduction of robot technology into the workplace promised to put more of the unskilled on the dole, while the elderly, dependent on government pensions, were an increasing percentage of the population. Typically, the governmental response at all levels was to cut back on unemployment insurance and welfare and to try to eliminate the indexation of pensions against inflation, the demands of heavy interest payments on the public deficit apparently outweighing the needs of the distressed. The problem of the late 1980s was likely to be how to pay for the social policies of the previous generation in the fiscal priorities of the present.

Even environmental restoration suffered, the Mulroney Government slashing research spending on wildlife, for example — while simultaneously increasing it elsewhere, notably on acid rain. Acid rain was a difficult issue for reasons other than the simply technical ones of resolving it. The Reagan administration in the United States, acutely sensitive to the concerns of big industry and those employed in the polluting sectors, continued to argue that acid rain was a subject that required more research, not action. The Trudeau Government had engaged in a tough battle with Washington on this issue, one Liberal minister even turning up at an environmental demonstration on Parliament Hill while the American president was visiting Ottawa. The Liberals got nowhere. The Mulroney Government, however, more concerned with the immediate needs of the Canadian economy and with its own popularity in the polls than the previous government, was visibly (and desperately) trying to build bridges to the White House. That demanded that acid rain be downplayed as a bilateral issue; the only result of a Mulroney-Reagan summit was the creation of yet another joint study. It also required cautious gestures — and maybe something more — toward a free trade arrangement with the United States.

Free trade was certain to be one of the great issues of the mid-1980s.

The protectionist pressures in the United States were growing as the American trade deficit worsened. The strength of the American dollar helped U.S. tourists in Europe while it simultaneously killed American exports to the Common Market. Observers of the confused Congressional scene suggested that soon those pressures might be such as to make any deal impossible for Canada, the "window of opportunity" closing rapidly. The simple fact was that the Canadian economy, proportionately much less strong than the American, less surefootedly on the way to recovery after the major recession of the early 1980s, was in difficulty in world markets despite a dollar worth about 70 cents U.S. More and more of Canada's trade was with the Americans — 75 per cent as compared to 7 per cent with Britain and Western Europe, and 10 per cent with Japan and the Pacific nations, and the vast majority of each country's goods already entered the other free of tariffs. Why not go all the way, Ottawa insiders and their friends in the business community asked, and create a giant continental free trade area, one that would give Canada a secure market to the south without the necessity of beating its head in vain against the tariff and non-tariff barriers of the European Community and Japan? Alternatively, why not negotiate free trade in certain key sectors such as steel or subway cars?

Those arguments sounded seductive to many. The leaders of many major Canadian industries now seemed to believe the historic move to the south could be made without overwhelming difficulty, and there were ministers in the Mulroney Government and Conservative premiers in the Maritimes and the West who looked to the idea with unbounded enthusiasm, a far cry from Robert Borden and the anti-reciprocity Conservatives of 1911. But the new Ontario Liberal Government of David Peterson was cautious, fearing the dislocation that the elimination of the few remaining trade barriers might bring to the industries of central Canada and the employment they provided in Toronto, Kingston, Hamilton, and Brantford. Agriculturalists, looking at the enormous productive capacity and huge surpluses of their American counterparts, were also frightened. Nationalists, although in disarray in the mid-decade, were predictably leery. What the Government would do was unclear, Mulroney cautiously playing his cards close to his three-piece suit, but clearly some of his key Tory ministers looking favourably on a sweeping trade package with the United States. The certainty was that if Canada moved to free trade across the board or even on a sectoral basis there could be no going back. The adjustments required in the Canadian economy to meet the challenge of free trade would be major ones as industry geared up to compete with or supply the U.S. market. But what would happen if the U.S. Congress or Administration ten years in the future decided that free trade no longer served American interests? The Americans could adjust their vastly larger economy in such an event without much difficulty. Could Canadians?

Equally important, what would occur if a U.S. Government asked Canada to agree, to cite only one example, to place major components of a "Star Wars" ICBM defence system in the North? Ottawa might be reluctant, but with the free trade arrangement, so vital to Canada, as a bargaining chip Washington might well be able to get its way after some delicate blackmail. That was purely hypothetical, of course, but it did suggest that there were implications in free trade that might extend to other areas

Defence certainly was going to be one more major problem of the decade. The Tories had made the restoration of Canada's defences one of their priorities after the election of September, 1984. They wanted to increase military spending and put more men and women into (new and distinctive) uniforms; they wanted to purchase new equipment for the country's N.A.T.O. contingent and build new ships for the navy's anti-submarine role. But the Tories, no less than the Liberals before them, wanted to keep Canada a non-nuclear power with no atomic weapons on Canadian soil. They also hoped that the United States and the Soviet Union might move toward a measure of nuclear disarmament or at least to an agreement to check the spiralling arms race. However, President Reagan's Strategic Defense Initiative, a scheme to spend billions of dollars on research for an anti-ICBM system, threatened to upset Ottawa's — and the world's — applecart. The S.D.I. was destabilizing to the nuclear balance; it frightened the Russians; and it upset the Allies, concerned that the research might produce a huge and costly system at some future point that would have to be deployed, and almost equally concerned that the technological breakthroughs S.D.I. could uncover would give the American economy a quantum leap forward into the twenty-first century — and leave them behind.

There was another area of uncertainty. Ottawa agreed that the radar lines in northern Canada, essentially unaltered since their installation in the mid-1950s, had to be updated at great cost to deal with the new threat posed by air-launched Cruise missiles. But did new radar defences commit Canada in some as yet unclear fashion to participating in S.D.I.? No one knew, but defence specialists were worried at the prospects.

This concern over the details of defence was only one sign of the continuing and overriding fear of nuclear war. The Americans and the Russians continued to increase their strategic weaponry, even while they engaged in desultory disarmament negotiations marked by what often appeared to be absolute insincerity on both sides. The prospect of Mutual Assured Destruction (or MAD) as the sole guarantor of an uneasy peace was not reassuring. The concept of deterrence had helped to preserve the world from a major war for a quarter century and more, but the uneasiness everywhere remained pronounced.

This textbook, then, cannot end with a ringing call to faith or with assurances that the future will be better than the unsettled present. One hopes, but one also fears. What does seem clear is that if the world can survive its present travails Canada will survive with it. That by itself is something; but Canada remains, as it has always been, a nation of hope and promise, one capable of providing a good life in peace for all its people. To many of those who came here from other lands in the eighteenth, nineteenth, or twentieth centuries, Canada was truly God's country. So it remains. But even God's country could not survive an atomic war and the nuclear winter that it might produce.

Index